PRIVATE PENSIONS AND PUBLIC POLICIES

PRIVATE PENSIONS AND PUBLIC POLICIES

WILLIAM G. GALE
JOHN B. SHOVEN
MARK J. WARSHAWSKY
Editors

BROOKINGS INSTITUTION PRESS
Washington, D.C.

Library of Congress Cataloging-in-Publication data

Private pensions and public policies / William G. Gale, John B. Shoven,
and Mark J. Warshawsky, editors.
   p. cm.
"The original versions of the contributions in this volume were presented
at a conference at the Brookings Institution in September 2000"—P.   .
Includes bibliographical references and index.
  ISBN 0-8157-0238-8 (cloth : alk. paper)
  ISBN 0-8157-0239-6 (pbk. : alk. paper)
  1. Old age pensions—United States—Congresses. 2. Pension trusts—
United States—Congresses. 3. Old age pensions—Government policy—
United States—Congresses. 4. Retirement income—Government
policy—United States—Congresses. 5. Social security—United States—
Congresses. I. Gale, William G. II. Shoven, John B. III. Warshawsky,
Mark. IV. Title.
HD7105.35.U6P75   2004
331.25'2'0973—dc22   2003026255

9 8 7 6 5 4 3 2 1

The paper used in this publication meets minimum requirements of the
American National Standard for Information Sciences—Permanence of Paper
for Printed Library Materials: ANSI Z39.48-1992.

Typeset in Adobe Garamond

Composition by Cynthia Stock
Silver Spring, Maryland

Printed by R. R. Donnelley
Harrisonburg, Virginia

Contents

Foreword

The creation of a lengthy, well-funded period of retirement at the end of most working lives has been one of the most striking economic transitions over the past century. In 1900, nearly two out of every three men aged 65 or older were in the work force. By 2000, the comparable figure had fallen to less than one in five. This is a historic achievement, but it also creates new challenges for public policy.

The long-term financial shortfalls facing Social Security and Medicare, the two cornerstones of public policy directed to the elderly, have received substantial attention over the past few decades. Somewhat less attention has focused on systematic reform of the private pension system, however, even though pensions play a sizable role in the welfare of retirees and form a second tier of retirement income support.

Tax incentives for employer-based pensions originated in 1921. Pensions expanded during World War II because pension contributions were exempt from wage controls and were deductible under the rapidly growing income tax. The spread of pensions continued after the war, and rules governing them have been modified repeatedly. The creation of Keogh accounts in 1962 and Individual Retirement Arrangements (sometimes called Individual Retirement Accounts or IRAs) in 1974 expanded eligibility for tax-sheltered saving plans beyond the employer-based system.

In recent years, pensions and tax-preferred saving plans covered more than 70 million workers, received more than $200 billion in new contributions, had total assets of more than $4 trillion, and provided one-fifth of the income of the elderly. Relative to Social Security, pension coverage is less universal—only about half of workers are covered at any one time and about two-thirds are covered at some point in their career. Coverage is particularly low among lower earners. Because pensions are intended to replace earnings rather than meet basic needs, pension income is distributed less equally than Social Security.

Strengthening the pension system is a crucial policy objective in light of the imminent retirement of the baby boomers and the likely shortfalls in Social Security and Medicare. Chronic pension problems, such as low coverage among low-income workers, and new problems, like those created by the extent to which employees hold their employers' stock in their portfolio, also suggest the need for change.

This book is the second of two concurrent volumes that take a hard look at pension realities and reform. The contributions in the first volume provide a framework for understanding the broad role of pensions in the American economy and paradigms for reform. The contributions in this volume supplement the bird's-eye view taken by the first volume and examine a variety of specific issues and facts that provide needed input into any reform effort. Thus, the analyses can be used, in conjunction with the broader analysis in the companion volume, to inform particular issues within the broader context and framework of pension reform.

This project was funded in part by Stanford University and its Institute for Economic Policy Research, as well as the American Council of Life Insurers. Brookings thanks them for their generous support.

Strobe Talbott
President

Washington, D.C.
January 2004

1

Introduction

WILLIAM G. GALE, JOHN B. SHOVEN,
AND MARK J. WARSHAWSKY

The private pension system is an intriguing combination of successes and
failures. In conjunction with Social Security, private pensions have helped
provide millions of Americans with adequate and secure retirement income.
Pensions help employers manage their work force and provide incentives to
employees. Pensions also help employees plan and save for retirement.

Yet pension coverage has stagnated over the last thirty years, and certain
groups appear to have fallen between the cracks of the pension system. Pension
regulations are notoriously complex. Shifts toward defined contribution plans
in recent years have exposed workers to more investment risk and required them
generally to be better-informed managers of their own retirement funds. Shifts
toward cash balance and other hybrid plans have raised concerns about the
effects on older workers caught in the transition.

This panoply of strengths and weaknesses can prove bewildering to policy
analyst and policymaker alike. This volume is the second of two that address
pension issues and reform. The contributions in the first volume, *The Evolving
Pension System: Trends, Effects, and Proposals for Reform,* provide a bird's-eye view
of the features, trends, strengths, and weaknesses of the pension system, as well
as three alternative paradigms for reform. The original versions of the contributions in this volume were presented at a conference at the Brookings Institution
in September 2000. The papers are intended to supplement the broader contributions of the first volume by focusing on a series of specific issues and facts

1

that provide needed input into any reform effort. These analyses can be used, in conjunction with the broader analyses in the earlier volume, to inform particular issues within the broader context and framework of pension reform.

The Transition to Hybrid Plans

The proportion of the labor force covered by an employer-provided pension plan has remained stable since the 1970s; however, the shape of the pension universe is being rapidly transformed. Since the passage of the Employee Retirement Income Security Act (ERISA) in 1974, there has been a strong and continued movement away from the use of defined benefit plans as more and more firms have chosen to offer defined contribution plans, especially 401(k) plans. The movement toward greater use of defined contribution plans has occurred primarily among smaller employers. However, in the most recent *Fortune* magazine list of the largest 100 publicly traded corporations in the United States, sixteen now have a defined contribution plan as their retirement plan.

During the 1990s another significant change to pension plan structure emerged: the conversion of traditional benefit plans defined by final levels of pay to hybrid plans, either cash balance or pension equity plans. Cash balance plans define a worker's "account" based on an annual contribution rate for each year of work plus a contractual rate of return on accumulated balances. A pension equity plan defines the benefit as a percentage of final average earnings for each year of service under the plan. Both types of plans specify and communicate the benefit in lump-sum terms payable at termination rather than as an annuity payable at retirement, which is typical for defined benefit plans. While these plans take on some characteristics of defined contribution plans from workers' perspectives, they continue to be funded, administered, and regulated as defined benefit plans. The recent shift toward hybrid pension plans is occurring primarily among larger employers. In a number of cases where corporate giants of America have switched to hybrid plans, there has been considerable publicity.

The paper by Robert Clark and Sylvester Schieber provides new evidence on the impact of plan conversions on workers and examines the full extent of the conversion process, including changes in supplementary defined contribution plans. The authors also analyze the use of transition benefits to moderate the effect of the conversion on senior workers and the ending of early retirement subsidies. The paper finds that younger workers with limited job experience gain from plan conversions because of the steadier accrual of benefits at all service levels and the high probability that they will change jobs before reaching retirement age. Senior workers with considerable job tenure at the time of conversion are more likely to receive lower benefits unless special transition rules are applied. The authors find that most plan sponsors provided at least some transition protection to workers with advanced tenure. An interesting new finding presented in the paper is that most of the reduction in benefits that these workers expect is not attributable to the plan conversion itself but is instead the result of eliminating subsidized early retirement. Recent court rulings, however, have raised questions about the viability of cash-balance plans.

Regulatory Issues

The regulation of pensions has attracted significant attention. Supporters view the regulations as necessary for ensuring that the revenue losses from pensions are limited and that the benefits are distributed fairly. Opponents view the rules as unduly complex and ultimately self-defeating.

Nondiscrimination Rules

The paper by Robert Clark, Janemarie Mulvey, and Sylvester Schieber examines the effects of nondiscrimination rules on private pension participation rates. In their empirical analysis, the authors account for the changes in pension participation caused by the three legislative acts that implemented more restrictive nondiscrimination rules: the Tax Equity and Fiscal Responsibility Act of 1982, the Tax Reform Act of 1986, and the Omnibus Budget Reconciliation Act of 1993. The authors employ regression and logit analysis to test whether the enactment of new regulatory provisions altered the ratio of high-income worker participation to low-income worker participation, and whether the legislation increased the probability that a worker will participate in a pension.

To answer the first question, the authors use time series regression analysis with the aggregate ratio of high-income worker participation rates to lower-income participation rates as the dependent variable and the legislative actions included in the model as explanatory variables. The authors find that all three legislative actions decreased the pension participation of lower-income workers relative to higher-income workers. To answer the second question, the authors test whether the legislative actions, and other variables including age, employment sector, and marginal tax rate, affect the probability that a worker will participate in a private pension. The results indicate that the first two legislative actions decreased lower-income worker pension participation rates, while the Omnibus Budget Reconciliation Act increased the rate of lower-income worker pension participation. The combined effect of the legislation, however, is negative on lower-income worker participation. The results also indicate that the sector in which the worker is employed is significant at all income levels and that marginal tax rates have a small effect on pension participation. The authors conclude that there is no evidence to suggest that the more restrictive nondiscrimination rules have forced or enticed employers to provide pensions to low-paid workers.

Contribution Limits

A key element of ERISA's defined contribution provisions is the setting of limits on the size of tax-deductible contributions. In both nominal and, especially, inflation-adjusted terms, these limits have been tightened over the years. As more and more workers are saving for retirement primarily through defined contribution and individual retirement account (IRA) plans, Congress is considering legislation to increase the various limits on tax-deductible contributions to retirement accounts.

The paper by Jagadeesh Gokhale, Laurence Kotlikoff, and Mark Warshawsky addresses several questions related to limits on defined contribution plans. The first is whether statutory limits on tax-deductible contributions to defined contribution plans are likely to be constraining, focusing on households in various economic situations. The second is how large is the tax benefit from participating in defined contribution plans. The third is how does the defined contribution tax benefit depend on the level of lifetime income. The paper finds that the statutory limits bind those older middle-income households who started their pension savings programs late in life, those households who plan to retire early, single-earner households, those households who are not borrowing-constrained, and those with rapid rates of real wage growth. Most households with high levels of earnings, regardless of age or situation, are also constrained by the contribution limits. By contrast, lower- or middle-income two-earner households that can look forward to modest real earnings growth are likely to be borrowing-constrained for most of their preretirement years because of the costs related to paying a mortgage and to having children who will go to college. These households are not in a position to save the 25 percent of earnings allowed as a contribution to defined contribution plans. Some of these middle-income households, however, are constrained by the $10,500 limit on elective employee contributions to 401(k) plans if the households have access to only these plans and their employers make no pension contributions for them. The borrowing constraints faced by many lower- and middle-income Americans mean that contributions to defined contribution plans must come at the price of lower consumption when young and the benefit of higher consumption when old. For a stylized household earning $50,000, consistently contributing 10 percent of salary to a defined contribution plan that earns a 4 percent real return means consuming almost two times more when old than when young.

The tax benefit from participating in a defined contribution plan can be significant. Assuming annual contribution rates at the average of the maximum levels allowed by employers in 401(k) plans and assuming a 4 percent real return on defined contribution and other assets, the benefit is 2 percent of lifetime consumption for two-earner households earning $25,000 a year, 3.4 percent for those earning $100,000 a year, and 9.8 percent for those earning $300,000 a year. Contribution limits effectively limit the benefit at the highest regions of the household earnings distribution. The extent of the benefit is also quite sensitive to the assumed rate of return on defined contribution and other assets.

Improving Participants' Information

The advent of self-directed, defined contribution plans places much heavier burdens on workers to understand and manage their accounts. A natural question, in this environment, is the extent to which workers understand the features and rules of their own pension plans.

What Do Pension Participants Know?

Alan Gustman and Thomas Steinmeier present a comprehensive analysis of the degree to which workers understand their retirement plans. In the research literature, the almost universal assumption is that workers are perfectly informed about the rules and regulations governing their employer- and government-provided pensions. However, to the limited extent that researchers have been able to test this assumption, results suggest that workers are less than fully informed and that providing information can affect their behavior. This analysis uses data from the Health and Retirement Study to compare individuals' responses concerning their pension plans with the actual characteristics of those plans as reported by employers.

The findings suggest that workers approaching retirement possess a great deal of misinformation about their pensions. Fewer than half of respondents could identify their eligibility for early and normal retirement benefits, and only about half could identify their plan type. Eighty percent of respondents with a defined benefit plan were unaware they were eligible for early retirement or did not know their plan's benefit reduction rate. Of the respondents who were willing to estimate the value of their expected Social Security benefits, only half were able to estimate their annual benefits within $1,500.

The authors find similar disparities for private pensions. In addition, the authors complete a preliminary analysis of the relation between knowledge of retirement plan benefits and the fulfillment of retirement expectations, including wealth accumulation. Their findings indicate that lack of knowledge about retirement plan benefits has some systematic, but modest, effects on retirement plans, the realization of those plans, and saving, and highlight these issues as productive areas for future research.

Financial Education

One mechanism for improving workers' knowledge of their pension plans in particular and saving and portfolio issues in general is financial education. The Department of Labor recently made increased financial education a significant priority.

Dean Maki examines the impact of financial education on households' financial knowledge. He notes that rather than changing the fundamental parameters in households' utility function or discount rate, financial education can affect saving behavior by increasing a household's knowledge of investment options. Defining financial education as exposure to financial topics in high school or to employer-provided educational programs and seminars, the paper tests for the effect of financial education of households' knowledge of their pension plan characteristics and understanding of the relative rate of return on major financial assets.

The paper finds that education at both the high school and workplace level can affect financial knowledge. Creating a dummy variable based on a survey response regarding relative asset returns to represent knowledge of personal finance, the paper finds that respondents with high school exposure to personal finance are more likely to understand personal finance and that employees of firms that offer workplace education are more likely to understand personal finance. In addition, the study finds that high school and workplace education reduces the probability that households will not understand their pension plans.

Worker Choices in Self-Directed Defined Contribution Plans

Another way to gauge how well workers are managing their defined contribution plans is to examine different aspects of employee behavior. In defined contribution plans, workers must choose not only whether to participate, but how much to contribute, how to allocate the assets across various investment vehicles, and when and in what form to withdraw the funds.

Asset Allocation

Asset allocation, the decision about how much of a portfolio to allocate to different types of securities, is one of the fundamental issues in financial economics. For taxable individual investors, the proliferation of tax-deferred opportunities for retirement saving, such as IRAs, 401(k) plans, Keogh plans, and 403(b) plans, has added a new dimension to the traditional asset allocation problem. A taxable investor needs to make choices not just about the amount to hold in various types of assets, but also where to hold these assets. Assuming assets are broadly defined as risky and riskless, a taxable investor with a tax-deferred retirement saving account faces the complex problem of deciding how much of the risky asset to hold in his tax-deferred account and how much to hold in his taxable account. These choices are likely to be most salient for upper- and middle-income households for whom tax-deferred assets represent a substantial fraction, but not all, of their financial wealth.

The paper by James Poterba, John Shoven, and Clemens Sialm uses data on actual returns on taxable bonds, tax-exempt bonds, and a sample of equity mutual funds over a thirty-seven-year period to compare two asset location strategies for retirement savers who invest in equities through equity mutual funds. The first strategy gives priority to holding equity mutual funds in a saver's tax-deferred account, while the second strategy gives priority to holding fixed-income investments in the tax-deferred account.

The study finds that asset location decisions can significantly affect the wealth accumulation of retirement savers who hold assets in both tax-preferred pension accounts and nonpension accounts. Savers would have accumulated a larger stock of wealth if they had held their actively managed equity mutual fund in their tax-deferred account than if they had held their fund in a conventional taxable form. The explanation for this apparent contradiction with conventional wisdom has two parts. First, many equity mutual funds impose substantial tax burdens on their investors, raising the effective tax rate on investing in equities through mutual funds rather than in a buy-and-hold personal portfolio. Second, taxable investors who wish to hold fixed-income assets can do so by holding either tax-exempt or taxable bonds. The interest rate differential between these two types of bonds suggests that the effective tax rate on fixed-income investments may be higher than the statutory rate for high-income investors.

Back-Loaded versus Front-Loaded Saving Choices

Another investment choice retirement savers need to make is between front-loaded and back-loaded structures. Back-loaded plans are becoming increasingly popular. In back-loaded saving plans, the contribution is not deductible, but earnings and withdrawals are not taxed at all. Back-loaded Roth IRAs have existed since 1997. The 2001 tax cut introduced the notion of a Roth 401(k). Since then, there have been proposals to expand back-loaded saving vehicles.

In contrast to back-loaded plans, most tax-preferred saving vehicles in the United States generally include an up-front tax deduction, tax deferral over the investment horizon, and taxation upon withdrawal—401(k) plans are an example. The tax benefit conferred under this structure is composed of two different parts: a trade-off of present for future tax rates and the inside buildup over the investment horizon. Both of these features are thought to convey significant benefits. The benefit of inside buildup is readily apparent in that asset values can grow at their pre-tax rate of return, offering significant deferral value. The trade-off between present and future tax rates benefits the investor to the extent that future retirement income is lower than income received during working years, when the contributions are made. However, the value of this benefit is uncertain because tax structures may vary considerably over an investor's life cycle.

Joel Dickson provides analysis showing how the uncertainty of future tax rates can affect individuals' savings and investment decisions between front- and back-loaded plans. These vehicles provide an alternative method of allowing investors to hedge against the uncertainty of future tax rates, which greatly affect the retirement income stream of a traditional pension investment vehicle. Depending on an investor's risk tolerance and expected future tax rate, back-loaded investment vehicles could represent part or all of an investor's retirement savings allocations.

Annuity versus Lump-Sum Choices

While defined benefit and defined contribution plans differ on several dimensions, one of the most important differences is the method of distributing retirement income. Traditional defined benefit plans typically pay benefits in the form of a life annuity and thus provide retirees with a form of insurance against outliving their resources. Defined contribution plans, in contrast, are much less likely to offer life annuities to retirees. Instead, most defined contribution plans offer some sort of lump-sum payment or "phased withdrawal" options (or both) upon retirement. While these alternative distribution methods offer retirees a high degree of flexibility and liquidity, they fail to provide a formal mechanism by which individuals can insure against the risk of outliving their resources.

The paper by Jeffrey Brown and Mark Warshawsky explores the extent to which retirees can and do insure themselves against longevity risk in private pension plans. The authors first review the theoretical and empirical results on the value of annuities, and discuss reasons why households may choose not to insure themselves further against longevity risk. Brown and Warshawsky then analyze current trends in the private pension market and find that the shift from defined benefit plans to defined contribution plans is likely to reduce annuitization rates among future retirees. This conclusion is driven primarily by the fact that the majority of defined contribution plans, such as 401(k) plans, do not even offer participants a life annuity option at retirement. Thus, individuals who wish to annuitize generally must do so in the individual market where payouts are lower because the life expectancy for annuitants is longer than for the population at large. Hence, the authors can forecast that in the coming decades, absent institutional and regulatory changes, overall annuitization rates may fall and households may be increasingly exposed to the risk of outliving their financial resources, while the currently small private individual annuity market may witness significant growth. Finally, the authors discuss several policy options designed to increase annuitization of retirement resources.

Interactions with Social Security Reform

Because Social Security provides retirement income to almost all elderly households, it is difficult to consider pension reform issues in isolation from the current status and potential reform of the Social Security program. Two papers address these issues.

Effects of Social Security Reform on the Pension System

Since the release of the report of the 1994–96 Advisory Council on Social Security, there have been many studies of Social Security reform. These studies have focused primarily on the reform experiences of other countries, the feasibility of various transition paths, the administrative aspects of a system of individual accounts, and the impact on workers and beneficiaries as participants in the system. To date, there has been no comprehensive discussion of the likely effect that Social Security reform would have on employer-provided pensions. This is a critical omission. Secure retirements are often depicted as a stool with three legs—Social Security, employer-provided pensions, and personal saving. Changing any one of the legs may necessitate changes in the other legs if the stool is to remain stable.

There are several possible changes through which firms and workers might modify the system of employer-provided pensions in response to Social Security reform. First, because the Social Security system operates through the workplace, closing the financial gap in Social Security will raise the cost of employing workers. Second, because pensions are primarily used as a means of accumulating wealth for retirement, the effect of Social Security reform on pension plans depends on the way reform affects workers' demand for retirement saving. Third, there is considerable heterogeneity in the reasons why people save and how well their pensions help them achieve their goals.

The primary objective of the paper by Andrew Samwick is to identify the important channels through which firms and workers might modify the system of employer-provided pensions in response to Social Security reform. The paper develops a model of pension plan design that incorporates heterogeneity in tastes for saving and sorting of workers in the labor market. The model is used to analyze the likely effects of a range of Social Security reform proposals on the design of employer-provided pensions. Several reform options are shown to change the relative benefits received by high- and low-income workers and to affect the ability of pension plan sponsors to comply with nondiscrimination rules for the distribution of pension contributions and benefits across workers of different wage levels.

Assessing Risk in Pension Guarantees

Many observers now believe that future retirement benefits provided by many public pension systems around the world, including the U.S. Social Security system, should be backed by more assets. Disagreement, however, exists about whether those new assets should be held in private accounts or by the public pension plan itself. The economics literature has traditionally focused on deterministic models and has concluded that the choice between the two is basically immaterial. However, sharp differences between the two approaches emerge when risks are explicitly taken into account.

The paper by Kent Smetters considers the design and cost of guaranteeing retirement benefits in the presence of political and market-based risks. The analysis focuses on two potential reforms to the Social Security system: the introduction of private pension accounts, and an increase in the asset holdings within Social Security while maintaining the existing structure. Smetters demonstrates that although the two approaches can be equivalent under certain circumstances, they generate very different risks. Each approach poses a different set of political risks, and each approach would typically differ in how market-based risk is shared between generations. Both sets of risks can dramatically affect the liabilities that future generations could inherit in the form of either increased taxes or reduced benefits. The author concludes that private accounts are typically superior in handling the most important political-economy risks, but that increasing the prefunding of public pension plans can be more effective at reducing market-based risks.

2

The Transition to Hybrid Pension Plans in the United States: An Empirical Analysis

ROBERT L. CLARK AND SYLVESTER J. SCHIEBER

O ver the past three decades, pension coverage rates have remained fairly constant, but the composition of pensions has changed dramatically. Plan sponsors have shifted away from defined benefit plans and chosen to offer defined contribution plans instead, especially 401(k) plans. This change has occurred primarily among smaller employers, but according to a recent *Fortune* list, sixteen of the largest one hundred publicly traded corporations in the United States had a defined contribution plan as their only retirement plan.

During the past decade, another significant change emerged: the conversion of traditional benefit plans to so-called hybrid plans, which take on some characteristics of defined contribution plans from workers' perspectives, but are funded, regulated, and insured as defined benefit plans. The first hybrid pension was created by BankAmerica in 1985, and initially only a few companies followed. By May 1999, however, at least 325 plan sponsors had adopted hybrid plans, and more have come into existence since then.[1] The number of new plans

The authors wish to thank Gordon Goodfellow, Tomeka Hill, and Lex Miller of Watson Wyatt Worldwide for their help in developing the statistical analysis included in this paper. They thank Richard Joss, Eric Lofgren, Richard Luss, Lex Miller, Steven Nyce, Lynn Phillips, and Kenneth Steiner of Watson Wyatt Worldwide for their comments. William Gale provided valuable, extremely helpful substantive and editorial comments on an earlier draft. A more detailed discussion of the issues and derivation and elaboration of the results may be found in Clark and Schieber (2001).

1. Pensions and Investments (1999).

continued to grow but slowed appreciably after 2000 because of uncertainty about how federal regulations were going to treat these plans. The shift toward hybrid plans is occurring primarily among larger employers and in a number of cases has attracted considerable adverse publicity.

Despite ongoing conversions and public controversies, hybrid plans have only recently attracted scholarly research.[2] This chapter provides new evidence of the impact on workers of conversions to hybrid plans, including the effects of changes in supplementary defined contribution plans, the use of transition benefits, and the termination of early retirement subsidies.

We find that younger workers gain from plan conversions because of the steadier accrual of benefits and the high probability they will change jobs before retiring. Senior workers with considerable job tenure at the time of the conversion are more likely to receive lower benefits unless special transition rules are applied. We find that most plan sponsors provided at least some transition protection to workers with advanced tenures. An interesting new finding is that most of the reduction in benefits for senior workers is due to the elimination of subsidized early retirement, not to the plan conversion itself. This suggests that conversions to hybrid plans should be evaluated in the broader context of whether it is appropriate to encourage later retirement.

Hybrid Plans: A Primer

Traditionally, pension plans have come in two types, defined benefit plans and defined contribution plans, which differ substantially in their basic structure. Hybrid plans contain features of both plans. This section contrasts the features of traditional and hybrid plans, discusses the causes of the shift toward hybrids, and raises key issues to be addressed in the subsequent analysis.

Characteristics of Traditional Plans

Defined benefit plans provide workers with a specified retirement benefit linked to preretirement earnings. Coverage is universal among qualified employees, and workers do not face any explicit investment choices or risks. Traditionally, benefits are paid as a life annuity, providing insurance against retirees outliving their wealth. Benefits are insured on a limited basis against the plan sponsor's insolvency.

Workers who change jobs frequently under defined benefit plans typically obtain considerably smaller total retirement benefits than if they remained with a single company. This occurs because benefits are typically based on earnings shortly before job termination and are not indexed for wage growth between termination and retirement. A related concern is that workers may not fully

---

2. Brown and others (2000), Clark and Munzenmaier (2001), Clark and Schieber (2001).

understand their benefits since the benefits upon leaving the firm differ from the ultimate benefit if they stayed.

Employers can use defined benefit plans to reduce turnover rates, reward loyal workers, and encourage timely retirement. The major disadvantage for sponsors is the relatively burdensome regulatory structure.

Defined contribution plans differ considerably. Under defined contribution plans, benefits depend on contributions over the working life and returns on those assets. If contributions are made at a stable rate during a worker's career, benefits will accumulate more smoothly over time than under a defined benefit plan of comparable lifetime generosity, because of the back-loaded structure of defined benefit plans. A related advantage is that defined contribution balances are portable with job changes. Thus, workers who change employers frequently typically accrue larger benefits during their career under a series of defined contribution plans than under a series of defined benefit plans of comparable lifetime generosity.

Workers in defined contribution plans must choose whether to participate, how much to contribute, how to allocate the funds, and when and in what form to withdraw the funds. This provides an opportunity for workers to fashion their retirement accounts to meet their personal preferences. But it also carries substantial risks: workers may make poor investment choices and end up with inadequate resources at retirement.

In addition, workers in defined contribution plans bear the investment risk on their saving, and they bear longevity risk. The plans tend to pay benefits as lump sums that do not provide the same insurance against longevity risk as annuities. Retirees can purchase individual annuities but not on terms as favorable as through a typical defined benefit plan. Retirees can also roll over lump sums into individual retirement accounts and withdraw funds incrementally over their life expectancy, but the participant still bears the risk of uncertain longevity.

Relative to defined benefit plans, defined contribution plans provide employers with more straightforward funding of benefits, easier matching of liabilities and assets, reduced administrative costs, increased ability to hand off fiduciary obligations and investment risks to participants, and simpler communications with employees. In addition, employer contributions to the plans can be disproportionately directed toward workers who demonstrate characteristics particularly associated with high productivity.[3]

But defined contribution plans also present disadvantages for employers. Employees who do not save enough may be reluctant to retire on a timely basis and have the potential to become hidden pensioners on active payrolls if their productivity falls below earnings at advanced ages. In addition, the plans are less

---

3. Ippolito (1997).

Table 2-1. *Features of Alternative Employer-Sponsored Retirement Plans*

Plan feature	Defined benefit plan	Defined contribution plan	Hybrid plan	Hybrid plan tendency
Employer contributes	Virtually always	Sometimes	Virtually always	DB
Employee contributes	Very rarely	Virtually always	Very rarely	DB
Participation	Automatic	Employee choice	Automatic	DB
Contribution level	Automatic	Employee choice	Automatic	DB
PBGC insurance	Yes but capped	Not needed	Yes but capped	DB
Early departure penalty	Yes	No	No	DC
Benefits easily portable	No	Yes	Yes	DC
Annual communication	Benefit at end of career	Current balance	Current balance	DC
Retirement incentives	Occur at specific ages	Neutral	Most are neutral	DC
Accrual of benefits	Loaded to career end	Level over career	Level or back-loaded	Mixed
Financial market risks	Employer bears	Employee bears	Shared	Mixed
Longevity insurance	Typically yes	Typically no	Not often taken	Mixed

DB = defined benefit, DC = defined contribution.

capable than defined benefit plans of retaining workers during prime career years, since workers lose benefits to a much greater extent under defined benefit plans by terminating prematurely than under defined contribution plans. Finally, it is impossible to put the same sort of retirement incentives into these plans to manage the orderly exit of workers at the end of their useful careers with the sponsors.

Characteristics of Hybrid Plans

Hybrid plans are intended to garner the relative advantages of traditional defined benefit and defined contribution plans (table 2-1). Cash balance plans, for example, define a notional worker account based on an annual contribution rate for each year of work plus accumulating interest on the account balance. In a pension equity plan, workers earn credits for each year of service under the plan. For example, a worker starting employment in her early twenties might earn seven points for each year of service initially. By the time she is in her fifties, the accrual rate might grade up to twenty points. When she terminates employment under the plan, her benefit is the accumulated point total times her final average salary divided by 100.

The participation and contribution features of hybrid plans are similar to traditional defined benefit plans. Likewise, hybrid plans are regulated, funded, and administered like defined benefit plans. But hybrid plans also feature portable, easily explained benefits, like defined contribution plans. Although hybrid plans must offer an annuity option, all of them also offer lump-sum options, which are the overwhelming choice of retirees.

The new plans alleviate some of the financial market risks of defined contribution plans. Account balances are credited with an annual rate of return equal to some specific rate such as the Treasury bill rate, thus reducing the explicit investment risk a typical defined contribution participant faces. Sponsors typically guarantee an investment return to workers, but that guarantee presumably includes an adjustment for the fact that sponsors now bear the risk of fluctuating asset returns. Workers retain investment risk in that sponsors may adjust the benchmark used or a given benchmark rate may fluctuate.[4]

Hybrid plans tend to be more age-neutral than traditional defined benefit plans and to date do not have early retirement incentives. It would be possible to structure a hybrid plan to include the same sorts of incentives that most traditional pensions currently include, although the actual occurrence of such incentives in hybrid plans is extremely rare.

Causes of Shift toward Hybrid Plans

There are many reasons why firms might shift to hybrid plans.[5] First, regulations limit employers to funding their plans on the basis of current liability, but accounting rules require that employers use projected liability. As a result, funding a defined benefit plan according to the regulations creates balance sheet liabilities and pension costs that plan sponsors may not want on their financial statements. Funding and accounting for hybrid plans allows sponsors to align accrued benefit obligations and projected benefit obligations more directly than they can with a traditional plan.

Second, employers may be responding to competitive labor markets and worker preferences for simpler pension arrangements. Attracting and retaining high-quality workers is a persistent problem for employers.[6] Restructuring pensions to give more benefits to younger workers in both real and perceived terms can help make the total compensation package more attractive to such workers. Eliminating the early retirement incentives for workers can also help retain workers even though it may generate negative feelings on the part of those affected.

Third, some employers have changed their retirement plans as part of a more comprehensive change to their compensation package. For example, as shown below, several employers have coupled enhanced pension benefits in the move to hybrid plans with reductions in future retiree health commitments. This is an effort by plan sponsors to get liabilities off their books as they rationalize the funding of retirement benefits under tax laws that do not allow retiree health

---

4. Some plans have recently begun to offer participants in cash balance plans returns keyed to a range of portfolio investment options, a feature that creates the same investment risks as exist in defined contribution plans where asset investment is self-directed.

5. Brown and others (2000).

6. Brown and others (2000).

benefit funding with pretax monies, but do encourage cash benefit funding. Other employers have modified their cash retirement programs in the move to hybrid plans as they spread stock options more broadly across their work forces than in the past.

Fourth, some employers have cut back on all costs due to market considerations. The three industries most heavily affected by the shift to hybrid plans have been health care, financial services, and utilities, all of which have undergone significant restructuring, which undoubtedly puts pressure on labor costs, including pensions.

A popular, but flawed, claim is that the conversions are merely a means for plan sponsors to gain access to surplus assets in the plans without having to pay the prohibitive taxes that would otherwise be applied.[7] This claim is flawed on both conceptual and empirical grounds.

Conceptually, it is not clear how a plan sponsor with excess assets benefits from converting to a hybrid plan. The sponsor cannot get at the assets for any purpose other than providing retirement benefits. If the new plan is less generous than the old one, then the plan becomes even more overfunded, thus defeating part of the alleged purpose of the conversion. If the new plan is more generous, that does not seem to be a policy problem.

The empirical problem with the claim that conversions are merely a mechanism to avoid reversion taxes is that the majority of plan conversions have taken place among plans that were not overfunded (box 2-1). The data simply do not support the notion that conversions were concentrated on overfunded plans or that conversions were simply a mechanism to avoid excise taxes.

Nevertheless, there are clearly strong incentives to move to hybrids for employers with overfunded traditional defined benefit plans who want a plan with defined contribution features. Shifting to a pure defined contribution plan requires termination of the existing plan and the purchase of annuities for all accrued benefits under that plan. There are costs associated with buying annuities. Second, the excise tax on conversions to traditional defined contribution plans is virtually confiscatory if the plan sponsor wants to recapture any of the excess assets. The excise tax can be avoided completely or partially, but only by taking steps that many employers are reluctant to pursue.[8] Converting to a hybrid plan does not incur any excise tax.

7. See Sheppard (2000) and Ippolito in this volume.

8. The excise tax can be avoided completely by allocating a pro rata distribution of assets across the participant population at the point of conversion subject to annual contribution limits. Employers seldom adopt this approach because it provides tremendous windfall benefits to the workers covered under a plan on the date of transition to the new one. A second alternative allows a sponsor with excess assets in a terminating defined benefit plan to reduce (but not eliminate) the tax obligation by transferring 20 percent of the excess to increase termination benefits across the board. A third alternative allows the sponsor to transfer 25 percent of excise taxes into a suspense account that can then be allocated to workers' defined contribution accounts over seven years. If

---

Box 2-1. *Did Overfunding Cause the Shift to Hybrid Plans?*

To examine the financial status of plans that were converted from defined benefit to hybrid plans, we used files generated by the Internal Revenue Service and the Department of Labor from the public disclosure filings—that is, Form 5500—required of employer-sponsored retirement plans. We examined data for the 1996 plan year.

After eliminating plans with fewer than 100 active participants, with less than $10 million in assets, or where the benefit formula does not depend on salary, the data file contained about 4,300 plans, of which 231 were hybrids. We compared the financial status of these plans with all pay-related defined benefit plans with more than 100 active participants.

One measure of overfunding compares assets and current liability obligations. In terminating a plan, the plan sponsor must immediately vest all benefits. Thus a reasonable measure of plan liability includes all vested and nonvested benefits as of a particular date. Figure 2-1 presents the results of such an analysis for the hybrid plans in our sample. The plans that have been converted to hybrid plans tended to be somewhat more concentrated at funding levels between 90 and 130 percent of their current liability than all defined benefit plans. At the tails of the funding distribution, hybrid plans were somewhat less represented compared with all defined benefit plans. The data do not support the contention that all plans were overfunded, as nearly one-quarter of the converted plans had assets totaling less than their current liability.

While the current liability may be a reasonable indicator of a plan sponsor's accrued pension obligation, it is not a reasonable measure of termination liability. In terminating a plan, the sponsor has to purchase annuities for all accrued benefits. Among the converting plans in our sample, 56 percent had assets of less than 120 percent of current liability, and 72 percent had assets of less than 130 percent of current liability at the end of their 1996 plan year. In comparison, the Pension Benefit Guaranty Corporation analyzed 10 large plans with assets in excess of 125 percent of current liability in 1995 and found that their assets would cover only 95 percent of the level needed to terminate the plans on average.[1]

1. Pension Benefit Guaranty Corporation (1995).

Issues Raised in the Shift toward Hybrid Plans

Almost every hybrid plan has replaced a traditional defined benefit plan. To illustrate the effects on retirement benefits, consider the accrual of benefits under a typical traditional defined benefit plan and a newly adopted cash balance plan. We assume the worker is hired at age 30 at a salary of $40,000 and

---

this option is chosen, the excise and income tax applies to only 75 percent of excess assets and the excise tax rate is reduced to 20 percent. A fourth variant allows the sponsor to transfer 100 percent of excess assets into a suspense account that can then be allocated to workers' defined contribution accounts over seven years. If this option is chosen, there is no income tax obligation on the excess assets and a 20 percent excise tax is applied to only 75 percent of excess assets.

Figure 2-1. *Funding Levels of Traditional Defined and Hybrid Plans Relative to Current Liability*[a]

Percentage of plans

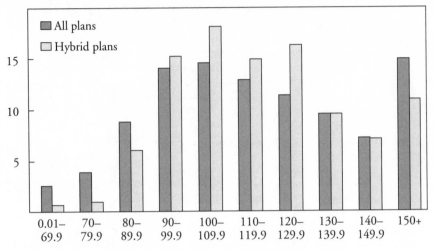

Asset level as percentage of full funding limit

Source: Authors' tabulation of 1996 Form 5500 files.
a. Based on 1996 plan year disclosure information.

obtains average wage growth over time. The results, shown in figure 2-2, assume the worker was employed throughout his career under each plan and that differences in pension accrual patterns had no offsetting effects on wages.

Whether the traditional plan or the hybrid plan is better for this worker depends on how long he works for the sponsor. If this worker were to quit at any age below 55, he would be better off under the cash balance plan. Around age 46 or 47, the difference in benefits is worth nearly one-half of a year's pay. The advantage under the cash balance plan changes dramatically with early retirement eligibility under the traditional plan. By age 60 the traditional plan value exceeds that of the cash balance by nearly a half-year's pay.

This typical case captures the main qualitative differences between the accrual patterns in traditional defined benefit plans and cash balance plans. But it masks a wide diversity of potential outcomes, due to differing plan features, wages, years of services, and expected retirement age among workers.

Transition Issues. The shift to hybrid plans raises difficult transition issues. For example, consider the case depicted in figure 2-3: a worker, age 50, has been covered under a traditional plan for twenty years before the transition to a cash balance plan. If the worker's initial cash balance in the new plan equals her accrued

Figure 2-2. *Value of Accrued Benefits at Various Ages for a New Hire at Age 30 with a Starting Wage of $40,000 under Alternative Plans*

Value of accrued benefit as a multiple of annual pay

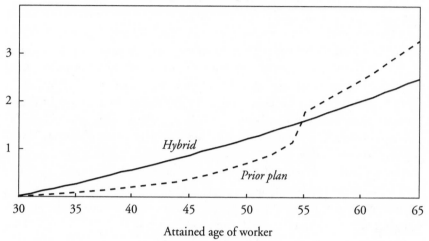

Source: Watson Wyatt Worldwide as described in the text.

Figure 2-3. *Potential Benefit Accruals as a Multiple of Annual Wage for a Worker Age 50 with 20 Years' Service at Conversion under Alternative Plans*

Value of accrued benefit as a multiple of annual pay

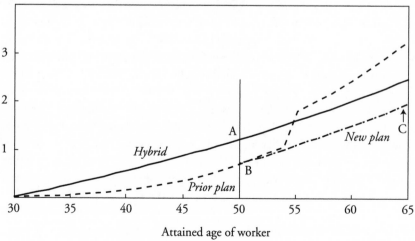

Source: Watson Wyatt Worldwide.

benefit under the previous plan, and the plan sponsor allows benefits to accrue under the new structure, the initial benefit would be set at point B. Benefits would accrue going forward at the same rate as under the new plan, and the worker would end up with a benefit of value C at age 65. This worker would essentially get the worst of both the traditional and hybrid plan worlds—she would have obtained the very low accruals in the traditional plan early in her career and missed the high accruals in that plan during the latter part of her career.

Plan sponsors have adopted a number of options to address this issue. One approach is create a starting balance as though the worker had participated in the hybrid plan from initial employment. In this case, the initial benefit would be set at point A, and future benefits would accrue from that point forward. This option still leaves the worker with lower benefits than if the traditional plan had stayed in place.

Another option is to grandfather workers who are close to retirement eligibility, letting them finish out their career as though no plan change has been implemented. A third possibility is having such workers convert to the new plan, but also providing them with supplemental benefits. Alternatively, some employers allow workers to choose among the plans.

None of these options is foolproof. Difficult equity issues arise in determining who should receive grandfathering treatment. Likewise, workers may choose a plan assuming they will stay at the firm but then leave prematurely or be laid off.

Wear-Away. Another concern arises when a worker is converted to the new plan with an opening balance that remains frozen for some period. This is commonly referred to as "wear-away" of earned benefits. There are essentially two situations under which this phenomenon arises.

The first situation arises when employers significantly curtail the benefit generosity in the adoption of the hybrid plan. In conversions to pension equity plans, initial balances are often set by assuming workers had been covered under the new plan from the time they were hired. Workers whose benefits under the new formula are less than accrued benefits under the previous plan will face a period of work without accruing added benefits, relative to the previous plan.

In conversions to cash balance plans, initial balances are typically set at the point of conversion on the basis of workers' age and service under the previous plan. If the sponsor uses a higher interest rate in calculating the value of initial benefits in the new plan than in determining the present value of the accrued benefit of the previous plan, initial benefits in the new plan will be less than accrued benefits in the previous plan. Participants would have to work for some period simply to allow the lump-sum benefit under the new plan to catch up to the benefit already accrued under the old plan.

The problem of wear-away of accrued benefits by establishing a low initial lump-sum benefit in the new plan appears to be have been resolved in recent years. In one survey, in 92 percent of plan conversions, participants' initial lump

Figure 2-4. *Potential Benefit Accruals for Fifty-Six-Year-Old Worker with Thirty-One Years' Service at Conversion under Alternative Plans*

Value of accrued benefit as a multiple of annual pay

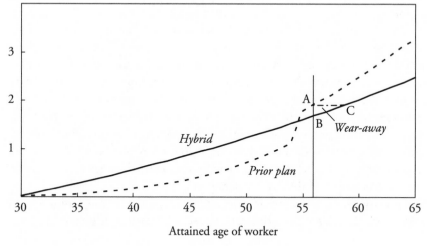

Attained age of worker

Source: Watson Wyatt Worldwide.

sums were equal to or greater than the present value of their normal retirement benefits under the old benefit formula.[9] The discount rates that sponsors can use are regulated by law.[10]

The second wear-away situation arises when the new plan does not offer a particular benefit that the old plan did (figure 2-4). In this case, the worker in question has already reached early retirement age under the previous plan, shown by point A, which is his accrued benefit under the old formula. Assume that under the new plan, the initial benefit is reflected at level B. This could apply for a pension equity plan because the formula results in a benefit accrual

9. Brown and others (2000).
10. There is another situation that may be perceived as creating wear-away but does not. It arises because of variations in interest rates used in establishing plan balances at the time of conversion. Under current rules, plans use thirty-year Treasury rates in determining the lump-sum values of benefits. While a plan can use the most recent month's closing rate, it can also use a closing quarterly, semiannual, or annual rate. To show how this may create the perception of wear-away, consider a plan that has traditionally used the closing September rate from the prior year. A sponsor transitioning to a hybrid plan in December might have used a given interest rate. One transitioning in the following January might have a higher rate because interest rates had changed in the interim. In this case, converting on the later date would have reduced the value of initial benefits significantly. Workers thus might have to work some period under their new plan to get back to the value of benefits in their old plan just before the transition, often thought of as wear-away. But in fact there is no added wear-away due to the rise in interest rates. The rise reduces the value of accrued benefits in the old plan just as much as under the new plan.

pattern shown by the solid line. The new plan eliminates the early retirement subsidy and simply provides a lower accrual at age 56. This could apply for a cash balance plan because the benefit value in the new plan is the lump-sum value of the accrued benefit; sponsors do not have to "vest" the value of early retirement subsidies if retirees take benefits in a lump sum.

The credited value of benefits under the new plan, at point B, would be less than his accrued benefit earned under the previous plan. While the worker's accrued benefit cannot be reduced, it can be frozen. The wear-away in this situation arises because benefits for this type of worker are frozen until the benefits in the new plan catch up with the accrued benefit under the old plan.

Given the widespread prevalence of early retirement incentives in traditional plans, this second wear-away situation has the potential to arise in almost all conversions to hybrid plans. Yet, as discussed below, many plan conversions do not create wear-away. The reason is that many sponsors include sweeteners in benefits under the new plan. In these cases, workers might receive added credits under the new plan, or the initial balance in the new plan might be calculated using a lower interest rate than that used to calculate the accrued benefit in the old plan.

Other Analytical Considerations

The discussion above focuses on changes in the defined benefit plans in isolation and ignores changes in the level or structure of other compensation. For example, among the seventy-seven plans we study, described below, twenty-four enhanced their defined contribution plans as they shifted to a hybrid plan. A substantial number of the sponsors who raised benefits in adopting a hybrid plan also curtailed retiree health benefits.[11]

Similarly, we cannot fully capture the implications of varying wage-growth patterns on the shift to hybrid plans. Allowing for changes in benefits and real wage patterns likely will result in more diverse outcomes across workers and plan types than our analysis suggests.

The Evolving Policy Discussion

The shift to hybrid plans has generated considerable outcry from affected workers, a series of congressional hearings, and several suggested legislative remedies to deal with perceived abuses. The policy issues generally revolve around the fair treatment of workers, in particular older workers.

One issue pertains to the information provided to participants. Regardless of whether workers are given a choice of plans, they need to understand the potential

---

11. In the latter case, the employers appear to be shifting from a benefit that cannot be effectively prefunded under the federal tax code to one that can be prefunded. Typically these employers allow retirees to continue to purchase retiree health insurance through the company, but they have to pay the full premium to do so. The enhancement of the cash benefits for retirement should facilitate retirees' ability to pay for their insurance.

benefits they will receive. It has been suggested that every worker affected by the adoption of a hybrid plan be given a report on the benefit they have accumulated at the point of transition in their old plan and estimates of future accruals in both the old and new plans. Much of this information is difficult to provide, however, at the point of the transition. Detailed information on divorce court orders, dependents' benefits, and so on that affect the benefit is often not accumulated until an actual pension determination is made at retirement.

A broader issue, with several interlocking themes, is whether firms should have the right to alter the employment contract in such a fashion. From a strictly legal viewpoint, there does not seem to be a problem. Firms already have the right to terminate a defined benefit plan. Firms also have the right to alter benefit formulas and retirement ages in defined benefit plans. Thus, the conversion to a hybrid plan does not seem at odds with existing law.

A key sticking point arises because firms do *not* have the right to reduce accrued benefits. To be clear, plans that provide an initial account balance in the hybrid plan, which is less than the accrued benefit in the previous, traditional plan on the date of conversion, would be required to pay the accrued benefits under the old plan if the worker were to retire before the accrued benefit in the new plan matched or exceeded it. Differences in the values of the discount rate used in these determinations can produce immediate gains in the present value of retirement benefits at the time of conversions and affect the subsequent rate of benefit accrual.

Wear-away is related to these concerns, but it represents a reduction in anticipated future benefits accruals, not in already accrued benefits. As noted above, wear-away arises from discount rate issues, which have been dealt with in the law, and from early retirement issues, discussed below. It can also arise when employers curtail benefits significantly and virtually freeze benefits for workers with substantial service. Here the problem seems to be one of reconciling the difficult issues of economic necessity that drive benefit reductions with a need to treat workers equitably. Some of the cost reductions related to plan restructuring are so severe that one can only conclude the plan sponsors must be struggling for economic survival. It is not clear that preservation of pension accruals at any cost makes sense.

A final issue is the role of early retirement subsidies. There is considerable sentiment that early retirement subsidies should be preserved and fully vested in the transition to hybrid plans. But this would provide more protection for early retirement subsidies in the transition to hybrid plans than current law provides in traditional plans. Early retirement benefits do not vest the way the normal retirement benefits do. Under current law, in order to receive an early retirement subsidy, an employee must work until the age of early retirement eligibility, retire, and take the benefit in the form of an annuity before reaching normal retirement age.

The Impact on Workers' Benefits

To investigate these issues more formally, we use a data set consisting of seventy-seven plan conversions, of which thirty-one are conversions to pension equity plans and forty-six are conversions to cash balance plans.[12] For purposes of comparability, we treat all of the conversions as though they occurred in 1999 even though they may have occurred several years earlier.

About 56 percent of the plans reduced their overall defined benefit costs upon converting to a hybrid, 20 percent adopted changes that were cost neutral, and 23 percent increased their pension costs. Overall, plan sponsors reduced long-term annual pension plan costs by about 10 percent.[13] Adding in changes to defined contribution plans, about 45 percent of sponsors reduced costs, 18 percent adopted changes that were cost neutral, and 37 percent increased costs. On average pension costs fell by only 1 percent.[14]

To provide more detail on how the plans were adjusted, we examine two hypothetical workers. The first is hired at age 30 for $25,000 a year at the time of transition to the hybrid plan. We evaluate his benefits under the hybrid plan and the previous plan when the worker is 40 and when he is 60. The second worker began employment at age 30, and at age 50 earns $50,000 per year when the new plan is adopted. We evaluate his benefits at ages 50 and 60.[15]

Table 2-2 shows that the overwhelming majority of the plan conversions provide increased benefits for the young new hire if he stays for ten years and then terminates. If he remains with the firm until age 60, however, only 22 percent of the hybrid plans would match or increase benefits relative to the previous plan. For the 50-year-old worker twenty years into a career at the transition, the story is similar. If the worker leaves just after the transition, he will be as well off or better off under the hybrid plan in 94 percent of the cases. But if the worker stays until age 60, he will be worse off under the hybrid plan in 55 percent of

12. Brown and others (2000) use data on seventy-eight plan sponsors. Clark and Schieber (2001) used seventy-seven of these sponsors in developing their analysis, eliminating one plan because of its relatively small size. We use the same sample here.

13. This figure is calculated using a projected unit credit basis, the actuarial method used for estimating pension costs under the Financial Accounting Standards Board rules for pension accounting.

14. Brown and others (2000).

15. In making these comparisons we had to make certain assumptions about wage growth, returns on account balances, and the like. We assumed each of the workers would realize steady wage growth of 4 percent per year over the calculation periods. For plans integrated with Social Security we assumed the wage base would grow at a rate of 3.5 percent per year. In the case of cash balance plans, most of them credit interest to accumulating balances by linking to some index measure. For those that follow long-term Treasury yields, we credited accounts with 7 percent interest per year. For those that follow intermediate yields, we credited them at 6.5 percent per year. For those using short-term rates, the crediting rate used was 5.5 percent. For those with a stated percentage credit rate in their plan, we used the stated percentage for annual interest crediting. In estimating the lump-sum values of traditional plans we used a 7 percent discount rate and the GAM-83 life table with a three-year setback.

Table 2-2. *Hybrid Plan Benefits Relative to Those under Prior Defined Benefit Plans for Selected Workers*
Percent of plans

Hybrid plan benefit as a percentage of prior plan's benefit	New hire age 30 at transition		Worker age 50 with 20 years' service at transition	
	At age 40	At age 60	At age 50	At age 60
25 to 49	0.0	10.4	0.0	7.8
50 to 74	1.3	41.6	1.3	23.4
75 to 99	0.0	26.0	5.2	23.4
100 exactly	2.6	5.2	20.8	24.7
100 to 124	3.9	9.1	20.8	18.2
125 to 149	5.2	6.5	19.5	2.6
150 to 199	23.4	1.3	16.9	0.0
200 to 299	41.6	0.0	14.3	0.0
300 to 399	15.6	0.0	1.3	0.0
400 or more	6.5	0.0	0.0	0.0
Minimum	68.5	25.4	68.4	37.4
Maximum	816.7	150.0	301.1	144.3
Mean	250.0	77.9	144.0	86.6
Standard deviation	126.3	28.3	50.9	23.0

Source: Authors' computations from data provided by Watson Wyatt Worldwide.

the cases. The story described in the previous section appears to be borne out in the vast majority of cases where employers have shifted to hybrid plans. The story seems to apply to many workers fairly far into their careers at transition as well as to younger workers.[16]

Early Retirement Subsidies

The one consistent element of change across virtually all of the conversions to hybrid plans has been the elimination of early retirement incentives.[17] This is such a universal phenomenon that it warrants special attention. Figures 2-1 through 2-3 indicate why table 2-2 shows such different results for workers leaving the firm at age 50 or less compared with those leaving at age 60. The step-up in benefits at age 55 in the figures corresponds to workers' eligibility for early retirement benefits under traditional defined benefit plans.[18]

16. There is no important difference between the results (not shown) for pension equity plans and the results for cash balance plans.

17. Clark and Schieber (2001).

18. The suggestion that a worker receives an actuarially subsidized benefit should not be confused with a discussion about who pays for the benefit. The marginal productivity theory of wages suggests that workers receive employee benefits, including pensions, at the cost of reduced wages. In that regard, a benefit that a worker may receive at age 55 has likely been financed out of the worker's reduced wages over the years he was covered under the plan (see McGill and others, 1996, ch. 20, for a full discussion).

Table 2-3. *Benefit Reductions Attributable to Eliminating Early Retirement Subsidies*
Percent of plans

Effect on benefit for hypothetical worker	At age 55	At age 60	At age 62
New hire at age 30, salary $40,000			
Cut exceeds subsidy	15.6	41.6	49.4
Cut less than subsidy	42.9	27.3	22.1
Maintained or increased	41.6	31.2	28.6
Worker at age 40 with 10 years' service earning $50,000 at transition			
Cut exceeds subsidy	15.6	39.0	48.1
Cut less than subsidy	45.5	28.6	19.5
Maintained or increased	39.0	32.5	32.5
Worker at age 50 with 20 years' service earning $60,000 at transition			
Cut exceeds subsidy	13.0	27.3	37.7
Cut less than subsidy	23.4	27.3	20.8
Maintained or increased	63.6	45.5	41.6

Source: Authors' computations from data provided by Watson Wyatt Worldwide.

Early retirement subsidies could be provided through hybrid plans, for example, by allowing workers to convert accumulated balances to an annuity at rates that are more favorable than their remaining life expectancy would suggest. Since that has not happened, it suggests that employers are deliberately eliminating these actuarial subsidies for early retirement.

Table 2-3 shows the effects of the shift to hybrid plans where early retirement subsidies were eliminated for three hypothetical workers and three scenarios: where costs of the hybrid plan fell by more than the cost of the early retirement subsidies; where costs fell, but by less than the saving if the subsidies had simply been eliminated; and where plan costs rose. In every case, the majority of the hybrid plans reduced benefits for the prototypical workers by less than the amount of the reduction that would have occurred if they had simply eliminated their early retirement subsidies. For many of the cases where the worker is assumed to retire at age 55, fewer than a fifth of the plans would reduce benefits by more than the elimination of the early retirement subsidies. For these workers retiring at 55, 39 to 64 percent of the plans would actually enhance benefits even though they had eliminated early retirement subsidies. Where benefits are reduced, eliminating these subsidies is the major aim, though not necessarily the sole aim, of plan sponsors. To the extent that it goes beyond eliminating the subsidy, the plan change is about a general reduction in retirement benefits. But plan sponsors can accomplish this reduction in correspondence with either the shift to a hybrid plan or within the context of the existing defined benefit plan.

Table 2-3 shows that employers used the cost savings from eliminating early retirement subsidies in very different ways. It also shows that conversion to a hybrid can reduce benefits for certain workers even in cases where the savings from eliminating the subsidies are plowed back into the plan, and that even where employers increased costs, some workers could be worse off. This is because the shift to a hybrid plan is, at least in part, a redistribution of pension benefits across a work force at a given point in time.

Wear-Away

Table 2-4 shows the percentage of plans that had some wear-away period for workers with selected characteristics.[19] In developing this analysis, we focused on 54-year-old workers, who are on the cusp of early retirement eligibility under their old plans, and 50-year-old workers, to show the extent to which workers further from early retirement eligibility were affected.

Clearly the wear-away phenomenon has been more prevalent for workers right at the eligibility age for early retirement than for workers a few years away. For workers age 54 about half of plans had no wear-away period, compared with about 85 percent for workers age 50. In most cases the duration of wear-away is less than five years, but the variation in wear-away periods is substantial. There are few plans with very extended periods of wear-away for the workers considered here. Most of the plans with more than six years of wear-away were adopted more than a decade ago. In a few cases, the protracted wear-away period amounted to freezing the old plan. Most of the cases with protracted wear-away involved substantial benefit cutbacks in the shift to a hybrid plan.

Table 2-5 shows the magnitude, or rate, of wear-away. For workers age 54 with earnings of $50,000 or $80,000, and with 25 years of service at transition, about half had no wear-away, between 36 and 41 percent had wear-away rates that were less than 10 percent of annual pay, and another 8-10 percent had wear-away rates between 10 and 15 percent pay. The rate of wear-away is lower for younger workers and those with shorter tenure.

Table 2-6 combines information on the duration and rate of wear-away to report the total potential exposure to wear-away. Total potential cumulative wear-away peaks for a worker with long service just before early retirement eligibility. Thus, we calculate wear-away for a 54-year-old worker with twenty-five years of service when the hybrid plan is adopted. Even for those workers, however, table 2-6 indicates that nearly half the hybrid plan conversions

---

19. For each prototypical worker, we calculate benefits at transition and in subsequent years until each worker reached 65. A year was considered a wear-away year if the end-year balance in the new plan did not exceed the accrued benefit under the old plan. The plan sponsor could not simply eliminate early retirement benefits for workers who were not yet 55 at the transition. Such workers would have the present value of the subsidy earned at the point of transition protected if they remained with the sponsor to age 55.

Table 2-4. *Plans with Wear-Away for Selected Workers by Duration*
Percent of plans in sample

| Duration of wear-away | Annual pay level | | | |
| | Age 54 at transition | | Age 50 at transition | |
	$80,000	$50,000	$80,000	$50,000
25 years' service				
None	49.3	49.3	83.1	85.7
1 year	7.8	9.1	3.9	2.6
2 years	7.8	6.5	1.3	2.6
3 years	7.8	9.1	1.3	0.0
4 years	15.6	14.3	2.6	3.9
5 years	2.6	3.9	1.3	0.0
6 years	3.9	2.6	0.0	0.0
7 to 9 years	2.6	2.6	2.6	2.6
10 years or more	2.6	2.6	3.9	2.6
15 years' service				
None	58.4	58.4	87.0	87.0
1 year	10.4	10.4	1.3	2.6
2 years	9.1	11.7	2.6	2.6
3 years	3.9	3.9	3.9	2.6
4 years	7.8	5.2	0.0	1.3
5 years	3.9	6.5	1.3	0.0
6 years	2.6	0.0	1.3	1.3
7 to 9 years	2.6	2.6	0.0	1.3
10 years or more	1.3	1.3	2.6	1.3
10 years' service				
None	57.1	56.1	87.0	88.3
1 year	14.3	16.9	3.9	2.6
2 years	9.1	10.4	1.3	2.6
3 years	7.8	5.2	2.6	1.3
4 years	5.2	5.2	2.6	1.3
5 years	1.3	1.3	0.0	1.3
6 years	2.6	1.3	0.0	0.0
7 to 9 years	1.3	1.3	1.3	0.0
10 years or more	1.3	2.6	1.3	2.6

Source: Authors' computations from data provided by Watson Wyatt Worldwide.

involved no wear-away at all, typically because of subsidies to the initial account or provision of some other transition protection. Another 14 percent of workers faced cumulative wear-away of between 1 and 25 percent of their annual pay at age 54 over potential employment ranging up to age 65. A few plans exposed workers to cumulative wear-away equaling multiples of their earnings at 54 for workers employed until 65 under the new plan. The maximum cumulative wear-away was 4.2 years of pay for such a worker.

Table 2-5. *Specified Annual Wear-Away Rates in the Transition to Hybrid Plans, as a Percentage of Annual Earnings for Selected Workers*
Percent of plans

| | Annual pay level at transition | | | |
| | Age 54 at transition | | Age 50 at transition | |
Wear-away rate as a percentage of annual pay	$80,000	$50,000	$80,000	$50,000
25 years' service at transition				
0	49.3	49.3	83.1	85.7
0.01–4.9	10.4	14.3	6.5	6.5
5.0–9.9	26.0	24.7	10.4	7.8
10.0–14.9	10.4	7.8		
15.0–19.9	2.6	3.9		
20.0–24.9	1.3			
15 years' service at transition				
0	58.4	58.4	87.0	87.0
0.01–4.9	22.1	22.1	10.4	10.4
5.0–9.9	13.0	11.7	2.6	2.6
10.0–14.9	5.2	6.5		
15.0–19.9	1.3	1.3		
10 years' service at transition				
0	57.1	56.1	87.0	88.3
0.01–4.9	27.3	27.0	7.8	6.5
5.0–9.9	13.0	16.9	5.2	5.2
10.0–14.9	2.6			

Source: Authors' computations from data provided by Watson Wyatt Worldwide.

While the discussion above estimates the extent, variation, and determinants of wear-away in the transition to hybrid plans, it does not provide a benchmark for comparison. The features of traditional defined benefit plans also contain a form of wear-away and therefore provide a useful benchmark. For example, a plan that provides a worker at age 62 with an actuarially subsidized benefit of 1.5 times annual pay, but eliminates the subsidy by the time the worker reaches 65, is reducing the present value of subsidized benefits each additional year from 62 to 65 by 50 percent of pay.[20] Despite the fact that the subsidy is "worn away" in this case, the lifetime value of benefits may still increase. In this latter situation, which is the norm in traditional plans, the wear-away reflects a slowing in the benefit accrual under the basic plan formula rather than a complete freeze in accruals. In this regard, wear-away that occurs in the transition to hybrid plans may be more apparent and may seem more severe even in cases where it is not.

20. Clark and Schieber (2001).

Table 2-6. *Comparison of Potential Wear-Away for a Worker Age 54 with 25 Years'*
Service in Hybrid and Traditional Plan
Percent of plans

Potential cumulative wear-away as a percentage of pay at base age	Potential cumulative wear-away in transition to hybrid plan at age 54	Potential cumulative wear-away in traditional plan at age 55
0	49.3	14.3
0.1–24.9	14.3	3.9
25.0–49.9	6.5	27.2
50.0–74.9	7.8	16.9
75.0–99.9	6.5	14.3
100.0–124.9	1.3	7.8
125.0–149.9	3.9	6.5
150.0–174.9	2.6	1.3
175.0–199.9	2.6	2.6
200.0–399.9	3.9	5.2
400 or more	1.3	0.0

Source: Authors' computations from data provided by Watson Wyatt Worldwide.

Figure 2-5 provides an example of accrual patterns in a traditional plan with and
without the early retirement subsidy and clearly shows the decline in benefits
from working past age 62.

For purposes of providing a benchmark, the last column of table 2-6 shows
the potential wear-away at 55 for a worker with twenty-five years of service in a
traditional plan. Under traditional plans, the magnitude of early retirement subsidies is maximized at age 55 in most plans.

In 14 percent of the plans, there is no potential wear-away from the erosion
of early retirement subsidies, even though less than 3 percent of all the former
plans did not subsidize early retirement. The reason that 14 percent show up as
having no potential wear-away at age 55 is that some of the plans did not subsidize early retirement benefits until a later age.

Thus, the results above show that in nearly half the cases, employers structured the new plans to make the wear-away issue moot. In the remaining plans,
the cumulative wear-away that workers faced in the hybrid plan was generally
not as great as what they faced in the previous plans.

Transition Benefits for Existing Workers

In 88 percent of the plans examined in this study, the plan sponsor provided
some form of transition benefit for some affected workers. The nature of the
transition benefits varied across plan sponsors and for workers based on their age
and tenure under the previous plan at the point of conversion. Table 2-7 shows
the effects of transition provisions for a worker who was 50 at the time of conversion with twenty-five years of service and a $60,000 salary under his old plan.

Figure 2-5. *Value of Accrued Pension Benefit for a New Hire at Age 30 with a Starting Wage of $40,000 per Year for a Typical Pension*

Accrued benefit as a multiple of annual pay

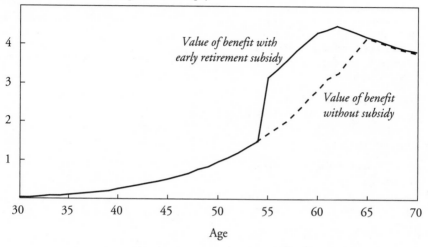

Age

Source: Authors' computations from data provided by Watson Wyatt Worldwide.

Transition benefits helped to ameliorate the adverse effects of the plan changes. For example, for a worker with twenty-five years of service and a $60,000 salary who is age 55, 49 percent of the plans would provide a benefit that was less than 75 percent of the previous plan benefit, ignoring transition provisions, and 78 percent of plans would have provided a smaller benefit than

Table 2-7. *Comparison of Benefits under Hybrid and Traditional Plans for Workers Age 50 with 25 Years of Service and a Salary of $60,000 at Conversion*
Percent of plans

Hybrid and transition benefit as percentage	At age 55 Hybrid benefit only	At age 55 Including transition	At age 60 Hybrid benefit only	At age 60 Including transition	At age 65 Hybrid benefit only	At age 65 Including transition
Less than 50	18.2	3.9	20.8	6.5	15.6	6.5
50–74.9	31.2	14.3	33.7	19.5	35.1	19.5
75–99.9	28.6	15.6	27.3	24.7	23.4	23.4
100–124.9	15.6	51.9	13.0	41.6	16.9	39.0
125–149.9	5.2	11.7	5.2	7.8	7.8	9.1
150 or more	1.3	2.6	0.0	0.0	1.3	2.6

Source: Authors' computations from data provided by Watson Wyatt Worldwide.
Note: Benefit changes include marginal improvements in defined contribution plans.

Table 2-8. *Effects on Hypothetical Workers' Benefits at Conversion*
Percent of plans

Age and service at time of conversion	Age at termination of employment			
	55	60	62	65
Age 50, 25 years' service, $60,000 salary				
No transition benefit, total benefits fall	3.9	7.8	9.1	15.6
Transition benefit but total benefits fall	32.5	42.9	41.6	37.7
Fully grandfathered or benefits increase	63.6	49.3	49.3	46.7
Age 50, 20 years' service, $60,000 salary				
No transition benefit, total benefits fall	6.5	13.0	14.3	18.2
Transition benefit but total benefits fall	31.2	42.9	45.5	39.0
Fully grandfathered or benefits increase	62.3	44.1	40.2	42.8
Age 50, 15 years' service, $60,000 salary				
No transition benefit, total benefits fall	9.1	16.9	18.2	19.5
Transition benefit but total benefits fall	29.9	40.3	44.2	41.6
Fully grandfathered or benefits increase	61.0	42.8	37.6	38.9
Age 50, 10 years' service, $60,000 salary				
No transition benefit, total benefits fall	19.5	27.3	31.2	31.2
Transition benefit but total benefits fall	26.0	33.8	35.1	35.1
Fully grandfathered or benefits increase	54.5	38.9	33.7	33.7
	50	55	60	65
Age 40, 10 years' service, $50,000 salary				
No transition benefit, total benefits fall	9.1	49.4	54.5	55.8
Transition benefit but total benefits fall	3.9	14.3	16.9	16.9
Fully grandfathered or benefits increase	87.0	36.4	28.6	27.3

Source: Authors' computations from data provided by Watson Wyatt Worldwide.
Note: Benefit changes do not include marginal improvements in defined contribution plans.

the prior plan. When transition benefits are considered, however, these figures fall to 18 percent and 34 percent, respectively.

The implications of transition benefits were similar for workers who continued to work later, including up until age 65. Table 2-8 shows that the provision of transition benefits rose for workers closer to retirement and with longer tenure. Nearly two-thirds of workers who were 50 with twenty-five years of service had a fully grandfathered benefit if they retired at 55 under their new plan. If they waited until 65, however, the share dropped to less than half. Workers who were 50 at the transition were more likely to be grandfathered or to receive higher benefits the more years of service they had at conversion. Just over half of those aged 50 with ten years of service at conversion were fully grandfathered for retirement at 55. Only about one-third of workers at this age and service would be grandfathered in their old plan benefit if they waited to retire until 65.

The bottom panel in table 2-8 shows the benefits for a worker age 40 with ten years of service at conversion. Note that the benefits are shown for a slightly different set of attained ages than those shown for the 50-year-old workers in the table. For the younger workers, the pattern of benefits under a hybrid plan for those who terminate employment before early retirement age under traditional plans tends to be extremely favorable. Even workers fairly far along into a career with some substantial tenure benefit from the shift to hybrid plans if they terminate employment before typical retirement ages in traditional plans. For these younger workers with relatively short tenures at conversion, grandfathering of benefits at early and normal retirement ages was not as generous as it was for their older counterparts. Slightly more than two-thirds of the 50-year-olds with ten years of service received some grandfather protection or actually came out better off under the new plan. Only half the 40-year-olds will fare so well if they delay retirement to age 60.

Table 2-9 provides somewhat more detail on two of the stylized workers included in table 2-8. In each case the 50-year-old worker is assumed to have a $60,000 annual salary. Of the seventy-seven plans under analysis here, twenty-four introduced some enhancement to their defined contribution plan in conjunction with the adoption of a hybrid plan. The added benefits from these plans reported in the table reflect only employers' contributions. The effects of adding in defined contribution plan changes in this case are quite moderate, especially for individuals affected late in their careers.

Table 2-10 is similar to table 2-9 except that it focuses on younger workers. Most but not all of these workers are better off under the new plans than the old ones. Clearly fewer of these workers are eligible for transition benefits. Still, substantial numbers of plans did provide transition benefits of some sort even for relatively young workers employed before the shift to hybrid plans.

Winning or Losing in the Shift to a Hybrid Plan

The benefit reductions we have documented are reductions against previous plans. While any changes to compensation packages raise certain equity questions, there have been questions for years about the fairness of traditional defined benefit pension accrual patterns. Specifically, these plans favor workers with longer tenures compared with workers who change jobs more frequently. Hybrid plans do not typically provide the same relative advantage to workers with long tenures and tend to distribute benefits more evenly than traditional plans.

To explore this issue further, we develop a case study of one of the plan conversions described earlier. The plan sponsor shifted to a cash balance plan on a relatively cost-neutral basis. The original plan did not have early retirement subsidies. This allows us keep total benefits in the two plans roughly constant and to highlight an additional issue below.

We use a synthesized work force of 30,000 workers, randomly drawn from work forces of fifteen large pension clients of Watson Wyatt Worldwide. In

Table 2-9. *Effects on Hypothetical Workers' Benefits at Conversion,*
Taking Defined Benefit and Contribution Changes into Account
Percent of plans

Age and service	At age 55	At age 60	At age 62	At age 65
Age 50, 25 years' service, including only the DB changes				
No transition benefit, total benefits fall	3.9	7.8	9.1	15.6
Transition benefit but total benefits fall	32.5	42.9	41.6	37.7
Fully grandfathered in old benefit	31.2	20.8	20.8	20.8
No transition benefit, total benefits rise	14.3	11.7	13.0	13.0
Transition benefit, total benefits rise	18.2	16.9	15.6	13.0
Age 50, 25 years' service, including DB, DC changes				
No transition benefit, total benefits fall	3.9	6.5	9.1	13.0
Transition benefit but total benefits fall	28.6	42.9	41.6	35.1
Fully grandfathered in old benefit	24.7	16.9	15.6	15.6
No transition benefit, total benefits rise	14.3	13.0	13.0	15.6
Transition benefit, total benefits rise	28.6	20.8	20.8	20.8
Age 50, 10 years' service, including only the DB changes				
No transition benefit, total benefits fall	19.5	27.3	31.2	31.2
Transition benefit but total benefits fall	26.0	33.8	35.1	35.1
Fully grandfathered in old benefit	20.8	15.6	14.3	14.3
No transition benefit, total benefits rise	18.2	15.6	14.3	14.3
Transition benefit, total benefits rise	15.6	7.8	5.2	5.2
Age 50, 10 years' service, including DB and DC changes				
No transition benefit, total benefits fall	19.5	27.3	31.2	28.6
Transition benefit but total benefits fall	20.8	31.2	33.8	32.5
Fully grandfathered in old benefit	22.1	15.6	11.7	11.7
No transition benefit, total benefits rise	18.2	15.6	14.3	16.9
Transition benefit, total benefits rise	19.5	10.4	9.1	10.4

Source: Authors' computations from data provided by Watson Wyatt Worldwide.
DB = defined benefit; DC = defined contribution.

simulating the workers through the remainder of their careers, we used employee turnover rates developed in a study for the Society of Actuaries under a sample of defined benefit plans.[21]

We simulate each worker through the remainder of his employment and calculate average pension accrual rates under the preconversion plans.[22] Table 2-11

21. Kopp (1997). The study's purpose was to value defined benefit pension plans in cases where the actuary does not have turnover experience measures on the actual work force covered under the individual plans.

22. To do this, we first calculate the present value of benefits under the preconversion plan. Then, we compare it to the pension benefit that would be paid and calculate the present value of the ultimate benefit at the point of termination of active employment. The difference is the expected value of additional pension that would be earned through continued service. From this

Table 2-10. *Effects on Hypothetical Younger Workers' Benefits at Conversion, Taking Defined Benefit and Contribution Changes into Account*
Percent of plans

Age and service	At age 55	At age 60	At age 62	At age 65
Age 40, 10 years' service, including only the DB changes				
No transition benefit, total benefits fall	9.1	49.4	54.5	55.8
Transition benefit but total benefits fall	3.9	14.3	16.9	16.9
Fully grandfathered in old benefit	5.2	7.8	7.8	10.4
No transition benefit, total benefits rise	64.9	19.5	13.0	11.7
Transition benefit, total benefits rise	16.9	9.1	7.8	5.2
Age 40, 10 years' service, including DB, DC changes				
No transition benefit, total benefits fall	7.8	48.1	50.6	49.4
Transition benefit but total benefits fall	2.6	13.0	16.9	14.3
Fully grandfathered in old benefit	5.2	9.1	6.5	7.8
No transition benefit, total benefits rise	66.2	18.2	16.9	18.2
Transition benefit, total benefits rise	18.2	11.7	9.1	10.4
Age 30, 5 years' service, including only the DB changes				
No transition benefit, total benefits fall	14.3	53.2	58.4	54.5
Transition benefit but total benefits fall	3.9	7.8	10.4	5.2
Fully grandfathered in old benefit	1.3	5.2	5.2	6.5
No transition benefit, total benefits rise	70.1	29.9	22.1	28.6
Transition benefit, total benefits rise	10.4	3.9	3.9	5.2
Age 30 with 5 years' service, including DB and DC changes				
No transition benefit, total benefits fall	6.5	42.9	48.1	41.6
Transition benefit but total benefits fall	3.9	7.8	7.8	3.9
Fully grandfathered in old benefit	1.3	5.2	6.5	5.2
No transition benefit, total benefits rise	77.9	40.3	32.5	42.9
Transition benefit, total benefits rise	10.4	3.9	5.2	6.5

Source: Authors' computations from data provided by Watson Wyatt Worldwide.
DB = defined benefit; DC = defined contribution.

shows the future average accrual of pension benefits for various workers under their previous plan. The top section reflects accrual rates for workers who would be at least as well off under the cash balance plan as under the old plan. The bottom section shows that those who would be better off staying under the old plan would accrue benefits over the remainder of their careers under that plan at about twice the rates of those in the top half of the table except at very advanced

---

we estimated an average accrual rate under the prior plan as though it continued to operate. The accrual rate is derived by dividing the added increment in pension value that each worker would earn from the beginning date of the simulation until termination by the present value of his future earnings while still with the employer. The result is what actuaries refer to as the aggregate normal cost, reflecting the accrual of future benefits as a constant percentage of pay over the remainder of workers' careers with the employer.

Table 2-11. *Simulated Future Pension Accruals by Tenure and Age at Conversion*
Percentage of pay under a prior plan

Tenure in years	Age					
	20–29.9	30–39.9	40–49.9	50–54.9	55–59.9	60–65
Future pension accrual rate as a percent of pay for those winning or held harmless						
0–4.9	1.10	2.01	3.50	5.07	6.24	7.58
5–9.9	1.36	2.23	3.79	5.65	6.70	8.32
10–14.9	1.85	2.68	4.14	5.97	7.02	10.18
15–19.9		2.80	4.13	6.08	7.02	9.77
20–24.9		3.03	4.14	6.06	6.88	10.01
25–29.9			4.60	6.12	6.99	10.60
30 +			5.12	6.34	7.58	10.53
Future pension accrual rate as a percent of pay for losers						
0–4.9	5.06	6.07	8.43	9.14	11.02	12.52
5–9.9	5.09	6.35	8.71	10.29	11.39	14.78
10–14.9		6.57	8.83	11.19	12.81	14.98
15–19.9		6.65	8.78	11.49	12.91	15.63
20–24.9		6.50	8.54	11.56	12.47	15.74
25–29.9			9.49	11.52	12.84	15.05
30 +			10.05	11.42	13.20	15.53

Source: Authors' computations from data provided by Watson Wyatt Worldwide.

levels of age and service. This simply reflects the fact that traditional defined benefit plans provide disproportionate benefits to a subset of workers, namely those who work until they are eligible for immediate benefits upon their termination.

In the conversion to a cash balance plan, the sponsor has to establish an initial value of benefit for workers. This is typically the value of the accrued benefit at the time of conversion payable at the normal retirement age discounted back to the present time. The value of the benefit that seeds the beginning cash balance in the conversion to the new plan is often not equivalent to the present value of the accrued benefit under the previous plan because of different interest rates used in deriving the two amounts.

Table 2-12 shows the net effect of using different discount rates for determining the present value of accrued benefits under the previous plan and for setting the initial balance in the replacement cash balance plan in this case. The table shows that the accrued benefits under the old plan are larger for the ultimate losers than they are for the winners. The reason is that in each cell, the losers tend to have longer tenure and thus larger pension accumulations under

Table 2-12. *Present Value of Accrued Benefits (PVAB) under Prior Plan and Increment in the Value of Cash Balance by Tenure and Age at Conversion*

Tenure in years	Age					
	20–29.9	30–39.9	40–49.9	50–54.9	55–59.9	60–65
Workers who ultimately gain benefits in the shift to a cash balance plan—						
PVAB at transition (dollars)						
0–4.9	504	982	2,225	3,331	4,930	10,152
5–9.9	1,221	2,887	6,424	11,287	15,275	19,136
10–14.9	2,452	4,889	10,417	18,397	23,688	27,668
15–19.9		6,069	10,595	21,766	24,148	37,360
20–24.9		4,698	10,062	17,698	21,334	30,144
25–29.9			12,687	18,974	30,105	48,484
30 +			10,716	18,645	26,924	52,724
Net wealth gain (percentage of PVAB)						
0–4.9	126.5	86.9	63.9	46.6	36.5	24.9
5–9.9	98.9	77.9	55.6	40.0	30.6	21.9
10–14.9	91.5	74.1	54.3	38.7	29.2	20.1
15–19.9		69.6	54.4	38.5	29.3	19.5
20–24.9		67.3	52.7	38.5	29.8	20.8
25–29.9			48.1	38.7	29.3	20.1
30 +			44.8	37.7	28.7	19.6
Workers who ultimately lose benefits in the shift to a cash balance plan—						
PVAB at transition (dollars)						
0–4.9	1,806	1,294	3,669	7,232	28,177	28,020
5–9.9	3,183	4,475	9,771	18,153	21,196	75,509
10–14.9	3,563	7,892	15,219	23,725	44,356	45,734
15–19.9		8,672	15,611	32,016	49,580	62,600
20–24.9		4,979	13,354	24,247	27,790	99,871
25–29.9			12,773	27,066	35,853	58,684
30 +			11,541	21,232	35,644	105,331
Net wealth gain (percentage of PVAB)						
0–4.9	110.9	84.1	63.5	46.6	33.2	25.6
5–9.9	93.7	74.3	54.6	40.3	31.1	22.6
10–14.9	91.0	70.6	54.6	38.3	30.0	22.0
15–19.9		68.5	53.9	38.0	29.7	21.8
20–24.9		67.0	51.0	38.7	29.6	21.9
25–29.9			48.6	37.9	29.3	22.3
30 +			45.3	37.6	28.3	21.8

Source: Authors' computations from data provided by Watson Wyatt Worldwide.

the plan. This reflects the phenomenon that at any given age, workers with long tenure are more likely to stay until retirement age than workers with shorter tenures.

The second and fourth panels in table 2-12 show the percentage increase in average pension wealth as the present value of accrued benefits under the old pension is converted into an initial cash balance under the new plan. In this case, correspondence between the two groups of workers is relatively close. This simply reflects that the average age of workers within each age and service cell will be similar for each of the two groups of workers. It is a worker's age that determines how many years are left until retirement, which determines the discounting period for calculating both the present value of accrued benefits under the prior plan and the cash balance in the new plan. The longer this period, the greater the relative wealth increment that will be realized from the differential in the two discounting rates.

The final important element of the shift to a hybrid plan is how workers benefit for future service under the new pension formula. Table 2-12 reports future accrual rates in the cash balance plan calculated in a manner analogous to the accrual rates in traditional plans reported in table 2-11. Controlling for age and years of service, those identified as losers in the transition to hybrid plans still accrue benefits in hybrid plans more rapidly than the winners. But the differential under the hybrid plan is much smaller than it was in the traditional plan documented in table 2-11.

If we had used a plan with an early retirement subsidy to develop this analysis, the results would have been even more pronounced than they are here. The larger the early retirement subsidy, the larger would be the differential in accrual rates for winners and losers and the greater would have been the effects of the leveling of accrual rates reflected in table 2-13.

In a number of highly publicized cases, workers who were shifted to a hybrid pension have been quite vocal about the inequity of the shift because their ultimate accrual of benefits will be comparatively inferior. If one focuses only on the erosion of benefits for big winners under traditional plans, the conclusion that some workers have been wronged is understandable. But if one focuses on the total distribution of benefits under the hybrid plan, the perspective can be entirely different. One can only make the case that hybrid plans are unfair if one believes that the accrual pattern in table 2-13 was fair to begin with.

Worker Preferences and Plan Choice

Consistent with the incentives embedded in pension plans, workers hired at older ages and those who are more likely to remain with the firm until retirement tend to prefer defined benefit plans while younger, more mobile workers tend to opt for defined contribution or hybrid pension plans. In most of the plan conversions over the past two decades, however, workers did not have a

Table 2-13. *Simulated Future Pension Accruals for Workers Shifted into Hybrid Plan with Same Cost as Prior Plan, by Tenure and Age*
Percentage of pay

	Age					
Tenure in years	20–29.9	30–39.9	40–49.9	50–54.9	55–59.9	60–65
Future pension accrual rate for those winning or held harmless						
0–4.9	1.98	3.26	4.80	6.42	6.43	6.60
5–9.9	2.17	3.24	4.75	6.19	7.02	7.41
10–14.9	2.57	3.37	4.52	5.81	6.70	7.74
15–19.9		3.49	4.51	6.16	6.48	7.75
20–24.9		4.13	4.62	6.01	6.98	7.32
25–29.9			4.95	6.26	5.78	7.61
30 +			5.51	5.84	6.29	6.55
Future pension accrual rate for losers						
0–4.9	4.27	5.31	6.30	7.76	8.36	9.01
5–9.9	4.80	5.29	6.25	7.71	8.43	9.08
10–14.9		5.33	6.25	7.71	8.47	9.13
15–19.9		5.40	6.24	7.59	8.50	9.14
20–24.9		5.39	6.30	7.60	8.53	9.13
25–29.9			6.68	7.62	8.53	9.14
30 +			7.12	7.69	8.54	9.13

choice. Media reporting on the subject has generally been based on a small number of interviews with senior workers who were very angry about conversions to cash balance plans.[23] More comprehensive studies reveal a different, more complex story. Older, more senior workers are more likely to view hybrids negatively, but many workers view the new plans very positively.

Generally, surveys suggest that relatively few workers are familiar with cash balance plans, but that many workers expect to leave their current employer before retirement and that workers tend to value portability, pensions that do not penalize job changers, and transparency in benefit calculation, all of which

23. Ellen E. Schultz, "Actuaries Become Red-Faced over Recorded Pension Talk," *Wall Street Journal,* May 5, 1999, pp. C1 and C19; Ellen E. Schultz, "Boomer Backlash: Controversy Besetting New Pension Plan Rises with IBM's Retreat," *Wall Street Journal,* September 20, 1999. p. A1; Ellen E. Schultz, "A 'Diagnostic' Takes a Role in Pension Debate," *Wall Street Journal,* September 22, 1999, pp. C1 and C13; Ellen E. Schultz, "Problems with Pensions: What You Don't Know about Cash-Balance Plans Can Hurt You," *Wall Street Journal,* November 8, 1999, p. 8; Ellen E. Schultz, "Pension Paternity: How a Single Sentence by IRS Paved the Way to Cash-Balance Plans," *Wall Street Journal,* December 28, 1999, p. A1; and Ellen E. Schultz, "Treasury Takes Serious Look at Whether Workers Get Enough Details on Pension-Payout Choices," *Wall Street Journal,* May 4, 2000, pp. C1 and C20.

are features of cash balance plans. At the same time, workers are concerned about the impact of plan conversions and the potentially adverse impact on those who had worked for many years under a previous plan.[24]

Policy Considerations

The conversion of traditional defined benefit plans to hybrid or defined contribution plans alters the age-tenure patterns of benefit accruals. Plan conversions increase the expected retirement benefits for most shorter-tenured workers, while long-tenured workers in many cases can expect reduced future benefits, especially if they retire at early retirement ages in traditional plans. In some instances of plans that cut benefits for early retirees, continued employment to normal retirement age or beyond will result in higher benefits under the new plans.

Our analysis shows that a large majority of workers who leave a firm before early retirement age will accumulate larger benefits under hybrid plans than under their old plans. Despite the decline in expected benefits, workers with long service with the same firm continue to have higher benefit accruals under the new hybrid plan compared with younger workers. Although the evidence available from surveys and case studies is limited, it shows that the characteristics of hybrid plans, such as account balances, lump-sum options, and portability, are highly popular with workers. For the most part, workers favor conversion to such plans.

Some workers caught in plan modifications that include very significant reductions in plan costs and overall generosity of benefits may realize extended periods of wear-away. We believe most employers undertaking such severe benefit reductions must be in relatively dire straits. It is unlikely that any legislative remedy can resolve this problem. If employers are precluded from cutting back benefits when in dire circumstances, they will be left at the margin with no other recourse than going out of business. If that occurs, workers' benefits will be just as frozen as they are under the plan modification. Concerns about sponsors who implement hybrid plans by using a relatively high interest rate in setting initial balances in cash balance plans appear to be an old problem that has generally been rectified.

The remaining wear-away that occurs in the transition to hybrid plans is largely related to the elimination of early retirement subsidies for workers who are close enough to eligibility that such benefits have substantial accrued value. Our analysis suggests that the wear-away created by the transition to hybrid plans is not generally longer or larger than the wear-away of subsidies that already existed in the plans being replaced. The timing of the wear-away may simply be different in a plan conversion. If this issue were deemed worthy of

24. Third Millennium (1999).

legislative remedy, it would seem to open the question of the legal treatment of early retirement subsidies in general. Such a review would undoubtedly touch on retirement, general labor, and macroeconomic policy issues that go well beyond the scope of the concerns raised in plan conversions.

The vast majority of firms have attempted to address the losses of certain workers, in whole or in part, through the adoption of transition benefits. Some firms offer workers the choice to remain in the old plan or grant larger pension credits to a wide range of existing workers. In these companies, the transition to hybrid plans has caused little outcry. Other companies have offered transitional benefits to a much smaller class of workers or ignored potential losses altogether. These companies have been the target of widespread criticism from their senior employees and been subject to considerable bad press and congressional review.

The era that we are entering is different from that we have just completed. Anticipating a significant change in our population's demographic makeup, Congress in 1983 legislated an increase in the normal retirement age under Social Security that began to take effect in 2000. Despite the long lead time and the open discussion about this development, there is some evidence that the general public remained largely oblivious of this development until the higher retirement age was being phased into effect. In contemporary discussions about Social Security or Medicare policy, the implications of demographic change appear to be well known. While there has been little done to adjust public retirement programs since 1983, political leaders now acknowledge that something must be done and are discussing what to do and when to do it. The demographics affecting public retirement programs are also facing employer-sponsored plans, and a number of parallel issues must be addressed.

Clearly, one of the reasons for raising Social Security's normal retirement age has been to encourage workers to remain in the work force longer. Not only have policymakers already adopted an increased retirement age for Social Security, some of them who have been particularly critical of the shift to hybrid pension plans have advocated that the normal retirement age under Social Security be raised even further.

In abstract terms, one cannot help but wonder about the compatibility of Social Security policy that is trying to get workers to stay in the work force longer and tax incentives for pensions that encourage them to retire much earlier than Social Security eligibility ages. If employer-based pensions are going to provide any support to Social Security, their early retirement incentives will have to be curtailed in relatively short order. Full grandfathering of anyone already in the shadow of an early retirement incentive is likely to extend such benefits to the majority of workers down to age 40 who are covered by plans offering early retirement incentives today. If employers exclude workers as young as 40 from the effects of reduced early retirement incentives, they might as well let all the baby boomers continue to enjoy them. It is the baby boomers that must be enticed to work longer if there is to be any practical relief to the financing problems that Social Security and Medicare are facing.

To the extent that employers are using the conversion from traditional pension plans as a mechanism to eliminate early retirement subsidies, there will be some who are going to be aggrieved. Such workers have a natural attraction and attractiveness to policymakers and reporters. At some juncture, however, policymakers must stand back from the anecdotal cases and decide what they want the U.S. retirement system to achieve. A federal retirement policy that is increasing retirement age under Social Security but hamstringing employers who are attempting to align with the national system's goals is schizophrenic and will serve neither the government nor workers in the long term.

Richard A. Ippolito

I concentrate my remarks on the core issue in cash balance plans, namely wealth transfers. The authors portray the sponsors who have engaged in cash balance conversions in a rather favorable light. They point out correctly that some firms (perhaps the majority) do not impose the *maximum* losses that they could on workers had they taken full advantage of the law, that many (mostly younger) workers can benefit from the change, and that, in any event, the conversions are consistent with good public policy, mostly because, in their view, cash balance plans encourage later retirement.

I interpret the evidence somewhat differently. I am sympathetic to the cash balance trend. Congress created an environment that is hostile to defined benefit plans[1] and at the same time set up a reversion tax scheme that assesses exorbitant exit fees from existing defined benefit plans that want to terminate (reversion and corporate taxes take upward of 85 percent of excess assets upon termination).[2] This leaves the cash balance conversion as the only economic option for firms to switch from the defined benefit to the defined contribution format, and the data are consistent with the hypothesis that tax avoidance is the raison d'être of cash balance conversions (Niehaus and Yu 2003). But while firms have escaped the high assessments in choosing this route, many have assessed similar exit fees on their employees in the conversion process. Firms *can* effect a cash balance conversion that effectively allows them to segue from a defined benefit to a defined contribution format without paying reversion taxes *and* without imposing large capital losses on workers. Few have chosen this route.

In principle, a cash balance conversion is tantamount to a unilateral breaking of an implicit contract, one that can and often does effect large wealth transfers from workers to shareholders. The implications of these actions are not confined to the parties directly affected. They also impose a negative externality on firms that want to honor their defined benefit plan commitments.

In effect, owing to the actions of perhaps upward of 10 percent of firms who have devalued their defined benefit pension promises through these conversions,[3] workers in *other* firms that offer defined benefit plans may now be suspicious that

1. See, for example, American Academy of Actuaries (1993), Clark and McDermed (1990), ERISA Industry Committee (1996), Gale (1994), Gustman and Steinmeier (1992), Hay Huggins (1989 and 1990), and Kruse (1995).

2. The first reversion tax (10 percent) was instituted in 1986; it escalated to 50 percent in 1990. An exception is made if all excess assets are given to workers, in which case the tax is 20 percent.

3. Estimates of coverage are found in Elliot and Moore (2000), Niehaus and Yu (2003), and U.S. Department of Labor (1999). Also see *Benefits Quarterly*, first quarter (January), which is devoted to cash balance plans.

their plans also will terminate. This means that sponsors of ongoing defined benefit plans will have difficulty convincing workers that their pension promises are worth the cash wages that workers must sacrifice to obtain them. If workers are unwilling to pay for their forthcoming benefits, competitive pressures will force firms to terminate the plan in order to rationalize the lower "price" that workers are willing to pay. The conditions are created that are favorable to a degenerating equilibrium, whereby all implicit promises are replaced with explicit defined contribution plan contracts. In effect, we end up with a "lemons" market.

Economic Consequences of Cash Balance Conversions

The establishment of a cash balance plan is the equivalent of terminating the original plan, replacing it with a defined contribution plan, and creating a tax-free trust fund earmarked to finance future accruals in the new plan. The transfer from the "old" defined benefit plan to the trust fund is subject to neither corporate nor reversion taxes. Sponsors "use up" their excess assets simply by devoting them to the purpose of funding future contributions to employees' accounts.

Virtually all cash balance plans are conversions of existing (presumably well-funded) defined benefit plans. In its extreme form, a conversion has the same impact on workers as a regular termination. As of the date of the plan amendment, workers effectively are given an account balance equal in value to the present value of the pension benefits to which they are legally entitled, whereupon they incur capital losses identical to a traditional termination. In a going forward sense, the cash balance plan looks very much like a classic defined contribution plan, in the sense that sponsors credit worker accounts with market interest rates and normally make contributions as a percent of pay for future periods.

Unless the sponsor is incurring serious financial problems, the substitution of termination benefits for projected (or ongoing) promised benefits violates the implicit pension contract. Workers sacrifice wages in exchange for the pension promise, which they expect a firm to honor in sound financial condition.[4] If the contract is terminated, workers suffer capital losses that are converted to shareholder value in the firm.[5] The losses are reminiscent of the spate of terminations that occurred in the early to mid-1980s and precipitated the sequence of reversion taxes.[6] Simply put, cash balance conversions can accomplish what reversion

4. Ippolito (1985); Pesando (1985).

5. Shleifer and Summers (1988); Pontiff, Shleifer, and Weisbach (1990).

6. Most pre-reversion-tax terminations were done as so-called reestablishments, which are transactions specifically designed to eliminate worker losses. The evidence suggests that most terminations that imposed capital losses on workers were associated with firms in weak financial condition but that a significant minority reflected true terminations not obviously characterized by financial stress (Ippolito and James 1992). Also see Mitchell and Mulherin (1989); Mittelstaedt (1989); Petersen (1992); Stone (1987); Thomas (1989); and VanDerhei (1987).

taxes were intended to eliminate: imposition of capital losses on workers when the plan was funded for substantially more than termination benefits.

Capital Losses from Leaving a Defined Benefit Plan before Normal Retirement Age

To illustrate the nature of pension capital losses, I use a simple model of pensions. The age at which full benefits are available in the plan (the normal retirement age) is R. There is an early retirement "window" starting at age a^* during which the worker can retire with a reduced benefit; the reduction is d percent for each year that early retirement precedes R. The pension annuity, A, is equal to service, s, times final wage, w, times some generosity factor, b; there are no cost-of-living increases after retirement. Thus the annuity based on current service and wage is denoted as:

$$(2\text{-}1) \qquad A_a = b w_a s_a.$$

Calculation of Pension Values

For any age within the window of early retirement, if a worker leaves immediately at age a, his pension is worth:

$$(2\text{-}2) \qquad PV_a^a(d) = A_a\, e^{-d(R-a)}\, \Omega_{aD},$$

where $\Omega_{aD} = {}_{t=a}\int^{D} e^{-it}\, dt$, $a^* < a < R$.

A_a is the full annuity from equation 2-1, i is the market interest rate, and Ω_{aD} is the present value of a \$1 annuity collected from early retirement age a ($a^* < a < R$) to age of death D, evaluated at current age, a, using interest rate i.

If the worker stays until age R, then the value of the benefit based on current service evaluated at age a based on *current* service level s_a is:

$$(2\text{-}3) \qquad PV_a^R = A_a\, e^{(g-i)(R-a)}\, \Omega_{RD},$$

where $\Omega_{RD} = {}_{t=R}\int^{D} e^{-it}\, dt,$

where g is the per annum wage growth (including overall increases plus within-firm merit or seniority increases), and Ω_{RD} is the present value of a \$1 annuity collected from normal retirement age R to age of death D, evaluated at age a using interest rate i.

To obtain the *economically fair reduction factor*, say d_{EF}, I set the two present values in equations 2-2 and 2-3 equal, which gives:

$$(2\text{-}4) \qquad d_{EF} = [\, -\ln(\Omega_{RD}/\Omega_{aD})\, /\, (R-a)\,] + [\, i-g\,].$$

Thus if the firm uses the reduction factor d_{EF}, then the worker's pension asset value based on service to date is invariant to his decision to continue working. The firm imparts no bias to his decision to leave.

To obtain the "actuarially fair" reduction factor, say d_{AF}, I set the two present values equal to each other with one important difference: *in the actuarial calculation, the wage growth factor is set to zero.* It is straightforward to show that the solution satisfies:

(2-5) $d_{AF} = d_{EF} + g;$

that is, the actuarially fair reduction factor equals the economically fair reduction factor *plus* the expected per annum growth rate in wages.

The actuary's calculation implicitly assumes that the worker's choice is either to retire now and wait until age R to start receiving his pension or retire now and start receiving his pension immediately. He ignores the issue at hand: the decision for the worker to retire now and start collecting now or retire *later* and start collecting later. Hence, by construction, the actuarial calculation cannot measure the incentive to leave or stay, since it assumes early departure in either calculation.

An "actuarially subsidized" early benefit exists anytime the reduction factor is set to some number less than d_{AF}. But, of course, this "subsidy" implies nothing about incentives as such unless it is compared against the economically fair reduction factor, d_{EF}. As long as the plan's reduction factor exceeds the economically fair reduction factor, $d > d_{EF}$, which is the usual condition, the pension encourages workers to postpone retirement until normal retirement age.

Treatment of Quits. If a worker leaves the firm *before* the earliest early retirement age a^* then he is a "quit," not a "retiree," and hence his pension normally is calculated on the basis of an actuarially fair reduction.[7] Thus a normal condition in defined benefit plans is that workers have an incentive to stay until early retirement age. Beyond this age and before the normal retirement age, the incentive to stay or leave on the margin is determined primarily by the plan's early reduction factor, but normally the incentive is tilted to favor a stay decision.

Capital Losses for All Departures before Normal Retirement Age. Assuming that the worker is vested (usually within five years of service), capital losses from leaving at any age before normal retirement age, CLa, are calculated as follows:

(2-6) $CL_a = [PV_a^R - PV_a^a(d_a)],$
$$d_a = d_{AF} \text{ if } a < a^*, \text{ and}$$
$$d_a = d \text{ if } a^* < a < R,$$

---

7. Some plans will award the early retirement subsidy to one who quits before a^*, subject to a service and age condition (U.S. Department of Labor 1999).

where d_a is the reduction factor that applies upon departure at age a. The capital loss from departing before normal retirement age equals the difference between the present value of ongoing benefits, PV_a^R, and the present value of benefits using the plan's early reduction factor, $PV_a^a (d_a)$, all calculated on the basis of current service. The extra cost of leaving before a^* is imposed because the reduction factor for plan d is replaced by the actuarially fair reduction factor d_{AF}.

Parameter Values for a "Typical" Defined Benefit Plan

The capital loss structure in equation 6 is straightforward and a fixture in pension economics. The particular way in which a sponsor chooses the pension parameters can have a significant influence on the path of these losses over age and service levels.[8] But the paths all share a similar "look"—namely, the hill-like function over tenure, often with a discrete drop at the earliest age of retirement eligibility, which reflects the switch of reduction factors, followed thereafter by various patterns between the early and normal retirement ages, depending on the plan's choice of its early reduction factor.

To show how this "hill function" looks for the typical pattern, I use data reported by the Bureau of Labor Statistics in its survey of medium and large firms.[9] The most popular normal and early retirement ages are 65 and 55, respectively.[10] As of 1997 the average early reduction factor was 4.9 percent,[11] and the mean generosity factor was 1.5 percent. Cost of living adjustments after retirement in defined benefit plans are rare, and so I set them to zero.[12]

In my model, I do not use mortality tables but instead assume that death occurs with certainty at 80. I have shown elsewhere that a reasonable assumption for 1997 is that nominal wages plus within-firm increases are about the same as nominal interest rates, and thus I set $g = i$.[13] The ten-year Treasury rate in 1997 was 6.4 percent.[14] I assume that workers who depart before early retirement age receive the "actuarially fair" benefit—that is, that the actuarially subsidized rate becomes available only upon reaching eligibility for early retirement.

---

8. Ippolito (1997).

9. U.S. Department of Labor (1999).

10. About 30 percent of workers are eligible for full benefits before age 60, but these almost always are union plans that are unlikely candidates for cash balance conversion. Union plans sometimes offer full benefits at 55 or less. In these plans, the incentive to retire early is significant at young ages.

11. This is the average for plans that use a uniform percentage (43 percent of plans); the rest use a sliding scale with different reductions for each age before normal retirement age. BLS gives no information for plans in the latter category (U.S. Department of Labor 1999).

12. As of 1995 only 7 percent of defined benefit plans have awarded a cost of living increase to retirees over the past five years (U.S. Department of Labor 1999).

13. Ippolito (2002).

14. White House (1998).

Figure 2-6. *Pension Capital Losses from Departing at Various Ages*

Pension loss divided by wage

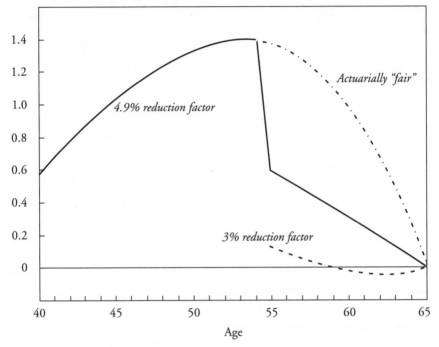

Source: Author's calculations.
Note: Assumes a 6.4% interest rate; start at age 35; wage growth equal to interest rate.

Graphical Depiction

The solid line schedule in figure 2-6 shows the schedule of losses (as a percent-age of annual wage) for my prototype plan for a worker from age 40 (with five years of service) to normal retirement age 65 (thirty years of service). At low service levels, the worker loses relatively little if he quits. As he accrues more service, the stakes become higher, until he approaches eligibility for early retire-ment (age 55 in this case).

If the plan pays only actuarially fair benefits at all ages before 65, then in pension parlance we would say that there is no early retirement age; effectively all departures before normal retirement age are treated as "quits." This policy is reflected by the schedule of capital losses depicted by the dash-dot line schedule in the figure.

"Early retirees" are distinguished from quits because the pension plan switches to a reduction factor that is more favorable than "actuarially fair," giv-ing rise to the term "subsidy." In my figure, the solid-line schedule of losses drops sharply at age 55, reflecting the use of a 4.9 percent reduction factor as compared with the actuarially fair 9.4 percent reduction factor used at age 54.[15] Clearly workers retiring after 55 are treated more generously than those who quit before, which explains the "spike" of retirements that typically occurs at the first age of eligibility for early benefits.[16] Notwithstanding the subsidy offer to early retirees, the plan does not favor retirement at 55 as compared with normal retirement age 65 because the reduction factor is not economically fair. Indeed, there is some bias toward encouraging work until 65. In effect, the typical pension plan charges early retirees an "early exit fee."[17]

The plan needs to set its reduction factor to the economically fair rate to generate conditions neutral to early retirement.[18] In 1997 this rate was about 3 percent. The dashed-line schedule from age 55 to age 65 depicts the capital losses from departing over this age range using a 3 percent reduction factor. This schedule of losses reflects a firm's intention to set up a pension plan that imparts neutrality to the retirement decision over this age range. No more than 10 percent of defined benefit pension plans used reduction factors as low as 3 percent in 1997.[19] (Many union plans offer full retirement at 55 or earlier, but these plans are not candidates for cash balance conversions.)

Getting a Handle on Losses

The capital loss structure depicted by the solid line schedule in figure 2-6 is a representation of the conversion issues raised by cash balance plans. If a defined benefit plan sponsor makes a conversion and awards workers only the legal value of its pension plan promise, then workers will absorb losses like those depicted by the solid line schedule. Older workers have more at stake than younger workers, especially those on the cusp of early retirement eligibility. That is, as long as the "old" plan is amended before workers attain the early retirement age, workers are not legally entitled to the early retirement subsidy.

Workers who have attained eligibility—for example, age 55 in the figure—are guaranteed by law to limit their capital loss from departure to a number that is about 60 percent of their annual wage in my prototypical plan. Under the old

15. The actuarially fair reduction factor is different at every age. At 54 it is roughly 9.4 percent; hence the switch to a 4.9 percent factor at 55 is what explains the sharp drop in capital losses at this age.

16. For example, see Gustman and Steinmeier (1994), Gustman, Mitchell, and Steinmeier (1994), and Quinn, Burkhauser, and Myers (1990).

17. One efficiency reason this schedule might be optimal is that early departures are more likely either to prefer leisure or to be unhealthy. In either case, these attributes might signify workers that are less valued by the firm (but not necessarily paid less if their health condition or zeal for leisure showed up late in tenure). Hence the firm has the opportunity to collect a rebate on compensation.

18. The rate is somewhat different for every age; a uniform rate of 3 percent is approximately correct for calculating economically fair benefits.

19. U.S. Department of Labor (1999).

plan, however, *based on service attained at 55*, this loss would have gone to zero by age 65, giving the worker the option to eliminate this loss by retiring later. Upon conversion, however, the plan can lock in the loss level at age 55 by simply awarding this worker the *actuarial equivalent* of his age-55 ERISA benefit if he decides to postpone retirement.

It is not hard to quantify wealth transfers upon conversion. All that is required are the ongoing and termination liabilities before conversion and excess assets that remain after employees' "accounts" have been credited with their starting lump-sum amounts. Aggregate losses are the summation of capital losses imposed on each worker in the plan. Suppose that the ongoing benefits in some plan before the conversion are denoted as L_0 and that termination benefits are L_T. Suppose also that the plan tempers the impact of the conversion by adjusting some of the conversion formulas or giving some workers a choice to stay in the old plan. I denote the present value of these adjustments by Δ. Thus the value of all worker "accounts" in the new plan is $L_T + \Delta$. Finally, let plan assets be denoted by A.

I make the following conjectures. For the vast majority of converted plans, wealth is transferred from workers to stockholders, and assets before the conversion are less than ongoing benefits but greater than the cumulative amounts of workers' accounts, meaning that the new plan is characterized by excess assets *EA*. These propositions are denoted as follows:

$$EA = A - (L_T + \Delta) > 0; \text{ and } A < L_0.$$

These propositions, which are testable, mean that the wealth transfers from workers to firms can be bounded. The lower bound is excess assets after plan conversion, *EA*, and the upper bound is the difference between ongoing and termination benefits, $L_0 - L_T$. These numbers, calculated for all conversions, give a reasonable range of wealth transfers occurring in these transactions since the mid-1980s.

Impact on Retirement Ages

Clark and Schieber seem to attach considerable importance to the impact of cash balance plans on retirement age. Their interpretation of cash balance plans is that they will encourage later retirement, which they assert is consistent with public policy.

What is the short-term effect of conversion on retirement decisions? Upon a conversion with no benefit enhancements, all workers incur losses, as depicted by the solid line in figure 2-6. Owing to these one-time wealth losses, all workers, and especially older workers, likely will remain in their jobs longer than anticipated to make up for these losses. Thus by expropriating older workers' pension wealth, firms essentially put workers in a position in which they have to postpone their retirement in order to recoup their lost wealth. I hardly think that these actions are consistent with public policy.

The long-run impact on retirement age is the opposite. The incentives that characterize defined benefit plans, as portrayed by the solid-line schedule in figure 2-6, are tilted to favor later retirement. In contrast, cash balance plans more or less are neutral to workers' decisions to stay or leave the firm at any age. The capital loss schedule for the typical cash balance plan lies exactly at zero over all ages because the value of the account and future guaranteed investment returns are invariant to the decision to stay or leave.[20] Viewed prospectively, workers who attain retirement ages after a lengthy period of coverage under a cash balance plan will retire at earlier ages, all other things being equal.

The Missing Empirical Work

Despite the authors' title, there is no empirical work reported in their paper. Clark and Schieber report stylized calculations from information they have on seventy-seven cash balance conversions. It is not clear that this sample is representative of all cash balance conversions. The authors do not calculate capital losses in each plan but rather evaluate the impact of conversion on the basis of hypothetical workers of varying ages that are standardized across plans. Thus we are unsure, for example, what weights to attach to young and old workers. Moreover, the algorithms that they use are not reported, making it difficult to evaluate the quality of their estimates.

The authors' general conclusion is that many (and perhaps a majority of) sponsors contribute more to workers than required by law, either in the form of grandfather provisions for some workers (that is, allowing older workers to stay in the old plan[21]) or the award of some credits beyond those legally required, notably in the form of some recognition of pending subsidized early retirement benefits for workers within a few years of eligibility.

The results also show, however, that sponsors generally award amounts substantially less than ongoing benefits from the old plan. In other words, their work conveys a kind of general impression of conversion practices but does not give us solid estimates to evaluate. The authors try to show that consideration of other pension plans in the firm softens the overall impact of conversion on workers, and they categorize conversions using "cost reducer," "cost neutral shifter,"

20. Often workers can take the value of the account with them as a lump sum and roll it over into an individual retirement account without triggering tax liability.

21. A prototype for this kind of option is the conversion of the federal government's plan from the old Civil Service Retirement System to the new Federal Employee Retirement System (FERS) in 1986. All new employees were required to join the new plan, but existing employees were given the option to switch to the FERS (see Ippolito 2002).

and "cost increaser" categories.[22] But these costs are compared on the basis of actuarial calculations for accounting purposes and do not necessarily reflect differences in the present value of contributions to either plan. Moreover, other data that are pertinent to an evaluation of the fair market value of a pension benefit are missing: notably, the bond ratings of the firms, quit rates at older ages, and retirement rates at various early retirement ages.

Even assuming that the calculations did reflect true economic cost, there is no evaluation of the distribution of these conversion costs across plans. In the implicit contract framework, one would expect that the conversion is most likely to be "cost reducing" (using Clark-Schieber terminology) if the sponsor evinces poor financial performance.

First, defined benefit plans sponsored by firms in financial difficulty are worth less because the probability of realizing the downside of the contract is higher. Second, these firms are less likely to be hiring in the labor market in the foreseeable future and thus are less likely to risk reputational damage associated with the imposition of capital losses on workers. I expect that the most generous conversions are affiliated with firms with strong growth characteristics. This empirical work is yet to be done with their data, although the outcome of that work promises to be informative to the new literature on cash balance plans.

It also is natural to be curious about the evolution of quit rates in the sample of conversions studied by Clark and Schieber. Have the higher predicted quit rates materialized? If not, did the sponsors arrange the cash balance plan to reflect incentives to stay, for example, by instituting graduated contribution rates with age or service? If quit rates increased, is there any evidence to suggest that conversions to cash balance plans are more likely in industries where higher quit rates are evolving as the norm?

To the extent that some firms' demand for low quit rates has fallen, then the retention of a defined benefit plan is an expensive way to award retirement benefits. The imposition of capital loss schedules makes it difficult for workers to move mid-career to a modestly higher paying job, requiring sponsors to pay wage premiums.[23]

Similarly, with regard to retirement effects, the question is begged whether firms in the Clark and Schieber sample evince characteristics different from some control sample that did not convert to cash balance. Economic incentives

---

22. There is some imprecision in these estimates because they are defined in an actuarial or accounting cost framework, which may be different from a calculation of true economic cost of various plan provisions. For example, the annual cost charge that actuaries make for defined benefit plans can sometimes be only vaguely related to the true present value of accruals and depends heavily on the funding status of the plan.

23. If the pay alternative is sufficiently high, then it still may pay to incur even substantial capital losses. Opportunities with more modest pay increases, however, become uneconomical. For a discussion of the pay premiums required in firms using deferred wage contracts such as defined benefit plans, see Ippolito (1997).

to retire across this sample must vary considerably in the preconversion defined benefit plans. Did the conversions occur in industries where new evidence suggests that worker productivity is uncorrelated with age? Do they occur in industries that have favored older retirement? And have retirement rates changed in the plans as the economic models predict?

A reasonable hypothesis is that the initial effect of conversion on retirement rates will depend on the rules of conversion: if older workers are given only termination benefits, then the negative wealth effect will encourage workers to postpone retirement. After an adjustment period, the neutrality of the cash balance plan suggests a mild drift toward earlier retirement, especially if reduction factors are large in the old versions of these plans.[24] Are conversions more likely in firms that offered generous early reduction factors? Offered subsidies to deferred vested quits? Set normal retirement age before age 65? These are all answerable questions in this database, but none are answered.

More generally, the amount of information that could be teased from these seventy-seven conversions, especially if matched to a control sample of equal size, seemingly is unlimited. Unfortunately, none of this potential is exploited.

Finally, but perhaps most important, the authors had data that permitted them to calculate upper and lower bounds on the capital losses referenced above. If they had done this, they would have produced a first-order approximation on the wealth transfers effected by their conversions. They also could have calculated these losses for every worker, or at least every service-age category for every conversion they studied. Thus there could have been estimates of losses across age-service profiles, along with appropriate standard errors. The authors report none of these data. In this case, however, I suspect that in saying nothing, they have said much.

Concluding Remarks

Reversion taxes are at the core of the trend toward cash balance plans. It is hard to imagine a public policy that has engendered a result so contrary to its original intent. In addition to reducing funding in most plans, it also gave rise to a new industry—namely, cash balance plans.[25] The reversion taxes gave firms the motive to abandon defined benefit plans. Cash balance plans gave firms the opportunity to terminate these plans without triggering the reversion tax. Thus Congress not only reduced the number of defined benefit plans but also encouraged

24. A notable exception exists if workers make it to normal retirement age. In the old version of the plan, it is almost certain that the pension cost of staying was high in relation to annual wage. But in the cash balance alternative, there are no pension costs to "staying too late." Of course, traditional defined benefit plans can be adjusted to eliminate the incentive to retire at normal retirement age.

25. Ippolito (2001).

transactions that imposed large losses on workers that may not have been incurred had Congress been more willing to live with imperfections in the old system.

Many hundreds, and perhaps thousands, of large defined benefit plans have been converted to cash balance plans.[26] Using preliminary data from the 1999 Form 5500 series, I find that approximately 25 percent of all workers in DB plans were in fact in the cash balance variety. Because these transactions are tantamount to a unilateral termination of promised benefits, in many cases they represent an abrogation of implied contracts. While the legal ramifications of these actions are nil, comporting as they do with federal laws governing terminations, the economic implications are more problematic. For the firms that engaged in conversions without adequate compensation for harmed workers, future compensation they pay in the market will be higher, all else constant, because their reputation for honoring implicit contracts has been diminished.

The aggregate impact of these transactions, however, goes beyond the firms that effected them because they have undoubtedly caused workers in other firms to question whether their plans also will be terminated. If workers in general expect plans to be terminated, then they will no longer be willing to forgo cash compensation in anticipation of ongoing benefits. This dynamic means that defined benefit plans become ever more expensive for reputable firms, encouraging them also to terminate or "convert" in order to rationalize workers' expectations. In other words, if workers are willing only to pay for a low-quality pension (one that will terminated), then it only pays for firms to offer low-quality pensions. We have the makings of a lemons market in pensions.[27]

A sensible public policy choice is to encourage, or require, firms that engage in conversions to provide full information to workers, articulating the quantitative impact on workers' pension asset values. This policy merely reflects the reality that workers are holding pension assets that involve substantial portions of their wealth. Thus, any change by the sponsor that substantially affects this wealth ought to be conveyed to the primary stakeholders. Widespread availability of information about the conversion offers the best protection not only to workers, but also to other sponsors of defined benefit plans, all of whom absorb some costs if some firms violate the implicit contract.

A sensible private policy for reputable sponsors is to use a model offered by the mutual fund industry. If a mutual fund advertises one investment policy in its prospectus and then wants to switch midstream to some other policy, then the *least* that they are required to do is inform investors of their intentions. In point of fact, they must obtain the votes of the majority of shareholders. A similar approach is not unreasonable for firms to follow when they fundamentally

---

26. Niehaus and Yu (2003) identify 358 cash balance plans using data sources in the private sector.
27. I present this model in Ippolito (2003).

alter the asset value of the contract previously in force. The firm's own reputation rides on its decision to alter an implicit contract with its workers, who are major stakeholders in it.

References

American Academy of Actuaries. 1993. "The Impact of Government Regulation on Defined Benefit Pension Plan Terminations." Special Report. Washington. March.

Brown, Kyle, and others. 2000. *The Unfolding of a Predictable Surprise: A Comprehensive Analysis of the Shift from Traditional Pensions to Hybrid Plans.* Bethesda, Md.: Watson Wyatt.

Clark, Robert, and Ann McDermed. 1990. *The Choice of Pension Plans in a Changing Environment.* Washington: American Enterprise Institute.

Clark, Robert, and Fred Munzenmaier. 2001. "Impact of Replacing a Defined Benefit Plan with a Defined Contribution or a Cash Balance Plan." *North American Actuarial Journal* vol. 5 (1): 32–56.

Clark, Robert, and Sylvester Schieber. 2001. "Taking the Subsidy out of Early Retirement: The Story behind the Conversion to Hybrid Pensions." In Olivia Mitchell and others, eds., *Innovations in Managing the Financial Risks of Retirement.* University of Pennsylvania Press.

Elliot, Kenneth, and James Moore. 2000. "Cash Balance Pension Plans: The New Wave." *Compensation and Working Conditions* 5 (Summer): 3–11.

ERISA Industry Committee. 1996. "Getting the Job Done: A White Paper on Emerging Pension Issues." Washington.

Gale, William. 1994. "Public Policies and Private Pension Contributions." *Journal of Money, Credit and Banking* 26 (3): 710–34.

Gustman, Alan, and Thomas Steinmeier. 1992. "The Stampede towards Defined Contribution Plans." *Industrial Relations* 31 (Spring): 361–69.

———. 1994. *Pension Incentives and Job Mobility.* Kalamazoo, Mich.: Upjohn Institute.

Gustman, Alan, Olivia Mitchell, and Thomas Steinmeier. 1994. "The Role of Pensions in the Labor Market: A Survey of the Literature." *Industrial Labor Relations Review* 47 (April): 417–38.

Hay Huggins Company. 1989. "OBRA 1987: The Impact of Limiting Contributions to Defined Benefit Plans." Washington.

———. 1990. *Pension Plan Expense Study for the PBGC.* Washington.

———. 2003. "Tenuous Property Rights: The Unraveling of DB Pension Contracts in the U.S." In O. Castellion and E. Fornero, eds., *Pension Policy in an Integrating Europe.* Cheltenham, U.K.: Edward Elgar.

Ippolito, Richard A. 1985. "The Labor Contract and True Economic Pension Liabilities." *American Economic Review* 75 (December): 1031–43.

———. 1997. *Pension Plans and Employee Performance: Evidence, Analysis, and Policy.* University of Chicago Press.

———. 2001. "Reversion Taxes, Contingent Benefits and the Decline in Pension Funding." *Journal of Law and Economics* 44 (1): 199–232.

———. 2002. "Stayers as Workers and Savers: towards Reconciling the Pension-Quit Literature." *Journal of Human Resources* 37 (Spring): 275–308.

———. 2003. "Tenuous Property Rights: The Unraveling of DB Pension Contracts in the U.S." In O. Castellion and E. Fornero, eds., *Pension Policy in an Integrating Europe.* Cheltenham, U.K.: Edward Elgar.

Ippolito, Richard, and William James. 1992. "LBOs, Reversions, and Implicit Contracts." *Journal of Finance* 47 (March): 139–67.

Koop, Steve. 1997. *Pension Plan Turnover Rate Table Construction Final Report.* University of Western Ontario, Department of Statistical and Actuarial Sciences, Canada.

Kruse, Douglas. 1995. "Pension Substitution in the 1980s: Why the Shift towards Defined Contribution Plans?" *Industrial Relations* 34 (April): 218–41.

McGill, Dan, and others. 1996. *Fundamentals of Private Pensions.* University of Pennsylvania Press.

Mitchell, Mark, and J. Harold Mulherin. 1989. "The Stock Price Response to Pension Terminations and the Relation of Terminations with Corporate Takeovers." *Financial Management* 18: 41–56.

Mittelstaedt, H. Fred. 1989. "An Empirical Analysis of the Factors Underlying the Decision to Remove Excess Assets from Overfunded Pension Plans." *Journal of Accounting and Economics* 11: 399–418.

Niehaus, Gregory, and Tong Yu. 2003. "Cash Balance Plan Conversions: Evidence on the Tax Avoidance Hypothesis." University of South Carolina.

Pension Benefit Guaranty Corporation. 1995. *Removing Pension Assets: Risks to Retirees and the Federal Pension Insurance Program.* Washington.

Pensions and Investments. 1999. "Special Report: Cash Balance Plans." May 31.

Pesando, James. 1985. "The Usefulness of the Windup Measure of Pension Liabilities: A Labor Market Perspective." *Journal of Finance* 40: 927–40.

Petersen, Mitchell A. 1992. "Pension Terminations and Worker-Shareholder Wealth Transfers." *Quarterly Journal of Economics* 107: 1033–56.

Pontiff, J., Shleifer, A., and M. S. Weisbach. 1990. "Reversions of Excess Pension Assets after Takeovers." *Rand Journal of Economics* 21 (Winter): 600–13.

Quinn, Joseph, Richard Burkhauser, and Daniel Myers. 1990. *Passing the Torch: The Influence of Economic Incentives on Work and Retirement.* Kalamazoo, Mich.: Upjohn Institute.

Sheppard, Lee A. 2000. "More Bad News about Cash Balance Plans." *Tax Notes*, October 2, pp. 14–18.

Shleifer, Andrei, and Lawrence Summers. 1988. "Breach of Trust in Hostile Takeovers." In A. Auerbach, ed., *Corporate Takeovers: Causes and Consequences.* University of Chicago Press.

Stone, Mary. 1987. "A Financing Explanation for Overfunded Pension Plan Terminations." *Journal of Accounting Research* 25: 317–26.

Third Millennium. 1999. *Public Attitudes toward Cash Balance Retirement Plans.* New York.

Thomas, Jacob. 1989. "Why Do Firms Terminate Overfunded Pension Plans?" *Journal of Accounting and Economics* 11: 361–98.

U.S. Department of Labor. 1999. *Employee Benefits in Medium and Large Private Establishments—1997.* Bureau of Labor Statistics Bulletin 2517, September.

VanDerhei, Jack. 1987. "The Effect of Voluntary Terminations of Overfunded Pension Plans on Shareholder Wealth." *Journal of Risk and Insurance* 54(1): 131–56.

White House. *Economic Report of the President, 1998.*

3

What People Don't Know about
Their Pensions and Social Security

ALAN L. GUSTMAN AND THOMAS L. STEINMEIER

The role of employer-provided pensions and Social Security in shaping employees' retirement and saving behavior has attracted an enormous amount of attention from both researchers and policymakers over the past twenty-five years.[1] In the research literature, the almost universal assumption is that workers are fully informed about the rules governing their employer- and government-provided pensions. However, to the limited extent that researchers have been able to test that assumption, results suggest that workers are less than fully informed (Bernheim 1988, Mitchell 1988, Gustman and Steinmeier 1989) and that providing information can affect their behavior (Clark and Schieber 1998; Bayer, Bernheim, and Scholz 1996; Bernheim and Garrett 1996; Madrian and Shea 2000).

Despite a general lack of research on the role of information in retirement planning, policymakers have made information a central issue. The Social

This paper is funded by a grant from the National Institute on Aging to the National Bureau of Economic Research. The authors would like to thank Richard Disney, William Gale, Olivia Mitchell, Joseph Piacentini, John Karl Scholz, Lawrence Thompson, Steven Venti, and participants in the Brookings Conference on Public Policies and Private Pensions, September 21–22, 2000, for their helpful comments. Data used in this study are from the Health and Retirement Study, which is supported by the National Institute on Aging.

1. See, for example, surveys by Lumsdaine (1996), Lumsdaine and Mitchell (1999), and Gustman and Juster (1996).

Security Administration (SSA), for example, recently began to mail workers statements of their accrued and projected benefits to improve their ability to plan for retirement; the SSA also has made a retirement planner available on its website. The U.S. Department of Labor has initiated several programs to examine the extent of workers' lack of information and to improve their knowledge of pensions and of saving for retirement in general. Following the 1997 Savings Are Vital to Everyone's Retirement (SAVER) Act, the National Summit on Retirement Savings, held in 1998, emphasized the need to educate the public about retirement planning through media campaigns and other means. In 2000 the Department of Labor celebrated the fifth anniversary of its Retirement Savings Education Campaign. And recent legislative proposals by Representative John Boehner of Ohio (HR 4747, 4748, and 4749) would significantly expand the scope of investment advice that employers are permitted to offer their employees.

This chapter provides a comprehensive analysis of what workers (don't) know about their pensions and Social Security. This analysis is based on information from the Health and Retirement Study, described below. Relative to previous findings and current policy issues, the paper provides five key sets of information. First, it uses more recent data than previous studies. This is important because of the significant changes in the pension universe and in Social Security that have occurred over the last fifteen years. Second, the paper focuses on the *distribution* of differences between respondents' reports of requested information and linked reports obtained from records provided by the Social Security Administration or from detailed pension plan descriptions obtained from firms, examining the patterns of discrepancies at the level of the individual respondent more than did previous studies. Third, the paper examines the effects of poor information on economic behavior in order to assess the potential benefits of providing better information. Fourth, to improve understanding of misreporting and to provide a foundation for imputing pension and Social Security outcomes when data are not available, the analysis explores whether the differences between the cases that have linked Social Security and pension records and those that do not are related to demographic or other measures. Fifth, the appendix provides information of use to researchers, including an analysis of the relation between respondent-reported earnings histories and linked earnings histories from Social Security records. It also includes a set of equations that researchers can use to impute pension characteristics and plan values for cases without employer-provided pension plan descriptions and for researchers who do not have access to linked pension data.

Our findings suggest that workers approaching retirement possess a great deal of misinformation about their pensions. Half of respondents with linked pension data correctly identified their plan type, but fewer than half could identify, within one year, the dates of their eligibility for early and normal retirement benefits. According to the firm-provided data, two-thirds of respondents would be eligible to retire by the time they reached age 55; however, less than half of respondents were aware that they were eligible. Those who were within three years of retiring forecast somewhat more accurately but did not do a much better job of forecasting their age of eligibility for early retirement than the sample as a whole. Eighty percent of respondents with a defined benefit plan either did not think that they were eligible for early retirement or did not know the benefit reduction rate for their plan.

Respondents did better in reporting the value of their pension than their age of eligibility, but the unexplained variation is still considerable. Only half of the respondents ventured to guess their expected Social Security benefits, and only half of those came within $1,500 of the actual annual amount. On the whole, respondents were somewhat pessimistic in evaluating their defined benefit pensions, in contrast to findings from earlier studies. Respondents' and firms' calculations of pension benefit amounts were in rough agreement in only 40 percent of the cases.

A preliminary analysis of how knowledge of Social Security and pension benefits affects retirement expectations, realization of those expectations, and wealth accumulation reveals complex relationships. Because it is easier to adjust saving downward than upward as one approaches retirement, even symmetric errors in expectations should affect retirement and saving outcomes. Yet respondents' lack of knowledge about Social Security and pension wealth and their inability to identify their plan type had only modest effects on retirement plans, on whether those plans were met, and on saving outcomes.

Although researchers would like to work with the true value of pensions and Social Security benefits, in many surveys only respondents' reports were available. Our findings show that respondents' reports and other information about the respondents accounted for 80 percent of the variation in linked employer-reported pension values and that respondent-reported work histories and other explanatory variables accounted for 75 percent of the variation in earnings obtained from linked Social Security records. Thus prospects are good for imputing pension and Social Security values, although they are not good for imputing the timing or size of incentives for early retirement.

Implications for policy depend to an important degree on two considerations: the precise behavioral channels through which misinformation affects retirement and saving and whether increased educational efforts affect behavior and planning in a timely manner. However, there is little information on which to base an answer to either question.

Previous Work

Several studies have shown that workers' knowledge of their Social Security and pension benefits is imperfect. Those studies compare respondents' reports with information gleaned from linked Social Security records or detailed employer-provided pension plan descriptions.

Bernheim (1988) compared the benefits expected by respondents to the 1969–79 Retirement History Study (RHS) with the benefits computed from linked Social Security records, concluding that expectations were quite noisy but unbiased, conditional on the incomplete information individuals used to form them. Bernheim faced a number of problems in his analysis that we also faced, among them the fact that fewer than half of the respondents guessed their likely Social Security benefits.[2] In addition, the RHS asked respondents about expected monthly Social Security benefits at age of receipt, but the question did not specify whether benefits were given in current (survey year) or future dollars. If the answer was interpreted as being given in future dollars, there was no information on the expected rate of inflation. Bernheim assumed that respondents reported in current dollars. Nevertheless, Bernheim concluded that "when the noise is filtered out appropriately, it appears that consumers do think seriously about future events and report expectations that may well reflect, albeit imperfectly, their true beliefs."[3]

Using data from the 1983 Survey of Consumer Finances, which linked employer-provided pension plan data with respondents' descriptions of their plans, Mitchell (1988) found that respondents were sometimes misinformed about plan type, contribution provisions, and age and length of service required to draw benefits. Regression analysis suggested that unionized employees, higher-income workers, better-educated workers, and those with seniority were better informed about those plan characteristics.

Gustman and Steinmeier (1989) evaluated the detailed benefit formulas from the Survey of Consumer Finances linked to employer-provided pension plan descriptions. They used respondents' work and earnings histories to determine dates of eligibility for early and normal retirement benefits as well as the values of those benefits. They found that plan type often was misreported and that pension values reported by respondents and their firms matched at the medians but not at the means. Some respondents seemed to be highly optimistic, expecting to be able to retire earlier than their plans permitted and with larger pensions.

Indirect evidence that workers are not fully informed comes from studies showing that financial education may affect individuals' behavior. Pension plan participation rates generally rise when firms offer information on retirement planning (Clark and Schieber 1998; Bayer, Bernheim, and Scholz 1996; Bernheim and Garrett 1996). In addition, when enrollment in a 401(k) plan was made automatic and a default contribution rate and investment allocation was selected by a firm, plan enrollment was increased and default contribution and

---

2. Bernheim (1988, tables 11.1 and 11.2, pp. 321–22).
3. Bernheim (1998, p. 313).

investment outcomes were observed much more frequently than before there was automatic enrollment and a default option (Madrian and Shea 2000). Employees whose pension plan offered a choice of investments were more likely to hold stock outside of their retirement plan (Weisbenner 1999), although that result may reflect selectivity on unmeasured characteristics. Respondents covered by pension plans did not reduce their saving in other forms; instead, their total wealth increased by only a fraction less than the value of their pensions (Gustman and Steinmeier 1999), suggesting perhaps that they were informed about the need for retirement saving through their pension plan. Lusardi (1999) suggests that some workers do not plan ahead for retirement and consequently do not save adequately. Maki (chapter 4 of this volume) provides a more detailed discussion of the effects of financial education. The evidence suggests that participation in retirement programs, patterns of investment, and related behaviors are influenced by private financial education. There is no reliable information on whether educational programs run by the government have a discernible impact on planning or saving for retirement.

The Data

The Health and Retirement Study (HRS) is a longitudinal, nationally representative study of older Americans that began in 1992 with an initial cohort of 12,652 individuals from 7,702 households in which at least one household member was born between 1931 and 1941. Participants were surveyed in 1992 and reinterviewed every two years through 1998.

Linked Social Security Data

The Social Security earnings records provided by the HRS are unique; only a few researchers, who work at or with the Social Security Administration, have access to comparable recent data. From these records, the amount of HRS respondents' covered earnings, computed as average indexed monthly earnings (AIME), and the values of their Social Security benefits, computed as the primary insurance amount (PIA), can be closely estimated. Although a small chance of mismatching records exists, the Social Security earnings records are the gold standard for employees' covered earnings history. Therefore patterns of discrepancies between respondents' reports of expected benefits and the benefits computed from the earnings histories are very informative.

Altogether, 75 percent of respondents gave permission to match their interview record with their Social Security earnings history. Records were matched for 95 percent of those who gave permission. Column 1 of table 3-1 reports the results of a probit in which the dependent variable is equal to 1 if respondents gave permission in wave 1 for HRS to match their self-report of benefits with their Social Security record. The independent variables are various characteristics

Table 3-1. *Probit for Probability of Permission Wave 1 to Match Social Security Earnings Record*

Independent variable	Partial effect	z
Female gender	0.000	0.01
Single marital status	−0.034	−2.94
Children		
None	−0.018	−0.99
Not known	−0.173	−4.81
Race		
Black	−0.028	−2.26
Hispanic	−0.061	−3.96
Education		
High school dropout	0.014	1.22
Some college	−0.021	−1.69
College graduate	−0.028	−1.70
Some graduate school	−0.041	−2.50
Home owner	−0.008	−0.56
Assets		
$0 to 10K	0.075	4.02
$10K to 25K	0.072	3.64
$25K to 100K	0.035	2.99
$250K to 1,000K	−0.038	−3.00
$1,000+K	−0.010	−0.44
Not known	−0.190	−4.12
Retirement horizon		
< 2 years	−0.001	−0.08
2 to 4 years	0.006	0.33
10+ years	0.001	0.09
Never	−0.040	−2.29
Not applicable	−0.042	−2.21
Not asked from proxy	−0.540	−23.64
Not known	−0.047	−2.70
Firm size		
0 to 4 employees	0.021	1.04
5 to 14 employees	0.008	0.38
15 to 24 employees	0.012	0.38
25 to 99 employees	0.039	1.88
500+ employees	0.029	2.01
Not known	−0.013	−0.54
Industry		
Nonmanufacturing	−0.002	−0.17
Not known	−0.035	−0.62
Occupation		
Management	−0.010	−0.89
White collar	−0.015	−1.19
Not known	−0.172	−1.84
Union member		
Yes	0.020	1.49
Not known	0.054	2.38
Annual earnings		
$0 to 15K	−0.015	−0.74
$15 to 30K	−0.029	−1.51
$30 to 50K	−0.036	−1.90
$100+K	−0.035	−0.96
Not known	−0.069	−2.02
Pension covered		
Yes	−0.009	−0.76
Not known	0.184	1.95
Summary statistics		
Log likelihood	−7,158.599	
Pseudo R^2	0.0652	
Number of observations	12,652	

Source: Authors' calculations based on data from the HRS.

of the respondent and the respondent's job;[4] they accounted for only a small part of the variation in the permission rate.[5] Black and Hispanic respondents, respondents with greater assets and in the highest education category, and those who expected never to retire or who did not report a specific retirement date were less likely to grant permission.[6]

Social Security Values Estimated from the Respondent Survey

The survey asked respondents about the starting date of their current job, starting and ending dates for the job last held by those not working in 1992, and starting and ending dates for the previous job held for at least five years before their current or last job. For ease of discussion, we call those jobs "current," "last," and "previous" jobs. Respondents also were asked about earnings during those periods. In addition, the survey asked respondents in wave 3 their date of entry into the labor force, how many years they worked before they secured their previous job, and how many years they worked in jobs covered by Social Security. From that information, we constructed a covered earnings history[7] that we used to calculate respondents' average indexed monthly earnings and the Social Security benefits respondents were entitled to (primary insurance amount).

Linked Pension Data

If a respondent was covered by a pension, the HRS also requested from the employer a detailed description of the pension plan.[8] Employer-provided pension plan descriptions proved to be more readily available for jobs that respondents currently held. The match rate was 65 percent for the 4,456 current jobs held at the time of the survey by respondents who reported that they were

4. Appendix table 3A-1, column 1, reports the Social Security matching rates in wave 1 for respondents according to individual and job characteristics.

5. Olson (1999) reaches similar conclusions.

6. Despite the relatively poor fit in the Social Security permission equations, in the appendix we include these covariates in regressions relating the value of benefits computed from Social Security records to the value computed from respondent answers. The inclusion of these variables will adjust predictions for whatever selection is systematically associated with these observables.

7. Wage profiles were forced through all observations, and values for missing years were projected backward off the profiles on the basis of experience and education. The wage profile coefficients were taken from the appendix to Anderson, Gustman, and Steinmeier (1999), which is available from the authors on request, and were based on data from the Survey of Consumer Finances. Coefficients are as follows: experience, .0138221; experience squared, −.0002827; and experience * education, .000996. Note that the wage profiles are not smooth, as they would be if they were based only on the coefficients in the wage equation. Rather, they have sharp discontinuous breaks at points where actual wage observations anchor the profile. Moreover, we did not use wage observations from all years, but only for the number of years worked as reported in the retrospective work history.

8. Question F37 of the HRS asks: "Are you included in any such pension, retirement, or tax-deferred plan?" If the respondent answered yes, the respondent was classified as covered and described as "covered by a pension" or "included in a pension."

included in a pension. The match rate was 66 percent for the 1,387 last jobs held by respondents with no current job in 1992 who reported that they were included in a pension on their last job. For the 2,839 previous jobs of five years' duration, the match rate was 35 percent. In addition, the survey identified another 750 jobs with pension plans that were held by respondents before the previous job. Since the survey did not ask for the employer's name and address for those jobs, respondents' reports could not be matched with plan descriptions.[9] Averaging over these jobs yields an exact-match percentage of 51 percent.

Table 3-2 reports probits where the dependent variable is an indicator of whether there was an employer-provided pension plan description for the respondent.[10] The first column indicates the correlates of plan description matches for all respondents who indicated that they were covered by a pension on some job. Separate equations are shown for matches for the current job held in 1992, the last job held for those with no current job, and the previous five-year job held before the last or current job. For the purpose of examining retirement incentives, the pension plan at the job held just before retirement is likely to be most important; although the survey had a lower plan description match for previous jobs, that is less crucial to retirement modeling. That is, HRS respondents were young enough that most had not phased into partial retirement or left their long-term job by 1992. (See Gustman and Steinmeier 2001.)

The likelihood of finding an employer plan description is not closely related to the independent variables included in table 3-2; however, the fit is somewhat better than it was for the Social Security permission rate in table 3-1. Across all pension plans, blacks, those with more education, homeowners, those with the shortest planning horizons, those with the longest job tenure, and those with nonmanufacturing jobs were more likely to have a match. Those with the greatest assets and earnings, those from firms with fewer than 100 employees, those in management jobs, and those who reported that they were covered by a defined contribution plan were less likely to have a matched plan description.

In addition, the more valuable an individual's pension plan was, the higher was the probability of a match. This finding suggests that if the sample were confined only to those with matched pension plan descriptions, the measured value of the pensions would overstate the value in the full covered population. Similarly, because higher-income individuals were less likely to give permission, the probability of a Social Security earnings record match was lower the higher an individual's earnings. If a sample is confined to those with a Social Security

9. These counts are for individual jobs, not individual pensions. That is, if an individual had both a DB and a DC pension in a job, it would be counted once in these tallies. However, an individual may have more than one entry if he or she had pensions in both the current job and a previous job or in the last job and a previous job.

10. Appendix table 3A-1, column 3, reports the pension matching rates in wave 1 for respondents according to individual and job characteristics.

match, a disproportionate number of those who will receive the highest Social Security benefits is omitted from the sample.

Pension Values Estimated from the Respondent Survey

Respondents also were asked a series of detailed questions about their pension plans. First respondents were asked whether they were covered, and if they were covered, about their plan type. If respondents indicated that their plan was a defined benefit (DB) plan, the subsequent questions asked the dates of early and normal retirement, the year of expected retirement, and the associated yearly benefits. If respondents reported that they had a defined contribution (DC) plan, the questions focused on the amount currently in the account and on contribution rates. When plan type was not reported, the questionnaire asked about plan characteristics of a defined benefit plan.

The Implications of Errors in Employer-Provided Pension Data and in Respondents' Reports

For those covered by defined benefit plans, the summary plan description (SPD) provided by the respondent's employer contained a full and accurate representation of the pension. To be sure, there were some possible sources of error. Most important, some plan descriptions were out of date, referring to provisions in place before 1992 but no longer relevant. Also, despite extensive checking, some plan features may have been miscoded. Moreover, if a firm had undergone complex merger activity, multiple plans may have covered different individuals with apparently similar backgrounds, creating the possibility of a mismatch.[11]

In the case of defined contribution plans, respondents' reports of the balance in their account may have been more accurate for estimating plan value. Because the HRS had to preserve respondent privacy when collecting pension plan descriptions, the amount in a particular respondent's DC account had to be estimated from the firm's contribution rate as reported in the plan description and the respondent's self-reported work history and contribution rate. In addition, the HRS collected plan descriptions at a particular moment in time, and both the contribution rates and the returns may have changed over time. Nevertheless, respondents' answers may have been subject to reporting error, perhaps, in some cases, to substantial error.

Many behavioral questions are raised by the existence of substantial reporting error, especially reporting error by a cohort that was so close to retirement.

11. Staff from the Health and Retirement Study coded the summary plan descriptions provided by employers. The coded plan descriptions were evaluated with software written for that purpose that generates pension values by applying the coded rules from the pension plan to respondent reports of earnings and tenure. The user specifies assumptions about interest rate, wage growth, and which respondent reports of retirement dates are to be used. Details about the procedures employed are available in Gustman, Mitchell, Samwick, and Steinmeier (2000).

Table 3-2. *Probit for Probability There Is a Matched Pension Provider Survey*

Independent variable	All pensions Partial effects	z	Current job pension Partial effects	z	Last job pension Partial effects	z	Previous job pension Partial effects	z
Female gender	0.010	0.75	0.010	0.54	0.073	2.08	−0.011	−0.49
Single marital status	−0.023	−1.40	−0.018	−0.87	−0.044	−1.03	−0.036	−1.30
Children								
None	0.014	0.54	0.004	0.11	0.015	0.24	0.051	1.29
Not known	−0.032	−0.66	−0.100	−1.62	−0.071	−0.61	0.093	1.18
Race								
Black	0.053	3.10	0.000	0.01	0.107	2.68	0.103	3.54
Hispanic	−0.020	−0.78	−0.041	−1.26	−0.123	−1.89	0.053	1.15
Education								
High school dropout	−0.076	−4.51	−0.034	−1.53	−0.114	−3.24	−0.102	−3.43
Some college	0.033	2.06	0.007	0.33	0.070	1.67	0.046	1.75
College graduate	0.082	3.89	0.087	3.04	0.133	2.28	0.042	1.30
Some graduate school	0.097	4.72	0.120	4.37	0.174	2.76	0.042	1.28
Home owner	0.050	2.35	0.018	0.63	0.133	2.46	0.055	1.61
Assets								
$0 to 10K	0.030	1.13	0.018	0.50	0.113	1.68	0.017	0.39
$10K to 25K	−0.009	−0.32	−0.021	−0.57	−0.022	−0.31	0.030	0.65
$25K to 100K	−0.001	−0.08	0.017	0.87	−0.031	−0.81	−0.004	−0.17
$250K to 1,000K	−0.005	−0.28	0.026	1.16	−0.049	−1.22	−0.010	−0.36
$1,000+K	−0.114	−3.18	−0.106	−2.08	−0.116	−1.34	−0.113	−2.07
Not known	−0.051	−0.65	0.060	0.60	0.157	0.66	−0.338	−1.94
Retirement horizon								
< 2 years	0.062	3.45	0.010	0.30	0.136	1.62	0.136	4.66
2 to 4 years	0.036	1.68	0.043	1.77	0.075	0.52	0.024	0.60
10+ years	−0.019	−1.12	−0.013	−0.65	0.142	1.42	−0.026	−0.86
Never	−0.037	−1.38	−0.040	−1.20	0.049	0.37	−0.011	−0.27
Not applicable	0.005	0.12			0.130	1.37	−0.009	−0.12
Not asked from proxy	−0.012	−0.39	−0.042	−1.14	0.129	1.19	0.042	0.82
Not known	−0.013	−0.49	0.005	0.15	−0.119	−0.95	0.010	0.24
Tenure								
0 to 1 years	0.013	0.37	−0.027	−0.69	0.029	0.35	−0.197	−1.20
2 to 4	0.024	0.99	−0.039	−1.36	0.083	1.27	0.089	1.50
10+	0.058	3.81	0.016	0.74	0.058	1.23	0.077	3.40
Not known	−0.138	−1.16	−0.333	−1.51	−0.124	−0.50	0.029	0.14
Firm size								
5 to 14 employees	−0.409	−9.05	−0.391	−8.33	−0.421	−4.08	n.a.	
15 to 24 employees	−0.254	−4.74	−0.283	−4.86	−0.165	−1.51	n.a.	
25 to 99 employees	−0.238	−8.86	−0.248	−8.63	−0.193	−3.43	n.a.	
500+ employees	0.014	0.88	0.012	0.68	0.025	0.75	n.a.	
Not known	−0.221	−3.98	−0.227	−3.74	−0.074	−0.55	n.a.	
Industry								
Nonmanufacturing	0.091	5.57	0.088	3.98	0.055	1.41	0.069	2.59
Not known	0.032	0.46	0.043	0.45	−0.090	−0.58	0.071	0.61
Occupation								
Management	−0.110	−7.09	−0.047	−2.27	−0.141	−3.67	−0.141	−5.47
White collar	−0.013	−0.75	−0.031	−1.38	−0.075	−1.83	0.040	1.46
Not known	−0.253	−2.08	−0.062	−0.33			−0.362	−2.09

Independent variable	All pensions Partial effects	z	Current job pension Partial effects	z	Last job pension Partial effects	z	Previous job pension Partial effects	z
Union member								
Yes	0.006	0.38	0.044	2.48	−0.007	−0.22	n.a.	
Not known	−0.120	−2.13	−0.169	−0.95	0.235	0.85	n.a.	
Annual earnings								
$0 to 15K	0.022	0.77	0.062	1.63	−0.109	−1.47	0.051	1.01
$15 to 30K	−0.007	−0.28	0.025	0.79	−0.105	−1.52	0.007	0.13
$30 to 50K	−0.001	−0.03	0.028	0.95	−0.125	−1.87	0.051	0.99
$100+K	−0.307	−5.35	−0.285	−4.59	−0.347	−1.56	−0.281	−1.97
Not known	−0.079	−1.04	−0.047	−0.45	0.224	1.01	−0.179	−1.35
Plan type								
DC plan	−0.185	−5.96	−0.190	−4.81	−0.074	−0.91	−0.165	−2.57
Combination plan	−0.044	−1.67	−0.055	−1.88	0.131	1.62	−0.072	−1.16
Not known	−0.226	−5.16	−0.189	−3.15	−0.070	−0.57	0.016	0.07
DB plan								
$0 to 2K	−0.089	−3.44	−0.073	−1.59	−0.151	−2.60	−0.037	−1.01
$2 to 5K	−0.065	−2.35	−0.087	−2.08	−0.074	−1.35	−0.009	−0.20
$10 to 25K	0.104	4.35	0.026	0.78	0.080	1.65	0.209	5.29
$25+K	0.143	4.54	0.152	3.41	−0.027	−0.42	0.203	3.84
Not known	0.005	0.19	−0.016	−0.50	−0.078	−1.07	−0.191	−0.85
DC plan								
$0–10K in account	0.047	1.70	0.085	2.69	−0.093	−1.10	0.032	0.52
$10–25K in account	0.070	2.29	0.073	2.18	0.141	1.39	−0.012	−0.16
$100–250K in account	0.088	1.88	0.084	1.70	−0.033	−0.23	0.150	1.09
$250+K in account	0.147	2.15	0.132	1.72	0.199	0.77	0.134	0.93
Not known	0.055	1.96	0.064	2.03	−0.079	−0.98	0.056	0.86
Summary statistics								
Log likelihood	−5,031.335		−2,539.922		−772.28188		−1,606.1744	
Pseudo R^2	0.1574		0.1164		0.1355		0.1221	
Number of observations	8,682		4,448		1,384		2,839	

Source: Authors' calculations based on data from the HRS.

Those questions are dealt with in later sections. But more mechanical questions related to the structuring of the Health and Retirement Study also are raised by reporting error. Answering one question incorrectly may lead the respondent to a subsequent series of questions that would be irrelevant to the respondent's current pension plan.

The questionnaire first asks about pension coverage, then plan type, then details about the particular plan. If a respondent initially misreports pension coverage, the error may be corrected as additional questions are asked. However, if respondents say that they are not covered by a pension when in fact they are, they skip the pension sequence entirely and no information is gleaned about the pension from a respondent or from an employer. The only hope that a person who incorrectly reports no pension will catch the mistake comes from a series of questions about whether the employer offered the plan to others, about eligibility in the future, and about plans for future participation. Those questions may jog a respondent's memory, leading the respondent to change the answer to the pension coverage question.

When respondents say that they do have a pension when they do not, they would have to answer a number of the subsequent detailed questions about the pension in a misleading fashion to be credited with a false pension value. Those questions not only ask about the plan, but also about vesting, personal dates of early and normal retirement, and expected benefits. Again, a person who proceeds down that path will have the opportunity to catch the error.

If respondents provide the wrong answer regarding plan type (a common occurrence), some of their answers to subsequent questions still will be useful, others will not. But the questions are not so inappropriate as to alert respondents that they made a mistake in reporting plan type. Consider, for example, what happens if a person has a defined benefit plan—which bases the future benefit on a formula that includes final salary and years of service—but reports having a defined contribution plan. The respondent is asked some then inappropriate questions requesting more details about what kind of DC plan it is— thrift or savings, 401(k), and so forth— how much is in the account, and whether the respondent can choose how to invest the money. The respondent can reasonably answer "Don't know" to those questions without being aware that he or she is in the wrong sequence. Other questions are relevant to a DB plan also, including those regarding years of coverage, employer and personal contribution, choice of a lump-sum payment or annuity, earliest retirement age, and expected age of retirement.

If the respondent has a defined contribution plan, which holds contributions in an account, but reports having a defined benefit plan, a different set of then irrelevant questions follow that may or may not result in "Don't know" answers. Those questions relate to earliest age for full or unreduced benefits (a question relevant to few DC plans), amount of benefits, benefit reduction rate for early retirement, and dependence of the benefit amount (as opposed to the employer contribution) on the respondent's Social Security benefits. Questions that also are relevant to DC plans, if sometimes confusingly worded for a person covered by a DC plan, ask the amount the respondent contributes to the plan; how many years the respondent has been included; when the respondent expects to start receiving benefits; how much the respondent expects benefits to be; what the respondent's pay will be at early retirement age; what the normal retirement age is; and whether the respondent can choose a lump-sum payment. But because the person has identified the plan as a defined benefit plan, the most important question about a defined contribution plan—"How much is in the account?"—will not be asked.[12]

The remainder of the chapter compares Social Security and pension data from the linked records and plan descriptions with the information gleaned from respondent surveys and then discusses the implications of the differences for retirement and wealth and ultimately for research and public policy. Because the HRS was unable to obtain linked data for each respondent, because coverage by Social Security and pension plans of different types varied among HRS respondents, and because data were missing, sample size varied with the question asked. Sample composition and sizes for the different tables in the chapter are reported in table 3-3.

Empirical Analysis

The discussion of the empirical data begins by comparing respondent reports of expected Social Security benefits with benefits respondents will be entitled to according to their matched earnings record from the Social Security Administration. It compares respondent and firm-provided reports of pensions, considering coverage, plan type, normal retirement age, early retirement age, benefit reduction rate, voluntary contributions, and plan values.

Social Security Comparisons

Table 3-4 relates respondents' reports of their expected Social Security benefits to the benefits they will receive based on their earnings histories. Expected Social Security benefits were not reported by many respondents and were subject to a number of other uncertainties.[13] Altogether, 43 percent of respondents provided an estimate of their benefits. Roughly half of those whose Social Security records said that they were entitled to benefits of from $7,500 to $15,000 provided an estimate of their benefits; only one-third of those whose benefits were below $7,500 or above $15,000 provided an estimate.

12. These questions are answered from memory. Respondents were not encouraged to collect financial documents in advance or to refer to them.

13. The benefit the respondent expected was reported in question N46 of the HRS. Problems with using the expected Social Security benefit amounts include the following: First, less than half of the respondents tried to guess the amount. Looking at the counts for question N46, 5,815 respondents reported that they expected to receive Social Security benefits, but only 2,563 guessed an amount. Second, since the question is in section N, the financial respondent answered the question for both spouses, meaning that a nonrandom sample of respondents answered the question for themselves. Third, there is a temporal mismatch: the amount constructed from the record pertains to earnings through 1991, but the self-reported amount presumably includes the effects of any future work. In addition, expected Social Security benefits are reported in dollars of some future year, and we do not have a good fix on the price levels in that year.

Table 3-3. *Sample Sizes by Table*

Table number and characteristics of sample	Number in sample
Table 3-1. Number of total HRS respondents in wave 1	12,652
Table 3-2. Respondents reporting coverage by a pension	8,682
Table 3-2. Respondents reporting coverage by a pension on current job	4,448
Table 3-2. Respondents reporting coverage by a pension on last job if no current job	1,384
Table 3-2. Respondents reporting coverage by a pension on previous job	2,839
Table 3-4. Respondents with matched Social Security records who were asked to project their Social Security benefits	3,443
Table 3-5. Respondents reporting whether they were covered by a pension in both 1992 and 1994	3,138
Table 3-6. Respondents reporting pension coverage on current job with a matched employer plan description	2,907
Tables 3-7, 3-8, 3-10, and 3-13. Respondents reporting DB coverage on current job, with plan description reporting DB coverage	1,881
Table 3-9. Respondents who intend to retire by 1995 reporting DB coverage on current job, with plan description reporting DB coverage	371
Table 3-11. Respondents with DC pension plans reporting voluntary contributions	873
Table 3-12. Respondents reporting DB plan and expected benefit amount, with matched pension plan description reporting DB plan	1,122
Table 3-14. Respondents reporting a DC pension plan on current job, with matched pension plan description reporting DC coverage	916
Table 3-12, 3-16. Respondents reporting a DC pension plan on current job and the amount in the account, with a matched pension plan description reporting DC coverage	641
Table 3-15. Respondents reporting a DC pension plan on their current job, with matched pension plan description reporting DC coverage with no voluntary contributions	188
Table 3-17. Respondents correctly reporting a DC pension plan with voluntary contributions on their current job and the amount in the account whose calculated balance was positive	467
Tables 3-18 and 3-19. Respondents with planned retirement dates	6,539

Source: Authors' calculations based on data from the HRS.

Reports of 383 of the 1,484 respondents who reported an expected Social Security benefit (26 percent) fall along the main diagonal. An additional 502 hazarded a guess that fell within one cell of the actual benefit they would receive. Altogether, 914 of those guessing (62 percent) picked an amount that fell within one cell of their actual benefit, but those who reported a benefit represented only 43 percent of those with a matched Social Security earnings record. So only about one-quarter (43 percent of 62 percent) of those with a matched record guessed an amount that was accurate enough to fall within one cell of the true value.

Table 3-4. *Distribution of Social Security Benefits Based on Respondent Reports and SSA Records*
Thousands of 1992 dollars

Respondent report	Social Security Administration records											Total
	0.0–1.5	1.5–3.0	3.0–4.5	4.5–6.0	6.0–7.5	7.5–9.0	9.0–10.5	10.5–12.0	12.0–13.5	13.5–15.0	15.0+	
0.0–1.5	5	4	5	3	2	2	3	3	3	1	0	31
1.5–3.0	9	18	16	9	6	1	3	4	0	1	0	67
3.0–4.5	13	9	25	20	14	9	7	3	2	2	4	108
4.5–6.0	14	14	35	56	49	29	30	12	6	1	1	247
6.0–7.5	3	2	9	21	39	38	24	8	12	1	1	158
7.5–9.0	0	2	9	19	27	49	54	21	6	9	5	201
9.0–10.5	0	2	4	16	23	26	109	56	26	17	2	281
10.5–12.0	1	1	2	7	8	32	61	60	34	21	7	234
12.0–13.5	0	0	0	0	1	1	5	6	2	6	0	21
13.5–15.0	0	0	0	0	1	7	11	15	10	18	7	69
15.0+	1	0	1	1	3	6	10	16	13	14	2	67
Total providing a value	46	52	106	152	173	200	317	204	114	91	29	1,484
Don't know	151	137	208	266	262	242	232	206	119	83	53	1,959
Total including *don't know*	197	189	314	418	435	442	549	410	233	174	82	3,443
Fraction providing a value	0.234	0.275	0.338	0.363	0.398	0.452	0.577	0.498	0.489	0.523	0.354	0.431

Source: Authors' calculations based on data from the HRS.

Table 3-5. *Pensions over Time in the Same Job*

	1994 observation	
1992 observation	*No pension*	*Pension*
No pension	1,075	271
Pension	73	3,138

Source: Authors' calculations based on data from the HRS.

Pension Coverage Comparisons

As noted, some individuals may not correctly report whether they are covered by a pension. One way to search for such errors is to compare responses in wave 1 and wave 2 for respondents who said that they still held the same job. If the respondents had said that they had pension coverage in wave 1, they were asked about changes in that pension in wave 2, whereupon they could deny that they had a pension. If the respondents said that they did not have a pension in wave 1, they were asked in wave 2 whether they had a pension. As seen from table 3-5, about 20 percent of those who said that they did not have a pension in 1992 reversed their stance in 1994, but relatively few who said that they did have a pension in 1992 denied it in 1994. Whether the asymmetry is due to the differences in the questions asked in 1994 or whether the respondents report being included in a pension only if they decide to participate is open to question. Because a denial is stronger than a simple fresh response, we would have expected that pattern to some degree, but perhaps not to that extent.

Pension Type Comparisons

Table 3-6 contains four panels describing the joint distribution of plan types reported by respondents and their firms on jobs held by respondents in 1992. The data are only for respondents with a matched employer-provided pension plan description.

Table 3-6A contains the frequencies of plan type reported by covered respondents and by their employers. If the firm reported two plans, one a DB plan and one a DC plan, the firm was classified as offering both, and there is one entry in the "Both" row. Table 3-6A shows 1,881 (777 + 380 + 409 + 315) cases in which both the individual and the firm reported having a DB pension plan, with or without a DC plan. When both the respondent and employer reported that the individual was covered by a DC plan, the comparable number was 916 (327 + 111 + 163 + 315).

The share of the total of 2,907 cases falling in each cell is reported in table 3-6B. The observations along the diagonal in table 3-6B represent only about half of the joint distribution of firm- and respondent-reported plan types, suggesting that respondents did a poor job of reporting the type of pension plan

Table 3-6. *Pension Plan Type as Reported by the Respondent and the Firm for Current Job Held in 1992, Including Only Respondents with a Matched Pension Plan*[a]

| Provider-reported | Self-reported | | | | |
	DB	DC	Both	Don't know	Total
A: Self-Reported versus Firm-Provided Plan Types					
DB	777	213	380	22	1,392
DC	160	327	111	10	608
Both	409	163	315	20	907
Total	1,346	703	806	52	2,907
B: Self-Reported versus Firm-Provided Plan Types (percent)					
DB	27	7	13	1	48
DC	6	11	4	0	21
Both	14	6	11	1	31
Total	46	24	28	2	100
C: Self-Reported Plan Type Conditional on Firm Report of Plan Type (percent of row total)					
DB	56	15	27	2	100
DC	26	54	18	2	100
Both	45	18	35	2	100
Total	46	24	28	2	100
D: Firm-Reported Plan Type Conditional on Respondent Report of Plan Type (percent of column total)					
DB	58	30	47	42	48
DC	12	47	14	19	21
Both	30	23	39	39	31
Total	100	100	100	100	100

Source: Authors' calculations based on data from HRS.

a. Numbers may not add due to rounding.

they were covered by. Some of the misreporting may be due to nonparticipation; even when the firm reported that it offered both plan types, some 14 percent of respondents reported that they were covered only by a DB plan. That may reflect respondents' failure to report coverage by a DC plan when they did not participate in the DC plan. Even allowing for misreporting, the discrepancy in plan types is substantial, occurring in more than one-third of the cases. Because the sequence of questions asked depends on the plan type reported by the respondent, this is a crucial problem in surveys that attempt to determine pension values solely from respondents' reports.

Comparisons of self-reported and firm-reported plan type based on means suggest more agreement between respondents' and firms' reports of plan type than is found in the individual data. At the micro (individual) level, respondents and firms agreed on plan type in 49 percent of the matched cases. In contrast, compare the fractions with only DB, only DC, or both types of plans computed separately. Table 3-6B shows that 46 percent of respondents reported that they were covered by DB plans only, 24 percent that they were covered by DC plans only, and 28 percent that they were covered by both types of plans. Similarly, 48 percent of firm-provided reports indicated that the plan was DB only, 21 percent that the plans were DC only, and 31 percent that the firm offered both types of plans. When the descriptive statistics from firm and individual reports are compared, they suggest a much higher level of agreement between reported and actual plan type than is found at the level of the individual observation.

One might ask whether respondents were doing much better than chance in identifying plan type. If they answered the plan type questions randomly, one-third would report DB plan only, one-third would report a DC plan only, and one-third would report both as a result of chance. However, in the case of firms for which we knew that the plan was DB only, respondents did much better than they would by chance. As seen in the first column of table 3-6C, which reports the distribution of respondent reports of plan type, conditional on the plan type reported by the firm, 56 percent of respondents whose employers reported that they were covered by a defined benefit plan only also reported that their plan was DB only. That is significantly different from the 33 percent that would be recorded if plan type were randomly chosen by the respondent. An additional 27 percent of those whose employers reported that their plan was DB only reported that their plan was both DB and DC. Thus 83 percent of respondents whose employers indicated that they were covered by a DB plan only reported coverage by a DB plan. Fifteen percent of those whose employers reported that they were covered by a DB plan only reported that they were covered by a DC plan only.

From the second row of table 3-6C, 54 percent of respondents whose employers indicated that they were covered by a DC plan only, slightly more than half, got the plan type right. If DB only, DC only, and both categories were equally likely, those covered by a DC plan did only little better than chance in reporting that they were covered by a DC plan. Altogether, among the cases in which the employer reported a DC plan only, the respondent reported a DC plan, held either exclusively or (mistakenly) together with a DB plan, in 72 percent of the cases. Of those whose employer reported their plan as DC only, 26 percent—representing 14 percent of the sample with a matched pension plan—reported their plan as DB only. Of those whose employer reported that they were covered by both a DB and a DC plan, slightly more than one-third, 35 percent, reported coverage by both a DB and a DC plan. Forty-five percent reported coverage by a DB plan only, and 18 percent reported coverage by a DC plan only.

The simplest way to determine plan type for those without a matched pension would be to use the respondent report, but respondent reports may be unreliable for two reasons. The first is selection bias; that is, the sample without a matched pension is different from the sample with a matched pension. Second, the respondent report will be wrong in roughly half the cases. Consider the distribution of firm reports conditional on respondent reports shown in table 3-6D. For those respondents who reported that they had a DB plan only, 58 percent of the firms indicated that they offered only a DB plan. Counting respondents whose firms reported DB and DC coverage, DB plan descriptions will be available for 88 percent of respondents reporting DB coverage, but DC plans will be missed for the additional 42 percent of those whose firms reported that they had only DC plans or both types of plans. Among respondents who reported that they had only a DC plan, 47 percent will have an exact match provided by an employer who reported offering a DC plan only. But we will have DB plan descriptions from employers for 53 percent of respondents who reported coverage by a DC plan only. Among respondents reporting coverage by both types of plans, descriptions of both plans were available from only 39 percent of their employers, suggesting that about 60 percent of respondents are misinformed.[14]

Pension Normal Retirement Age

Table 3-7 examines the joint distribution of *normal* retirement dates predicted from provider plan descriptions and from respondent data. The median normal retirement age is 62 in both the respondent-provided data and the firm-provided plan descriptions. When normal retirement ages are computed from firm-reported plan provisions and respondent expectations, the means are 61.3 and 60.7 respectively. Once again, however, the discrepancies are much wider in the individual data than they appear from the medians or means. For those with normal retirement dates of between 50 and 65 computed from employer-provided plan descriptions, 33 percent of the observations lie along the diagonal in table 3-7. Among the same group, 40 percent have an expected normal retirement age within one year of the date calculated from employer-provided data. The correlation between the normal retirement dates from provider and self-reports is 0.352.

Pension Early Retirement Age

Age of early retirement when both the respondent and the firm reported a defined benefit plan is reported in table 3-8 for respondents in jobs held in

14. More than 80 percent of those in table 6D who responded that they did not know their plan type had a DB plan, according to their employers. Of the same group, 58 percent had a DC plan. The convention in the HRS was to ask those who did not know their plan type questions that applied to a DB plan. As noted in the previous section, many of those questions also provided information that was relevant for a DC plan. However, respondents were not asked their plan balance.

Table 3-7. *Self-Reported Compared with Provider-Reported Dates of Normal Retirement for Plans Reported as Defined Benefit by Both the Respondent and the Firm*

Provider-reported	Self-reported																		Don't know	Total
	< 50	50	51	52	53	54	55	56	57	58	59	60	61	62	63	64	65	> 65		
< 50	1	1			2		6				1	3		5			1			22
50		7					6	1	1			5		7	2		7		5	41
51	1	1					1					1		1			2		1	8
52	1	1		1	1	1	2					2		2		1			1	13
53				4	1		5		1	2		1		2					1	16
54	1	1	1	1	1		3	1				1					1		1	13
55	4	2	1	1	2	2	81	2	3	1	3	5		15	2	2	13	2	7	146
56							9	3	1	1	1	1		3			3	2	1	26
57							13	4	7	2	1	2		2	1		4	1	1	37
58	1				1		8	2	5	4	1	1		5		1	6		2	38
59					1		11		3	4	3	4		3	1	1	4		3	39
60	1	2	1	1		4	63	6	9	5	15	69	6	67	7	2	50	9	26	343
61							4	1	1			13	2	5	5		5	2	2	35
62	5	2	1	3	2		19	4	5	7	8	13	10	95	10	4	68	16	21	293
63							2		1		1	1		5	1	1	3	1	3	19
64							3			2	1	1		1		1	2	1	2	17
65	5	2	2	4	3	3	74	3	12	15	21	41	7	188	6	7	287	17	42	739
> 65												1		3	1		4	6	2	17
Don't know	1									1		1		6		1	6	1	2	19
Total	20	19	8	17	14	12	310	27	49	44	56	166	25	415	31	21	466	58	123	1,881

Source: Authors' calculations based on data from the HRS.

Table 3-8. *Self-Reported Compared with Provider-Reported Dates of Early Retirement for Plans Reported as Defined Benefit by Both the Respondent and the Firm*

Provider-reported	Self-reported																			
	< 50	50	51	52	53	54	55	56	57	58	59	60	61	62	63	64	65	> 65	Don't know	Total
< 50	19	5	5	3	5	2	54	1	2	2		7		23	1	1	2		7	138
50	7	24	6	3	4	1	65	3	4	4	4	8	1	14	1	1	1		17	168
51	3	6		2	1		5	1	2	2		3	2	5			1		3	36
52	1	3	2	8		1	11		1		1			1					2	31
53	2			1	1	2	9	1		1	2	3	1	1			1		3	32
54					1	2	8	1			2	5	2	4			1		3	31
55	15	11	4	6	9	12	314	22	22	22	28	37	2	160	5	4	46	7	43	769
56	3	2	2	2			20	2	2	1	1	6	2	9	1		5	2	4	62
57	3		1				11	4	2	3	3	6	2	9	2		1		7	53
58		1				1	6	1	8	6	3	3	1	9			3		4	46
59	1		1	2	2	1	11	3	3	4	3	9	1	6			5		6	52
60	9	5	1	3	1	6	26	8	4	7	8	40	5	68	2	2	17	1	25	236
61		1					4	1	1	1		7	4	7	1		1		2	29
62	2	1			1		13	1	3	3	3	7	3	28	2	2	11	1	7	88
63							1			1		1		6	2			2	1	13
64	1						1		1		1	1		8	2	1	1		3	18
65						2	2	2					1	21	4	1	8		5	44
> 65							1			2		1		3	1		5	1	3	17
Don't know							1	1		2				8			2	1	3	18
Total	66	59	20	31	25	26	562	48	52	58	61	152	22	390	20	11	111	15	152	1,881

Source: Authors' calculations based on data from the HRS.

1992. When based on the firm-provided plan description, the early retirement date was about two years earlier than the date reported by the respondent. The median age of early retirement reported by the respondent is 57. When the formula reported by the firm is applied to respondents' self-reported work histories, the median age of early retirement across plans is 55. The average early retirement age is 57.6 when calculated from respondent reports and 55.4 when calculated from the firm-provided plan description. According to the firm-provided data, two-thirds of respondents would be able to retire by the time they reached age 55, but less than half of respondents thought that they could. Thus respondents to the HRS appear to be more pessimistic about their eligibility for early retirement than is warranted by the provisions of their plans. We will see that some respondents may simply be ignorant of the opportunity to retire early or perhaps consider it to be irrelevant.

It also is useful to examine the distribution of differences between the early retirement dates expected by respondents and the dates they would attain early retirement eligibility according to their firm reports. Among the observations with firm-reported retirement ages in the range from age 50 to 65, only 28 percent (434/1,569) lie along the diagonal in table 3-8, indicating that the respondent- and firm-based early retirement dates are identical. Moreover, no more than 39 percent of those respondents (609/1,569) reported an early retirement date within one year of the firm-based date. The simple correlation between the provider-reported and self-reported retirement dates is 0.353.

We also considered the relation between errors in respondent-reported early retirement and normal retirement ages. On one hand, among those estimating their early retirement age for whom a matched provider-based age was available, 36 percent (609/1,714) of respondent reports of age of eligibility for early retirement were within one cell of the age calculated from the plan description and 41 percent (714/1,741) of reports of normal retirement age were within one cell.[15] If there were no correlation, then the number of reports within one year of both the actual early and normal retirement ages would be 249 (= 1,714* 0.355*0.410). The actual number, 225, is close. On the other hand, the correlation between the two errors is 0.311, which indicates some tendency for the estimate of one age of eligibility to be high if the estimate of the other age of eligibility is high.

How accurately are pension rules described by respondents closest to retirement? Table 3-9 compares respondent-reported early retirement dates with the dates calculated from firm plan descriptions and respondent-reported records, this time confining the sample to the 371 respondents in the 1992 wave 1 HRS survey who indicated that they wanted to retire by 1995. For that sample, the

---

15. Except for cells at the limits of the range, being within one cell of the eligibility age for early or normal retirement implies being within one year of the eligibility age for early or normal retirement.

Table 3-9. *Self-Reported Compared with Provider-Reported Dates of Early Retirement for Plans Reported as Defined Benefit by Both the Respondent and the Firm, Including Only Observations of Wave 1 Respondents Who Plan to Retire by 1995*

Provider-reported	Self-reported																		Don't know	Total
	< 50	50	51	52	53	54	55	56	57	58	59	60	61	62	63	64	65	> 65		
< 50	6	2	1	2	1		17	1				3		5					2	40
50	1	5	1	2	2	1	17		2	1	1	2	1	1		1			2	36
51	1	3					2					1	2	2					1	10
52		1	1			1	4		1			1							2	10
53			1				3				1	1							1	8
54							4				1	3								8
55	4	3	1	2	3	1	57	2	5	1	5	10	1	27	2	1	4	1	5	135
56	1	1					9					2		1	1			1		15
57	2						2	1					2	1					1	10
58							2	1	3	1		1		1					1	10
59					1		1					1							1	4
60	1	1		2		3	8		1		2	10		10		1	3		3	45
61							2					3							1	7
62									1		1		1	6	1		1		1	13
63												1		2						4
64							1				1	1		1						3
65							1					1		4	1		1		3	10
> 65												1		1						2
Don't know																		1		1
Total	16	16	4	6	7	6	132	5	13	3	11	41	4	62	6	3	9	3	24	371

Source: Authors' calculations based on data from the HRS.

median age of early retirement eligibility expected by respondents is the same as that reported by their firms, age 55, as it was for the full sample. However, the mean early retirement date based on respondent data is later than the mean date based on firm data, 57.0 and 54.8 respectively. Moreover, when we confine the sample to those who intended to retire by 1995, we continue to observe the same wide discrepancy between the early retirement dates computed from provider formulas and from respondent data that characterized the full sample in table 3-8. Thus for the full sample, 28 percent of the observations lie along the diagonal, while for those who expect to retire by 1995, 26 percent of the observations lie along the diagonal. The correlation coefficient is 0.359 for the data in table 3-9, virtually identical to the correlation coefficient of 0.353 found for table 3-8.

Pension Benefit Reduction Rate

A key characteristic of the defined benefit plan is the benefit reduction rate, the rate at which benefits are reduced for each year a covered worker retires before the normal retirement date. If the reduction rate is relatively low, early retirement is subsidized so that benefit accrual peaks at early retirement age.

Respondents themselves had almost no idea how much the benefit reduction rate was. The benefit reduction rate was available from both the individual and the firm for relatively few of the 1,881 jobs for which both the respondent and the firm reported coverage by a defined benefit plan. As can be seen in table 3-10, we can compute early retirement reductions for only about 58 percent of firm observations; most of the remainder are cases in which the worker had joined the firm so recently that he or she was not eligible to retire before early retirement age. The median benefit reduction rate reported by firms was 4 to 5 percent. Of 1,881 respondents with a defined benefit plan in their 1992 job, 1,512, or 80 percent, either did not think they were eligible for early retirement or did not know the benefit reduction rate for their plan. Indeed, half of the respondents did not think that they could retire before the normal retirement age. Of the remaining 369 respondents, the median reported benefit reduction rate was 5 to 6 percent, well above the average from provider data. Altogether, only 234 observations on benefit reduction rates were reported by both the respondent and the firm. Of those, only 26 lie along the diagonal. For this limited number of observations, the correlation coefficient is 0.524.

Pension Voluntary Contributions

As table 3-11 shows, there is agreement in a majority of cases about whether a DC plan allows voluntary contributions.[16] In 392 of 873 observations, providers

---

16. The self-reported voluntary contribution variable is a dummy variable for whether the plan has a 401(k) component. Because of that, it would be incorrect to infer that a plan with voluntary contributions does not also have required contributions.

Table 3-10. *Self-Reported vs. Provider Annual Early Retirement Reduction Rates, for Plans Reported as Defined Benefit by Both the Respondent and the Firm*

Provider-reported	Self-reported										Don't know/ not available	Total
	0–1%	1–2%	2–3%	3–4%	4–5%	5–6%	6–7%	7–8%	8–10%	> 10%		
0–1%	1	9	4	6	1	4	4	4		5	102	136
1–2%	5	3	3	2	2	4	4	4	1	6	83	117
2–3%	1	3	2	5		8	2	6		4	97	128
3–4%	2	2	4	7	3	10	3	2	1	3	123	157
4–5%	3	7	4	5		5	4	4	2	9	191	237
5–6%	4	1	3	1	1	6	4	2		7	102	131
6–7%				1		1			1		47	50
7–8%		1		1							27	30
8–10%	2			2		2	1	1	1	2	31	41
> 10%		1		1		2	3			3	62	72
Not available	7	28	14	20	2	16	7	9	6	26	647	782
Total	25	55	34	51	9	58	32	27	13	65	1,512	1,881

Source: Authors' calculations based on data from the HRS.

Table 3-11. Self-Reported Compared with Provider-Reported Voluntary Contributions

	Self-reported		
Provider-reported	No	Yes	Total
No	121	57	178
Yes	303	392	695
Total	424	449	873

Source: Authors' calculations based on data from the HRS.

and respondents agreed that voluntary contributions were allowed; in another 121 cases, both respondents and firms agreed that they were not. Thus, 59 percent of the cases lie along the main diagonal. Respondents and firms disagreed about voluntary contributions in 41 percent of the cases. The most likely misreport occurs when the firm reported voluntary contributions and the respondent did not; those misreports account for 35 percent of the observations.

Defined Benefit Plan Values Derived from Self-Reports and Firm Reports

Table 3-12 and the next several tables pertain to cases in which the respondent and the firm agreed on the type of pension plan and in which the principal components of the plan (earnings, expected benefits, accumulations, and so forth) were available and not imputed. Table 3-12 examines results for pensions from the job held at the time of the survey. The results for the first two columns pertain to respondents who said that they had a defined benefit plan when the plan's value could be computed from the respondents' answers and when their firms indicated that the individuals were indeed covered by a defined benefit plan. Combination plans with a defined benefit component also are included in these numbers. Individuals who reported that they had both defined benefit and defined contribution parts to their pension and whose firms agreed that the pension had both components are in the columns in table 3-12 for both plan types. Individuals who said that they had only a defined benefit plan but whose firm indicated only a defined contribution plan, or vice versa, are not included in this table, although they are included in later tables.

Table 3-12 shows the dollar amounts associated with various points on the univariate distributions of defined benefit pension amounts, calculated by using both the respondents' answers and the formulas in the pension documents obtained from the firms.[17] For defined benefit plans, the survey asked when the

17. In table 3-6 there were 1,881 plans for which both the respondent and the firm reported plan type as defined benefit. Table 3-12 reports pension values for 1,122 defined benefit plans. The difference is accounted for by missing data, primarily because only two-thirds of respondents in table 6 reported expected pension amounts (or percentage of pay). For similar reasons, table 12

Table 3-12. *Distribution of Pension Values for Current Jobs Held at Time of the Survey*
1992 dollars

	Defined benefit plans		Defined contribution plans	
Percentile	Respondent-reported	Provider-reported	Respondent-reported	Provider-reported
95	385,497	523,704	200,000	347,265
90	311,775	387,276	128,322	223,951
75	211,733	227,373	45,000	100,030
50	116,327	112,380	15,000	29,067
25	48,084	49,767	4,500	6,093
10	16,805	24,223	1,200	750
5	9,231	11,252	400	0
Mean values	148,015	168,405	59,105	85,790
Number of observations	1,122		641	

Source: Authors' calculations based on data from the HRS. Columns 1 and 2 are present values as of the date of expected retirement, discounted to 1992. They are not prorated to allow comparisons between individual and firm reports of DB plan values, as the individual reports were as of the date of expected retirement. The DB and DC amounts in this table are not comparable since the DC amounts are account balances as of 1992, and do not include future contributions.

respondent expected to start collecting the pension and how much the pension would be. The pension value in column 1 of the table is the present value (discounted to 1992) of the expected benefits from the date of expected retirement forward, assuming that the pension remained the same in nominal terms.[18] If the respondent failed to provide either the age when the pension would start or the amount of the pension, the pension value was not imputed. The second estimate of the pension value, in column 2 of the table, came from applying the respondent's earnings and tenure at the expected collection date to the rules found in the pension documents.[19] Those rules give the value of the annual benefit, year by year. The value of the pension again is the discounted value of the

---

reports results for 641 observations, whereas there were 916 observations in table 6 for which both the respondent and the firm reported a defined contribution plan.

18. By assuming that benefits stay constant in nominal terms, we ignored the fact that some pensions had benefits that were reduced when the participant became eligible for Social Security. About 12 percent of participants in defined benefit plans indicated that their pensions were subject to such provisions. The pension calculator program incorporates the automatic cost of living adjustment in the few plans that offered one, but it does not include the ad hoc cost of living increases that historically have accounted for most cost of living adjustments.

19. The projected future earnings are calculated using Social Security Administration projections, increasing the 1992 earnings by 5 percent per year. See the 1994 Annual Report of the Board of Trustees of the Federal Old-Age and Survivors Insurance and Disability Insurance Trust Funds, p.11.

stream of benefits.[20] If the respondent's 1992 earnings were imputed, the value of the pension was not imputed, since the imputed earnings may not be a very accurate indication of actual earnings for individual respondents.

Table 3-12 indicates that for defined benefit plans, the mean present value of benefits based on the employers' reports ($168,405) exceeds the mean value based on the respondents' report ($148,015). At the median, there is remarkable agreement between the defined benefit amounts based on the respondents' answers and those based on calculations from the pension documents. In fact, looking at the values in the 25th and 75th percentiles, the middle part of the distribution is almost identical. Only in the two tails are the pension amounts calculated from the firm documents noticeably higher than the amounts calculated from the respondents' reports.

Although the distributions are similar for the defined benefit pension amounts calculated from the respondents' expectations and the pension documents, table 3-13 indicates that there are substantial differences between the two amounts at the individual level. To some degree, that result could have been expected after looking at tables 3-7, 3-8, and 3-9. If respondents are that inaccurate in reporting the early and normal retirement ages under their plans, it seems unlikely that they would be more accurate in reporting their pensions, which presumably involve more complex calculations than do the early and normal retirement ages. That the joint distribution is more or less symmetric around the main diagonal reflects the fact that the two individual distributions are similar, and the fact that the largest entries are down the main diagonal is indeed encouraging. However, only about 40 percent of the observations fall along the main diagonal. Moreover, the ranges of the categories in this table are very wide.

---

20. Some difference might arise because the respondent might have assumed future wage growth that differed from the 5 percent growth (the Social Security Administration's intermediate projection) we assumed when evaluating the firm pensions. Therefore, we adjusted the respondent's projected benefits to allow for implied differences in wage growth assumptions. To be more specific, the survey asked about expected benefits on the date the individual expected to receive them and about wages both in 1992 and at the normal retirement age. To project the wage to the benefit start date, we interpolated the wage between 1992 and the normal retirement age; we then calculated the implied ratio of the benefit to the wage that the respondent was expecting at the benefit start date. Finally, we multiplied that ratio by the wage that the respondent would have if the 1992 wage grew by 5 percent per year. That essentially adjusted the reported benefit for differences in wage growth assumptions. However, there were some observations for which this procedure did not work very well; they had in common the feature that the individual was almost at normal retirement age but expected to work several more years. For instance, the individual might be 59, have a normal retirement age at 60, expect to retire at 65, and report earnings of $40,000 at 59 and $80,000 next year. Continuing that rate of growth until 65 yields a value that clearly is nonsense. Therefore, we compared the computed wage at expected retirement to the wage that would be obtained by simply increasing the 1992 wage by the growth rate assumed in the Social Security projections. In the relatively few cases in which the former exceeded the latter by more than 50 percent, we took the expected pension benefits at the expected retirement age at face value and did not try to make any adjustments.

Table 3-13. *Self-Reported Compared with Provider-Reported Amounts Accumulated in Defined Benefit Plans*

Provider-reported	Self-reported											
	0	0–5K	5–10K	10–20K	20–50K	50–100K	100–200K	200–500K	500K–1M	>1M	Don't know	Total
0		6	3	3	5	4	6	5	1		157	190
0–5K			2	1	1			1			7	12
5–10K		3	2	2	1	1	3	2			6	20
10–20K		5	13	7	6	3	3	1			42	80
20–50K		3	19	31	65	38	25	9	1		133	324
50–100K		2	3	8	51	91	55	14			141	365
100–200K	1	1	5	3	21	63	131	62	1		113	401
200–500K				6	7	16	84	147	2		63	325
500K–1M		1			3		5	43	7	2	6	67
>1M								2	2			4
Don't know		1			5	2	2	1			82	93
Total	1	22	47	61	165	218	314	287	14	2	750	1,881

Source: Authors' calculations based on data from the HRS.

Even being one entry off the main diagonal is consistent with the respondent's estimate of pension value being half or twice the corresponding amount calculated from the pension documents.[21]

Defined Contribution Plan Values Derived from Self-Reports and Firm Reports

The last two columns of table 3-12 pertain to individuals who said that they had defined contribution plans and whose firms agreed. The value of the pension as reported by the respondent, in column 4 of the table, is simply the answer to the question regarding the current value of the accumulation. To derive the amount from the plan documents, the required contribution amounts were calculated for each year that the participant had been employed by the firm. If that amount was expressed as a percentage of annual earnings, the percentage was multiplied by the earnings in the year. Those contributions were accumulated forward using a 6.3 percent nominal interest rate from the long-run projections of the Social Security Administration, and the sum of the contributions constitute the implied present value.[22] If the plan allowed for voluntary contributions, the percentage of contributions in the survey year was extrapolated backward and the individual was assumed to have contributed the same percentage of previous years' earnings. The plans themselves indicated whether the contributions began after the respondent began to work for the firm. If an individual's 1992 earnings were imputed or if the respondent did not respond to the question about contributions and the plan allowed voluntary contributions, the present value was not imputed. The resulting calculated defined contribution pension values are in column 5 of the table.

The situation for defined contribution plans is considerably different from that for defined benefit plans. The mean pension value of $85,790 based on firm reports greatly exceeds the mean value of $59,105 based on respondent reports. While the upper tail for the distribution of DB plans exhibits provider values that exceed the values reported by respondents, the same is true for the top 90 percent of DC recipients; that is, for DC pensions the *entire* distribution of accumulations reported by respondents is much lower than the amounts calculated from the plan documents. In the middle and upper parts of the distribution, the respondents' accumulations are about half as much as the amounts from the plan documents at the corresponding percentiles.

Table 3-14 shows the joint distribution for the defined contribution plans. The scatter of the plans is about the same as for the defined benefit plans, with 28 percent of the observations falling on the main diagonal.[23]

---

21. The correlation coefficient, which is heavily influenced by the larger values, is 0.615.
22. The 1994 Annual Report of the Board of Trustees of the Federal Old-Age and Survivors Insurance and Disability Insurance Trust Funds, p. 11.
23. The correlation coefficient for the observations in table 14 is 0.302.

Table 3-14. *Self-Reported Compared with Provider-Reported Amounts Accumulated in Defined Contribution Plans*

Provider-reported	Self-reported											
	0	0–5K	5–10K	10–20K	20–50K	50–100K	100–200K	200–500K	500K–1M	> 1M	Don't know	Total
0	2	28	8	9	6	4	2				38	97
0–5K	1	58	14	7	5	1	1				25	112
5–10K		22	13	5	2	1		1			12	56
10–20K	1	18	22	23	13	3	2				26	108
20–50K	1	18	19	21	37	10	2	2	1		31	142
50–100K		9	12	13	27	18	15	3	1		35	132
100–200K		5	5	11	27	16	12	6	2	1	21	106
200–500K		1	1	3	14	15	14	14	2	3	12	79
500K–1M						1		4			1	6
> 1M						1	1	1	1			4
Don't know		4	1	4	11	3					51	74
Total	5	163	96	96	142	73	48	31	6	4	252	916

Source: Authors' calculations based on data from the HRS.

Imperfect Information: Implications and Comparisons of Discrepancies over Time

The many differences between the firm reports and respondent reports of plan features and values raise questions about studies that take the respondent reports as error free. Although undoubtedly errors arise in the matched employer-provided plan descriptions, the discrepancies in both the Social Security and the pension descriptions and extensive "don't know" responses from respondents suggest that many of the errors originate with the respondents. Yet until the availability of the Health and Retirement Study, almost all nationally valid studies of retirement were based on self-reported pension plan descriptions. We explain why errors in pension plan descriptions can have major consequences for studies of retirement and saving and further explore the reasons for these errors. We document the changes in discrepancies between respondent and firm reports of pensions in surveys taken in 1983 and 1992.

Implications of Misreporting the Early Retirement Date

The wide variation between respondent- and firm-reported dates of eligibility for early retirement is a particularly important problem for analysts wishing to model retirement behavior. For many pension plans, benefit rules give covered workers a substantial benefit increment for working up to the age of early retirement. By working the year they became eligible for early retirement, HRS respondents with a defined benefit plan typically increased the present value of the pension by an amount equal to two-thirds of a year of pay or more (Gustman and Steinmeier, 2000). That provides a powerful incentive for respondents to remain at the firm. If, in formal models of retirement behavior, individuals appear to leave their firms before reaching that date, retirement models will indicate that individuals are not sensitive to economic incentives when making their retirement decisions. As seen in the responses tabulated in table 3-8, many individuals reported an early retirement date that was later than the date that they actually would become eligible for early retirement benefits. As they approach retirement age, however, in many cases the firm may inform them of the correct date. But that new information may not be reflected in the individual responses to the survey, and the analyst will not have the correct answer unless the firm-provided plan description is available. Unless an adjustment is made when one uses respondent-reported data for those who seem to leave just before becoming eligible for early retirement benefits, this form of reporting error will cause the effects of pension incentives on retirement to be understated and the parameter estimates also will lead to an understatement of the influence of Social Security benefits on retirement.

Implications of Misreporting of Pension Values for Defined Contribution Plans

The systematic difference between the accumulated balances in defined contribution plans reported by participants and those calculated from pension documents could have several potential explanations. First, participants could be systematically underreporting plan accumulations. Second, the rate of return used by the pension program in calculating the pension reports may be higher than the actual return experienced by the participants. Third, for the plans with voluntary contributions, participants may have contributed substantially less in prior years than their current contribution rates would suggest.[24] Note that the first explanation implies that the respondents' answers are systematically incorrect, while the last two imply that the amounts calculated by the pension program are incorrect.

To distinguish among these competing explanations, table 3-15 presents the results for those DC plan participants whose plans do not allow for voluntary contributions. In table 3-15 almost twice as many observations lie above the main diagonal as below it, in contrast to the results in table 3-14, where the opposite is true. Although the number of observations is much lower than in table 3-14, table 3-15 suggests that among those participating in plans without voluntary contributions there is no systematic tendency for the pension values calculated from the plan documents to be more than the accumulations reported by the respondents.

The fact that values from firm reports are lower than those from self-reports for plans without voluntary contributions but are greater for those with voluntary contributions suggests that participants contributed less in prior years. The other two potential explanations should have equal force whether the firm permits voluntary contributions or not. That point is expanded on in table 3-16 and in figure 3-1. Table 3-16 groups defined contribution pensions according to the value calculated by the pension program on the basis of the pension documents. The top part of the table deals with defined contribution pensions without a provision for voluntary contributions. The first row indicates the median accumulation reported by respondents, and the second row indicates the median value calculated by the pension program. The solid line in figure 3-1 calculates the ratio between the two. The ratio is about 1.5 for small pensions (below $5,000 in present value) and about 1.0 for pensions between $5,000 and $50,000. Above $50,000, the number of pensions is low and the ratio fluctuates more widely, but there is no evidence of a systematic bias. All in all, over most of the range the reported accumulations exceed the values calculated from the plan

24. The pension calculation program assumes a constant contribution rate for participants of plans with voluntary contributions.

Table 3-15. *Self-Reported Compared with Provider-Reported Amounts Accumulated in Defined Contribution Plans for Plans without Voluntary Contributions*

Provider-reported	Self-reported											
	0	0–5K	5–10K	10–20K	20–50K	50–100K	100–200K	200–500K	500K–1M	> 1M	Don't know	Total
0	1	10	3	1	1	1					11	28
0–5K		15	4	2	2	1	1				9	34
5–10K		4	4	3	1	1					2	15
10–20K		4	2	6	5	2	2				6	27
20–50K		3	4		8	2	2	2	1		8	30
50–100K		2		2	2	3	6	2			10	27
100–200K		2	1		3	1	1	2	1	1	4	16
200–500K					1	1		1		2		5
500K–1M												
> 1M												
Don't know				1	1						4	6
Total	1	40	18	15	24	12	12	7	2	3	54	188

Source: Authors' calculations based on data from the HRS.

Figure 3-1. *Ratios of Median Reported Accumulations to Median Calculated Pension Values for DC Plans with and without Voluntary Contributions*

Ratios of median reported accumulations to median calculated pension values

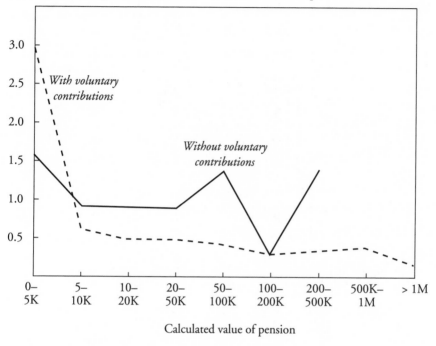

Calculated value of pension

Source: Authors' calculations based on data from the HRS.

descriptions, but for pensions without voluntary contributions the differences are small.

The lower part of table 3-16, which is reflected in the dotted line in figure 3-1, indicates the results for pension plans with voluntary contributions. For those plans, for values above the first category, there is evidence of a systematic difference between accumulations reported by respondents and those estimated by the pension program. There is some indication that the degree of underestimation is worse for larger pensions.

This brings us to the question of what the most accurate estimate of the true value of the pensions is. The inaccuracies in respondent reports are obvious. However, it also is likely that the values calculated from the pension documents are not completely accurate, in part because the calculations still employ uncertain information from the respondents, such as earnings, years of service, and the like. Another reason is that the program is forced to make assumptions about information not collected from respondents, such as the time path of

Table 3-16. *Reported Accumulations and Calculated Values of Defined Contribution Pensions*

	Calculated value of pension								
Type of pensions	0–5K	5–10K	10–20K	20–50K	50–100K	100–200K	200–500K	500K–1M	> 1M
Pensions without voluntary contributions									
Median accumulation reported by respondents	1,900	7,000	14,000	24,850	92,000	40,000	400,000	—	—
Median value calculated from pension documents	1,207	7,668	15,924	27,972	67,050	142,295	287,970	—	—
Number of observations	42	13	21	22	17	12	5	—	—
Pensions with voluntary contributions									
Median accumulation reported by respondents	3,375	4,200	7,000	15,000	30,000	37,500	94,500	206,000	201,750
Median value calculated from pension documents	1,146	6,945	15,090	30,389	69,141	131,885	292,690	550,933	1,151,112
Number of observations	104	31	61	89	80	73	62	5	4

Source: Authors' calculations based on data from the HRS.

earnings and of voluntary contributions. Is the value calculated from the pension documents or the value calculated from respondent information the more accurate estimate of the true value of the pension? Is it better to somehow combine the information in the two sets of numbers?

For defined benefit plans, the most accurate estimate is almost certainly the one calculated from the pension documents. It is subject to errors in earnings and years of service, but it captures details of the pension plan that most respondents may be unaware of unless they already have retired and asked the firm how their benefits were calculated. In cases where there are sharp differences, it seems much more likely that the respondent is making an uninformed guess than that the provider's calculations are substantially wrong. The fact that the two distributions are similar is not cause to think that one or the other of the estimates is systematically biased.

Many of the same arguments hold for defined contribution plans when contributions are completely specified by the plan. In addition to uncertainties regarding earnings and years of service, there is an additional uncertainty here regarding investment returns. This uncertainty would be an argument in favor of the accuracy of respondents' reports of their accumulations. However, in many cases the discrepancy between the accumulation reported by the respondent and the accumulation calculated from the firm-provided plan description is larger than can be plausibly attributed to uncertainties in investment returns. Since there do not appear to be systematic differences between the two sets of values that would indicate that one or the other was biased, perhaps the accumulation calculated from the plan description is the more accurate measure of the value of the plan.

For defined contribution plans *with voluntary contributions*, the situation is murkier. There is a tremendous amount of scatter in table 3-14, which means that in a substantial number of cases there is an order of magnitude of difference between the amounts calculated from the pension document and the amounts reported by respondents. Although increasing contribution rates could contribute to some of the scatter, it seems unlikely that they could explain a scatter of that magnitude. Moreover, the scatter appears to be approximately as wide as the scatter in table 3-13, for which the arguments that the scatter is due to respondents' inaccuracies are more persuasive. This leads to the conclusion that while the amounts calculated from the pension documents are too high, much of the scatter in table 3-14 is due to respondent misreporting.

It therefore would appear that the amounts calculated from the pension documents, while too high, probably are better guides to the value of accumulations than are the respondent reports. In this situation, taking the values calculated from the pension documents and applying a correction to reduce the apparent bias may yield the most accurate estimates. Table 3-17 presents the results of a median regression attempting to quantify that overestimation for the sample of

Table 3-17. *Median Regression for the Over-Prediction of Pension Values Calculated from Plan Documents, Defined Contribution Plans with Voluntary Contributions*[a]

Explanatory variables	Coefficient	t-statistic
Constant	3.1822	3.56
ln (pension value calculated from plan documents)	−0.4200	2.39
[ln (pension value calculated from plan documents)]^2	0.0152	1.77
Number of observations	467	

Source: Authors' calculations based on data from the HRS.

a. Dependent variable is the ratio of the accumulation reported by the respondent to the value of the pension calculated from plan documents.

plans with voluntary contributions. The dependent variable is the ratio of the value of the accumulations reported by respondents to the value calculated from the plan documents, which is the amount plotted on the vertical axis in figure 3-1. The independent variable is the log of the pension value calculated from the plan documents and its square. This value is plotted on the horizontal axis of figure 3-1. The estimated function has a value of approximately unity at a pension value of $1,000 and drops to 0.48 for a pension value of $25,000 and to 0.36 for a pension value of $100,000. To correct for the apparent bias in the values calculated from the pension documents when estimating the value of DC plans with voluntary contributions, it is appropriate to reduce those values according to the results implied by the regression in table 3-17.[25]

How Has Worker Knowledge Changed over Time?

The 1983 Survey of Consumer Finances (SCF) collected pension plan descriptions from respondents and detailed pension plan descriptions from firms. In many ways the SCF pension data and firm-provided plan descriptions were precursors to the HRS; therefore the SCF data afford the opportunity to explore changes in worker knowledge of key pension plan features documented in surveys taken a decade apart.

Comparing Plan Type. Comparing plan type reported in the HRS with plan type reported in the Survey of Consumer Finances, we report the percentages from Gustman and Steinmeier (1989),[26] which provided results analogous to those in table 3-6C using the 1983 SCF. In the SCF, 63 percent of respondents whose firms reported a DB plan only also reported coverage by a DB plan only, compared with 56 percent from the HRS in table 3-6C. In the SCF, of respondents whose

25. Regressions with additional variables were tried, but in those regressions only a small number of variables were significant and they suffered from the problem that they yielded negative predicted values for some of the pensions.

26. Gustman and Steinmeier (1989, table 6, p. 72).

employers reported a DC plan only, 37 percent reported that they had a DC plan only. That compares with 54 percent in table 3-6C. Although the HRS respondents did a bit worse in identifying DB plans only, they did much better identifying DC plans only than respondents in the SCF sample did, perhaps due to the increasing popularity of DC plans between 1983 and 1992.

Comparing Retirement Age. In contrast to our findings in the HRS data, SCF respondents ten years earlier did not overstate the age of eligibility for early retirement benefits. In the data from the 1983 SCF, we found that the median early dates expected by respondents and those computed from plan provisions and earnings histories were both age 55.[27] Moreover, the SCF included workers from age 40 on, so that those sampled were further from retiring than the HRS sample. Yet the median expectations of age of eligibility for early retirement benefits in the SCF sample were more accurate than in the HRS sample.

Another piece of evidence suggests that, in relation to the rules in place, people are less optimistic today about when they will be able to retire than they were in the past. In previous work using SCF data, we found that in the self-reported data mean early retirement dates were lower than the median dates by about three years.[28] Because the medians of self-reported and firm-reported data were equal, that suggests that a few people may have been highly optimistic about when they would be eligible for early retirement benefits. In the HRS, evidence of such optimism has disappeared: mean and median dates of expected eligibility for early retirement benefits are the same. That result corresponds with findings from direct comparisons of early retirement dates based on respondent- and firm-provided data. People were more pessimistic about the age of eligibility for early retirement in the HRS than they were in the past.

Comparing Plan Values. In our earlier analysis of data for the Survey of Consumer Finances, we found that mean pension values based on respondent reports were higher than mean pension values based on the plan formula.[29] The findings in the HRS are the opposite. We also found that, unlike in our earlier findings, people on average were more pessimistic about their ages of eligibility than was warranted by their pension plan. Perhaps the finding that people were less optimistic about their pensions than they were ten years ago reflects a shift of attitudes in response to changing firm policies over the intervening decade.

Relation of Misreports to Retirement Planning and Wealth Accumulation

What difference does misinformation about pensions and Social Security make for actual behavior? In tables 3-18 and 3-19 we examine the relationship of

27. Gustman and Steinmeier (1989, table 5, p. 70).
28. Gustman and Steinmeier (1989, table 5, p. 70).
29. Gustman and Steinmeier (1989, table 5, p. 70).

Table 3-18. *Effect of Pension and Social Security Knowledge on Accuracy of Retirement Expectations*[a]

	Planned retirement						
	Before last survey		After last survey		Don't know		Number of observa-
Respondents arrayed	Actual retirement (relative to last survey)						
by their knowledge	Before	After	Before	After	Before	After	vations
All respondents	18.0%	10.7%	13.8%	46.0%	3.9%	7.6%	6,539
Social Security benefits (expected/actual)							
Less than 75%	12.5	7.5	12.9	61.3	0.7	5.1	296
75–125%	24.8	13.5	12.5	42.4	2.6	4.1	847
More than 125%	20.6	14.9	13.2	41.5	3.0	6.8	341
Don't know	14.3	9.7	14.4	47.8	5.0	8.7	1,959
Knowledge of DB pension							
Correct	25.5	13.5	10.4	44.5	1.3	4.7	1,754
Incorrect or *don't know*	20.8	12.3	13.6	47.8	1.9	3.6	536
Pension benefits (expected/actual)							
Less than 75%	26.6	13.2	11.8	44.2	0.9	3.3	567
75–125%	29.4	17.3	8.8	40.5	0.5	3.4	341
More than 125%	26.1	17.7	9.5	43.8	1.4	1.5	383
Don't know	20.6	10.0	12.6	48.2	2.2	6.4	971

Source: Authors' calculations based on data from the HRS.
a. Social Security and pension observations are restricted to those with matched social security or employer-provided records.

reporting errors to retirement outcomes and wealth accumulation. Here we address three questions: How does knowledge of Social Security and pensions affect retirement plans? Realization of retirement plans? Wealth accumulation? These analyses are descriptive.[30]

We looked for but did not find simple patterns in the data. For example, we might have found that those who understated their Social Security and pension benefits had a nice surprise in store. If respondents always thought their benefits were less valuable than in fact they were, one might expect them to plan on a later retirement, to be disproportionately represented among those planning for a later retirement, to actually retire earlier than planned, and to have accumulated greater wealth to compensate for their expected lower benefits. The patterns we found are more complex and require a more complex model to explain.

30. For careful analyses of the economic factors determining the differences between retirement expectations and realizations, see Bernheim (1989) and Disney and Tanner (1999).

Retirement Plans

From line 1 in table 3-18, we see that in the first survey in which they were asked, 29 percent (18 + 10.7) of all respondents expected to retire before the last survey in which they were interviewed. Dividing respondents into groups according to whether their expectations of Social Security benefits were accurate, in the second row of the table, we find that those whose expected benefits were less than 75 percent of their actual benefits were more likely to plan a late retirement than respondents with accurate benefit expectations or respondents who overestimated their Social Security benefits. That finding is consistent with our naive expectations. More than half (57 percent) of the sample responded that they did not know their expected Social Security benefits; of those, 24 percent, slightly less than for the sample as a whole, planned to retire before the last survey.

Those who correctly stated that they had a DB plan were more likely to plan to retire before the last survey (39.0 percent versus 33.1 percent) and less likely to plan to retire after the last survey (54.9 percent versus 61.4 percent) than were those with incorrect knowledge or those who reported that they did not know their plan type. There also was a difference in plans for retirement between those who indicated their expected pension benefits and those who did not know what their benefits would be. Sixty-one percent of those who did not know their benefits predicted that they would retire after the last survey. Only 49 percent of those with accurate benefit expectations expected to retire after the last survey, and those who overstated or understated their pensions expected to retire after the final survey in 56 percent and 53 percent of the cases respectively—a result that was the opposite of our naive expectation.

Realization of Retirement Plans

Typically, the respondent was interviewed first in wave 1, and retirement status was determined in wave 4 or in an earlier wave if the respondent dropped from the survey. The figures in columns 1 and 4 pertain to those who retired according to their plans. A majority of those planning to retire early in fact did so. Sixty-three percent [18.0/(18.0 + 10.7)] of those planning to retire before the last wave in which they were interviewed succeeded in their plans. Of the 59.8 percent of the respondents planning to retire after the last survey, 77 percent [46.0/(13.8 + 46.0)] did retire after the last survey. Thus almost two-thirds (18 + 46) of all respondents had a planned retirement date and realized their plan.

Respondents whose expected Social Security benefits were less than 75 percent of their actual benefits were more likely to meet their planned retirement date than respondents in general—with three-fourths of those who underestimated their benefits retiring according to plan. Sixty-one percent of those whose benefit expectation was too low both planned to and succeeded in retiring after the last survey, and 12.5 percent of the group both planned to and succeeded in retiring earlier. Altogether, among those who understated their Social Security benefits, 83 percent of those planning to retire after the last survey actually retired after the last survey. Our naive expectation was the opposite: that those who were pleasantly surprised to learn that their benefits were more valuable than they thought would retire earlier due to the windfall. Perhaps they were not well informed even by the last wave of the survey, or perhaps those who understated their benefits had more wealth or were younger. That is, those closest to early retirement age may have had the most accurate expectations. We will explore these findings in more detail in subsequent work.

Those who had an accurate expectation of their Social Security benefits were slightly more likely to meet their plans for retirement than were respondents as a whole, but they were less likely to meet their retirement plans than were those who underestimated their benefits.

Those who overestimated their Social Security benefits were least likely to meet their plans for retirement, with 62 percent retiring before or after the last survey, as they had forecast. One-fifth of those who overestimated their benefits planned to retire before the last survey and carried out their plans, despite having overstated their expected benefits by 25 percent or more. Contrary to naive expectations, the number of those who planned to retire after the last survey and in fact did so was lower among respondents who overstated the value of their pensions than among those who understated it.

More than half (57 percent) of the sample responded that they did not know their expected Social Security benefits. Nevertheless, 62 percent of that group accurately forecast their retirement behavior. They were slightly less likely than the sample as a whole to plan to retire before the last survey.

We considered next the relation between the accuracy of retirement expectations and the accuracy of pension expectations. Those who correctly identified their pension plan type were only slightly more likely to retire as planned than those who did not. The most identifiable difference between those groups is that one-fifth of those who did not know what type of pension plan they had planned to retire before the last survey and succeeded in doing so, whereas one-quarter of those who correctly identified their plan type both planned to and succeeded in retiring before the last wave of the survey.

Last, the relationship between expected pension amount and accuracy of retirement expectations is in accordance with simple expectations. A larger share of those who understated their pensions and planned on a later retirement did in fact retire earlier than of those who overestimated their pensions. The effect, however, is small. Moreover, conditional on planning to retire after the last survey, the share retiring before the last survey was the same for those who overestimated the value of their pensions as it was for those who estimated the value of their pensions correctly.

Table 3-19. *Median Ratios of Wealth to Lifetime Earnings, Excluding Pension and Social Security Wealth*

Respondents arrayed by their knowledge	Planned retirement					Number of obser- vations
	Before last survey	After last survey	Never	Don't know	All	
All respondents	0.19	0.15	0.18	0.19	0.17	6,539
Social Security benefits (expected/actual)						
Less than 75%	0.17	0.13	0.14	0.23	0.14	296
75–125%	0.15	0.13	0.17	0.16	0.15	847
More than 125%	0.17	0.17	0.26	0.21	0.17	341
Don't know	0.15	0.13	0.16	0.13	0.14	1,959
Knowledge of DB pension						
Correct	0.17	0.14	0.13	0.15	0.15	1,754
Incorrect or *don't know*	0.18	0.16	0.14	0.06	0.16	536
Pension benefits (expected/actual)						
Less than 75%	0.19	0.18	0.09	0.14	0.15	567
75–125%	0.13	0.14	0.13	0.09	0.14	341
More than 125%	0.18	0.14	0.40	0.14	0.17	383
Don't know	0.17	0.15	0.13	0.13	0.16	971

Source: Authors' calculations based on data from the HRS.

Wealth–Lifetime Earnings Ratios

Table 3-19 addresses the relationship between planned retirement dates, errors in knowledge about Social Security or pension benefits, and accumulated wealth as a share of lifetime earnings. As seen in the first row of the table, there is some relation between planned retirement and wealth–lifetime earnings ratios. Those who planned to retire before the last survey had higher wealth–lifetime earnings ratios than those who planned to retire after the last survey. However, causality is unknown. Moreover, those who planned to never retire had higher wealth–lifetime earnings ratios than those who planned to retire after the last survey. Those who did not know when they would retire also had high wealth–lifetime earnings ratios.

There also is some relationship between knowledge of benefits and wealth–lifetime earnings ratios. From column 5 in table 3-19, those who overstated their Social Security benefits had higher wealth–lifetime earnings ratios (.17) than those with accurate expectations, those who understated their benefits, or those who did not know what benefits to expect, with wealth–lifetime earnings ratios of .14 to .15 for those in each group. There are some differences in the patterns of wealth–lifetime earnings ratios with planned retirement and errors in Social Security values, but the reasons for those patterns are not obvious.

Knowledge of plan type was related to wealth–lifetime earnings ratios. Those who did not know their plan type or when they planned to retire had very low wealth–lifetime earnings ratios (.06). Those who did know their plan type and when they expected to retire had slightly lower wealth–lifetime earnings ratios than those who did not know their plan type.

The ratio of expected to actual pension amount and planned retirement also interacted in influencing wealth–lifetime earnings ratios. Among those giving specific planned retirement dates, those with accurate expectations of pension benefits had lower wealth-earnings ratios than those who overestimated or underestimated their pension benefits. Those who planned never to retire and who were overly optimistic about their pension benefits had wealth–lifetime earnings ratios that were more than twice as large as those in any other category.

Much more could be done to analyze the relation between knowledge about pension and Social Security benefits and retirement and wealth outcomes. For example, we would like to consider not only the ratio of wealth to lifetime earnings, but also the level of wealth. One may have poor knowledge of Social Security benefits for a number of reasons, one of them being that with more wealth, those benefits are less important. On the other hand, a person with low lifetime earnings may have low absolute wealth, but a reasonable wealth–lifetime earnings ratio, as long as Social Security benefits provide a high replacement rate. For analogous reasons, it would be useful to standardize for age when analyzing how knowledge of Social Security or pension benefits affects retirement plans and whether those plans are realized. An obvious next step is to embed indicators of knowledge of Social Security and pension benefits into standard models of planning and saving for retirement to determine how that knowledge relates to retirement and wealth outcomes. It also would be interesting to see whether variables measuring the accuracy of knowledge continue to behave differently from variables measuring the effects of planning activity on wealth accumulation.[31]

In sum, we have conducted a very preliminary analysis of the relation between knowledge of Social Security and pension benefits on one hand and retirement expectations, realization of those expectations, and wealth accumulation on the other. It appears that lack of knowledge about Social Security and pension benefits and error in determining plan type have some systematic but modest effects on plans for retirement, on whether those plans are met, and on saving outcomes. However, those relations are complex, and no obvious overriding themes emerge. For example, we did not find that those who understated the value of their pension or Social Security benefits planned disproportionately

---

31. See Lusardi (1999) for an example of a study that measures the effect of retirement planning on wealth accumulation.

to retire later but ended up retiring earlier than they planned when they realized the windfall. Nor did they have consistently higher wealth–earnings ratios.

Conclusions and Questions for Further Research

Our analysis shows that respondent reports of Social Security and pension values and characteristics differed extensively from comparable information obtained from linked data provided by the Social Security Administration or employers. Respondent reports misstated the wealth that older individuals would have in retirement and the budget sets that eventually govern their decisions to retire. Although some of the errors are random, respondents were on the whole somewhat pessimistic. Most important, the misreports were extensive at the level of the individual.

These findings have implications for both researchers and policymakers who wish to determine whether individuals' preparations for retirement are adequate. They also have implications for those who wish to understand retirement and saving behavior and for policymakers who would like to improve the information available to those approaching retirement in order to allow them to better plan their retirement.

Implications for Researchers

When respondent reports differ from employer-provided plan descriptions, the researcher must address a number of issues. For some purposes, it may be possible to impute pension and Social Security benefit wealth for those with missing records. We discuss the methodology for such imputations in the appendix to this chapter. We report equations that relate pension and Social Security values estimated by using linked employer-provided pension data or Social Security records to the values obtained from respondent reports and to other independent variables. In addition, we will produce files for distribution to HRS users that contain the predicted values of those variables for all observations, including the observations for which linked data are available. That will make information from the linked data available to a wider group of researchers, including those who do not apply for or obtain permission to use the linked data directly.[32]

32. A procedure has been established at HRS, in coordination with the National Institute on Aging and the Social Security Administration, to protect respondent confidentiality when linked data are made available. A researcher must apply for access to restricted data, and the application requires a research plan, a data protection plan, a demonstration of grant support from a federal agency, and a promise not to link the restricted data to any but specified respondent files. The basic respondent survey, without linked data, is available on an unrestricted basis.

Implications for Behavioral Analyses of Retirement and Saving Decisions

Our findings have implications for the specification of models of retirement and saving behavior. Many people are approaching retirement age with a misunderstanding of both the wealth they will have in retirement and the criteria for eligibility for benefits. As they approach retirement age they will learn what their Social Security and pension benefits are worth and when they will be able to claim them, if only when they are on the doorstep of retirement. Behavioral models should be modified to determine the effects of learning and reoptimization as correct information is absorbed. Our findings suggest that models of retirement and saving that assume perfect foresight and planning are likely to misestimate the key parameters that supposedly drive retirement and saving behavior. The result will be a misunderstanding of how the provision of pension and Social Security programs affects retirement and saving outcomes.

It will take a sophisticated model to isolate the effects of misinformation. Those who undersave because they initially overestimated the value of their Social Security and pension benefits may not be in a position to easily correct their errors. They may have to work longer, consume less once they retire, or both. They will have a great deal of difficulty in substantially increasing their savings if they are close to retirement. Those who find that they have underestimated the value of their benefits are in a position to correct their error without significant sacrifice, beyond the reduction in consumption they experienced in order to save more before their retirement. Moreover, those who expect the date of early retirement to be earlier than it actually is will have a surplus of funds left to support their retirement by the time they reach the true age of eligibility under their retirement program—that is, if they do not also overstate the value of their pension. Those who do not expect to be eligible for benefits until well after they in fact are eligible would in theory be in a position to retire at the plan's retirement age, unless they have undersaved, expecting a later retirement date. Thus not only do asymmetries exist in terms of how respondents adjust to errors on the high and low sides, but outcomes depend on how errors in expectations about the timing of eligibility for retirement correlate with errors in expectations about the levels of those benefits.

There also are more fundamental questions facing behavioral analysts: What is the source of the errors we have observed? What are the implications of the particular reasons for the errors for saving and retirement behavior? Does misinformation affect the perceived budget set or the perceived risk associated with the budget set, or is poor information simply the result of a high time preference rate that makes the individual less forward looking?

One might argue that the errors in reported retirement dates and plan values are relatively modest at the aggregate level and that they are random at the level of the individual, so they can be treated using standard approaches to measurement error. Even if one ignores the implications of reporting error for behavioral modeling, it would be a mistake to ignore the implications for econometric estimation. In nonlinear retirement models, we have noted that the consequences for parameter estimates of those errors may be severe. If the errors are ignored, so that some seemingly retire before the measured date of eligibility for early retirement benefits, the investigator will conclude, mistakenly, that retirement is not responsive to economic rewards.

If information is imperfect because respondents are heavily discounting the future, that raises questions about the efficacy of the life-cycle model, in which the rewards from work, to be realized in future periods, and consideration of future consumption play such central roles in shaping saving and labor market outcomes.

Implications for Policy Analysts and Policymakers

Our findings suggest that much more work has to be done before we can evaluate current programs and policies designed to increase information for those planning for retirement. We need to know how the major errors in respondent-reported plan features, eligibility dates for benefits, and benefit amounts enter into the retirement model. Different behavioral models of the role of misinformation imply very different reactions to various policies. If the rate of time preference is very high for those who are misinformed and they are not paying attention because retirement is a few years away, then provision of general information programs may not be very effective. On the other hand, if there is genuine confusion about how much saving is required to ensure an adequate replacement rate in retirement, information programs may be much more effective.

Perhaps a continuous stream of general information on the need for retirement planning will make those who would not otherwise plan more sensitive to the need for earlier and systematic retirement planning. Currently there is little information on the effectiveness of recent government efforts to educate workers about their pensions and Social Security. Employer financial education seems to be helpful. But we do not have enough systematic information about the causes of misinformation to have confidence in what types of educational programs might be most useful.

Once we have addressed fundamental questions about how imperfect information affects behavior, we can turn to more fundamental questions about the effectiveness of current policies.

Appendix 3A

In this appendix, we explore the degree to which it is possible to predict pension and Social Security values given the information available in respondent interviews. We use employer-provided pension records and Social Security

Administration (SSA) data to calculate relatively good estimates of the true benefit values and then attempt to explain those values by using information from respondent interviews, including respondent perceptions of pension amounts and earnings histories. In general, our results suggest that it is possible to predict pension and Social Security values fairly well on the basis of the relationship between respondent-reported outcomes and SSA or firm-provided data. The equations we estimate can be used to predict benefit values for those in the HRS without an attached pension or Social Security record. The accompanying files not only can be used to impute pension and Social Security wealth levels for those without a matched record, but also can be used by researchers who require that information but do not wish to or cannot obtain permission from the HRS to use restricted data. Basic descriptive data, indicating how matching rates vary with respondent characteristics, are reported in table 3A-1. The first two columns report matching rates for Social Security records; the last two columns report matching rates for pension records. Table 3A-2 reports matching rates for employer-provided pension plan descriptions by type of pension and pension value reported by the respondent. In many cases, the matching rates vary systematically with respondent characteristics or reported plan type or value.

Projecting Pensions from Linked Data for Those without a Linked Employer Record

In this subsection we focus on predicting pension values given the information available in the respondent survey. One possible strategy would be to project defined benefit and defined contribution plans separately, using the respondent's estimate of the values of those plans plus other information gathered in the respondent interview. However, that approach is complicated by the fact that a substantial number of respondents were misinformed about the type of plan they had (table 3A-6). Therefore we use an alternative strategy, projecting the total value of the pension including both defined benefit and defined contribution components.

Table 3A-3 tabulates total pension values calculated from plan documents and those calculated only from respondents' information. The table includes only those respondents for whom the HRS obtained pension plan documents. To allow for the overstatement of respondent contributions because the contribution rate observed in 1992 was assumed to hold in all previous years, the amounts calculated from pension documents for defined contribution plans with voluntary contributions were reduced according to the coefficients in table 3-17. Another issue with both values calculated from plan documents and those calculated from respondent interviews is that defined contribution amounts are accumulations as of the survey date but defined benefit amounts are amounts expected at retirement. To put the two types of pensions on comparable footing, for defined benefit plans we multiply the amount expected at retirement by the fraction of years until retirement that already have been served before we add the two types of pensions to get the total pension value.

Note that unlike previous tables, table 3A-3 includes cases in which the respondent said that he or she had one type of pension plan but the plan documents indicated another. The table looks reasonably symmetric around the main diagonal, as would be expected since we eliminated systematic discrepancies between calculated values and reported accumulations for the defined contribution plans. However, there is a wide scatter, indicating that a large difference remains between the amounts calculated from the plan documents and those reported by the respondents.

Table 3A-4 reports on regressions to explain the values calculated from plan descriptions, which were taken to be approximately correct.[33] In total there are six regressions. The first four regressions use observations in which pension value estimates are available from both the provider and the respondent. The first and third of these regressions use only the value of the plan calculated from the survey questions as an explanatory variable. The second and fourth include additional explanatory variables. The second and fourth regressions use the preferred specification, and the results give some idea of how much adding explanatory variables improves the fit of the regression. The fifth and sixth regressions explain the value of pensions obtained from provider plan descriptions, but they pertain to observations for which pension amounts are not available in the respondent survey. Since the final two regressions use only observations for which the pension value cannot be calculated from the survey questions, it perforce does not include that value. In table 3-13 we saw that on average, values calculated from the plan documents were lower for respondents who did not report amounts for their pensions than for respondents who did. Hence, it would not be advisable to take a mechanical approach, applying a regression for those who did report pension values to impute pensions for those who did not without any further adjustment.

Equations 1 and 3 and equations 2 and 4 of table 3A-4 are related regressions. Because the distributions of pension values appear to be roughly loglinear, if regressions were run on the linear values computed from the plan documents and the linear values calculated from the survey questions, the regressions would give enormous weight to very high-value pensions. To avoid that, we take the log of the pension values. However, doing so creates another problem because some of the pensions, especially those calculated from plan documents, have

---

33. Note that the provider plan values for defined contribution plans with voluntary contributions in table 3A-4 are adjusted according to the coefficients in table 3-17. The regressions include variables for missing values for plan characteristics. The value for the missing variable indicator is set to 1 if the characteristic is relevant to the type of plan and the characteristic is missing, and the value of the missing variable is set to zero so that the value is picked up in the coefficient of the variable indicating that the value is missing.

Table 3A-1. *Matching Rates of Social Security Records and Pension Plan Descriptions with Respondent Records*[a]

Characteristics of respondents and their jobs	Matching rates for Social Security records (%)	Number of observations	Matching rates for pension plan descriptions (%)	Number of observations
Gender				
Men	71.1	5,867	55.5	4,972
Women	72.2	6,785	54.6	3,710
Combined	71.6	12,652	55.2	8,682
Age				
<= 50	73.7	1,595	60.7	971
51–61	71.3	9,742	54.7	6,951
>= 62	72.4	1,315	57.7	1,008
Marital status				
Married	72.4	9,896	56	6,997
Single	70.1	2,756	53.4	1,685
Parents				
Yes	72.2	11,743	55	8,003
No	68.3	754	57.9	547
Race				
White	71.8	9,415	54.7	6,870
Black	71.7	2,064	62.7	1,360
Hispanic	69	1,173	48.4	452
Education				
< High school	73.4	3,696	47.6	1,675
High school graduate	74.1	4,424	54.5	3,064
Some college	69.4	2,320	55.7	1,812
College graduate	68.6	1,040	56.3	951
Graduate school	66.7	1,172	62.4	1,180
Residence status				
Homeowner	71.1	10,205	56.2	7,517
Renter	73.3	2,447	49.6	1,165
Assets				
< 10K	75.8	1,949	49.9	781
10–25K	77.5	812	51.8	447
25–100K	74.6	3,565	56	2,571
100–250K	70.8	3,304	57.7	2,744
250K–1M	65.2	2,393	57.5	1,809
1M+	63.9	534	33.1	280
Retirement horizon				
< 2 years	73.5	2,939	62.7	2,146
2 to 4 years	74.2	1,040	61.6	972
4 to 9 years	74.5	2,071	55.6	1,794
10+ years	74.1	2,396	50.1	2,077

Respondent characteristic	Matching rates for Social Security records (%)	Number of observations	Matching rates for pension plan descriptions (%)	Number of observations
Never retire	71.1	1,069	45.5	549
Self-employed				
Yes	67.9	1,564	0	184
No	72.8	10,022	56.8	8,498
Combined	72.1	11,586	55.2	8,682
Tenure with firm				
< 2 years	72.6	578	51.7	269
2 to 4 years	71.2	775	52.5	657
5 to 9 years	73.8	2,286	41.7	1,825
10+ years	71.7	7,944	60	5,894
Size of firm				
< 5	71	805	17	90
5–14	72.4	609	25.3	163
15–24	65.4	242	45.4	97
25–99	74.6	611	40.3	432
100–499	75.2	750	56.5	710
500+	72.7	1,634	73.9	1,784
Industry				
Manufacturing	74.7	2,520	49.5	2,318
Other	71.5	8,971	57.5	6,283
Occupation				
Management/professional	69.2	3,318	57	3,006
White collar	70.7	2,871	52.6	2,113
Blue collar	75.4	5,356	55.2	3,528
Union status				
Union	72.1	2,122	70.1	2,253
Nonunion	71.9	5,448	62.1	3,576
Annual earnings				
< 15K	74.4	4,630	44.2	2,427
15–30K	71.9	3,519	54.6	3,169
30–50K	70.3	2,089	63.5	2,069
50–100K	72.4	879	67.2	810
100K+	63.5	191	30.4	128
Pension				
Yes	72.6	5,056		
No	71.8	6,530		

Source: Authors' calculations based on data from the HRS.

a. The observations in this table use the HRS survey weights. Percentages in column 2 are for permissions as reported in V136, wave 1. Job characteristics in column 1 are for the longest job. Calculations for columns 4 and 5 include only jobs offering pensions. Percentages are weighted averages.

Table 3A-2. *Matched Pension Plans by Type of Pension and Pension Value*[a]

Respondent-reported pension characteristic	Matching rates for pension plan descriptions	Number of observations
Pension type		
Defined benefit	59.1	4,528
Defined contribution	40.8	2,446
Combination	69.2	1,368
DB annual benefit		
< 2K	41.8	664
2–5K	49.8	663
5–10K	61.4	794
10–25K	71.6	1,475
25K+	76.9	642
DC account value		
< 10K	46.9	1,258
10–25K	58.9	627
25–100K	54.5	641
100–250K	68.1	184
250K+	52.0	86

Source: Authors' calculations based on data from the HRS.
a. The observations in this table use the HRS survey weights.

zero values. For the explanatory variable (the value calculated from the survey questions), we compensate by creating a binary variable that takes on a value of one if the pension value is zero. For the dependent variable, the pension value must be estimated in two steps. The first step is a probit for the probability that the pension value calculated from the plan documents will be zero. As might be expected, that probability declines rapidly as the pension value calculated from the survey questions increases. The second step is a regression of the log of the value from the plan documents on a set of explanatory variables, if the value is positive.

For those who have positive employer-provided and respondent pension value, equation 3 suggests an elasticity of employer pension value with respect to respondent-reported value of around .73. The R^2 for that equation is 0.63, suggesting that self-reported plan value is associated with about two-thirds of the variation in the plan value calculated from firm reports. Holding other plan features and job characteristics constant, equation 4 suggests an elasticity of firm-reported plan values with respect to respondent values of .24, but that holds constant a number of plan characteristics that are associated with higher plan value. Thus equation 4 should be used to predict pension values, but care should be exercised in attempting to interpret any particular coefficients.

Table 3A-3. *Pension Value Calculated from Plan Documents Compared with Pension Value Calculated from Respondent Reports, All Plans*

Provider-reported	Self-reported											Total
	0	0–5K	5–10K	10–20K	20–50K	50–100K	100–200K	200–500K	500K–1M	> 1M	Don't know	
0	5	67	30	35	31	14	11	4	2	0	295	494
0–5K	1	77	20	7	11	1	2	1	0	0	88	208
5–10K	0	26	24	22	14	2	5	0	0	0	81	174
10–20K	1	20	26	43	49	18	4	2	0	0	98	261
20–50K	0	11	12	38	92	61	31	14	2	0	176	437
50–100K	0	3	4	9	39	90	72	21	2	0	163	403
100–200K	0	1	5	2	15	59	121	56	4	2	111	376
200–500K	0	1	0	4	4	15	67	128	9	1	53	282
500K–1M	0	0	0	0	2	0	3	26	6	2	6	45
> 1M	0	0	0	0	0	0	0	2	2	1	0	5
Don't know	1	4	2	2	10	4	3	1	0	0	143	170
Total	8	210	123	162	267	264	319	255	27	6	1,214	2,855

Source: Authors' calculations based on data from the HRS.

Table 3A-4. Regression of Provider Total Pensions on Self-Reported Pensions Plus Other Variables

Dependent variable	Binary variable for provider pension = 0		Binary variable for provider pension = 0		ln provider pension		ln provider pension		Binary variable for provider pension = 0		ln provider pension	
Self-reported values	Yes		Yes		Yes		Yes		No		No	
Provider values	All		All		Positive values only		Positive values only		All		Positive values only	
Estimation method	Probit		Probit		Regression		Regression		Probit		Regression	
Independent variable	Coefficient	z	Coefficient	z	Coefficient	t	Coefficient	t	Coefficient	z	Coefficient	t
Constant	1.852	7.61	1.908	1.17	2.882	17.52	0.506	0.79	2.580	1.29	−1.354	−1.38
Respondent reports zero pension value	−1.558	−3.63	−0.165	−0.31	6.275	14.30	2.089	5.85				
ln of value respondent reports	−0.300	−12.30	−0.133	−3.16	0.735	48.89	0.239	11.82				
Current age			0.002	0.16			0.064	13.09	−0.004	−0.34	0.093	14.58
Age at hire			0.003	0.45			−0.059	−24.54	0.026	4.08	−0.078	−23.67
Age expects benefits to begin			0.023	1.12			−0.030	−4.04	−0.046	−2.27	−0.014	−1.68
Age benefit expected missing									−0.468	−0.37	−1.685	−3.25
Respondent has only DC plan			2.151	1.67			−2.763	−6.06	0.313	0.23	−3.044	−5.42
Respondent has DB and DC, or combination plan							−0.263	−3.31			−0.282	−2.46
Early retirement age, DB plan, = 0 for DC plan			−0.289	−1.25			0.003	0.46	−0.432	−1.80	−0.026	−3.31
Respondent reports can collect benefits at any age			0.017	0.84			−0.004	0.01	0.020	1.06	−1.728	1.92
Early retirement age missing			0.882	0.72			0.102	0.28	1.403	1.23	−1.698	−3.56
Normal retirement age, DB plan, = 0 for DC plan			−0.019	−1.09			−0.003	−0.63	0.006	0.35	0.003	0.33
Normal retirement age missing			−1.525	−1.32			−0.161	−0.47	0.371	0.32	0.211	0.42
Annual reduction factor, DB plans, = 0 for DC plans			−3.553	−0.95			−0.014	−0.27	1.013	0.64	−0.058	−0.07
Reduction factor missing			−0.287	−1.01			−0.020	−0.32	−0.013	−0.05	0.157	1.38

Variable	(1)	(2)	(3)	(4)	(5)	(6)
Contribution rate for 401k/403b/ SRA plans, 0 otherwise		−0.845 (−0.58)		1.270 (2.03)	−4.323 (−2.26)	1.665 (1.89)
Contribution rate missing		−0.140 (−0.87)		0.152 (1.98)	0.238 (1.15)	0.374 (3.28)
Female		0.012 (0.18)		0.137 (3.00)	−0.386 (−2.80)	0.243 (3.51)
High school dropout		0.114 (0.76)		−0.016 (−0.25)	−0.268 (−1.66)	0.098 (1.19)
Some college		0.111 (0.78)		−0.036 (−0.68)	0.360 (2.38)	0.146 (1.76)
College graduate		0.202 (1.07)		0.082 (1.20)	−0.032 (−0.14)	0.219 (2.03)
Some graduate school		0.438 (2.42)		0.015 (0.24)	0.646 (2.84)	0.238 (2.06)
ln earnings		−0.359 (−3.24)		0.786 (15.27)	−0.312 (−2.10)	1.154 (14.72)
Earnings missing		−3.407 (−2.50)		8.128 (12.93)	(dropped)	
Full-time		−0.065 (−0.40)		−0.119 (−1.75)	−0.121 (−0.66)	−0.310 (−3.14)
Union		0.255 (2.25)		0.025 (0.61)	0.137 (1.18)	0.178 (3.00)
Manufacturing		0.227 (1.39)		−0.042 (−0.63)	−0.221 (−1.02)	−0.245 (−2.77)
Public employment		0.357 (2.15)		0.403 (6.86)	0.000 (0.00)	0.443 (4.44)
Manager or professional		0.242 (1.41)		0.244 (3.84)	0.183 (0.88)	−0.064 (−0.65)
White collar		−0.020 (−0.13)		0.238 (4.16)	0.414 (2.43)	0.047 (0.56)
Firm size >100		0.046 (0.30)		−0.045 (−0.67)	−0.407 (−2.38)	0.078 (0.70)
Firm size missing		0.703 (1.72)		0.033 (0.16)	−0.235 (−0.50)	−0.094 (−0.26)
Health is good		−0.084 (−0.77)		0.006 (0.14)	0.093 (0.75)	0.006 (0.95)
Health is poor		0.032 (0.17)		−0.037 (−0.50)	0.016 (0.08)	−0.079 (−0.82)
Planning horizon < 2 years		0.164 (1.39)		−0.002 (−0.05)	0.099 (0.74)	−0.004 (−0.05)
Planning horizon > 10 years		0.065 (0.38)		0.069 (1.02)	−0.042 (−0.19)	−0.011 (−0.10)
Planning horizon not available		0.273 (0.85)		0.225 (1.59)	−0.328 (−1.12)	−0.064 (−0.42)
Number of words recalled in second test		−0.019 (−1.02)		0.017 (2.39)	−0.018 (−0.89)	0.002 (0.02)
Missing recall measure		−0.008 (−0.03)		−0.037 (−0.27)	0.141 (0.44)	0.164 (0.99)
Number of observations	1,614	1,611	1,415	1,415	1,067	776
Adjusted or pseudo R^2	0.1525	0.2738	0.6297	.7969	.4288	.7267

Source: Authors' calculations based on data from the HRS.

Comparing Earnings from Respondent Reports and Linked Earnings Histories

Next we examine how well we can impute the value of Social Security benefits from the information in the respondent questionnaire; again, two approaches can be taken. One is to use the information about the date the respondent expects to receive benefits and the amount of benefits expected to calculate the present value of benefits. A drawback of this approach is that only one-quarter of respondents were willing to provide an amount and knew the amount to within about $1,000 per year of the true value of benefits. A more indirect approach, but one that yields considerably better results, is to impute an earnings history based on information in the respondent questionnaire and to calculate benefits based on the imputed earnings history. This has the advantage that a rough earnings history can be estimated for most of the sample, and the estimates usually are fairly close compared with those using the respondent's report of expected Social Security amounts.

Tables 3A-5 and 3A-6 report the relations between the present values of own benefits computed from respondent earnings reports and those obtained from the Social Security Administration. Overall, the present value of own benefits is seen in table 3A-5 to be 5.9 percent too high when computed from respondent-reported earnings. For men the lifetime benefits are about 1.2 percent too high when computed from respondent earnings histories, and for women they are 13.6 percent too high. From table 3A-6, we find that 68 percent of the observations are within one cell of the main diagonal (6,428/9,472) and that the observations along the main diagonal account for 34 percent of the observations (3,251/9,472).

Rather than estimate an equation for the present value of benefits, however, we estimate equations for the average indexed monthly earnings (AIME), on which benefits are based. We do this for several reasons. First, benefits are a non-linear function of the AIME, and it probably is better to estimate the relation before the transformation. Second, the AIME frequently is of interest in its own right, since it is roughly proportional to lifetime covered earnings. Finally, the AIME provides a means to calculate family Social Security benefits, which often are more than simply the sum of the values of the benefits of a married couple on the basis of their own earnings records.

Table 3A-7 reports coefficients for equations that relate the AIME on an annual basis, computed from the Social Security earnings record, to the value imputed on the basis of variables available in the survey. When separate equations are estimated for men and women, the regression accounts for 60 percent of the variance in annualized AIME for men and 66 percent of the variance for women. Because this equation is to be used for predictive rather than analytical purposes, it includes a number of different measures of earnings and benefits, including the AIME implied by the respondent's expected Social Security benefits. Consequently, the coefficients on particular variables are not readily interpretable.

Table 3A-5. *Social Security Administration Compared with Respondent Report of Present Value of Social Security Benefits*[a]
1992 dollars

	All respondents			Male respondents			Female respondents		
	Respondent	SSA	Difference	Respondent	SSA	Difference	Respondent	SSA	Difference
Mean	55,745	52,622	-3,123	71,880	71,035	-844	42,170	37,130	-5,041
Percentile									
95	113,163	109,625	28,315	119,057	117,684	32,868	97,495	85,268	24,281
90	100,862	97,570	17,501	110,794	108,923	20,649	83,782	72,367	14,584
75	81,624	76,572	5,558	94,583	92,596	7,374	62,816	54,192	4,128
50	55,678	50,471	-1,423	75,379	72,692	-400	42,207	36,548	-2,585
25	29,682	26,637	-11,635	51,592	49,702	-9,327	13,963	13,511	-13,789
10	3,331	6,807	-26,340	26,403	30,988	-23,195	0	2,977	-27,956
5	0	2,031	-38,845	4,891	14,643	-36,082	0	665	-40,012
Number of observations		9,472			4,328			5,144	
Correlation		0.81			0.75			0.77	

Source: Authors' calculations based on data from the HRS.

a. This table includes the Social Security records obtained with permission of respondents to HRS waves 1, 2, and 3.

Table 3A-6. *Distribution of Present Values of Own Social Security Benefits Based on Respondent and Social Security Administration Reports*[a]
Thousands of 1992 dollars

Respondent-reported	SSA records														Total
	0–10	10–20	20–30	30–40	40–50	50–60	60–70	70–80	80–90	90–100	100–110	110–120	120–130	130+	
0–10	788	249	104	73	69	30	17	13	9	6	6	6	1	1	1,372
10–20	137	151	92	71	40	20	8	5	2	3	0	1	0	0	530
20–30	78	101	126	91	52	20	6	4	3	2	2	2	1	0	488
30–40	54	91	112	225	130	53	18	13	8	3	2	2	0	1	712
40–50	57	63	95	213	343	132	70	20	21	5	0	3	1	0	1,023
50–60	32	44	46	98	285	286	157	58	23	12	2	4	1	0	1,048
60–70	24	19	18	52	131	210	227	138	50	20	3	5	0	1	898
70–80	20	12	22	30	73	118	195	231	125	40	16	1	3	2	888
80–90	10	1	9	13	30	60	102	204	206	100	29	9	3	1	777
90–100	7	8	7	13	25	35	53	92	157	260	63	17	2	4	743
100–110	3	5	1	6	9	7	12	23	50	103	155	38	4	1	417
110–120	9	0	1	4	5	7	8	15	19	20	67	127	23	8	313
120–130	1	2	1	0	1	4	1	6	4	7	13	29	52	7	128
130+	3	0	1	1	0	4	3	4	1	4	10	11	19	74	135
Total	1,223	746	635	890	1,193	986	877	826	678	585	368	255	110	100	9,472

Source: Authors' calculations based on data from the HRS.
a. This table includes the Social Security records obtained with permission of respondents to HRS waves 1, 2, and 3.

Table 3A-7. Regressions of Average Indexed Yearly Earnings Calculated from Social Security Records on Average Indexed Yearly Earnings Calculated from Earnings Imputed from Survey[a]

Independent variables	All observations with matched Social Security earnings records				Observations for males with matched Social Security earnings records		Observations for females with matched Social Security earnings records	
	Coefficient	t	Coefficient	t	Coefficient	t	Coefficient	t
Constant	1,863	−19.02	5,404	14.65	3,990	4.24	1,757	5.27
AIME calculated from earnings imputed from survey	0.778	137.80	0.511	45.63	0.499	26.27	0.466	32.49
AIME imputed from expected benefit amount			0.097	11.91	0.097	7.86	0.080	7.89
AIME from expected benefit missing			600	2.97	−71	−0.15	574	2.91
AIME from earnings imputed from survey interacted with missing value indicator			−0.014	−1.23	0.020	0.94	−0.023	−1.47
Female			−5,019	−37.64	(dropped)		(dropped)	
Married			149	1.10	1,568	5.57	−711	−5.51
High school dropout			−645	−4.69	−795	−3.20	−592	−4.21
Some college			−407	−2.67	−1,064	−3.82	204	1.32
College graduate			242	1.12	292	0.80	21	0.09
Some graduate school			972	4.27	464	1.24	1,482	5.73
Respondent working at time of survey			502	1.99	896	1.05	596	2.76
Earnings in current job			0.031	5.95	0.018	2.29	0.041	5.95
Indicator respondent had section G job			−628	−2.32	−1,131	−1.29	−317	−1.35
Earnings from section G job			0.040	5.56	0.044	3.78	0.060	6.11
Self-employed			−1,247	−7.56	−1,205	−4.36	−1,358	−7.48
Worked for federal government in past			−1,349	−7.16	−2,281	−7.39	−198	−0.93
Worked for a state government in past			−402	−3.03	−414	−1.76	−304	−2.20

(Table continues on the following page.)

Table 3A-7 (continued)

Independent variables	All observations with matched Social Security earnings records		Observations for males with matched Social Security earnings records		Observations for females with matched Social Security earnings records	
	Coefficient	t	Coefficient	t	Coefficient	t
Reported a non–Social Security job in past	−1,027	−6.94	−1,172	−4.69	−1,113	−6.88
Current or last five-year job was full time	−312	−2.12	−671	−2.09	−7	−0.05
Respondent had a pension in any job	2,347	17.15	2,950	11.68	1,987	14.29
Union in main job	155	1.12	313	1.37	−49	−0.31
Management/professional in main job	807	5.38	1,068	4.23	636	3.88
Manufacturing in main job	1,708	12.11	1,923	8.54	1,289	7.80
Indicator survey available for 1996	34	0.21	675	2.43	−813	−4.49
Reported health excellent or very good	24	0.19	85	0.39	57	0.44
Reported health fair or poor	−548	−3.55	−718	−2.61	−373	−2.34
Planning horizon < 2 years	−306	−2.52	−520	−2.33	−89	−0.74
Planning horizon > 10 years	−186	−0.97	69	0.20	−394	−1.99
Planning horizon not available	−432	−1.45	−387	−0.74	−567	−1.78
Words recalled in second test	16	0.81	33	0.86	20	1.04
Recall variable missing	356	1.10	454	0.84	323	0.87
Number of observations	9,472		4,328		5,144	
Adjusted R^2	0.7549		0.6016		0.6587	

Source: Authors' calculations based on data from the HRS.

a. This table includes the Social Security records obtained with permission of respondents to HRS waves 1, 2, and 3. Average indexed yearly earnings equal AIME x 12.

Table 3A-8. *Social Security Administration Compared with Respondent-Reported Earnings*[a]

	All respondents			Male respondents			Female respondents		
	Respondent	*SSA*	*Difference*	*Respondent*	*SSA*	*Difference*	*Respondent*	*SSA*	*Difference*
Mean	13,738	12,548	–1,190	19,909	19,230	–680	8,545	6,926	–1,620
Percentile									
95	31,958	30,820	7,720	33,341	32,587	10,221	24,526	20,228	4,702
90	29,422	28,252	4,785	32,022	31,034	6,915	20,330	16,211	2,950
75	22,922	20,773	1,481	28,356	27,261	2,609	13,280	10,425	778
50	12,110	10,070	–453	21,866	20,551	–245	6,554	5,067	–611
25	3,969	3,513	–3,660	12,366	11,570	–3,778	1,850	1,754	–3,572
10	462	903	–8,225	3,853	4,772	–8,815	0	394	–7,730
5	0	264	–11,952	757	2,180	–13,526	0	91	–10,945
Number of observations		9,472			4,328			5,144	
Correlation		0.82			0.72			0.76	

Source: Authors' calculations based on data from the HRS.

a. This table includes the Social Security records obtained with permission of respondents to HRS waves 1, 2, and 3. Average indexed monthly earnings, expressed on an annual basis, equal AIME x 12. AIME, expressed on an annual basis, in 1992 dollars.

Table 3A-9. *Distribution of Respondent and Social Security Administration Reports of Average Indexed Yearly Earnings*[a]
Thousands of 1992 dollars

Respondent-reported	SSA records											Total
	0–4	4–8	8–12	12–16	16–20	20–24	24–28	28–32	32–36	36–40	40+	
0–4	1,803	358	105	34	27	21	18	14	2	0	0	2,382
4–8	395	519	182	70	32	16	10	4	2	0	0	1,230
8–12	173	338	358	136	49	25	10	6	2	0	0	1,097
12–16	72	148	264	228	144	63	22	9	0	0	0	950
16–20	47	62	145	217	178	125	75	18	3	1	0	871
20–24	31	40	63	117	195	184	136	41	10	0	0	817
24–28	32	13	46	50	94	206	287	125	16	0	0	869
28–32	13	20	14	23	39	76	188	334	83	0	0	790
32–36	6	6	16	14	24	25	44	141	172	0	0	448
36–40	0	1	0	0	0	1	3	3	4	3	0	15
40+	0	0	0	0	1	0	1	0	1	0	0	3
Total	2,572	1,505	1,193	889	783	742	794	695	295	4	0	9,472

Source: Authors' calculations based on data from the HRS.

a. This table includes the Social Security records obtained with permission of respondents to HRS waves 1, 2, and 3. Average indexed yearly earnings equal average indexed monthly earnings, expressed on an annual basis, which equals AIME x 12.

Table 3A-8 summarizes the distributions of AIME based on Social Security records compared with respondent reports of earnings histories for the 9,472 respondents for whom HRS had a matched earnings record.[34] The data in the table are AIME computed on an annual basis, that is, AIME multiplied by 12. Using respondent reports—including earnings on the current or last job in 1992, at the start of the current or last job, in a previous job, and in past pension-covered jobs—and incorporating information from wave 3 on the age that the respondent initially entered the labor force, years of full-time work, and years of covered work, the computed AIME amounts overestimate the true amounts by about 9.5 percent overall, about 3.5 percent for men and about 23 percent for women. The last column in table 3A-8 first orders the differences, then presents the results for different parts of the distribution. Thus the median of the differences is not equal to the difference of the medians. When the differences are ordered from low to high, however, the median difference is greatly reduced.

Table 3A-9 displays the joint distribution of the AIME on a yearly basis. The dispersion is considerably narrower than the dispersion of pension values. In this table there are a total of 9,472 observations; of those, 7,303 (77 percent) fall within one cell of the diagonal, and 4,066 observations (43 percent) fall exactly on the diagonal. The correlation of these two amounts is 0.82.

---

34. Table 3A-8 includes the Social Security records obtained through permissions granted by respondents in wave 1, as analyzed in table 3A-1, and in addition it includes Social Security records obtained through permissions granted by respondents in waves 2 and 3.

John Karl Scholz

Alan Gustman and Thomas Steinmeier have written many high-quality papers exploring aspects of pension and Social Security data and wealth using the Health and Retirement Study (HRS). In pursuing their research, they have set a high standard for careful HRS data work. This chapter continues their strong tradition.

What do they do in this chapter? There are two sources of pension data in the HRS. First, respondents are asked a series of questions about pension coverage and, if they have a pension, about the details of their pension, including its value. Second, the survey matched respondents with detailed descriptions of the pension provided by employers. The central contribution of the chapter is to compare the two sources of pension information.

The idea behind this chapter is sensible. Understanding changes in pension wealth is important to understanding many issues. Any study using the life-cycle model as a point of departure needs to consider pension wealth, since pensions can be a sizable element of lifetime wealth for people who have them. Efforts to assess the adequacy of saving for retirement or efforts to analyze the effects of policies to promote saving must consider pensions. Yet the leading data sets used to analyze these issues include, at best, limited pension data.

Until recently, the most important data sets with information on wealth in the United States have included very little pension information. Over the past fifteen years, for example, the Survey of Consumer Finances has collected little information on defined benefit (DB) pensions. The wealth supplements from the Panel Study of Income Dynamics contain only a very limited set of pension-related questions. This makes the HRS an exceptionally important resource for understanding behavioral issues related to pensions.

The strength of this chapter is in its detailed comparisons of self-reported values of defined contribution (DC), defined benefit, and Social Security wealth with values drawn from employer surveys in the case of private pensions and from government records in the case of Social Security benefits. The authors also report descriptive, preliminary analyses of the degree to which poor information is related to economic behavior and the degree to which discrepancies across data sets are related to observable characteristics.

What do they find? The chapter is packed with nineteen tables (with nine more in the appendix), but I take away the following five central findings:

—When the distribution of benefits is considered, mean and median DB pension values are similar to those calculated from plan documents.

—There are significant discrepancies between self-reports and calculations based on plan details for DB pensions when observations are examined on a case-by-case basis, but it is not clear that the errors are systematically biased. It is likely, given the difficulty of valuing DB pensions, that employer-based values reflect actual future pension benefits.

—There are large discrepancies between the values of DC pensions from self-reports and those computed from plan documents. Mean accumulations reported by respondents are only 69 percent of the amounts calculated by using pension documents. The authors present compelling evidence that the values computed from plan documents are overstated.

—Researchers can generate reasonably accurate Social Security parameters—such as average indexed monthly earnings and primary insurance amounts—for men by using retrospective earnings data. Discrepancies are much larger for women.

—People generally are badly informed about the early retirement date and benefit reduction rates associated with their pensions. That suggests that self-reported pension data are likely to be more useful for studies of wealth accumulation than they are for studies of the effects of pensions on retirement decisions.

What does this mean for empirical work on pensions and wealth? Consider the case of DC pensions. There are large discrepancies between reported DC pension amounts and amounts imputed from plan documents. The amounts imputed from plan documents are too large, probably because the plan-based calculations assume that discretionary contributions observed in the survey year reflect the level of contributions made throughout the employee's tenure with the employer. But current contributions of the HRS cohort are likely larger than their historical contributions. The plan-based DC pension calculations will be overstated, therefore, if families increase saving when faced with the prospect of retiring in ten years or if families increase their discretionary pension contributions when their children leave home.

The authors do not think the self-reports are necessarily more accurate, however, since even for those without discretionary DC contributions there are large differences between self- and provider-reported amounts. In those cases, they believe that the provider reports are more accurate. In general, therefore, they believe that provider-based values are more accurate when there are no discretionary contributions. They think that the *median* of the distribution of the self-reported amounts is accurate when there are discretionary contributions but that the distribution is flawed. Hence, they use information on the level of self-reports to scale the DC pension values computed from provider plans. Specifically, they do regression-based adjustments that lower the calculated DC pension amounts by roughly half for a calculated pension of $25,000 and almost two-thirds for a calculated pension of $100,000. If this view is correct—that the provider-based values are accurate and the self-reports are very noisy—two immediate implications follow:

—First, use of self-reported values in many empirical studies will be highly problematic. Recall that classical measurement error in the dependent variable has no consequence for empirical specifications, so if researchers are seeking to explain pension wealth accumulations, perhaps the self-reports will work fine. But if researchers are trying to study the effects of pensions on saving or wealth, retirement, or a host of other issues, measurement error in the right-side variable will result in biased coefficient estimates of an indeterminate direction. Put differently, you have a mess.

—Second, confusion over pension amounts and plan provisions suggests that many people are unlikely to be making anything close to optimal life-cycle consumption and retirement decisions and, as a consequence, that increased financial education may generate large returns. Others have made this point, and they would probably find much in this chapter to strengthen their conviction. *I am not sure either interpretation is warranted, however.* Four concerns immediately come to mind:

—First, my guess is that only a small percentage of Americans know that the State Department issued a travel advisory on the Solomon Islands on June 30, 2000. Yet I suspect that a large fraction of those interested in ecotourism in the South Pacific were aware of it. More generally, it may be the case that people seek out information that is critical for optimal decisionmaking at the time that they need to have it.

—Second, information on pension values is readily accessible. There are strict reporting requirements on DC pensions, so beneficiaries get regular updates on investment returns. DB pension programs have an annual reporting requirement, although DB statements typically are more difficult to interpret than DC balances, except for workers nearing retirement.

—Third, misperceptions of pension wealth of even tens of thousands of dollars can still be a trivial fraction of lifetime wealth and consequently have little practical effect on optimal life-cycle planning. While the chapter does a nice job of documenting discrepancies between different sources of pension information, it would be helpful to provide a context for the discrepancies by comparing them with the expected value of Social Security benefits, private wealth, and lifetime earnings.

—Fourth, despite the institutional detail provided by the plan supplements, the pension provider data still require assumptions. Hence, unlike the Social Security earnings record, which is described as the gold standard for earnings information, it is never clear whether the employer reports or the self-reports are more accurate. The authors seem to believe the employer reports are generally better. But to make calculations with the employer reports, wage trajectories must be imputed for many households. Coefficients on wage regressions can move around considerably depending on the chosen empirical specification, so these imputations surely lead to errors in estimated wage profiles, particularly for women whose labor market experiences may be interrupted when they have children. Errors in these profiles may, in turn, result in errors in estimated pension and Social Security wealth. I do not have a sense of how the magnitudes of these errors might compare with reporting errors made by respondents, but I would be nervous venturing a guess that one type is necessarily larger than the other type.

For other issues the self-reports are almost surely in error: most people do not know the early retirement date in their pension plan, most have a poor understanding of the effect on their pension of working additional years, and some do not even know their pension type. But it is not clear to me how important the erroneous self-reports are for understanding behavior or designing policy.

What does all this mean? The chapter clearly and convincingly demonstrates that there are significant discrepancies between the pension values calculated from self-reported data and those from employer-provided data. A much harder question, which the chapter does not make a great deal of progress on, is What do the discrepancies in pension reports mean for behavior and policy?

—The answer to that surely depends on the question being asked. The authors argue convincingly that misreported data on early retirement provisions in pensions will likely lead to underestimates of the effects of pensions on retirement.

—If DB pension errors are random, however, or small in relation to lifetime wealth or nonpension wealth, the errors may have little consequence for a person's well-being. More generally, if people have a reasonable understanding of the value of their pension, other discrepancies documented in the chapter may be largely irrelevant in determining a near-optimal life-cycle consumption profile.

—Stepping back, it is not obvious what should matter: expectations or actual values. Too little attention has been paid in microeconomics to how people form and act on their expectations. The crucial issue when thinking about the behavioral effects of pension policy changes is how technical and other changes in pension rules affect people's *perceived* budget sets and how, in turn, they act on those changes.

I think we are a long way from having adequate answers to these issues.

To conclude. The authors have provided a tremendous service by making files available for distribution to HRS users that contain predicted values for pension variables based on their work, incorporating information from the pension-provider records. The amount of work that goes into this is extraordinary. I believe that with the 1983 Survey of Consumer Finances, if there were 1,800 people with pension plans, there were something like 1,600 different plans. One-size-fits-all has not hit the world of pension administration, and a lot of us, myself included, owe a big debt to the authors for their efforts, both to illuminate important dimensions of the very rich data in the Health and Retirement Study and to share the results of their efforts with other interested scholars.

References

Anderson, Patricia M., Alan L. Gustman, and Thomas L. Steinmeier. 1999. "Trends in Male Labor Force Participation and Retirement: Some Evidence on the Role of Pensions and Social Security in the 1970s and 1980s." *Journal of Labor Economics* 17(4), pt. 1, October: 757–83.

Bayer, Patrick J., B. Douglas Bernheim, and John Karl Scholz. 1996. "The Effects of Financial Education in the Workplace: Evidence from a Survey of Employers." Working Paper 5655. Cambridge, Mass.: National Bureau of Economic Research (July).

Bernheim, B. Douglas. 1988. "Social Security Benefits: An Empirical Study of Expectations and Realizations." In *Issues in Contemporary Retirement,* edited by Rita Ricardo-Campbell and Edward P. Lazear, 312–50. Stanford, Calif.: Hoover Institution Press.

———. 1989. "The Timing of Retirement: A Comparison of Expectations and Realizations." In *The Economics of Aging,* edited by David A. Wise, 335–55. University of Chicago Press for National Bureau of Economic Research.

Bernheim, B. Douglas, and Daniel M. Garrett. 1996. "The Determinants and Consequences of Financial Education in the Workplace: Evidence from a Survey of Households." Working Paper 5667. Cambridge, Mass.: National Bureau of Economic Research (July).

Board of Trustees of the Federal Old-Age and Survivors Insurance and Disability Insurance Trust Funds. 1994. *1994 Annual Report.* U.S. Government Printing Office.

Clark, Robert L., and Sylvester J. Schieber. 1998. "Factors Affecting Participation Rates and Contribution Levels in 401(k) Plans." In *Living with Defined Contribution Pensions: Remaking Responsibility for Retirement,* edited by Olivia S. Mitchell and Sylvester J. Schieber, 69–97. University of Pennsylvania Press.

Disney, Richard, and Sarah Tanner. 1999. "What Can We Learn From Retirement Expectations Data?" Working Paper W99/17. Nottingham, England: Institute for Fiscal Studies.

Gustman, Alan L., and F. Thomas Juster. 1996. "Income and Wealth of Older American Households: Modeling Issues for Public Policy Analysis." In *Assessing Knowledge of Retirement Behavior,* edited by Eric A. Hanushek and Nancy L. Maritato, 11–60. Washington: National Academy Press.

Gustman, Alan L., Olivia S. Mitchell, Andrew A. Samwick, and Thomas L. Steinmeier. 2000. "Evaluating Pension Entitlements." In *Forecasting Retirement Needs and Retirement Wealth,* edited by Olivia S. Mitchell, P. Brett Hammond, and Anna M. Rappaport, 309–26. University of Pennsylvania Press for the Pension Research Council.

Gustman, Alan L., and Thomas L. Steinmeier. 1989. "An Analysis of Pension Benefit Formulas, Pension Wealth, and Incentives from Pensions." In *Research in Labor Economics,* vol. 10, edited by Ronald G. Ehrenberg, 53–106. Greenwich, Conn.: JAI Press.

———. 1999. "Effects of Pensions on Saving: Analysis with Data from the Health and Retirement Study." Carnegie-Rochester Conference Series on Public Policy 50 (June): 271–324.

———. 2000. "Employer-Provided Pension Data in the NLS Mature Women's Survey and in the Health and Retirement Study." In *Research in Labor Economics*, vol.19, edited by Solomon W. Polachek, 215–52. Greenwich, Conn.: JAI Press.

———. 2001. "Retirement Outcomes in the Health and Retirement Study." *Social Security Bulletin* 64 (4).

Lumsdaine, Robin L. 1996. "Factors Affecting Labor Supply Decisions and Retirement Income." In *Assessing Knowledge of Retirement Behavior,* edited by Eric A. Hanushek and Nancy L. Maritato, 61–122. Washington: National Academy Press.

Lumsdaine, Robin L., and Olivia S. Mitchell. 1999. "New Developments in the Economic Analysis of Retirement." In *Handbook of Labor Economics,* edited by Orley Ashenfelter and David Card, 3261–3307. Amsterdam: North Holland.

Lusardi, Annamaria. 1999. "Information, Expectations, and Savings for Retirement." In *Behavioral Dimensions of Retirement Economics,* edited by Henry J. Aaron, 81–115. Brookings Institution.

Madrian, Brigitte C., and Dennis F. Shea. 2000. "The Power of Suggestion: Inertia in 401(k) Participation and Savings Behavior." Working Paper 7682. Cambridge, Mass.: National Bureau of Economic Research (May).

Mitchell, Olivia S. "Worker Knowledge of Pension Provisions." *Journal of Labor Economics* 6 (1): 21–39.

Olson, Janice A. 1999. "Linkages with Data from Social Security Administration Records in the Health and Retirement Study." *Social Security Bulletin* 62 (2).

Weisbenner, Scott. 1999. "Do Pension Plans with Participant Investment Choice Teach Households to Hold More Equity?" Finance and Economics Discussion Series Paper Number 1999-61. Federal Reserve Board.

4

Financial Education and Private Pensions

DEAN M. MAKI

Because of the shift in the United States over the past two decades from defined benefit pension plans to defined contribution plans, American households increasingly shoulder the responsibility of planning for retirement.[1] To take full advantage of the opportunities now available, households must possess sufficient financial knowledge to make wise decisions. Bernheim (1998) raises concerns about whether households are financially literate enough to make wise decisions with regard to participating in and contributing to a pension plan.

A related concern is the amount of personal saving by households in the United States. Starting with the third quarter of 2000, the personal saving rate measured in the National Income and Product Accounts dipped below zero, and many economists have concluded that additional measures to increase saving are needed to ensure that members of the baby boom generation have an adequate standard of living when they retire. Indeed, tax-incentive plans such as 401(k)s and IRAs have been created specifically to increase the incentive for households to save.

I would like to thank Doug Bernheim for providing me with the data used in this chapter, Merrill Lynch for collecting the data, and William Gale and Bill Even for helpful comments. Much of this chapter was written while I was on the staff of the Federal Reserve Board; however, the views expressed are mine and do not necessarily reflect the views of the Federal Reserve Board or of JPMorgan Chase.
    1. See, for example, tables 11-5 and 11-6 in chapter 11 of this volume.

In recent years there has been increased interest in financial education as one possibility for increasing households' financial literacy and thereby, perhaps, improving their financial decisionmaking. An increasing number of employers have begun offering education in retirement planning to their employees, often with the goal of increasing their participation in and contributions to 401(k) pension plans. Recently H.R. 4747, the Retirement Security Advice Act of 2000, was introduced as a bill in the U.S. House of Representatives; the bill aims to make it easier for firms to contract with financial institutions to give individualized financial advice to their employees without the firm being liable as a fiduciary adviser.

School-based financial education has a longer history. In the 1970s, a number of states instituted policies to encourage or require financial education in high school.[2] Although the pace of change slowed markedly in the 1980s, a number of organizations still promote financial education at the high school level, including the Jump$tart Coalition for Personal Financial Literacy and the National Endowment for Financial Education.

This chapter reviews the literature on the effects of financial education, which has been found to increase household saving and wealth accumulation. Possible reasons for those effects are discussed, among them that education changes parameters in a household's utility function. Household-level data are then used to investigate a different channel by which financial education may have an impact: increasing a household's knowledge of the financial choices that it has. The results suggest that financial education in the workplace is associated with greater financial knowledge, both of relative asset returns and of the features of the household's pension plan. The importance to policymakers of that and other findings is discussed.

What Is Financial Education?

Two main types of financial education are examined in this chapter. The first is workplace financial education, which may consist of written materials, seminars, workshops, and newsletters. Topics covered often include asset allocation strategies and methods of estimating the amount of money a household needs to save for retirement. Often those educational programs are linked to a firm's 401(k) plan, and sometimes they are implemented specifically to increase participation in and contributions to the plan. See Bernheim and Garrett (2000) and Bayer, Bernheim, and Scholz (1996) for a more detailed discussion of workplace financial education.

---

2. Bernheim, Garrett, and Maki (2001).

The second is high school financial education, which may be required or optional and which may be included in another course or a full course in its own right. The topics covered may include budgeting, money management, credit, and saving and investing. Within saving and investing, the topics may include discussion of various types of financial instruments, the relationship between risk and return, the effect of inflation and taxes on investments, and the advantages of portfolio diversification.

A number of states passed financial education mandates in the 1970s. Those mandates differ in their impact; some require state education agencies to assemble and distribute materials to local districts, some require districts to offer financial education, and some require each student to receive instruction, either through a separate course or as part of an existing course. I consider the effects of mandates that require each student to receive financial education, which exist now or have existed in fourteen states. See Bernheim, Garrett, and Maki (2001) for a more detailed discussion of the types of high school financial education.

Previous Research

In recent years, more employers have been offering financial education to their employees. Several recent studies have attempted to measure differences in behavior between households that were exposed to educational programs and households that were not. Bayer, Bernheim, and Scholz (1996), using data from the KPMG Peat Marwick Retirement Benefits Survey, analyzed differences in participation in and contributions to 401(k) plans between firms that offered financial education to their employees and other firms. Using cross-sectional variation, they found that participation and contribution rates were significantly higher in firms that offered educational programs. Retirement seminars were found to be the most effective means of communication, raising participation rates by about 8 percentage points and contribution rates by .66 of a percentage point. The effect was higher for workers who were not highly compensated: their participation rates increased by 11.5 percentage points, and their contribution rates rose by .8 of a percentage point.[3] Similar results were found when *changes* in participation and contribution rates were regressed on changes in educational programs.

Clark and Schieber (1998) used a survey of firms collected by Watson Wyatt Worldwide, a benefits consulting firm, to analyze determinants of participation and contribution rates in 401(k) plans. They found that generic employer newsletters raised participation rates, as did materials specifically tailored to the employer's 401(k) plan. If both types of information were used, the participa-

---

3. Bayer, Bernheim, and Scholz (1996, table 5).

tion rate increased 36 percentage points.[4] Generic newsletters had no effect on contribution rates, while specifically tailored information raised contribution rates by about 2 percentage points.[5]

Bernheim and Garrett (2000) also looked at the effect of workplace financial education, using a survey of households conducted for Merrill Lynch in fall 1994. They found that being exposed to financial education raised a household's probability of participating in a 401(k) plan 12 percentage points and raised the median balance by $2,800. Also, for households at or below the median, exposure to financial education was associated with 1 or 2 percentage points higher *overall* saving rates. Because they were using a single cross-section of data, the authors investigated several alternative explanations for the relationship, concluding that the higher saving rate was best explained as the result of financial education and was unlikely to have been caused by spurious correlation.

Bernheim, Garrett, and Maki (2001) look at the effect of financial education at the high school level on adult financial decisionmaking. The authors compile a database of state financial curriculum mandates that shows that a wave of mandates was passed in the 1970s as part of the broader consumer education movement; that wave of mandates provides a unique opportunity to compare households exposed to mandates with other households. The data are matched with a survey of households conducted for Merrill Lynch in fall 1995 that obtained information on household demographics and saving rates and, most important, on whether the respondent took financial education courses in high school, whether they were required, and in which state the respondent attended high school. The authors find that financial education mandates raised the likelihood that a respondent took financial education in high school and that they are associated with higher levels of saving and net worth among respondents in adulthood.

Presumably because of lags in implementation, the effects of mandates on exposure to financial courses and on saving appear to rise with the number of years since the mandate was enacted. Five years after the mandate, saving rates were 1.5 percentage points higher for exposed households than for unexposed households and exposed households' net worth was estimated to be higher by about one year's worth of earnings.

Muller (2000a) used the Health and Retirement Study (HRS) to look at the effect of retirement planning education on asset allocation in defined contribution pension plans. No general effects were found, although there did appear to be an effect for households with a "high" degree of risk aversion (the second-highest of four risk aversion categories). Muller noted that the relatively coarse nature of the survey question—it asked whether the households' assets were

---

4. Clark and Schieber (1998, p. 85).
5. Clark and Schieber (1998, p. 92).

mostly or all in stocks, mixed, or mostly or all in bonds—may have masked small changes in portfolios resulting from exposure to education.

Muller (2000b) used the HRS also to analyze the effect of retirement education on whether a household spends or saves a lump-sum distribution from its DC pension. Little effect was found for the sample as a whole, but separating the sample suggested that younger workers—especially men—who were exposed to financial education were more likely to save their distribution after receiving financial education, whereas better-educated households—especially women—were more likely to spend theirs. Muller suggests one possible explanation: education might make younger workers more likely to realize the importance of saving for retirement and therefore to save their distribution. On the other hand, college graduates, who may be more likely to have ample outside assets, may learn through the education program that they can access their money—albeit with penalties—and may be more willing to treat their pension plan as a short-run saving instrument. Muller's work emphasizes that the effects of retirement education may be heterogeneous, with different workers learning different lessons. Further research into those differences would be useful.

The existing literature points to one strong conclusion: financial education, either in the workplace or at school, increases household saving and wealth. In the next section, I discuss possible reasons for that relationship.

Why Does Financial Education Increase Saving?

The finding that financial education increases saving is not easily reconciled with standard models of consumption and saving behavior. Simple versions of the life-cycle model assume that there is no uncertainty and that households optimally allocate their consumption across periods in preparation for retirement. More sophisticated models of intertemporal choice allow for households to be uncertain about future income and to build precautionary balances to prepare for possible future income shocks. Also, the intertemporal consumption capital asset pricing model allows for uncertainty about the return on a risky asset. Even within models that allow for such uncertainty, however, it is not clear why financial education would have an impact. Although households do not know what particular draws they will receive from the distributions of possible future income and asset returns, they are assumed to have full information about the distributions themselves. If this assumption were true, there would be no additional information for the household to acquire through financial education.

One way to reconcile the results on education with standard models would be to assume that some parameter in the household's utility function is changed by financial education. One possibility is that financial education might lead to higher saving by reducing a household's discount rate. However, why that might occur is not obvious. Typically, financial education in the workplace covers topics like the features of a firm's pension plan, asset allocation strategies, and historical returns on different types of assets. No clear link exists between those topics and the discount rate, which measures a household's preference for current consumption relative to future consumption. It seems especially implausible that other behaviors that are affected by a household's discount rate, such as the propensity to smoke, would be affected by exposure to financial topics.

Another parameter to consider is a household's level of risk aversion. One might imagine that, if anything, exposure to the types of topics covered in a financial education course might cause households to become less risk averse as they learn that riskier assets, such as corporate equities, typically do better than other investments over the long term. However, in order for financial education to increase saving in most models of saving under uncertainty, financial education would have to make households *more* risk averse. It is not at all clear which topics covered in financial education courses would have that effect.

Thus, it seems implausible that financial education has its primary effect on saving by changing the parameters of households' utility functions, such as risk aversion or discount rates. A third possibility is that education changes a household's knowledge of its set of choices. While that explanation may seem plausible, it is a radical departure from the standard assumptions used in saving models because these models assume that all households have perfect information about the choices available to them. The analysis in this chapter provides evidence on a necessary, though not sufficient, condition for the third possibility: that households that are exposed to financial education become more knowledgeable about their choices as a result.

Data

This analysis is based on a unique cross-sectional household survey fielded in November 1995.[6] Respondents (households) were between the ages of 30 and 49. Most presumably graduated from high school between 1964 and 1983, a period that spans the transition to high school financial education in many states. A total of 2,000 surveys were completed. The survey gathered standard economic and demographic information including household earnings; total

6. The survey was designed in cooperation with Doug Bernheim and fielded for Merrill Lynch by Survey Communications, Inc. The original purpose of the survey was to monitor the adequacy of saving among members of the baby boom generation (see Bernheim 1996). Existing public-use data sets such as the Survey of Consumer Finances (SCF) and the Panel Study of Income Dynamics (PSID) do not contain data on the state in which the respondent attended high school or on exposure to financial education curricula. See also Bernheim, Garrett, and Maki (2001).

Table 4-1. *Summary Statistics*

Variable and subsample	Full sample	Covered by financial education mandate	Not covered by financial education mandate
Percent married	67.9	67.7	68.0
Percent single male	16.5	16.2	16.5
Percent single female	15.6	16.2	15.5
Percent white	80.4	75.3	81.0
Percent nonwhite	19.6	24.7	19.0
Percent no degree	5.9	4.5	6.1
Percent high school degree only	61.8	64.1	61.6
Percent college degree	32.3	31.3	32.3
Percent homeowners	71.7	66.2	72.3
Average age of respondent	39.6	34.7	40.1
Percent required to take consumer education course with financial topics	•11.4	21.2	10.4
Median household earnings	50,000	45,000	50,000
Median net worth	77,000	93,000	75,250

Source: Author's calculations based on data from a survey conducted for Merrill Lynch by Survey Communications, Inc., in November 1995.

income; rates of saving; assets and liabilities;[7] pension coverage;[8] employment status; gender, age, and marital status; ethnic group; education; and household composition. It also solicited information on childhood influences of possible relevance to future financial decisionmaking. Most important, it asked respondents to identify the state in which they attended high school, and it requested information concerning exposure to financial education, both in high school and at the workplace.

Table 4-1 contains summary statistics for the full sample.[9] The net worth and income figures are higher than benchmarks such as those in the Survey of Consumer Finances (SCF); that pattern is to be expected in a telephone survey, because homeowners are more likely than renters to answer the phone. Bernheim, Garrett, and Maki (2001) find that when the sample is adjusted for demographic variables such as homeownership status, marital status, and age,

7. Respondents were given separate questionnaires about the value of financial assets, houses, other real property, business interests, and debt.

8. Respondents were asked to identify the type of pension plan (defined benefit plan, voluntary tax-deferred salary reduction plan, or other defined contribution plan) and to provide total assets for defined contribution plans.

9. Earnings are defined as income from employment or self-employment. Net worth equals the sum of financial assets (including defined contribution pension plan balances), home equity, other real property, and business interests, net of debt.

the net worth and income of respondents line up reasonably well with data in the SCF. Columns 2 and 3 show the figures separately for households that were exposed to financial education mandates and those that were not. Differences in demographic variables are relatively minor, but, as would be expected, households that were exposed to mandates were significantly more likely to have been required to take a course in personal finance than were other households. Median net worth was higher among households exposed to mandates.

Results

As noted, the goal of the empirical work discussed in this chapter was to investigate whether financial education changes household members' financial knowledge. Specifically, we checked to see whether financial education increased their knowledge of relative asset returns. Also, Gustman and Steinmeier (chapter 2) point out an area in which household members' knowledge is quite imperfect: they find that many respondents to their survey did not understand the features of their pension plan. That appears to be an area in which financial education would be particularly likely to have an impact, so this analysis also tests whether financial education increases respondents' knowledge of the features of their pension plan.

In the 1995 Merrill Lynch survey, participants were asked, "Over the last 20 years, which of the following investments would have offered you the best returns on your money? Stocks, bonds, a savings account, or certificates of deposits (CDs)?" As noted by Ibbotson Associates (2000), stocks have been the highest-yielding investment over every twenty-year period since 1926 (when Ibbotson began collecting data), including the period from 1976–1995—the twenty-year period immediately preceding the survey. Yet only 52 percent of households in the survey correctly chose stocks as the investment with the highest return. In the analysis to follow, I use a dummy variable that equals one if the respondent answered the question correctly and zero if not: I refer to this variable as *know_return*.

The first analysis assesses whether workplace financial education influenced respondents' ability to answer the question correctly. Thus I use *know_return* as the dependent variable and use demographic control variables and a dummy variable equal to one if a respondent received financial education at the workplace. To focus on households that received information relevant to the question through their education, only respondents whose employer offered education that included information on asset allocation or options in their investment plan (about 83 percent of all households who received any form of employer-provided financial education) are counted as having received financial education. Also, for comparability with later results on respondents' knowledge about their pension plan, the sample is restricted to respondents whose employer offered a 401(k)-type of defined contribution plan, leaving 848 respondents in the sample.

The first column of table 4-2 shows the results. The coefficient estimates indicate that respondents whose employers offered financial education were about 10 percent more likely to answer the question correctly, and the coefficient is significant at the 5 percent level. Other coefficients indicate that women were less likely to answer correctly, as were African Americans (although the coefficient is significant only at the 10 percent level). Respondents with more education were more likely to answer correctly, as were older respondents.

To investigate the effect of education at the high school level, I use as an independent variable a dummy equal to one if the respondent was exposed to a financial education mandate and zero if not. To control for the possibility that households in states that imposed mandates are somehow different from households in other states, I also include a variable that equals one if the respondent's state *ever* imposed a mandate. The regression is essentially a "difference-in-difference" estimation; we examine the difference between households in mandate and nonmandate states to see whether that difference is changed by financial education mandates.

The results of the estimation are shown in column 2 of table 4-2. The coefficients indicate that respondents whose state ever imposed a mandate were nearly 10 percent less likely than other households to answer the question correctly. However, the coefficient on "exposed to mandate" indicates that respondents who were exposed to mandates were nearly 15 percent more likely to answer the question correctly than unexposed respondents living in states that eventually imposed mandates, and that estimate is significant at the 5 percent level. In other words, respondents who were exposed to the mandates were about 5 percentage points more likely to answer the question correctly than households living in nonmandate states, while respondents who lived in mandate states but were not themselves exposed to the mandates scored about 10 percentage points lower than households in states that never imposed a mandate. Thus, the results indicate that mandates were successful in increasing the number of households answering the relative return question correctly.

Next we look at whether households were more likely to understand the features of their pension plan if their employer offered financial education. Respondents were asked whether they were given a choice about the allocation of their funds, whether those choices included equity mutual funds, whether their employer matched their contributions to the pension plan, what the matching rate was, and whether the plan had a provision allowing employees to take loans against their plan balance. To test the respondent's understanding, I constructed an "ignorance" variable for each of those questions that equals one if the respondent replied "I don't know" or refused to answer the question. I

Table 4-2. *Probit Estimations for Knowledge of Relative Asset Returns*[a]

Variable	(1) Workplace financial education	(2) High-school financial education
Availability of financial education at respondent's workplace	0.096 (2.31)	
State ever imposed mandate		−0.096 (−1.93)
Exposed to mandate		0.145 (2.21)
Marital status	0.163 (0.66)	0.183 (0.72)
Female	−0.109 (−2.71)	−0.112 (−2.79)
Black	−0.114 (−1.68)	−0.107 (−1.59)
Other nonwhite	−0.054 (−0.99)	−0.053 (−0.97)
Education, respondent	0.054 (4.40)	0.054 (4.47)
Education, spouse	0.022 (1.16)	0.020 (1.09)
Age, respondent	0.009 (2.30)	0.012 (2.90)
Age, spouse	−0.004 (−1.12)	−0.005 (−1.20)
Log earnings, respondent	0.050 (2.72)	0.057 (3.12)
Log earnings, spouse	−0.009 (−0.37)	−0.010 (−0.41)
Self-employed, respondent	−0.089 (−1.50)	−0.131 (−2.23)
Self-employed, spouse	−0.030 (0.44)	0.041 (0.59)
Not working, spouse	−0.071 (−0.58)	−0.089 (−0.71)
Part-time, respondent	0.094 (1.50)	.074 (1.18)
Part-time, spouse	0.099 (1.26)	.086 (1.08)
Number of observations	848	848

Source: Author's calculations based on data from a survey conducted for Merrill Lynch by Survey Communications, Inc., in November 1995.

a. Dependent variable equals one if respondent answered the question correctly. *T* statistics in parentheses. Sample includes all households eligible to participate in a 401(k)-type of defined contribution pension. Coefficients are scaled to reflect incremental effects on probability evaluated at sample means.

constructed another dummy variable equal to one if the respondent answered "I don't know" or refused to answer *any* of the five questions. To test whether financial education reduces ignorance, I use probit regressions in which the ignorance dummies are the dependent variable and the dummy variable for employer education and demographic variables are the independent variables. Results of those estimations are shown in table 4-3. Very few of the demographic variables are significant. Notable exceptions are that higher-income respondents were less likely to be ignorant about a loan option and part-time workers were more likely to be ignorant about the employer's match rate.

The striking result of table 4-3 is that for every feature of the pension plan, respondents whose employer offered financial education were less likely to be ignorant of the features of the pension plan, with the percentage of "I don't know" answers decreasing anywhere from 5 percentage points for the question about an employer match to 14 percentage points for the question about a loan option. As shown in column 6, respondents whose employer offered financial education were 20 percentage points less likely to be ignorant of at least one feature of their pension plan. Column 7 shows whether financial education at the high school level was related to respondents' knowledge of their pension. The results indicate that respondents who were subject to mandates were 11 percent less likely to be ignorant of at least one feature of their pension plan, and the effect is significant at the 5 percent level. The coefficient on "state ever imposed mandate" is 12 percentage points, so that respondents in mandate states who were not subject to the mandate were more likely to be ignorant than households in nonmandate states. The coefficient on "exposed to mandate" indicates that that differential was largely wiped out for those households that were subject to the mandate. That is an important result that implies that a high school financial education course had long-lasting effects on respondents' propensity to acquire knowledge of their pension plan.

Thus, both employer and school-based financial education appear to reduce employees' ignorance of their pension plans. The finding that high school financial education also improved respondents' knowledge of relative asset returns and their knowledge about their pension plans gives considerable support to the idea that workplace-based financial education results are not due to some type of spurious correlation.

Policy Implications

Recent research has found that financial education increases a respondent's saving and net worth, and the results in this chapter indicate that education may work by increasing respondents' understanding of the choices available to them. These results have a number of policy implications. Policymakers who aim to increase saving should consider financial education a policy tool, one that seems

Table 4-3. *Probit Estimations for Ignorance of Pension Plan Features*[a]

Variable	(1) Asset choice	(2) Equity	(3) Match	(4) Match rate	(5) Loan	(6) Any feature	(7) Any feature
Availability of financial education at respondent's workplace	−0.064 (−4.48)	−0.066 (−2.90)	−0.048 (−3.01)	−0.087 (−2.41)	−0.140 (−5.15)	−0.200 (−5.61)	
State ever imposed mandate							0.122 (2.91)
Exposed to mandate							−0.114 (−2.29)
Marital status	0.060 (1.96)	−0.013 (−0.13)	−0.005 (−0.06)	0.002 (0.01)	0.063 (0.54)	0.188 (1.17)	0.186 (1.13)
Female	0.007 (0.65)	0.017 (0.99)	0.007 (0.50)	−0.024 (−0.75)	−0.011 (−0.45)	0.008 (0.23)	0.013 (0.38)
Black	0.422 (2.04)	0.004 (0.13)	−0.003 (−0.13)	0.009 (0.19)	−0.008 (−0.20)	0.017 (0.31)	0.008 (0.15)
Other nonwhite	−0.013 (−1.03)	−0.009 (0.44)	0.006 (0.33)	0.030 (0.71)	0.003 (0.09)	0.023 (0.52)	0.018 (0.40)
Education, respondent	−0.002 (−0.62)	0.007 (1.39)	−0.001 (−0.27)	0.001 (0.06)	0.007 (0.93)	0.009 (0.95)	0.006 (0.59)
Education, spouse	−0.010 (−1.95)	−0.003 (−0.48)	0.003 (0.40)	0.005 (0.36)	−0.007 (−0.60)	−0.011 (−0.74)	−0.010 (−0.65)
Age, respondent	−0.001 (−0.98)	−0.001 (−0.88)	0.001 (0.41)	−0.002 (−0.51)	0.003 (1.35)	−0.001 (−0.31)	−0.004 (−1.17)
Age, spouse	−0.001 (−1.11)	0.002 (1.70)	−0.002 (−1.38)	−0.002 (−0.49)	−0.003 (−1.17)	−0.003 (−0.78)	−0.002 (−0.54)
Log earnings, respondent	0.000 (0.07)	−0.003 (−0.53)	−0.006 (−1.45)	−0.009 (−0.76)	−0.017 (−2.02)	−0.030 (−2.24)	−0.041 (−3.01)
Log earnings, spouse	−0.008 (−2.02)	0.001 (0.15)	−0.001 (−0.17)	−0.003 (−0.14)	−0.008 (−0.68)	−0.022 (−1.27)	−0.023 (−1.29)
Self-employed, respondent	0.000 (0.01)	−0.020 (−0.98)	0.007 (0.40)	0.041 (0.83)	−0.017 (−0.55)	0.030 (0.62)	0.103 (2.09)
Self-employed, spouse	−0.002 (0.10)	−0.009 (−0.34)	0.032 (1.19)	−0.049 (−0.89)	0.046 (1.09)	0.018 (0.32)	0.016 (0.28)
Not working, spouse	−0.025 (−2.13)	−0.011 (−0.25)	−0.002 (−0.05)	−0.038 (−0.42)	−0.064 (−1.22)	−0.139 (−1.81)	−0.126 (−1.57)
Part-time, respondent	0.027 (1.50)	−.000 (−0.02)	0.015 (0.69)	0.106 (1.97)	0.020 (0.53)	0.095 (1.72)	0.152 (2.71)
Part-time, spouse	−0.015 (−0.93)	−0.002 (−0.07)	−0.02 (−0.74)	−0.028 (−0.48)	−0.015 (−0.35)	−0.063 (−1.05)	−0.055 (−0.88)
Number of observations	848	566	848	538	848	848	848

Source: Author's calculations based on data from a survey conducted for Merrill Lynch by Survey Communications, Inc., in November 1995.

a. Dependent variable equals one if respondent answered "I don't know" or refused to answer the question. *T* statistics in parentheses. Probit coefficients are scaled to reflect incremental effects on probability evaluated at sample means. Sample includes all households eligible for a 401(k) pension plan, except for columns 2 and 4, which are restricted to those who report having a choice of investments in their pension plan and those who have an employer match, respectively. Each column is a question about a feature of the household's pension plan. Column 1 refers to whether the household has a choice of investments in its pension plan, column 2 to whether the household has an equity mutual fund as a choice in its plan, column 3 to whether the employer matches employee contributions, column 4 to the matching rate that the employer offers, column 5 to whether the plan allows participants to borrow against their balance, and columns 6 and 7 to whether the household answered "I don't know" or refused to answer any of the questions in the first five columns.

to have a number of advantages over other tools such as increasing the limits on saving incentives like individual retirement accounts (IRAs) and 401(k) pension plans. First, there is substantial disagreement among economists about whether those incentives actually increase saving or simply substitute for other forms of saving (see Engen, Gale, and Scholz (1996) and Poterba, Venti, and Wise (1996) for a review of the debate). Even if one believes that the incentives increase saving, one may be concerned about their regressive nature, since wealthy households make disproportionate use of them.

Financial education has neither of those drawbacks. There is no possibility of substitution; if financial education increases total household saving, as several studies have found, it does not come at the expense of some other kind of saving (except for the relatively small cost of the educational materials, which would come out of business or government saving).[10] In addition, if one group might be said to benefit most from educational programs, it would seem to be lower-income households. Bayer, Bernheim, and Scholz (1996) found that workplace financial education seemed to increase the 401(k) contributions of non–highly compensated workers most, and Bernheim, Garrett, and Maki (2001) found that the effects of high school financial education were highest among respondents who reported that their parents did not save more than the average household.

In addition, financial education—especially at the high school level—might have other benefits besides its effect on saving. Presumably, respondents who are more knowledgeable about finances handle other aspects of their financial affairs better. Some suggestive evidence on that point comes from Mandell (1998), who found that states where students have greater financial literacy have lower levels of personal bankruptcy filings.

For all of these reasons, using financial education as a policy tool should attract little opposition from most economists. While I am not aware of work that tries to quantify the direct financial costs to the government of providing financial education, it would seem that they would be relatively minor compared with the potential benefits. That is especially true when private employers pay the cost of education and the government need only encourage it and reduce barriers to providing it. At the high school level, the costs probably are similar to those of any other course. Of course, the opportunity cost of requiring students to take financial education may be important, in that students then will not be able to take some other course. Given the relatively large benefits that education appears to confer, however, it seems that requiring students to

---

10. It is important to distinguish here between the finding that financial education increased 401(k) participation and contributions and the finding that it increased total household saving. In the first case, there is the usual possibility of shuffling between retirement and nonretirement saving. However, for the studies that found that financial education increased *total* household saving, there is no corresponding decrease in other saving. See Bernheim and Garrett (2000) and Bernheim, Garrett, and Maki (2001). It is to the latter findings that the text refers.

acquire at least some knowledge of personal finance during high school would be justified. One possibility would be to require a course in personal finance but allow students to test out of the course if they can show that they have mastered the concepts through independent study.

Finally, the results suggest that policymakers should not rely solely on the results of standard intertemporal optimization models to assess the effects of policy changes on household behavior. While those models may give accurate predictions for some households, the results here suggest that at least some households imperfectly understand their set of choices.[11] The results from standard optimization models need to be rigorously checked against the data before policy is made on the basis of those models. In addition, developing formal models of household saving behavior that allow at least some households to be imperfectly aware of their choices seems like a profitable area for future research.

---

11. One might argue that the standard model can fit the data if transaction costs are added to the model. The argument would be that there is a cost to acquiring financial knowledge and that respondents for whom financial choices are especially important—such as those who are near retirement or who have large amounts of assets to manage—are more willing to incur that cost. However, given the enormous consequences of undersaving or misallocating retirement assets over a lifetime and the large effect on behavior that the knowledge obtained even in just a short seminar appears to have, in my view the transaction costs of learning basic asset allocation and saving strategies would have to be implausibly large to deter a household from getting the information. It seems more plausible that households who have not taken a seminar do not *understand* the large potential payoff and the small cost of such a seminar.

William Even

Dean Maki's chapter adds to the growing literature examining the effect of financial education on saving behavior. Earlier work has established that financial education in high school or in the workplace increases saving; Maki's chapter extends this work by asking why it does. He proposes three possible answers. First, financial education may lower a person's discount rate. Second, it may alter a person's degree of risk aversion. Finally, it may improve a person's knowledge of the relevant choice set. Maki dismisses the first two explanations as unlikely and focuses instead on the role of improved financial knowledge.

One reason that this line of research is so important is that in the United States there is incredible heterogeneity in terms of wealth accumulation. Traditional economic models of saving explain relatively little of the variation in saving behavior. Venti and Wise, for example, find that differences in lifetime earnings and other factors that might influence saving explain less than one-fourth of the variation in asset accumulation among people approaching retirement.[1] They conclude that "differences in saving choices among households with similar lifetime earnings lead to vastly different levels of asset accumulation by the time retirement age approaches." Formation of policies to stimulate saving requires better knowledge of the factors that shape savings preferences. The research on the effect of financial education may be an important piece of the puzzle.

Maki argues that one possible way in which financial education could affect saving is by improving worker financial knowledge. The chapter shows that financial education increases the chance that a worker will know that stocks outperform bonds over long periods of time and that a worker will know about various features in his or her 401(k) plan. Maki admits that the empirical evidence is a necessary but not sufficient condition for claiming that financial education increases saving by improving worker financial knowledge.

The empirical analysis in Maki's chapter is relatively straightforward. I believe that there is fairly convincing evidence that financial education mandates increase workers' knowledge of relative returns on assets and the provisions of their 401(k) plan. I have a modest reservation about the analysis of how the availability of financial education in the workplace affects workers' knowledge. Given that many workers did not know what type of pension they were offered, it seems equally plausible that they could be unaware of the availability of financial education. Workers who intend to save would be more likely to know about their 401(k) plan and seek out information about financial education. If this is

---

1. Venti and Wise (2001).

true, misreports on the availability of financial education could create an upward bias in the estimated effect of financial education on pension knowledge. This caveat aside, I believe that there is strong evidence that financial education is associated with improved financial knowledge.

While the empirical analysis in Maki's chapter suggests that financial education improves knowledge of asset returns and pension plan design, it is not yet safe to conclude that this is the way in which savings are increased. Bernheim points out that a positive correlation between financial knowledge and financial wealth could be the result of individuals acquiring economic knowledge only after accumulating wealth so that they can manage their resources more competently.[2] For example, it is possible that financial education merely convinces people that saving is vital to having a comfortable retirement and thus induces them to save more. Having made a decision to save more, they have a greater incentive to seek out information on asset returns and the features of their 401(k) plan.

Knowing why financial education increases saving is vital to designing a program to stimulate saving. If improved worker knowledge regarding asset returns and pension plans is the reason saving increases, then programs should provide such information. If the effect on saving comes through another channel—for example, the importance of saving to a comfortable retirement—the emphasis could be placed elsewhere.

While improved financial knowledge could be the reason that financial education increases saving, I remain somewhat skeptical. The bulk of the evidence from the existing literature suggests that financial education increases saving for those groups that ordinarily have low saving rates but that it has little or no effect on the saving of those with high saving rates. In order for misinformation to cause people to save too little, it would have to be systematically biased in one direction. For example, if all misinformed people believe that Social Security will be more generous than it really is, then they will save too little. However, I am not aware of any basis for the belief that misinformation is systematically skewed in a way that causes too little saving.

There are alternative explanations of the effect of financial education on saving. One possibility is that financial education simplifies saving decisions. Madrian and Shea provide evidence that the default option for employee participation in a 401(k) can have large effects on worker saving.[3] Originally, the default option was that the employee contributed nothing to the pension plan; the firm then switched to "automatic enrollment," with a default contribution of 3 percent of salary to a money market fund. Even though workers could opt out of the 401(k) plan, the switch to automatic enrollment caused an enormous

2. Bernheim (1999).
3. Madrian and Shea (2001).

change in worker participation: participation rates among recent hires increased from 37 to 86 percent as a result of the switch. The authors concluded that "automatic enrollment appears to be a much more effective means of increasing 401(k) participation than either employer-provided financial education or increasing the 401(k) employer match."

An interesting question is why such a simple change in the default option would cause such an enormous change in employee behavior. Madrian and Shea propose that the reason is that saving decisions are complicated, and they cite several studies supporting the hypothesis that people tend to procrastinate when they have to make complex decisions. Automatic enrollment may simplify the decision for employees and thereby reduce procrastination. Consistent with procrastination being the problem for low savers is the fact that automatic enrollment increased saving among the most among recent hires. It is also worth noting that this effect on saving behavior **is** consistently in one direction. Those who have procrastinated in making their decision begin saving, and those who already have made the decision to save continue to do so. This matches the pattern discovered for the effect of financial education.

Duflo and Saez provide additional evidence that benchmarks could be important, finding peer effects in the participation and investment decisions of employees.[4] According to their results, workers' participation and investment behavior is influenced by the behavior of other workers in their department. Co-worker effects are larger for workers who are peers—for example, of the same gender or age. Possible explanations for the peer effect are that workers imitate each other's saving behavior or that they share information with each other.

To further emphasize alternative channels for the effect of financial education on saving, it is worth noting that workplace financial education generally covers three topics. According to a survey of 401(k) plans described in Bernheim (1998), 97 percent of workplace financial education programs cover principles of asset allocation, 83 percent discuss retirement income needs, and 79 percent cover retirement income sources. Unfortunately, there is no evidence indicating which of these components has the most important influence on saving behavior.

In conclusion, if financial education programs are to be used to improve saving, further research needs to be done. First, we need to improve our understanding of which components of financial education are most important. For example, is establishing a saving target the key to improved saving? Or would time be better spent on the principles of asset allocation and the importance of diversification? Second, research needs to improve our ability to identify beforehand those students or workers who will benefit most from these programs. For example, given the aforementioned role of peer effects, should certain types of schools be targeted? Should students who choose the college prep track in high

4. Duflo and Saez (2002).

school be exempted from such courses? Will financial education programs be of greatest value to firms with a low-skill work force?

Overall, I agree with Maki's assertion that financial education has the potential to improve the savings of a significant portion of the U.S. population and has some advantages over tax incentives for saving. At this point, however, it is not clear that financial education mandates would be cost effective. More research needs to be done to determine what particular aspects of financial education increase saving and to identify the workers who will benefit most from financial education.

References

Bayer, Patrick J., B. Douglas Bernheim, and John Karl Scholz. 1996. "The Effects of Financial Education in the Workplace: Evidence from a Survey of Employers." Working Paper 5655. Cambridge, Mass.: National Bureau of Economic Research (July).

Bernheim, B. Douglas. 1996. "The Merrill Lynch Baby Boom Retirement Index: Update '96." Stanford University, Department of Economics.

———. 1997. "Rethinking Saving Incentives." In *Fiscal Policy: Lessons from Economic Research,* edited by Alan J. Auerbach, 259–311. MIT Press.

———. 1998. "Financial Illiteracy, Education, and Retirement Saving." In *Living with Defined Contribution Pensions: Remaking Responsibility for Retirement,* edited by Olivia S. Mitchell and Sylvester J. Schieber, 38–68. University of Pennsylvania Press.

———. 1999. "Taxation and Saving." Working Paper 7061. Cambridge, Mass.: National Bureau of Economic Research (March).

Bernheim, B. Douglas, and Daniel M. Garrett. 2000. "The Determinants and Consequences of Financial Education in the Workplace: Evidence from a Survey of Households." Stanford University.

Bernheim, B. Douglas, Daniel M. Garrett, and Dean M. Maki. 2001. "Education and Saving: The Long-Term Effects of High School Financial Curriculum Mandates." *Journal of Public Economics* 80 (June): 435–65.

Bernheim, B. Douglas, and John Karl Scholz, 1993. "Private Saving and Public Policy." In *Tax Policy and the Economy,* edited by James M. Poterba, 7, 73–110. Cambridge, Mass.: National Bureau of Economic Research and MIT Press.

Clark, Robert L., and Sylvester J. Schieber. 1998. "Factors Affecting Participation Rates and Contribution Levels in 401(k) Plans." In *Living with Defined Contribution Pensions,* edited by Mitchell and Schieber, 69–97.

Duflo, Esther, and Emmanuel Saez. 2002. "Participation and Investment Decisions in a Retirement Plan: The Influence of Colleagues' Choices." *Journal of Public Economics* 85 (1): 121–48.

Engen, Eric M., William G. Gale, and John Karl Scholz. 1996. "The Illusory Effects of Saving Incentives on Saving." *Journal of Economic Perspectives* 10 (4): 113–38.

Highsmith, Robert J. 1989. *A Survey of State Mandates for Economics Instruction.* New York: Joint Council on Economic Education.

Ibbotson Associates. 2000. *Stocks, Bonds, Bills, and Inflation 2000 Yearbook.* Chicago: Ibbotson Associates.

Madrian, Brigitte C., and Dennis F. Shea. 2001. "The Power of Suggestion: Inertia in 401(k) Participation and Savings Behavior." *Quarterly Journal of Economics* 116 (4): 1149–87.

Mandell, Lewis. 1998. *Our Vulnerable Youth: The Financial Literacy of American 12th Graders.* Washington: Jump$tart Coalition for Personal Financial Literacy.

Mayer, Robert N. 1989. *The Consumer Movement: Guardians of the Marketplace.* Boston: Twayne Publishers.

Muller, Leslie A. 2000a. "Investment Choice in Defined Contribution Plans: The Effects of Retirement Education on Asset Allocation." Social Security Administration, Division of Policy Evaluation (November).

———. 2000b. "Retirement Education and Pension Preservation: Does Retirement Education Teach Individuals to Save Pension Distributions?" Social Security Administration, Division of Policy Evaluation (November).

National Institute for Consumer Education. 1994. *Consumer Approach to Investing: A Teaching Guide.* Ypsilanti: Eastern Michigan University.

Poterba, James M., Steven F. Venti, and David A. Wise. 1996. "How Retirement Saving Programs Increase Saving."*Journal of Economic Perspectives* 10 (4), 91–112.
Venti, Steven F., and David A. Wise. 2001. "Choice, Chance, and Wealth Dispersion at Retirement." In *Aging Issues in the United States and Japan,* edited by S. Ogura, T. Tachibanaki, and David Wise. University of Chicago Press.

5

Life-Cycle Saving, Limits on Contributions to DC Pension Plans, and Lifetime Tax Benefits

JAGADEESH GOKHALE, LAURENCE J. KOTLIKOFF,
AND MARK J. WARSHAWSKY

I t is now more than a quarter of a century since the Employee Retirement Income Security Act (ERISA) was passed. ERISA regulates employer-sponsored
tax-favored vehicles for retirement saving, including defined contribution (DC)
pension plans; a key element of the law's provisions governing DC plans is to
limit the amount of tax-deductible contributions. In both nominal and, especially, inflation-adjusted terms, those limits have been tightened over the years.
Rules current in 2000 allow workers and their employers to contribute a combined total of 25 percent of a worker's earnings or $30,000, whichever is less, to
a DC plan each year; of that total, the employee can contribute no more than
$10,500.[1] For 401(k)–type plans in which the employer makes no contribution,
$10,500 becomes the total limit. If the employer does not sponsor any plan, a
worker is limited to an annual contribution of $2,000 to an individual retire-
ment account (IRA).[2]

We thank Mary DiCarlantonio and Shana Neiditch for research assistance and William Gale,
Leslie Papke, Annika Sundén, Peter Weinberg, David Wise, and others for helpful comments.
Laurence Kotlikoff thanks the National Institute of Aging for research support. The findings and
views expressed in this chapter are those of the authors and not necessarily those of Boston University, the National Bureau of Economic Research, TIAA-CREF, or the Federal Reserve Bank of
Cleveland.
1. Internal Revenue Code, sections 415 (c)(1) and 402 (g).
2. Internal Revenue Code, section 408 (a).

146

In recent years, Congress has raised the limits on tax-deductible contributions to retirement accounts. And it is currently contemplating even further increases in the limits. Policymakers' interest in the issue is understandable: more and more workers are saving for retirement primarily through DC and IRA plans, and limiting their contributions raises concerns about the adequacy of retirement savings. Those concerns are consistent with the results of studies by Warshawsky and Ameriks (2000), Bernheim, Forni, Gokhale, and Kotlikoff (2000), and others suggesting that many Americans are saving too little to sustain their current standard of living into old age and with the fact that many workers are not covered by pension plans.

Would raising the joint employer-employee contribution limit in DC plans increase saving for retirement? Or is the real issue raising the limits on employee or IRA contributions or the limits for older workers—or simply getting employers and employees to set up retirement plans if they do not have one or to increase their contributions if they are contributing less than the allowed maximum? To encourage full participation in retirement plans, the government does provide a significant tax benefit for most households: contributions are tax deductible. Although withdrawals are taxable, no federal or state tax on capital income accrues before withdrawal.[3] Unlike with saving outside a retirement account, the deferral of tax payments gives workers an interest-free loan on the taxes they otherwise would have paid on the original contribution plus all capital income subsequently earned on the contribution. As a result, the capital income component of income tax is effectively eliminated for income earned and invested in retirement accounts.

Because poor and low-income workers are assessed low rates of income tax and have significantly more of their preretirement earnings replaced by Social Security benefits, the DC joint employer-employee contribution limits seem to have been set with middle-, upper-middle-, and high-income groups in mind. The goal of the joint limit appears to be to permit middle- and upper-middle-income households to save significant sums on a tax-favored basis in order to fund a comfortable retirement, while limiting the tax break available to the rich. That approach also limits short-term losses in aggregate tax revenues for the federal government.[4]

3. This discussion ignores Roth IRAs.
4. DC contribution limits also constrain the amount of tax arbitrage possible under the system. Tax arbitrage, in this context, refers to borrowing on a tax-deductible basis and using the proceeds to make contributions. Borrowing on a tax-deductible basis means that interest paid on such borrowing is tax deductible. Because, as just indicated, interest earned on funds invested in DC plans is effectively untaxed, tax arbitrage here amounts to borrowing on an after-tax basis and lending on a pretax basis. Current tax law permits deducting interest payments only on mortgages and home equity loans, and therefore such tax arbitrage is constrained by the degree to which DC contributors can leverage their homes.

This chapter addresses three questions related to limits on DC contributions: The first is whether employees' personal economic situation would permit them to contribute more to defined contribution plans if no statutory limit on tax-deductible contributions existed—in other words, whether those limits are "binding." The second concerns the extent of the tax benefit of participating in a DC plan. The third concerns the dependence of the amount of the tax benefit on the level of lifetime income. Specifically, we determine whether stylized households that differ by age, level of lifetime earnings, past pension coverage, planned retirement date, and so on would want to contribute more than the allowed maximum amounts. We also measure, as a percent of lifetime consumption, the lifetime tax benefit to households from participating in a DC plan and show how that benefit varies by level of lifetime earnings. Stated differently, we calculate the percentage increase in the present value of households' lifetime consumption resulting from their participation in DC plans.

We ran a number of stylized households through Economic Security Planner (ESPlanner), a sophisticated planning model of optimal saving and consumption over the life cycle, and used the model to address the questions posed above, and, more broadly, to discuss current federal government policy toward retirement saving.

We found that the statutory limits were binding on older middle-income households that started their pension saving program late in life, households that planned to retire early, single-earner households, households that could borrow freely, and households that had rapid rates of real wage growth. Most households with high levels of earnings, regardless of age or situation, also were constrained by the contribution limits. Lower- or middle-income two-earner households that anticipated modest real earnings growth were unlikely to be able to borrow significant amounts for most of their preretirement years because of the costs of paying a mortgage and raising children who go to college; these households were not in a position to contribute the 25 percent of earnings allowed to them and their employer as a contribution to DC plans. Some of these middle-income households, however, are constrained by the $10,500 limit on elective employee contributions to 401(k) plans if they have access to only those plans and if their employers make no pension contributions for them.

The constraint on borrowing faced by many lower- and middle-income Americans means that their contributions to DC plans come at the price of lower consumption when they are young and with the benefit of higher consumption when they are old. In one scenario that we considered, if the household consistently contributed 10 percent of salary to a DC plan that earned a 4 percent real return, it consumed more than twice as much when the householders were old than it did when they were young.

The tax benefit of participating in a DC plan can be significant. Assuming annual contribution rates at the average of the maximum levels allowed by employers and assuming a 4 percent real return on DC and non-DC assets, the benefit was 1.9 percent for two-earner households earning $25,000 per year, 3.5 percent for those earning $100,000 per year, and 9.8 percent for those earning $300,000 per year. Contribution limits effectively limit the benefit only in the highest ranges of the household earnings distribution. The extent of the benefit also is quite sensitive to the assumed rate of return on DC and non-DC assets.

The significant value of the DC tax benefit combined with the distortions it creates in age-consumption patterns suggests the need to reexamine the structure of the tax preference provided to defined contribution plans. In theory, limits on contributions to DC plans should be lifetime limits and should take into account a household's contribution history and the extent of other provisions made for funding retirement. In practice, the administrative requirements and costs of an individualized approach are extremely high; therefore, simple, one-size-fits-all rules must be designed. A practical implication of our research results is that consideration should be given to increasing contribution limits for older workers, unconstrained by nondiscrimination requirements. Similarly, increasing the 401(k) and 403(b) contribution limits also seems appropriate, as they are a potential constraint to saving for many upper-middle-income households. Furthermore, modification of the nondiscrimination requirements to easily allow age-weighted DC plans may be warranted given the general indication that savings should be more concentrated in the ages just before retirement. And fairness would seem to dictate that all workers should share the benefits of participation in tax-advantaged savings plans regardless of whether their employer sponsors a pension plan and regardless of how much the employer contributes, if anything. Under current conditions, raising the limits on tax-deductible IRA contributions could achieve more uniform treatment of employees.

Limits on DC Contributions

Section 415 was added to the Internal Revenue Code by ERISA in 1974, limiting contributions to DC plans to $25,000 or 25 percent of compensation, whichever amount was less. The dollar limitations were adjusted for inflation, and by 1982 they had risen to $45,475. The law was amended, reducing the contribution limit to $30,000, effective in 1983.[5] Although the new limit was supposed to be adjusted for inflation after 1986, legislation passed in 1984 froze adjustments through 1988.[6]

The Tax Reform Act of 1986 governed policy current in 2000. Under the act, contributions for and by an employee to all DC plans maintained by an employer may not exceed $30,000 (or, if greater, they may not exceed one-quarter of the

---

5. The Tax Equity and Fiscal Responsibility Act of 1982, P.L. 97-248, section 235(a)(2).
6. The Deficit Reduction Act of 1984, P.L. 98-369, section 15 (a).

Figure 5-1.   *Contribution Limits to DC Plans: Nominal and Inflation-Adjusted*

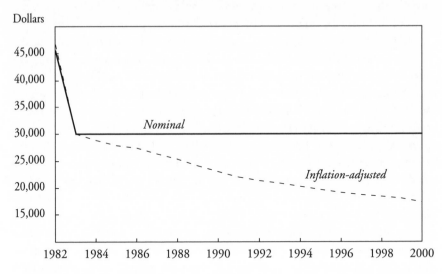

Source: From nominal contribution limits as described in text and the Consumer Price Index.

benefit dollar limit for defined benefit plans) or 25 percent of the participant's compensation, whichever is less. The Tax Equity and Fiscal Responsibility Act of 1982 set the dollar limit for defined benefit (DB) plan benefits at $90,000 through 1986 and the Deficit Reduction Act of 1984 froze that limit until 1988. The law provides that any inflation adjustment that is not a multiple of $5,000 will be rounded to the next lower multiple of $5,000.[7] Hence even though the DB limit reached $135,000 in 2000, the dollar limit for DC plans still remained $30,000. The DC limit will increase to $35,000 in 2001, as the DB limit increases to $140,000.

Figure 5-1 shows contribution limits to DC plans since 1982 in nominal and inflation-adjusted terms. Inflation eroded the contribution limit, in July 1983 dollars, from $30,000 to about $17,500 in 2000. If the $30,000 limit of 1983 had been allowed to keep pace with inflation, it would have been almost $52,000 in 2000; if the $45,475 limit in effect in 1982 had been allowed to keep pace with inflation, it would have been almost $79,000 in 2000. Effectively, contribution limits to DC plans have been progressively tightened for the last two decades.

In addition to the overall limit on joint employer-employee contributions to the lesser of $30,000 and 25 percent of salary, there are separate limits on employee contributions. In 2000, employee pretax (elective) contributions were

7. Internal Revenue Code, section 415 (d).

limited to a total of $10,500 for 401(k) and 403(b) plans, and they were counted toward allowable elective contributions to Simplified Employee Pensions (SEPs), section 457 state and local government plans, tax-deferred 403(b) annuities, and 501(c)(18) trusts.[8]

Contributions may be further restricted by nondiscrimination rules in sections 401(a) 4, 401(k), and 401(m) under which a DC pension plan, in the actual experience of the plan every year, generally cannot allow higher-paid workers to receive higher contribution rates than lower-paid workers. Furthermore, an employer is limited in making tax-deductible contributions to a DC plan it sponsors to 15 percent of the aggregate compensation of the employees covered by the plan.[9] An additional contribution limit known as the maximum exclusion allowance (MEA) applies to 403(b) plans. It applies to both employer and employee contributions and generally limits contributions to 20 percent of an employee's compensation multiplied by the number of years of service with the employer minus any amounts previously contributed to a retirement plan.[10]

The current maximum total annual new contribution permitted to IRAs (including traditional deductible IRAs, Roth IRAs, and nondeductible IRAs) is $2,000 or 100 percent of an individual's compensation, whichever is less; that limit has been in place since 1981. Starting in 1997, the limit for married couples was gradually increased to $4,000 ($2,000 per spouse). An individual may make deductible contributions to an IRA if neither the individual nor the individual's spouse is an active participant in an employer-sponsored pension plan. If an individual or a spouse is an active participant, the $2,000 deduction limit is phased out for single taxpayers with adjusted gross incomes of more than $42,000 and for married taxpayers with adjusted gross incomes of more than $62,000.[11]

A substantial overhaul of the tax rules governing retirement plans was contemplated as part of the Taxpayer Relief Act of 2000, which was passed by the House of Representatives in October 2000 following several years of discussions and the introduction of various bills containing pension reform provisions. The act was approved overwhelmingly by the House of Representatives, but dropped by the Senate in response to a threatened presidential veto.

---

8. A special catch-up election under 403(b) plans applies to employees of educational organizations, home health service agencies, health and welfare service agencies, and church organizations. It applies only to employees with fifteen or more years of service, and it may increase the section 402(g) limit by $3,000 in any given year. The total of such additional elective deferrals can never exceed $15,000 over the employee's lifetime. We did not consider this special catch-up elective deferral for the purposes of this chapter.

9. Internal Revenue Code, section 404 (a)(3)(AXi).

10. Internal Revenue Code, section 403 (b)(2)(A).

11. See Internal Revenue Code, section 219 (g), for information regarding IRA contribution limits.

The act would have raised the limit on combined employer-employee contributions for DC plans to $40,000, subject to inflation indexing in $1,000 increments in future years. The limit on elective employee contributions to 401(k), 403(b), and 457 plans would have been raised to $15,000 over five years, subject to indexing in $500 increments thereafter. And the annual contribution limit for IRAs would have been raised over three years to $5,000, subject thereafter to indexing in $500 increments. The act also would have increased the percentage of earnings limit for DC plans from 25 to 100 percent and repealed the 403(b) MEA calculation.

Finally, the act would have permitted workers aged 50 and older to make additional annual "catch-up" contributions to DC plans of up to $5,000 (phased in over five years), subject to indexing in $500 increments. Those additional contributions would not have been subject to any other contribution limit, but they would have been subject to nondiscrimination tests.

It is important to bear in mind that the effective limits on workers' retirement saving are determined by their employers' decisions as well as by statute. Employers who offer no DC plan are, in effect, setting their workers' DC contribution limits to zero and leaving their workers only the option of saving through IRAs, which have very low contribution limits. At any point in time, less than half of the private sector work force has access to a DC or DB plan.[12] As Poterba, Venti, and Wise document, recent growth in DC plans had raised the share of the U.S. workforce covered by such plans to more than 40 percent by 1993.[13] Nearly three-quarters of workers with 401(k)-type plans reported that they considered that plan their primary retirement plan. At least one-fifth of all participants in 401(k)-type plans in 1993 were enrolled in plans with no employer contributions, and about 35 percent of workers at firms sponsoring those plans either could not or did not participate.[14]

Employers who offer a DC plan with an employer match of employee contributions of up to, say, 5 percent of pay are, perhaps unwittingly, suggesting that their workers contribute no more than 5 percent of their salary. In 1997, the modal employer match was 50 percent on employee contributions of up to 6 percent of pay.[15] The average employee elective contribution to those plans was 7.1 percent of compensation.[16]

The maximum pretax employee contribution allowed by employers in saving and thrift plans in 1997 averaged 13.7 percent of pay; the maximum contribution rate allowed by employers ranged from 5 percent or less to 20 percent, with

12. U.S. Department of Labor, Pension and Welfare Benefits Administration (1999, table E4).
13. Poterba, Venti, and Wise (1999, table 1, p. 33).
14. Employee Benefit Research Institute (1997, tables 12.3 and 12.4).
15. See U.S. Department of Labor, Bureau of Labor Statistics (1999, table 152, p. 121).
16. See Employee Benefit Research Institute (1997, table 12.3).

the mode at 15 percent.[17] Apparently many plan sponsors are influenced by their workers' preferences as well as by the operation of nondiscrimination requirements and other legal factors in setting maximum contribution rates.

Why do employees who have DC plans not contribute to the maximum extent possible? The reasons given by 401(k) participants in the 1996 Retirement Confidence Survey were that they could not afford to save, that they were too young to start saving, that they were saving for a house or for their children's college education, and that it was difficult to withdraw funds.[18] The survey also generated the following distribution of principal factors cited as determining the amount of participants' 401(k) contributions: the maximum amount that their employer would match (21 percent), the maximum that they could afford to contribute (31 percent), the maximum amount that they were allowed to contribute (30 percent), the amount that they determined that they should contribute (16 percent), and other factors (2 percent).[19]

ESPlanner

The decision of when and how much to contribute to a DC plan involves a complex set of economic factors. First, workers have to consider their current federal and state income-tax brackets to assess their immediate tax saving from making DC contributions. Second, they have to project their future federal and state income-tax brackets to assess the rate at which their future DC withdrawals will be taxed. For some households, contributing to DC plans smoothes the time-path of taxable income—that is, lowers taxable income when workers are young and raises it when they are older—and lowers the levels of marginal tax rates they face, on average, as they age.

A third factor is workers' ability to contribute without reducing their current consumption. Workers who are in a position to borrow as much as they want can perfectly smooth their consumption over time regardless of how much they contribute to a DC plan; those who are not have to reduce their consumption when they are young in order to finance their contributions.[20] Whether a worker faces borrowing constraints depends on his or her household's projected growth in future income and its "off-the-top" expenditures on housing, college, and other special expenditures.

17. See U.S. Department of Labor, Bureau of Labor Statistics (1999, table 150, p. 120).
18. Employee Benefit Research Institute (1997, chart 13.1).
19. Employee Benefit Research Institute (1997, chart 13.2).
20. This will alter their entire time-path of non-tax-favored asset accumulation, which, in turn, will mean a different time-path of income taxes than would otherwise have been the case. It also leaves workers with a higher living standard in retirement than in young adulthood. For such workers, participation in DC plans, rather than smoothing marginal tax rates, may do the opposite because it leaves them with so much more taxable income in old age than would otherwise have been the case.

A fourth factor influencing the amount of the benefits gained from participating in and contributing to a DC plan is Social Security, specifically its progressive provision of benefits and regressive taxation of payroll. As documented in Gokhale and others (2001), the Social Security system represents a lifetime net benefit to the very poor but a lifetime net tax to low-income, middle-income, and high-income households; the rate of lifetime net taxation is highest for those with middle incomes. In addition to affecting the level of lifetime consumption differentially for different households, Social Security differentially affects different households' liquidity. That arises, in part, because Social Security's benefit replacement rate is higher for low contributors and, in part, because the program's payroll-tax ceiling makes payroll-tax contributions a smaller share of earnings the higher earnings are above the ceiling.

Because the amount of consumption that can be financed out of earnings depends on Social Security's net lifetime taxation and because the denominator in the DC tax-benefit rate is the household's level of consumption, the DC benefit rate also will be influenced by Social Security. In raising the lifetime consumption of the very poor, Social Security lowers their DC benefit rate. It does the opposite for those with higher incomes, especially for those who are in the middle class.

Taking into account the previously mentioned factors requires a life-cycle model that incorporates the fine details of federal and state income taxes and Social Security taxes and benefits. It also requires a model that considers housing and special expenditures and recognizes household borrowing constraints.[21] ESPlanner meets those requirements. ESPlanner smoothes a household's living standard over its life cycle to the extent permitted by its capacity to borrow. As described in the appendix, the program has highly precise federal and state income tax calculators and Social Security tax and benefit calculators. The income tax calculators determine whether households should itemize their deductions and place households in their appropriate tax brackets. They also properly deduct DC contributions and include DC withdrawals in determining taxable income.[22] The program also takes into account a variety of additional factors involved in life-cycle consumption planning, including the nonfungible nature of housing, bequest plans, and the desire of households to make special off-the-top expenditures on college tuition and so forth. Finally, ESPlanner recognizes that a household's expenditures do not directly translate into its standard

---

21. "Borrowing constraints" refers to a household's inability to get credit on the security of its future anticipated earnings, for example, through a credit card or an unsecured line of credit. Liquidity often is affected by that as well as by the inability to sell assets (whether financial or real) to finance consumption. The term "borrowing contraints" is more appropriate for the experiments considered in this chapter.

22. See Gokhale, Kotlikoff, and Warshawsky (2001) for a comparison of ESPlanner to more conventional retirement planning software.

of living. Adjustments are made for household composition and household economies of scale—the fact that people can live more cheaply together than apart.[23] To be more precise, ESPlanner has a household provide for children until they reach age 19, and it considers that children may cost more or less than adults and that the relative costs of children can vary by age. It also adjusts for the number of adult equivalents—that is, how much a couple saves by living together rather than apart—based on a user-specified degree of economies of scale in shared living.

ESPlanner's principal outputs are recommended time-paths of consumption expenditures, taxable savings, and term-life insurance holdings (for each spouse in the case of married households). All outputs are displayed in current-year dollars. Consumption in this context is everything the household gets to spend after paying its off-the-top expenses—for housing, special expenditures, life insurance premiums, taxes, and net contributions to tax-favored accounts. As mentioned, the recommended amount of consumption expenditures varies from year to year in response to changes in the household's composition. It also rises when the household moves from being borrowing constrained to being unconstrained. Finally, recommended household consumption will change over time if users specify that they want to change their living standard. For example, if users specify that they want a 10 percent higher living standard after a certain year in the future, the software will incorporate that preference in making its recommendations, provided that it does not violate a borrowing constraint.

ESPlanner's recommended taxable saving in a particular year equals the household's total income (asset plus nonasset income) in that year minus that year's sum of

—recommended spending on consumption and insurance premiums

—specified spending on housing and special expenditures

—taxes

—net contributions to tax-favored accounts (contributions less withdrawals).

Given the household's data inputs, preferences, and borrowing constraints, ESPlanner recommends the highest and smoothest possible living standard over time, leaving the household with zero terminal assets.[24]

We used ESPlanner to determine how much households should save in the absence of a DC pension plan and then compared the recommended amount

23. From the perspective of economic theory, the household is viewed as maximizing a Leontief intertemporal utility function with year-specific time-preference and demographic weights subject to borrowing constraints and nonnegativity constraints on life insurance.

24. ESPlanner's recommendations for annual term insurance are either positive or zero. If recommended term insurance is positive for a particular person (the household head or, if married, spouse) in a particular year and if that person dies at the end of that year, the surviving household will have precisely the same living standard as it would have had if the person had not died. If the person's recommended insurance in a particular year is zero and the person dies in that year, the living standard of the surviving household will be the same or higher.

Table 5-1. *Total and Out-of-Pocket Saving Rate by Age and Annual Earnings with No Initial Assets*[a]

Earnings	Age				Maximum DC contribution rate
	25	*35*	*45*	*55*	
$25,000	19.4	26.7	37.0	54.5	25.0
$50,000	20.3	27.0	36.6	52.0	25.0
$100,000	20.4	26.3	34.6	48.1	25.0
$150,000	20.8	26.2	33.7	46.1	25.0
$200,000	20.7	29.0	35.8	46.7	25.0
$250,000	20.5	25.4	32.4	43.5	24.0
$300,000	20.3	27.9	34.3	44.4	20.0
$1,000,000	19.3	23.8	29.8	39.2	6.0

Source: Authors' calculations based on ESPlanner.

a. For a married couple with no children, no Social Security benefits, no earnings growth, and no housing. The total saving rate is defined as total saving divided by total income. The out-of-pocket saving rate is defined as total saving minus capital income divided by total labor earnings.

with the DC contribution limit. ESPlanner's recommended saving includes saving for education, saving for retirement, and saving to smooth the household's living standard before retirement. As indicated, ESPlanner considers a variety of key factors that influence actual saving decisions, but not all factors. The principal factor it ignores is uncertainty in earnings and rates of return. Hubbard, Skinner, and Zeldes (1995) conducted one of a number of theoretical and simulation studies that show that earnings uncertainty can raise a household's desired saving rate. Clearly then, optimal overall saving will be larger than saving recommended by ESPlanner.

Are Statutory Limits on Contributions to Defined Contribution Plans Binding?

Table 5-1 evaluates the DC limits for a Massachusetts household that has no Social Security benefits, no children, no life-cycle earnings growth, no housing, and no DB or DC pension account. It also assumes that the household's total earnings, which range in the table from $25,000 to $1 million per year, are divided equally between spouses; that each spouse works to age 65; that each spouse's maximum life expectancy is 95; that the household has no assets at the age the household is being considered; and that the household earns a 4 percent real return on its savings. The household has no access to any nonsecured borrowing, such as credit card debt. The household's desired standard of living remains flat over the life cycle; that assumption is conservative for purposes of public policy analysis because it does not demand that the government help finance through tax benefits for retirement savings a continually rising standard of living.

We start with this highly unrealistic household to illustrate how ESPlanner works and to make the strongest case possible that statutory limits on DC contributions can bind—that is, that households with Social Security benefits, children, life-cycle earnings growth, and a mortgage to pay will naturally save less when workers are young and more when they are old.

In table 5-1 and subsequent tables we consider two definitions of the household saving rate. The first is the "total" rate, which refers to total saving (including capital income) divided by total income (including capital income). The second is the "out-of-pocket" saving rate, which refers to total saving (excluding capital income) divided by total income (excluding capital income). The denominator in the out-of-pocket saving rate is simply current labor earnings, making it directly comparable to the 25 percent DC limit, which also is expressed in relation to labor earnings. Table 5-1 considers households at various initial ages when they are assumed to have no assets; therefore they have no capital income initially and total and out-of-pocket saving rates are identical.

The characterization in this analysis of poor, middle-income, and upper-income households and so on is somewhat informal because the households are stylized. A more formal frame of reference comes from ERISA itself; federal law, in establishing nondiscrimination requirements for pension plans, defines the dividing line between highly compensated and non–highly compensated workers as $85,000 in 2001.[25] That, of course, is for a single worker, not a household; therefore we might characterize two-earner households with an income of $150,000 or less as non–highly compensated, or not upper-income, households.

Table 5-1 delivers a number of findings. First, without Social Security and with the previously mentioned factors, smoothing consumption requires a very high rate of saving. A middle-income ($50,000 a year) couple needs to save 20.3 percent of its income at age 25; if the couple fails to save and arrives at age 35 with no assets, it then needs to save 27.0 percent of its income. At ages 45 and 55, the corresponding saving rates are 36.6 percent and 52.0 percent. Clearly, the 25 percent of earnings statutory limit on DC joint employer-employee contributions would bind for that household at ages 35, 45, and 55.[26] That is the second finding: DC joint contribution limits are more likely to bind for older households that have engaged in little or no past saving. Indeed, the DC limits

---

25. Internal Revenue Code, section 414 (q).

26. The fact that this saving would be done in tax-favored form would not change this statement. The tax benefits would raise recommended consumption when households are young and old but also lower taxes when young and raise them when old. The net impact would be more disposable income when young. Hence, if the household can save X percent when young in non-tax-favored form without feeling liquidity constraints, it can save an even higher percent in tax-favored form when young without being constrained.

Table 5-2. *Total Saving Rate by Age and Annual Earnings with Life-Cycle Assets*[a]

Earnings	Age 25	35	45	55
$25,000	19.4	23.2	27.1	30.9
$50,000	20.3	24.1	26.3	27.7
$100,000	20.4	22.3	23.8	24.9
$150,000	20.8	22.3	22.9	23.1
$200,000	20.7	21.2	21.7	22.0
$250,000	20.5	21.1	21.4	21.4
$300,000	20.3	20.6	20.8	21.0
$1,000,000	19.3	19.8	20.1	20.3

Source: Authors' calculations based on ESPlanner.

a. For a married couple with no children, no Social Security benefits, no earnings growth, and no housing. The total saving rate is defined as total saving divided by total income.

bind for all earnings classes at ages 35, 45, and 55, but only for the two highest-earning households at age 25. A third finding is that appropriate life-cycle saving rates can vary considerably across households with different levels of earnings, particularly at older ages, because of the progressivity of income taxes—specifically, the fact that higher-earning households face relatively higher income taxes during their working years than in old age. That is particularly true of high-earnings households that begin to accumulate wealth late in life.

Table 5-2 considers the same type of household but assumes that the households properly save for their retirement as they age. As comparison with table 5-1 indicates, that makes a huge difference in the rate at which those households need to save late in life. For example, households at 55 that earn $25,000 per year need to save only 30.9 percent of their wages if they have saved in the past, compared with 54.5 percent if they have not.

Proper saving over the life cycle dramatically reduces the potential for hitting the DC contribution limit. Table 5-3 shows the out-of-pocket saving rates that correspond to the total saving rates shown in table 5-2; out-of-pocket rates are the rates that relate directly to the evaluation of contribution limits. The statutory DC joint employee-employer contribution limit now binds only for the household earning $300,000 per year at age 25 and for the household earning $1 million per year at ages 25, 35, and 45. The limit on employee elective contributions would, however, constrain optimal contributions at earlier ages among the middle-income as well as the upper-income groups for workers whose employers contribute little or nothing on their behalf.

Comparison of tables 5-2 and 5-3 indicates how much of a household's required life-cycle saving can be achieved in middle age by simply saving the capital income earned on past savings. Compare, for example, the 23.1 percent

Table 5-3. *Out-of-Pocket Saving Rate by Age and Annual Earnings with Life-Cycle Assets*[a]

	Age				Maximum DC contribution rate
Earnings	25	35	45	55	
$25,000	19.4	16.6	12.9	7.8	25.0
$50,000	20.3	17.3	11.5	3.7	25.0
$100,000	20.4	15.6	9.6	2.0	25.0
$150,000	20.8	15.5	8.9	.3	25.0
$200,000	20.7	14.6	7.7	0.0	25.0
$250,000	20.5	14.5	7.4	−.4	24.0
$300,000	20.3	14.1	7.2	−.5	20.0
$1,000,000	19.3	13.5	6.9	−.4	6.0

Source: Authors' calculations based on ESPlanner.

a. For a married couple with no children, no Social Security benefits, no earnings growth, and no housing. The out-of-pocket saving rate is defined as total saving minus capital income divided by total labor earnings.

total saving rate recommended in table 5-2 for a 55-year-old household earning $150,000 with the corresponding 0.3 percent out-of-pocket rate in table 5-3. For that household, there is almost no need to actively save out of earnings to smooth its future living standard; all it needs to do is reinvest its capital income. For households with even higher earnings, the recommended out-of-pocket saving rates are slightly negative. The clear finding of table 5-3 is that for the types of households that we are examining that do their homework and save early in life, the DC limits will not bind unless the household has unusually high labor earnings when young or has an employer that makes little or no contribution on workers' behalf.

Table 5-4 turns to a more realistic set of households: The real earnings of both husband and wife grow by 1 percent per year each year prior to retirement. The households own their homes, have two children, and pay Social Security taxes and receive Social Security benefits. The first child is born when the couple is age 25, and the second when the couple is age 30. The market value of a couple's house is set at three times its annual labor earnings at age 25. The couple is assumed to purchase its house at age 25, to borrow at 8 percent, to put 20 percent down, and to take out a 30-year mortgage. Annual homeowner's insurance, property taxes, and maintenance are set at .17 percent, 1 percent, and 1 percent of house value, respectively. Each child is assumed to attend college for four years. A couple earning $25,000 per year is assumed to spend $7,500 per child for each year of college; college expense is set at $15,000 for couples earning $50,000 and $30,000 for couples earning $100,000 or $150,000. For couples earning $200,000 or more per year, annual college expenses are capped at

Table 5-4. *Total and Out-of-Pocket Saving Rate by Age and Annual Earnings with No Initial Assets at Age when Saving Begins*[a]

Earnings at age 25	Type of saving	Age							
		25	30	35	40	45	50	55	60
A. Saving beginning at age 25									
$25,000	Total	0	−3.1	.1	6.1	−8.9	−2.9	15.6	20.0
	Out-of-pocket	0	−3.1	.1	5.6	−10.0	−3.1	15.0	16.9
$50,000	Total	0	−2.8	.2	5.2	−8.7	−3.1	20.2	23.2
	Out-of-pocket	0	−3.0	.2	4.8	−9.7	−3.3	19.4	19.4
$100,000	Total	0	−2.7	1.5	5.5	−10.1	−3.2	21.8	24.6
	Out-of-pocket	0	−2.9	1.5	4.9	−11.4	−3.5	20.9[b]	20.5[b]
$150,000	Total	0	−2.4	0	2.5	−4.4	−.2	24.3	26.3
	Out-of-pocket	0	−2.6	0	2.4	−4.9	−.4	23.2[b]	21.6[b]
$200,000	Total	0	−2.8	0	1.9	−3.3	5.7	26.7	28.1
	Out-of-pocket	0	−3.0	0	1.8	−3.7	5.1	24.6[c]	22.2[c]
$250,000	Total	0	−2.8	0	2.8	.4	9.5	27.3	28.4
	Out-of-pocket	0	−3.0	0	2.6	−.3	8.1[b]	24.1[c]	21.4[c]
$300,000	Total	0	−2.9	0	3.7	3.1	11.6	27.6	28.5
	Out-of-pocket	0	−3.0	0	3.4	2.1	9.5[b]	23.7[c]	20.8[c]
$1,000,000	Total	0	−1.2	3.3	6.9	12.0	19.2	28.5	29.2
	Out-of-pocket	0	−1.6	2.8[b]	5.6[c]	9.4[c]	14.6[c]	21.7[c]	18.5[c]

Earnings at age 35	Type of saving	Age					
		35	40	45	50	55	60
B. Saving beginning at age 35							
$25,000	Total	2.1	4.9	−11.6	−3.6	14.5	19.0
	Out-of-pocket	2.1	4.1	−13.1	−3.9	14.3	16.2
$50,000	Total	.4	6.3	−10.4	−3.7	19.2	22.3
	Out-of-pocket	.4	5.8	−11.8	−4.0	18.7	18.7
$100,000	Total	1.4	6.5	−11.5	−3.9	21.4	24.3
	Out-of-pocket	1.4	5.9	−12.9	−4.3	20.7[b]	20.3[b]
$150,000	Total	0	3.2	−5.5	−2.0	24.7	26.8
	Out-of-pocket	0	3.1	−6.1	−2.2	23.8[b]	22.3[b]
$200,000	Total	0	2.2	−4.1	2.4	27.4	29.1
	Out-of-pocket	0	2.2	−4.5	2.0	25.9[c]	23.7[c]
$250,000	Total	0	1.0	−2.2	6.9	28.6	29.7
	Out-of-pocket	0	1.0	−2.4	6.2	26.4[c]	23.6[c]
$300,000	Total	0	1.6	.6	9.4	28.8	29.8
	Out-of-pocket	0	1.5	.1	8.2[b]	25.9[c]	23.1[c]
$1,000,000	Total	.4	5.0	10.2	17.4	29.7	30.5
	Out-of-pocket	.4	4.6[b]	8.6[c]	14.0[c]	24.3[c]	21.0[c]

		Age			
Earnings at age 45	Type of saving	45	50	55	60
C. Saving beginning at age 45					
$25,000	Total	0	−4.6	6.3	9.9
	Out-of-pocket	0	−5.0	6.3	8.6
$50,000	Total	0	−4.4	12.5	15.9
	Out-of-pocket	0	−4.8	12.5	13.6
$100,000	Total	0	−4.6	19.7	22.6
	Out-of-pocket	0	−5.1	19.3[b]	19.2[b]
$150,000	Total	0	−2.4	23.4	25.7
	Out-of-pocket	0	−2.6	22.7[b]	21.6[b]
$200,000	Total	0	−1.9	27.6	29.3
	Out-of-pocket	0	−2.0	26.8[c]	24.7[b]
$250,000	Total	0	2.6	28.9	30.5
	Out-of-pocket	0	2.2	27.5[c]	25.2[c]
$300,000	Total	0	5.5	29.6	30.9
	Out-of-pocket	0	5.0	27.8[c]	25.2[c]
$1,000,000	Total	7.3	14.9	31.4	32.3
	Out-of-pocket	7.3[c]	13.2[c]	27.9[c]	24.6[c]

		Age	
Earnings at age 55	Type of saving	55	60
D. Saving beginning at age 55			
$25,000	Total	0	0
	Out-of-pocket	0	0
$50,000	Total	9.2	13.1
	Out-of-pocket	9.2	11.3
$100,000	Total	19.8	22.8
	Out-of-pocket	19.8[b]	19.7[b]
$150,000	Total	24.4	26.8
	Out-of-pocket	24.4[b]	23.2[b]
$200,000	Total	28.8	30.3
	Out-of-pocket	28.8[c]	26.4[c]
$250,000	Total	30.9	32.3
	Out-of-pocket	30.9[c]	28.2[c]
$300,000	Total	32.1	33.2
	Out-of-pocket	32.1[c]	29.0[c]
$1,000,000	Total	35.4	36.4
	Out-of-pocket	35.4[c]	32.0[c]

Source: Authors' calculations based on ESPlanner.

a. For a married couple with two children, Social Security benefits, increasing earnings, and a house. The total saving rate is defined as total saving divided by total income. The out-of-pocket saving rate is defined as total saving minus capital income divided by total labor earnings.

b. Desired saving would be restricted by an elective contribution limit of $10,500 were the employer to make no contributions to the plan.

c. Desired saving would be restricted by a maximum DC contribution rate of 25 percent or a combined total contribution of $60,000.

$35,000. Nonsecured borrowing is constrained to zero, as in the simple cases above. Also as in previous tables, we assume for the time being that the household does not participate in a defined contribution plan.

Table 5-4 has four panels that differ with respect to the age at which the household begins saving. For example, panel C assumes the household begins saving at age 45 and, therefore, has no accumulated savings at age 45. Each panel shows the total and out-of-pocket saving rates at the age when the household begins to save and at subsequent ages. Consider first panel A, which examines the household at age 25. The table shows zero recommended saving at age 25, negative recommended saving at age 30, low recommended saving at age 35, modest recommended saving at age 40, negative recommended saving at ages 45 and 50 (except for the top-earning households), and high recommended saving at ages 55 and 60. What is going on there? The household is borrowing constrained when it starts out, then does some small saving before the arrival of the second child; those savings are spent down when the second child arrives. Between ages 25 and 40, the household is spending much of its resources paying down its mortgage; once the real value of the mortgage payments is lowered by the assumed annual 3 percent inflation, the household begins to save for the children's college education. At household ages 45 and 50, the children are in college, and we see the household dissaving as it makes tuition payments. When the children have completed college, the household can begin saving in earnest for retirement. Indeed, consider the $50,000-per-year household: its recommended out-of-pocket saving rates at age 55 and age 60 are both a substantial 19.4 percent.

This recommended life-cycle saving pattern may seem surprising, but it corresponds to what one observes empirically. As shown in Kotlikoff and Summers (1981), Gokhale, Kotlikoff, and Sabelhaus (1996), and Carroll and Summers (1991), longitudinal age-consumption and age-earnings profiles track each other very closely before late middle age, so that the *hump* saving that does occur accrues only in the 15 or so years before retirement.

In panel A we indicate with a superscript c cells in which the households would not be able to do all of their recommended saving through a defined contribution plan, assuming that the plan permitted the maximum allowable joint employer-employee contribution. As shown, the constraints bind only for the four top-earning households, and only in middle and late-middle age. We indicate with a superscript b cells in which the households would not be able to do all of their recommended saving if their employers made no contributions to their plans and if they were limited by the elective (individual) contribution limit. The elective contribution limit also binds only at older ages, but across a wider range of earnings.

In addition to the interesting pattern of recommended saving rates by age, panel A shows remarkable variation at a given age across households with different levels of earnings. At age 55, the household earning $25,000 a year needs to save 15.6 percent of its income to smooth its future living standard; in contrast, the household earning $150,000 a year needs to save 24.3 percent of its income. What explains the difference? The answer, for the most part, is Social Security, which replaces a much larger share of the lower-income household's earnings.

Panel B repeats the exercise, but considers the household at age 35 under the assumption that the household failed to save in the past. The pattern of recommended saving rates from age 35 onward is similar to that in panel A, but the magnitudes of recommended saving rates are somewhat different. For example, in panel A, the recommended out-of-pocket saving rate for the $50,000-a-year household at age 40 is 4.8 percent, compared with 5.8 percent in panel B. If the household waits until age 45 to start saving, the saving rates are again quite different, as shown in panel C. Now the recommended age-45 saving rates are zero, except for the highest-earning household, because the households, which have no assets, need to spend every free dollar on college tuition and mortgage payments. That is, they are borrowing constrained and so do the best that they can do, which in this case is to save nothing. Once the household's children are out of college, saving picks up, but at a generally lower rate than would have been the case had the household started saving before age 45. Waiting until later in life to save does not significantly alter the number of cells that violate the DC limits.

Sensitivity Analysis

Although we believe that the set of households examined in table 5-4 are closer to reality than the initial cases, they still are highly idealized in that they represent a remarkable degree of earnings stability and equality over a long horizon. In particular, while in table 5-4 we assume long and equal labor force participation at a steadily growing wage by both husband and wife, both implicitly having access to the opportunity to save through a pension plan, that still is an unusual occurrence. Hence, for policy analysis purposes, the sensitivity analysis in tables 5-5A, 5-5B, and 5-5C is particularly relevant.

Tables 5-5A, 5-5B, and 5-5C make alternative assumptions in recalculating out-of-pocket saving rates at ages 35, 45, and 55, assuming the households saved appropriately in the past. The alternative assumptions include a 6 percent rather than a 4 percent real return, extra initial assets equal to one year's earnings at age 25, no second child, maximum life expectancy of 100, 2 percent rather than 1 percent real growth in earnings, and retirement at age 60. Other alternative assumptions include no borrowing constraints, the decision by the wife to remain at home while the children are young, and paying state taxes in Indiana rather than Massachusetts. A final set of alternative assumptions assumes a two-thirds/one-third, rather than a fifty/fifty, split of earnings between the husband

Table 5-5A. *Age-35 Out-of-Pocket Saving Rate for Variants on the Base Case*[a] *with Age-35 Life-Cycle Assets*

Earnings at age 25	Base case	6 percent real return	Extra initial assets equal to first year's earnings	No second child	Maximum life span equals 100	2 percent growth in labor income[b]	Retirement at age 60	No borrowing constraint	Wife at home with children for 15 years[c]	Live in Indiana	Earnings split: 2/3 husband-1/3 wife[d]	Husband earns total income[e]	1 percent growth in standard of living until retirement	Maximum DC contribution rate
$25,000	.1	0	-4.4	0	.2	0	0	-8.3	0	0	0	.1	1.7	25.0
$50,000	.2	0	-4.9	0	.2	0	.1	-5.8	0	0	.1	.3	1.4	25.0
$100,000	1.5	1.3	-4.6	.9	1.5	0	2.5	-2.8	0	1.3	1.4	1.4	2.0	25.0
$150,000	0	0	-5.3	0	0	0	1.1	-2.9	0	0	0	0	2.0	25.0
$200,000	0	0	-4.9	1.3	0	0	4.3	-.3	0	0	0	1.0	4.0	25.0
$250,000	0	0	-4.4	2.4	.6	0	4.7	.3	0	0	0	1.4	4.3	21.7
$300,000	0	0	-3.8	3.1	1.4	0	5.2	.7	0	0	0	1.7	4.7	18.1
$1,000,000	2.8[f]	0	-1.8	5.9[g]	4.0[f]	0	7.1[g]	2.9[f]	0	2.7[f]	2.9[f]	3.2[g]	6.3[g]	5.4

Source: Authors' calculations based on ESPlanner.

a. Couple with two children, Social Security benefits, increasing earnings, and housing.

b. Maximum DC contribution rates for 2 percent growth in labor income scenarios are 25, 25, 25, 25, 24.6, 19.7, 16.4, and 4.9 for the respective earning categories.

c. Maximum DC contribution rates for wife at home scenarios are 25, 25, 25, 25, 25, 20.0, and 10.8 for the respective earning categories.

d. Maximum DC contribution rates for earnings split scenarios are 25, 25, 25, 25, 21.9, 19.2, 17.4, and 5.4 for the respective earning categories.

e. Maximum DC contribution rates for husband earning all income scenarios are 25, 25, 25, 18.1, 13.6, 10.9, 9.1, and 2.7 for the respective earning categories.

f. Desired saving would be restricted by an elective contribution limit of $10,500 if the employer were to make no contributions to the plan.

g. Desired saving would be restricted by a maximum DC contribution rate of 25 percent, combined total contribution of $60,000, or an annual contribution of $10,500 to a 401(k) plan per person.

Table 5-5B. *Age-45 Out-of-Pocket Saving Rate for Variants on the Base Case[a] with Age-45 Life-Cycle Assets*

							Variants							
Earnings at age 25	Base case	6 percent real return	Extra initial assets equal to first year's earnings	No second child	Maximum life span equals 100	2 percent growth in labor income[b]	Retirement at age 60	No borrowing constraint	Wife at home with children for 15 years[c]	Live in Indiana	Earnings split: 2/3 husband-1/3 wife[d]	Husband earns total income[e]	1 percent growth in standard of living until retirement	Maximum DC contribution rate
$25,000	-10.0	-10.3	-13.5	-8.5	-10.1	-4.6	-10.0	-14.4	-9.7	-9.9	-9.9	-10.1	-14.5	25.0
$50,000	-9.7	-9.9	-13.3	-8.6	-9.7	-5.6	-9.6	-13.3	-9.5	-9.4	-9.7	-9.9	-13.6	25.0
$100,000	-11.4	-11.6	-15.3	-9.7	-11.4	-5.9	-10.7	-13.0	-10.4	-11.1	-11.3	-11.2	-15.1	25.0
$150,000	-4.9	-5.0	-6.9	-3.7	-4.9	-1.9	-2.9	-5.3	-5.3	-4.6	-4.7	-4.6	-5.8	25.0
$200,000	-3.7	-3.8	-5.9	-.5	-3.0	-1.0	-.8	-2.4	-4.1	-3.5	-3.5	-1.9	-4.4	24.6
$250,000	-.3	-1.7	-2.9	2.9	.5	1.0	2.2	-.9	0	0	-.2	1.1	-1.2	19.7
$300,000	2.1	.2	-.8	5.1	2.8	3.0	4.1	2.7	1.7	2.3	2.1	3.0	.8	16.4
$1,000,000	9.4[f]	7.7[f]	6.0[f]	11.9[f]	9.8[f]	10.3[f]	10.9[f]	9.4[f]	9.7[f]	9.7[f]	9.4[f]	9.3[f]	7.9[f]	4.9

Source: Authors' calculations based on ESPlanner.

a. Couple with two children, Social Security benefits, increasing earnings, and housing.

b. Maximum DC contribution rates for 2 percent growth in labor income scenarios are 25, 25, 25, 25, 25, 20.2, 16.2, 13.5, and 4.0 for the respective earning categories.

c. Maximum DC contribution rates for wife at home scenarios are 25, 25, 25, 25, 21.2, 17.6, and 5.2 for the respective earning categories.

d. Maximum DC contribution rates for earnings split scenarios are 25, 25, 25, 24.7, 20.6, 18.2, 16.4, and 4.9 for the respective earning categories.

e. Maximum DC contribution rates for husband earning all income scenarios are 25, 25, 24.6, 16.4, 12.3, 9.8, 8.2, and 2.5 for the respective earning categories.

f. Desired saving would be restricted by a maximum DC contribution rate of 25 percent, combined total contribution of $60,000, or an annual contribution of $10,500 to a 401(k) plan per person.

Table 5-5C. *Age-55 Out-of-Pocket Saving Rate for Variants on the Base Case*[a] *with Age-55 Life-Cycle Assets*

													1 percent	
			Extra						Wife at		Earnings		growth in	
			initial			2			home with		split:	Husband	standard	Maximum
		6 percent	assets equal to	No	Maximum	percent	Retire-	No	children	Live in	2/3 husband-	earns	of living	DC con-
Earnings	Base	real	first year's	second	life span	growth	ment at	borrowing	for 15	Indiana	1/3 wife[d]	total	until	tribution
at age 25	case	return	earnings	child	equals 100	in labor income[b]	age 60	constraint[c]	years[c]			income[e]	retirement	rate
$25,000	15.0	13.0	15.3	13.7	16.0	16.8	30.5[f]	31.6[f]	15.3	15.0	17.3	10.6	19.0	25.0
$50,000	19.4	17.3	19.6	17.1	20.5	19.4	31.5[f]	32.6[f]	20.6	19.9	19.6	16.1[g]	22.8	25.0
$100,000	20.9[g]	19.3[g]	21.1[g]	17.6[g]	22.0[g]	22.9[g]	29.4[f]	29.1[f]	21.8[g]	22.0[g]	21.9[g]	23.8[f]	23.5[f]	25.0
$150,000	23.2[g]	21.8[g]	23.3[g]	19.7[g]	24.1[g]	24.4[f]	27.7[f]	28.8[f]	24.2	23.9[g]	24.6[f]	26.8[f]	23.3[f]	25.0
$200,000	24.6[f]	22.5[f]	23.2[f]	19.6[g]	25.1[f]	25.1[f]	25.1[f]	25.8[f]	24.9[f]	25.2[f]	24.7[f]	25.5[f]	20.7[g]	22.3
$250,000	24.1[f]	22.6[f]	22.2[f]	19.2[f]	24.4[f]	25.0[f]	23.7[f]	24.7[f]	24.8[f]	24.7[f]	23.9[f]	24.5[f]	19.6[f]	17.8
$300,000	23.7[f]	22.1[f]	21.6[f]	19.3[f]	23.9[f]	24.9[f]	23.1[f]	24.2[f]	24.4[f]	24.3[f]	23.4[f]	23.8[f]	19.1[f]	14.8
$1,000,000	21.7[f]	19.7[f]	19.1[f]	18.0[f]	21.4[f]	24.2[f]	20.4[f]	21.7[f]	23.2[f]	22.4[f]	21.4[f]	21.1[f]	17.2[f]	4.5

Source: Authors' calculations based on ESPlanner.

a. Couple with two children, Social Security benefits, increasing earnings, and housing.

b. Maximum DC contribution rates for 2 percent growth in labor income scenarios are 25, 25, 25, 22.1, 16.6, 13.2, 11.0, and 3.3 for the respective earning categories.

c. Maximum DC contribution rates for wife at home scenarios are 25, 25, 25, 23.9, 19.2, 15.9, and 4.8 for the respective earning categories.

d. Maximum DC contribution rates for earnings split scenarios are 25, 25, 23.2, 19.5, 17.2, 14.8, and 4.5 for the respective earning categories.

e. Maximum DC contribution rates for husband earning all income scenarios are 25, 25, 22.3, 14.8, 11.1, 8.9, 7.4, and 2.2 for the respective earning categories.

f. Desired saving would be restricted by a maximum DC contribution rate of 25 percent, combined total contribution of $60,000, or an annual contribution of $10,500 to a 401(k) plan per person.

g. Desired saving would be restricted by an elective contribution limit of $10,500 if the employer were to make no contributions to the plan.

and wife; the husband earning all household income; and a desired 1 percent annual growth in the household's standard of living through age 65.

A quick glance at tables 5-5A, 5-5B, and 5-5C indicates that the variants of 2 percent growth in wages, no borrowing constraints, and early retirement make the greatest difference to recommended saving rates. DC joint employee-employer contribution limits bind more frequently in those cases as well as those in which one spouse accounts for most of the household's earnings. However, with the exception of the early retirement scenario and the no-borrowing constraint cases in table 5-5C, all the cells in which the joint employee-employer contribution limit binds involve older, upper-income households.

With higher real wage growth, households are borrowing constrained for longer periods of time and recommended saving at age 35 is zero. At age 45, recommended dissaving rates are roughly half as large, in absolute value, for the low- and middle-income households as in the base case. Because households experiencing higher earnings growth are borrowing constrained for longer periods of time, their capacity to save and their subsequent ability to dissave, when children enter college, are both diminished. The absence of borrowing constraints leads the five lowest-earning households to dissave at both ages 35 and 45; those households then save at dramatically higher rates at age 55. Indeed, households at every level of earnings that can borrow freely are bound by the joint DC contribution limits at age 55. When there is no borrowing constraint, the household borrows extensively early in the life cycle; in order to repay its debts and to fund retirement, it must increase its savings rate substantially when older.

Households that retire early have fewer years to prepare for retirement and longer retirements to finance, which explains why they save at higher rates while working. Although allocating most or all of a household's earnings to one spouse does not change recommended saving rates very much, it does change the dollar limit applied to the household's total DC contribution. With two earnings, the limit is $60,000, but with only one earner, it is only $30,000; that explains why more of the cells in the tables under those variants would be bound by the contribution limits.

The other variants make relatively little difference in recommended saving rates. Consider, for example, having no second child. Table 5-5A shows that saving rates at age 35 are lower for low-income but higher for high-income households. The elimination of future college costs increases a low-income household's sustainable consumption level by enough to make it borrowing constrained when young; at middle- and upper-income levels the opposite occurs because college costs do not rise in proportion to lifetime income. With one child less, borrowing constraints no longer bind at age 35 because the increase in sustainable consumption due to lower college expenses is less than the reduction in one child's consumption expenses when young. Thus, middle- and upper-income households save more at age 35 than in the base case. Table 5-5B shows that, at age 45, saving rates are higher (less negative) at all income levels because one child less implies smaller current college expenses. Table 5-5C shows that saving rates at age 55 are lower at all income levels because, with only one child, households save more earlier in life.

When the household wants an increasing, rather than a flat, standard of living during its working years, the out-of-pocket saving rate is higher in early years, lower in the middle years when children go to school, and significantly higher for middle-income households in the years preceding retirement. But those changes in saving rates do not change the conclusion that the DC joint limits are not binding except for older, upper-income households.

The Impact of Participating in DC Plans on the Age-Consumption Profile

Because most of the households in our analysis are borrowing constrained when young, participating at any level in a DC plan comes at the cost of a decline in current relative to future living standards. Tables 5-6 and 5-7 show that contributing even small percentages of wages to a DC plan can have a large impact on relative consumption when one is young and old. The calculations in table 5-6 assume a 4 percent real return, while those in table 5-7 assume a 7 percent real return; both tables focus on the household that earns $50,000 per year.

Consider first the results in table 5-6 for the base case, with no contribution to a DC plan. The first column shows the base case with borrowing constraints; the second column shows no borrowing constraints. Without borrowing constraints, the household enjoys the same living standard each year, but its consumption expenditures vary with the size of the household. With borrowing constraints, the profile of the household's living standard is irregular, although it is smoothed as much as possible. The first two columns of table 5-6 show that when the borrowing constraint is imposed, consumption is 17 percent lower at age 25 and 25 percent higher in the final year than when it is not.

Consider next how a 10 percent contribution to a DC plan affects those results at age 25. Consumption at age 25 under the borrowing constraint is one-third less than it would be with no borrowing constraint. At the end of the household's life, it is a remarkable 71 percent greater. Stated differently, with a 10 percent contribution and with borrowing constraints, consumption expenditures at the end of life are more than twice as large as they are at the beginning. In contrast, when the household is not borrowing constrained, it consumes 18 percent less when old than at age 25.

Those results are magnified if the DC contribution rate is 25 percent rather than 10 percent of earnings. In the borrowing-constrained case, consumption when the household is old now is almost five times greater than when it is

Table 5-6. *Life-Cycle Consumption Profile for the Base-Case Household with $50,000 in Annual Earnings at Age 25 for Different Rates of Contribution to a DC Plan*[a]

						Variants						
Age	Base case, no contribution	Base case, no contribution and no borrowing constraint	5 percent employee contribution rate	5 percent contribution with no borrowing constraint	10 percent employee contribution rate	10 percent contribution with no borrowing constraint	15 percent employee contribution rate	15 percent contribution with no borrowing constraint	20 percent employee contribution rate	20 percent contribution with no borrowing constraint	25 percent employee contribution rate	25 percent contribution with no borrowing constraint
25	26,511	32,020	24,514	33,130	22,518	33,906	20,529	34,624	18,538	34,956	16,546	34,932
35	33,566	37,437	31,289	38,735	28,958	39,642	26,631	40,482	24,317	40,871	22,002	40,842
45	28,709	32,020	26,761	33,130	24,767	33,906	22,777	34,624	20,798	34,956	18,818	34,932
55	32,619	26,124	39,364	27,030	42,540	27,663	40,013	28,249	37,352	28,520	34,688	28,500
65	32,619	26,124	39,364	27,030	47,434	27,663	58,192	28,249	68,140	28,520	78,089	28,500
75	32,619	26,124	39,364	27,030	47,434	27,663	58,192	28,249	68,140	28,520	78,089	28,500
85	32,619	26,124	39,364	27,030	47,434	27,663	58,192	28,249	68,140	28,520	78,089	28,500
95	32,619	26,124	39,364	27,030	47,434	27,663	58,192	28,249	68,140	28,520	78,089	28,500

Source: Authors' calculations based on ESPlanner.

a. Assuming 4 percent non–tax-favored and tax-favored real rates of return in 2000 dollars.

Table 5-7. *Life-Cycle Consumption Profile for the Base-Case Household with $50,000 in Annual Earnings at Age 25 for Different Rates of Contribution to a DC Plan*[a]

Age	Base case, no contribution	Base case, no contribution and no borrowing constraint	Variants									
			5 percent employee contribution rate	5 percent contribution with no borrowing constraint	10 percent employee contribution rate	10 percent contribution with no borrowing constraint	15 percent employee contribution rate	15 percent contribution with no borrowing constraint	20 percent employee contribution rate	20 percent contribution with no borrowing constraint	25 percent employee contribution rate	25 percent contribution with no borrowing constraint
25	26,662	31,055	24,663	32,462	22,664	33,268	20,668	33,552	18,678	33,670	16,698	33,713
35	33,818	36,309	31,710	37,954	29,433	38,897	27,108	39,229	24,714	39,366	22,330	39,417
45	29,013	31,055	27,134	32,462	25,174	33,268	23,185	33,552	21,137	33,670	19,099	33,713
55	34,923	25,337	44,787	26,485	42,540	27,143	40,013	27,374	37,352	27,470	34,688	27,505
65	34,923	25,337	55,649	26,485	83,481	27,143	110,273	27,374	135,999	27,470	159,821	27,505
75	34,923	25,337	55,649	26,485	83,481	27,143	110,273	27,374	135,999	27,470	159,821	27,505
85	34,923	25,337	55,649	26,485	83,481	27,143	110,273	27,374	135,999	27,470	159,821	27,505
95	34,923	25,337	55,649	26,485	83,481	27,143	110,273	27,374	135,999	27,470	159,821	27,505

Source: Authors' calculations based on ESPlanner.

a. Assuming 7 percent non-tax-favored and tax-favored real rates of return in 2000 dollars.

young. Next consider what happens if the borrowing-constrained household earns a 7 percent rather than a 4 percent real return on both its DC and non-DC assets (table 5-7): in that case, consumption when old is almost four times greater than at age 25. If the contribution rate is 25 percent, consumption when young is half of what it would be if the household were not borrowing constrained and consumption when old is almost ten times greater than when young! The most telling comparison is between levels of consumption at age 25 for this case, in which contributions are set at the legal maximum, and in the base case, in which there are no DC contributions. Consumption in this case is roughly one-third less than in the base case. In order to contribute up to the statutory ceiling, the household therefore would have to be willing to lower its immediate living standard by one-third—a sacrifice that most young households would appear to be unwilling to make.

The Size of the DC Tax Benefit

By comparing, for different rates of DC contributions, the levels of consumption in the non–borrowing-constrained cases in tables 5-6 and 5-7 one can see the tax advantage of participating in a DC plan. Table 5-8 presents the DC benefit for different rates of return under the assumption that the real rates of return on non-DC assets and DC assets are the same. It captures the pure tax advantage of contributing to a DC plan. To examine the potential benefit afforded by DC plans, the calculations assume elective employee contributions and employer matching contributions equal to the average of maximum contributions allowed across DC plans. The household's elective contribution is set at 13.5 percent of earnings and the employer matching contribution is set at 3 percent of earnings, bringing the total DC plan contribution to 16.5 percent of earnings.[27]

Table 5-8 shows that with a return of 4 percent, the lifetime tax benefit from consistently participating in a DC plan increases from 1.9 percent at household earnings of $25,000 to 3.5 percent at earnings of $100,000 and to 9.8 percent at earnings of $300,000. The dollar limit on contributions reduces the subsidy to 7.7 percent at earnings of $1,000,000. With a 6 percent real return, the poor and low-income households get a small tax break, while the high-income households continue to receive significant benefits. With an 8 percent real return, poor and low-income households actually lose from 1.5 to 1.9 percent of their lifetime consumption by participating in a DC plan. Even those earning

---

27. At this contribution rate, the dollar contribution ceiling limits the household's contribution to $60,000 at earnings exceeding $363,636.36. In our use of ESPlanner to make these calculations, we treat all contributions as if they were made by the employee so that when we run the same case without DC contributions, there is no difference in the gross income earned by the workers.

Table 5-8. *Tax Benefit from Participating in a DC Plan for Base-Case Household*[a]

| Earnings at age 25 | Real rate of return on tax-favored and non–tax-favored assets | | | | |
	2 percent	4 percent	6 percent	8 percent	10 percent
$25,000	3.96	1.89	.59	–1.53	–3.26
$50,000	3.21	1.97	.11	–1.94	–3.88
$100,000	4.25	3.45	1.88	–.07	–1.47
$150,000	4.77	4.52	2.26	.29	–1.05
$200,000	7.66	6.63	4.11	2.02	.54
$250,000	10.35	8.83	5.71	3.66	2.19
$300,000	11.05	9.80	6.46	4.22	2.78
$1,000,000	7.19	7.67	7.21	6.48	4.31

a. Tax benefit was measured as percent of lifetime consumption at a 16.5 percent contribution rate for alternative rates of return and levels of annual earnings at age 25. For $1,000,000 earnings, the 10 percent contribution rate was constrained to the limit of a $60,000 annual contribution. Subsidy is calculated as the percentage difference in the present value of the household's lifetime consumption, discounted at the specified real rate of return (the assumed return on both tax-favored and non–tax-favored assets) to age 25.

$100,000 a year end up slightly worse off by participating. In contrast, households with earnings of $1 million per year enjoy a tax benefit equal to 6.5 percent of their lifetime consumption. Clearly, there are large gains and also a few not-trivial losses to be had by contributing to DC plans. The table also shows that the tax benefit of DC plans is regressive.

Summary and Conclusion

Our analysis yields four central findings. First, among the model households that engage in life-cycle saving and have Social Security benefits, children, their own homes, and modest life-cycle earnings growth, joint employer-employee DC contribution limits bind only for those with very high levels of earnings. However, the elective employee contribution limit binds across a wider range of earnings if employers make no DC contributions on behalf of their employees. Second, the DC limits bind for middle-class as well as upper-income households at older ages if those households fail to save when young, plan to retire early, are single-income households, are not borrowing constrained, or experience rapid real wage growth. Third, given borrowing constraints, participating in DC plans comes at the cost of having dramatically lower household consumption when young than when old. For example, assuming a 10 percent contribution rate and a 4 percent real return, our stylized household's consumption in retirement is more than twice as great as in young adulthood. Fourth, assuming moderate rates of return, all income classes benefit from participating in DC plans, although the tax break as a percent of lifetime consumption is higher for those with high incomes. At those rates of return, the statutory limit on joint contributions is effective in lowering the subsidy to the rich. However, at much higher rates of return, participating in a DC plan actually generates higher lifetime net taxes for low- and middle-income households because it pushes them into higher marginal tax brackets.

At most income levels and rates of return, the tax breaks from participating in a DC plan can be significant, but those breaks are available only to those fortunate enough to work for employers that offer DC plans with high contribution rates. Taking advantage of the DC tax break, when it exists, requires not only finding the right employer, but also, in many cases, being willing to forgo some current consumption in order to enjoy higher consumption in old age. For our middle-income stylized household, participating in a DC plan that sets contributions at the statutory limit and earns a 4 percent real return means spending almost five times more on consumption when old than when young.

ERISA does not delineate principles for setting DC contribution limits. It does not say, for example, that households with specific incomes should be able to save enough in tax-deferred form to finance their retirement fully. In focusing on benefit security, rather than saving adequacy, Congress appears to have set ERISA's contribution limits primarily on the basis of equity and revenue considerations.[28] Had Congress instead tried to establish lifetime, rather than annual, contribution limits to achieve a particular retirement saving target, it would have had a difficult time. As demonstrated here, the right target is critically dependent on a range of household-specific demographic and economic factors. In addition, regulating lifetime contribution limits would be a more difficult administrative task than regulating annual limits.

If, in the context of our current income-tax structure, having annual retirement account contribution limits represents the only practical approach, what principles should guide the setting of those limits? We offer four. The first is to treat workers equally no matter who their employer is; that could be accomplished by allowing workers to make IRA contributions equal to the difference between the DC statutory limits and the maximum joint employer-employee contribution permitted by their DC plans.[29] If the first principle cannot be honored, a second, less ambitious one is to treat all workers participating in DC plans equally regardless of their employer. That could be achieved by allowing workers to make elective contributions equal to the difference between the DC

---

28. This criterion for setting limits can be contrasted with state-sponsored Section 529 tuition savings plans. There the law makes explicit that the policy goal is to enable families to pay five years' tuition and other educational expenses at the most expensive college included in the plan and that the state sponsor is to set lifetime contribution limits to allow achievement of that goal (see Ma and others 2000).

29. Thus, workers with no DC plan would be able to contribute this year the lesser of 25 percent of their earnings or $30,000 to an IRA.

statutory limits and the employer's contribution on the worker's behalf. A third principle would be to give older workers more scope to save for their retirement than younger ones. That principle recognizes that many, if not most, households are liquidity constrained when young and that they will be able to save significant amounts for retirement only in the fifteen or so years before they retire. A fourth principle is to view the tax breaks afforded to DC participants in the context of the advantages certain households obtain from Social Security, Medicare, and other government tax-transfer programs. Establishing public policies that meet all four principles requires a careful balancing of both equity issues and administrative concerns.

Appendix 5A
ESPlanner's Tax and Social Security Benefit Calculations

Federal Income Tax Calculations

ESPlanner's calculations of federal income taxes in each future year take into account the household's year-specific marital status. Thus, in the case of married households, marital status is "married" when both spouses are alive and "single" when one is deceased. Married households are assumed to file jointly. Tax schedules for each filing status are taken from the federal income-tax booklet for the latest available tax year—usually the year before the "current" year entered by the user. The tax schedule is applied to the program's calculation of federal taxable income, which equals federal adjusted gross income (AGI) minus personal exemptions and minus the standard or itemized deduction, whichever is larger.

AGI for each year includes projected income in current dollars from the following sources: labor income (wages and salaries), self-employment income, and asset income projected by the program on the basis of user inputs of initial non–tax-favored net worth and rates of return and of the optimal spending plan computed by the program. AGI also includes taxable asset income, taxable Social Security benefits, taxable special receipts, taxable distributions from defined benefit pension plans, and taxable withdrawals from tax-favored saving plans. Each of those items is based on the user's inputs and preferences. Nontaxable special receipts and withdrawals from nondeductible tax-favored accounts are not included in AGI, and deductible contributions to tax-favored retirement accounts are subtracted from income in calculating AGI for each year. Employer contributions to tax-favored retirement accounts are not included in AGI. However, withdrawals from those accounts are included.

Tax Schedules. The tax schedules for the two types of filing status implemented in ESPlanner are taken from the federal income-tax booklet for the 1998 tax year. Those schedules are shown in table 5A-1.

Table 5A-1. *1998 Tax Schedule by Filing Status in ESPlanner*

1 *If taxable* *income is over—*	2 *but not* *over—*	3 *the tax is—*	4 *of the* *amount over—*
Married filing jointly			
$ 0	$ 42,350	——— 15 %	$ 0
42,350	102,300	$ 6,352.50 + 28 %	42,350
102,300	155,950	23,138.50 + 31 %	102,300
155,950	278,450	39,770.00 + 36 %	155,950
278,450	———	83,870.00 + 39.6 %	278,450
Single			
$ 0	$ 25,350	——— 15 %	$ 0
25,350	61,400	$ 3,802.50 + 28 %	25,350
61,400	128,100	13,896.50 + 31 %	61,400
128,100	278,450	34,573.50 + 36 %	128,100
278,450	———	88,699.50 + 39.6 %	278,450

Indexation for the Tax Schedule. Tax-rate brackets and inframarginal tax amounts of all of the dollar amounts listed in the tax schedules are adjusted for inflation in each year over the household's lifetime to ensure that the schedule keeps pace with the growth of income in current dollars. Indexation is done by applying the user-specified rate of inflation.

Adjustment for the Current Year. Because the tax schedules shown apply to the 1998 tax year and the user will enter 1999 as the current year, all tax brackets and inframarginal tax amounts (the dollar amounts shown in column 3 of the schedules) are indexed for inflation at the user-specified annual rate. That is done to avoid applying tax schedules appropriate for 1998—that is, based on wage and price levels prevailing in 1998—to 1999 taxable income.

Standard Deductions and Exemptions. The standard deduction and personal exemption amounts also are taken from the tax year before the "current" year (tax year 1998 in the current version). The amount subtracted from AGI for each personal exemption was $2,700. The standard deductions were $7,100 for the married filing jointly filing status and $4,250 for the single filing status. Those amounts also are indexed for inflation for each future year based on the user-specified future rate of inflation. The number of personal exemptions allowed equals two plus the number of children for married filing jointly status and one plus the number of children for the single filing status. The personal exemption amount that can be deducted from AGI in calculating taxable income is phased out if AGI is above certain dollar limits, depending on filing status. ESPlanner takes account of the phase-out of personal exemptions based on those dollar limits, indexed for inflation.

The Decision to Itemize. ESPlanner takes the maximum standard deduction or itemized deduction when the latter includes mortgage interest payments, property taxes, state and local income-tax payments, and tax-deductible special expenditures that the user specifies, such as alimony payments, charitable contributions, and deductible medical expenses. State and local income tax payments are deductible only if they are being withheld from pay or if the user makes estimated tax payments during the tax year. ESPlanner assumes withholding or prepayment in every case.

The Phaseout of Itemized Deductions. Federal income tax rules phase out itemized deductions for high-income-tax payers (both married filing jointly and single payers). For the 1998 tax year, the amount of the deduction is reduced by 3¢ for every dollar of AGI in excess of $124,500, with the total reduction limited to 80 percent of the original amount. The reduction does not apply to certain components of the itemized deductions claimed, such as medical care expenses, investment interest, and casualty and theft losses. Because ESPlanner does not distinguish between those and other sources of itemized deductions, the phase-out rules are applied to the entire itemized deduction.

The Child Tax Credit. The child tax credit equals $400 multiplied by the number of qualifying children in the household. The tax credit is phased out if AGI is more than $110,000 for married filing jointly status and $75,000 for single filing status. The phase-out rate is $50 for each $1,000 of income in excess of the applicable amount. The amount of the child tax credit equals the computed amount or the federal income-tax liability net of the earned income tax credit, whichever is less. If the earned income tax credit exceeds the federal income-tax liability, the child tax credit is applied against the payroll tax liability.

The Earned Income Credit. The program's calculation of the earned income credit (EIC) adheres to the EIC worksheet for Form 1040. ESPlanner first checks for eligibility to take EIC on the basis of thresholds for investment income and taxable and nontaxable earned income—employer contributions to 401(k) plans, for example—for households with no qualifying child and for those with at least one qualifying child (adopted, foster, step- and grandchildren are excluded in ESPlanner's calculations). Next, EIC is computed according to the EIC schedule for taxable and nontaxable income. If the EIC is non-zero, it applies if AGI is less than certain dollar thresholds ($5,600 for households without a qualifying child and $12,300 for households with at least one qualifying child). If AGI is greater than those dollar amounts, EIC is based on the AGI.

Payroll Taxes

In each year, the payroll tax for a married household is the sum of the two spouses' payroll taxes. Each spouse's tax equals the employee share of the Old

Age, Survivors, and Disability Insurance (Social Security) tax rate (6.2 percent) applied to labor earnings up to the taxable maximum level plus the employee share of the hospital insurance (HI) tax rate for Medicare (1.45 percent) applied to total labor earnings. If there are earnings from self-employment, they are included in the calculation only to the extent that labor earnings fall short of the taxable maximum limit for the OASDI tax. The entire labor income from self-employment is taxed because of the HI tax. In the case of self-employment income, the employer plus employee tax rates for OASDI and HI are applied.

Taxation of Social Security Benefits

Social Security benefits are taxed by including them in the federal income tax base in the following manner. If the sum of AGI and 50 percent of Social Security benefits falls short of $25,000 (adjusted for inflation in future years) for single filers and $32,000 (same qualification) for married filers, none of the benefits are taxable. If the sum exceeds the applicable amount but the excess is less than $9,000 (single) or $12,000 (married), one-half of the excess or 50 percent of the benefit, whichever is smaller, is taxable and is included in the federal income tax base. In addition, if the excess is greater than the thresholds, 85 percent of the excess or 85 percent of the benefit, whichever is smaller, also is added to the federal income tax base.

State Income Tax Calculations

State income taxes are calculated for each state that imposes an income tax according to the tax rules applicable in the user's state of residence. In most cases, the state income tax base equals the federal AGI readjusted for taxable Social Security benefits. State income tax calculations incorporate features peculiar to each state: for example, some states (such as Massachusetts) impose special taxes on asset income. State-specific personal, spousal, and dependent exemptions (including additional exemptions for the elderly) and the applicable standard deductions are used to calculate state taxable income. State taxes are calculated by applying the state's tax rate schedule to the taxable income.

Social Security Retirement Benefit Calculations

—*Eligibility.* Before ESPlanner provides Social Security retirement benefits, it checks to make sure that an individual is *fully insured* on the basis of his or her earnings record.[30] Becoming fully insured requires sufficient contributions at a job (including self-employment) covered by Social Security. For those born after 1929, acquiring 40 *credits* prior to retirement suffices to qualify for fully insured status. Earnings between 1937 and 1950 are aggregated and divided by $400,

---

30. See also the documentation provided with ESPlanner Software in Bernheim and others (2000).

and the result (rounded down to an integer number) becomes the number of pre-1951 credits, which are added to the credits earned after 1950 to determine insured status. In 1951, workers began to earn one credit for each quarter of the year that they work in Social Security–covered employment and earn above a specified minimum amount. The year of *first eligibility* for retirement benefits is the year in which the individual reaches age 62. The individual is *entitled* to retirement benefits after an application for benefits is submitted but never before age 62.

—*Determination of Primary Insurance Amount.* The primary insurance amount (PIA) is the basis for all benefit payments made on the basis of a worker's earnings record. There are several steps in computing the PIA. *Base years* are computed as the years after 1950 up to the first month of entitlement to retirement benefits. For survivor benefits, base years include the year of the worker's death.

Elapsed years are computed as those after 1950 or after attainment of age 21, whichever occurs later, up to (but not including) the year of first eligibility. The maximum number of elapsed years for an earnings record is 40; it could be shorter, for purposes of calculating survivor benefits, if the person dies before the age of 62.

Computation years are calculated as the number of elapsed years less five, or two, whichever is greater. Earnings in base years (up to the maximum taxable limit in each year and through age 60 or two years before death, whichever occurs earlier) are wage indexed according to economywide average wages. Of these, the highest earnings in years equaling the number of computation years are added together and the sum is divided by the number of months in computation years to yield *average indexed monthly earnings* (AIME).

—*Bend Points.* AIME is converted into the PIA using a formula with *bend points.* The bend-point formula is specified as 90 percent of the first X dollars of AIME plus 32 percent of the next Y dollars of AIME plus 15 percent of AIME in excess of Y dollars. The dollar amounts X and Y also are wage indexed and are different for different eligibility years. The dollar amounts pertaining to the year of attaining age 60 (or, for survivor benefits, the second year before death, whichever is earlier) are applied in computing the PIA.

—*Benefits.* A person who begins to collect benefits at his or her normal retirement age (currently age 65) receives the PIA as the monthly retirement benefit. In subsequent years, the monthly benefit is adjusted according to the consumer price index (CPI) to maintain its purchasing power.

—*Increases in Normal Retirement Age.* Beginning in 2003 the normal retirement age is scheduled to increase by two months for every year that a person's 65th birthday occurs later than the year 2003. This progressive increase in the normal retirement age ceases between the years 2008 through 2020; those attaining age 65 in those years have a normal retirement age of 66. The postponement in retirement age resumes after 2020 so that those who retire after 2026 have a normal retirement age of 67. All cohorts attaining age 65 after that year have a normal retirement age of 67.

—*Reductions for Age.* Retirement benefits of a person who begins to collect benefits earlier than the normal retirement age are subject to a *reduction for age.* The reduction factor is 5/9 of 1 percent for each month of entitlement before the normal retirement age. The reduced benefit payment (except for the inflation adjustment) continues even after the person reaches or surpasses normal retirement age. If the number of months of reduction exceeds 36 months (for example, in case of entitlement at age 62 when the normal retirement age is 67), the reduction factor is 5/12 of 1 percent for every additional month of early entitlement.

—*Delayed Retirement Credits.* Those who begin to collect benefits after their normal retirement age (up to age 70) receive *delayed retirement credits.* The amount of the delayed retirement credit for each month of delayed entitlement depends on the year in which a person attains normal retirement age. For example, those attaining age 65 in 1997 receive an additional 5 percent in monthly benefits for each year of delayed entitlement. However, those attaining age 65 in the year 2008 will receive an additional 8 percent in benefits for each year of delay.

—*Earnings Test.* If a person continues to work and earn after the month of entitlement but before normal retirement age, benefits are reduced according to provisions of the *earnings test.* Beneficiaries under the normal retirement age lose $1 for each $2 earned above an earnings limit. The earnings limits are scheduled to grow with average wages in future years. All benefits payable on a worker's earnings record, including the worker's own retirement benefits and spousal and child dependent benefits, are proportionally reduced by applying the earning test.

—*Recomputation of Benefits.* Earnings in any year after entitlement to benefits are automatically taken into account in recomputing the PIA to determine the subsequent year's benefit amount. However, those earnings are not indexed before they are included in the AIME calculation. If the earnings are higher than some previous year's earnings (indexed earnings through age 60 or unindexed earnings after age 60), they result in an increase in the PIA and benefit payable. If they are lower than all previous years' earnings, they will not lower the PIA or benefits since only the highest earnings in base years are included in the calculations.

Social Security Spousal and Child Dependent Benefit Calculations

—*Eligibility.* Wives and husbands of insured workers are entitled to *spousal benefits* if the spouse is over age 62 or has in care a child under age 18 who is entitled to benefits under the insured worker's record and if the insured worker is collecting retirement benefits. Children of insured workers under age 18 are entitled to *child dependent benefits* if the child is unmarried and the worker is collecting retirement benefits. Spousal benefits are allowed for a divorced spouse of an insured worker only if the marriage lasted at least ten years.

—*Benefits.* Spousal and child dependent benefits equal 50 percent of the insured worker's PIA each. Child dependent benefits may be lower only if the *family maximum* applies. Spousal benefits may be lower because of the family maximum, reduction for age, application of the earnings test, or spouse's receipt of retirement benefits based or her or his own earnings record.

—*Family Maximum.* All benefits paid under a worker's record (except retirement benefits or divorced spousal benefits) are reduced proportionately to bring them within the family maximum benefit. The maximum benefits payable on a worker's earnings record are determined by applying a bend-point formula to the PIA similar to that applied to AIME in calculating the PIA. For example, the family maximum equals 150 percent of the first $X of the PIA plus 272 percent of the next $Y of the PIA plus 134 percent of the next $Z of the PIA plus 175 percent of the PIA greater than $X + $Y + $Z. The values X, Y, and Z are adjusted for each year of the calculation according to the growth in economy-wide average wages. In case the spousal benefit is eliminated for any reason, the benefits payable on the insured worker's record are subjected to the family maximum test again; that may result in higher benefits for any children who are eligible for dependent benefits under the worker's record.

—*Reduction of Spousal Benefits for Age.* Spouses eligible for the spousal benefit may elect to receive (may become entitled to) their benefits before normal retirement age. In that case the spousal benefit is reduced by 25/36 of 1 percent for each month of entitlement before normal retirement age. If the number of months of reduction exceeds 36 months (for example, in case of entitlement at age 62 when the normal retirement age is 67), the reduction factor is 5/12 of 1 percent for every additional month of early entitlement.

—*Earnings Test and Redefinition of Spousal Benefits.* If a spouse is earning above the amount allowed by the earnings test, the spousal benefits he or she is eligible to receive will be earnings tested according to the pre–normal retirement schedule described above. If a spouse already is collecting retirement benefits, the spousal benefit is redefined as the excess of the spousal benefit over the spouse's own retirement benefit or zero, whichever is greater.

Social Security Survivor Benefit Calculations

—*Eligibility.* The surviving spouse of a deceased worker is eligible for *widow(er) benefits* if the widow(er) is at least age 60; if the widow(er) is entitled to (has applied for) widow(er) benefits; if the worker died fully insured; and if the widow(er) was married to the deceased worker for at least nine months. The widow(er) of a deceased worker is eligible for *father/mother benefits* if the widow(er) is entitled to (has applied for) benefits; if the worker died fully insured; and if the widow(er) has in care a child of the worker. A surviving child is eligible for *child survivor benefits* on the deceased worker's record if the child is under age 18 and is entitled to (an application has been filed for) benefits and the worker was fully insured.

—*Survivor Benefits.* Monthly survivor benefits equal 100 percent of the worker's PIA for a widow(er); they equal 75 percent of the PIA for father/mother and child survivors. Widow(er) and child survivor benefits may be lower only if the family maximum applies. Widow(er)s may become entitled to (elect to receive) survivor benefits earlier than normal retirement age but not earlier than age 60. In that case the reduction is 19/40 of 1 percent for each month of entitlement before normal retirement age. After the widow(er) is 62, she(he) may become entitled to (elect to receive) retirement benefits on the basis of his or her own past covered earnings record. In that case the widow(er) benefits are redefined as the excess over own retirement benefit or zero, whichever is greater. Finally, widow(er) and own retirement benefits also are subject to the earnings test. If the deceased worker already was collecting a reduced retirement insurance benefit, the widow(er)'s benefit cannot be greater than the reduced widow(er) benefit or 82.5 percent of the worker's PIA or the worker's own retirement benefit, whichever is greater. If the deceased worker already was collecting a retirement insurance benefit greater than the PIA because of delayed retirement, the widow(er) is granted the full dollar amount of the delayed retirement credit over and above the (reduced) widow(er) benefit. Father/mother benefits are not similarly augmented by delayed retirement credits that the deceased worker may have been receiving.

—*Father/Mother Benefits.* Father/mother benefits may be reduced if the family maximum applies or if the father or mother is entitled to his or her own retirement benefit. In that case the father/mother benefit is redefined as the excess over the father's or mother's own retirement benefit or zero, whichever is greater. Father/mother benefits also are subject to the earnings test. On the other hand, they are not reduced for age. For those eligible to receive both widow(er) and father/mother benefits, the program calculates both and confers the larger benefit.

—*Calculation of a Deceased Worker's PIA.* Two alternative methods are used to calculate a deceased worker's PIA, the "wage indexing" method and the "reindexing" method. Widow(er)'s benefits equal the larger of the two results. The year up to which the worker's wages are indexed may be different depending on whether the deceased worker would have become age 62 before or after the widow(er) attains age 60.

Using the wage-indexing method, the last year for indexing earnings is the year the worker dies minus two years or the year the worker would have attained age 60, whichever is earlier. Bend-point formula dollar amounts are taken from the earlier of the year the worker dies and the year the worker would have attained age 62. The PIA thus calculated is inflated by the CPI up to the year the widow(er) turns age 60 (if later) to obtain the PIA value on which widower benefits are based. Where applicable, those benefits are then adjusted for family maximum, reduction for age, delayed retirement credits, and the earnings test.

Under the reindexing method, the worker's original earnings are indexed up to the earlier of the year the widow(er) attains age 58 and the year the worker attains age 60. The elapsed years are computed as the number of years from 1951 (or the year the worker reaches age 22, if later) through the year the widow(er) attains age 60. The computation years equal elapsed years minus five (computation years cannot be less than two). Bend-point formula dollar values are applied from the year the widow(er) attains age 60. There is no subsequent indexing of the PIA for inflation.

—The Sequencing of Widow(er) Benefit Calculations. Widow(er) benefit reductions follow these steps: First, the widow(er) plus children's benefits are subjected to the family maximum. Second, the widow(er) benefit is reduced for early entitlement of the widow(er) before normal retirement age. Third, the widow(er) benefit is compared with the widow(er)'s own retirement benefit if the widow(er) is entitled to the latter. Fourth, the widow(er) benefit is redefined as the excess over own benefit if own benefit is positive. Finally, the earnings test is applied, first to the widow(er)'s own benefit and then to the widow(er) benefit that is in excess of own benefit. If the widow(er) benefit is eliminated as a result of these tests, the benefits payable on the insured worker's record are subjected to the family maximum test again, treating the widow(er) as though he or she were not eligible for the widow(er) benefit. That procedure may increase children's benefits if the family maximum limit was binding the first time through.

Annika Sundén

According to the life-cycle hypothesis, workers save over their working lives and spend down their assets during retirement. They make consumption and savings decisions to smooth consumption over the life-cycle and retire at the desired time. If they are covered by a pension plan, one important decision they must make is how much saving should be done through their pension plan and how much should be done through other types of saving. The nature of pension plans has changed dramatically over the past decade as the defined contribution plan—in particular the 401(k) plan—has to a large extent replaced the traditional defined benefit plan. The defining characteristics of 401(k) plans have shifted a substantial portion of the burden of providing for retirement to the worker, who must decide whether or not to participate, how much to contribute, and how to invest the assets.

The analysis in this chapter examines the decision of when and how much to contribute to a defined contribution plan. To create an incentive to participate in such a plan, both employee and employer contributions are tax deferred. No income taxes are levied on the original contributions or on the earnings on the contributions until the funds are withdrawn from the plan. Because the saving is tax favored, the Internal Revenue Code limits the amount that employees and employers can contribute to 401(k) plans. Tax-deferred 401(k) elective employee contributions could not exceed an indexed amount of $10,500 in 2000 and total contributions could not exceed $30,000 or 25 percent of the participant's compensation, whichever was lower. The limits are governed by the Tax Reform Act of 1986; recent legislation has increased limits on 401(k) contributions and IRA contributions. To evaluate these changes, the chapter asks three questions: are limits on defined contribution plans in 2000 binding if households follow a recommended savings path; how large is the tax benefit from participating in a defined contribution plan; and how does the tax benefit depend on the level of lifetime income?

To answer these questions, the authors employed a financial software package, the Economic Security Planner (ESPlanner). A wide range of financial planning software packages has emerged in recent years, and compared with most other software programs, the ESPlanner is a highly sophisticated and complex financial planning tool. The planner is based on a life-cycle model that incorporates federal and state taxation, households' borrowing constraints, and additional features involved in life-cycle planning. The goal of the planner is for a household to achieve the highest standard of living over the life cycle; the outputs are recommended time-paths of consumption and savings.

Using a set of stylized households, the analysis shows that for the recommended savings paths, the defined contribution limits are binding only for households in the top earnings classes and only for middle-aged and older workers. In particular, constraints tend to bind households whose members started to save late in life and plan to retire early. Most workers are liquidity constrained when they are young because of the need to pay down a mortgage and pay for college tuition; they are in no position to save the 25 percent of earnings allowed by the tax code. For them, the ESPlanner recommends that saving for retirement begin when the children are out of college. But even with this recommendation, contribution limits are binding only for households in the upper earnings classes. As expected, the results also show that most of the gain from the tax subsidy goes to high-income households; in fact, the subsidy rate for high-income households is twice that for low- and middle-income households.

It should be emphasized that the outputs of the model are *recommended* savings paths and not a description of what households actually do. In order to interpret the results, it is useful to examine how households provide for their retirement. The retirement income system in the United States is often described as a three-legged stool consisting of Social Security, employer-provided pensions, and individual savings. Although the government is spending close to $100 billion per year in tax relief for employer-sponsored pension plans in order to encourage participation, only about half of all workers are covered by a pension plan of any sort.[1] About 40 percent of workers were covered by some type of defined contribution plan, the most common being the 401(k) plan; however, among workers offered a 401(k) plan, roughly one-fourth—predominately low-income workers—elect not to participate.[2] Among workers who participate in defined contribution plans, less than 10 percent contribute at the limit. This means that for a majority of workers, Social Security is the main source of retirement income. The major concern is not whether they are going to bump up against the contribution limit, but how they will be able to provide for an adequate retirement income at all.

How then should contribution limits be determined? The chapter discusses four principles for setting contribution limits. First, the authors argue that all workers should be treated equally, regardless of employer: if the employer does not sponsor a pension plan, the employee should be allowed to contribute an equal amount to an IRA. Second, if employers do not make matching contributions, employees should be allowed to contribute up to the maximum limit— that is, $30,000 or 25 percent of compensation. Third, the authors suggest that contribution limits should allow older workers to contribute more. Finally, they argue that in setting limits, tax subsidies to defined contribution participants

---

1. Halperin and Munnell (2004).
2. Munnell, Sundén, and Taylor (2000).

should not be viewed in isolation but should be evaluated together with subsidies created by Social Security, Medicare, and other government programs.

In effect, the first three principles all argue for higher limits. The question is whether that makes sense. The IRA limit in 2000 was $2,000 per year. Would an increase in the limit increase participation and contributions to these plans by households without a pension plan? Currently, about one-fourth of all households own IRAs. The majority of owners are from high-income households and most of them also have pension coverage from an employer. Among households with annual incomes of between $10,000 and $25,000, only 14 percent had an IRA in 1998. It is not likely that the limit of $2,000 is binding for these households. This implies that IRA contribution limits are binding only for middle- and high-income households and that increasing limits is not likely to increase participation or contributions by low-income households. An increase in limits would simply increase the tax benefit going to high-income earners and possibly reduce the incentive for firms, and in particular small firms, to sponsor pension plans. If employers can make a large contribution to an IRA for themselves, they may be less inclined to provide pensions for their employees.[3]

Both the second and third principle increase the contribution limits for defined contribution plans. The authors argue that making the maximum total contribution equal for all workers with a pension plan is a way of treating workers in an equal manner. It gives workers who do not receive matching employer contributions a chance to contribute that amount themselves. They also argue that since their recommended saving paths indicate that retirement savings should be done later in life, limits should be age-weighted. However, the results from their analysis show that even if households follow the recommended saving path and start saving for retirement after the mortgage has been paid off and the children have finished college, limits are binding only for high-income households. Hence, increasing limits will do very little to increase overall saving and instead shift even more of the tax subsidy to high-income workers. It also is unclear whether an increase in limits would increase savings for these households. Contributions to pension plans will increase savings as long as they represent *new saving* rather than just shifting other forms of savings into a pension account. The relationship between pensions and other savings has been the topic of much research. New evidence in this debate from Engen and Gale shows that the effects of 401(k) contributions vary significantly with level of earnings.[4] Their analysis shows that 401(k) wealth held by high-income earners is less likely to represent new saving than the 401(k) wealth held by low-income earners.

Finally, the authors argue that all tax subsidies should be evaluated together.

---

3. Perun (2000).
4. Engen and Gale (2000).

This is an important point in designing pension policy, a main goal of which must be to promote increased coverage and contributions among low- and middle-income workers. The results from this chapter together with other research indicate that increasing limits does not help reach that goal but would further increase subsidies to high-income households. A better way to ensure adequate retirement income would be to promote policies that increase retirement savings for all, for example, by establishing a system of savings accounts with a federal match for low-income workers.

References

Bernheim, B. Douglas, and others. 2000. *ESPlanner 2000.* MIT Press.

Bernheim, B. Douglas, Lorenzo Forni, Jagadeesh Gokhale, and Laurence J. Kotlikoff. 2000. "How Much Should Americans Be Saving for Retirement?" *American Economic Review* 90 (May): 288–92.

Carroll, Christopher D., and Lawrence H. Summers. 1991. "Consumption Growth Parallels Income Growth: Some New Evidence." In *National Saving and Economic Performance,* edited by B. Douglas Bernheim and John B. Shoven, 305–43. University of Chicago Press.

Employee Benefit Research Institute. 1997. *EBRI Databook on Employee Benefits,* 4th ed. Washington.

Engen, Eric, and William Gale. 2000. "The Effects of 401(k) Plans on Household Wealth: Differences across Earnings Groups." Working Paper W8032. Cambridge, Mass.: National Bureau of Economic Research (December).

Gokhale, Jagadeesh, and Laurence J. Kotlikoff. "Social Security's Treatment of Postwar Americans: How Bad Can It Get?" In *Distributional Aspects of Investment-Based Social Security Reform,* edited by Martin Feldstein and Jeffrey Leibman. National Bureau of Economic Research and University of Chicago Press.

Gokhale, Jagadeesh, Laurence J. Kotlikoff, and John Sabelhaus. 1996. "Understanding the Postwar Decline in U.S. Saving: A Cohort Analysis." *BPEA* 1: 315–407.

Gokhale, Jagadeesh, Laurence J. Kotlikoff, and Mark J. Warshawsky. 2001. "Comparing the Economic and Conventional Approaches to Financial Planning." In *Essays on Saving, Bequests, Altruism, and Life-cycle Planning,* edited by Laurence J. Kotlikoff. MIT Press.

Halperin, Daniel, and Alicia H. Munnell. 2004. "Ensuring Retirement Income for All Workers." In *The Evolving Pension System: Trends, Effects, and Proposals for Reform,* edited by William G. Gale, John B. Shoven, and Mark J. Warshawsky. Brookings.

Hubbard, R. Glenn, Jonathan Skinner, and Stephen P. Zeldes. 1995. "Precautionary Saving and Social Insurance." *Journal of Political Economy* 103 (April): 360–99.

Kotlikoff, Laurence J., and Lawrence H. Summers. 1981. "The Role of Intergenerational Transfers in Aggregate Capital Accumulation." *Journal of Political Economy* 89 (August): 706–32.

Ma, Jennifer, and others. 2000. "An Economic Approach to Setting the Contribution Limits in Qualified State-Sponsored Tuition Savings Programs." TIAA-CREF Institute Working Paper (September).

Munnell, Alicia H., Annika Sundén, and Catherine Taylor. 2002. "What Determines 401(k) Participation and Contributions?" *Social Security Bulletin,* vol. 64, no. 3.

Perun, Pamela. 2000. "The Limits of Saving," Occasional Papers 7. Washington: Urban Institute (August).

Poterba, James M., Steven F. Venti, and David A. Wise. 1995. "Do 401(k) Contributions Crowd Out Other Personal Saving?" *Journal of Public Economics* 58 (September): 1–32.

———. 1994. "401(k) Plans and Tax-Deferred Saving." In *Studies in the Economics of Aging,* edited by David A. Wise, 105–38. University of Chicago Press.

———. 1997. "The Effects of Special Saving Programs on Saving and Wealth." In *The Economic Effects of Aging in the United States and Japan,* edited by Michael D. Hurd and Naohiro Yashiro, 217-40. University of Chicago Press.

———. 1999. "Implications of Rising Personal Retirement Saving." Working Paper 6295. Cambridge, Mass.: National Bureau of Economic Research (March).

U.S. Department of Labor, Bureau of Labor Statistics. 1999. *Employee Benefits in Medium and Large Private Establishments: 1997.* Bulletin 2517 (September).

U.S. Department of Labor, Pension and Welfare Benefits Administration. 1999. "Abstract of 1996 Form 5500 Annual Reports." *Private Pension Plan Bulletin 9* (Winter 1999–2000).

Warshawsky, Mark J., and John Ameriks. 2000. "How Prepared Are Americans for Retirement?" In *Forecasting Retirement Needs and Retirement Wealth*, edited by Olivia S. Mitchell, P. Brett Hammond, and Anna M. Rappaport, 33–67. University of Pennsylvania Press.

6

The Effects of Social Security Reform on Private Pensions

ANDREW A. SAMWICK

Over the past decade, two primary factors transformed the Social Security program from the "third rail" of American politics to a leading reform issue of the day. The first was the report of the 1994–96 Advisory Council on Social Security,[1] which focused renewed attention on the financial crisis in the Social Security system.[2] Though unable to agree on a single proposal to resolve the crisis, three subgroups of members of the council devised plans with varying degrees of benefit cuts and tax increases. A common element of all the plans was to invest a portion of Social Security funds in private securities; two of the plans explicitly called for establishment of a system of individual accounts.

The second factor was the appearance in the late 1990s of federal budget surpluses, which were projected to persist for more than a decade. In a pay-as-you-go (PAYGO) system, current payroll tax revenues pay the benefits of current

I would like to thank William Gale, Alan Gustman, David Wise, and conference participants for helpful comments and Safoa Sackey-Acquah for research assistance. I am grateful to the National Institute on Aging for research support.

1. Advisory Council on Social Security (1997).

2. According to the 2003 Trustees' Report (2003 Annual Report of the Board of Trustees of the Federal Old-Age and Survivors Insurance and Disability Insurance Trust Funds, table IV.B1, pp. 47–48), the cost rate will first exceed the income rate in 2018 and the gap will widen to an annual deficit of 6.67 percent of taxable payroll in 2080. All descriptions of the financial status of the Social Security program are based on the intermediate cost assumptions.

retirees, and those revenues cannot be diverted unless another mechanism is found to pay current beneficiaries. Alternatively, new revenues may be raised in order to prefund future liabilities. On several occasions between 1998 and 2001, projections of federal government revenues were revised upward, resulting in projected increases in the surplus. Those unanticipated surplus revenues generated political discussion of how to ease the tax burden on the transition generation of workers that would exist if certain proposed reforms took place, who would have to pay current payroll tax rates to provide for current retirees while prefunding a portion of their own future benefits.

Many studies of Social Security reform have appeared since the Advisory Council's report was published, focusing primarily on reform in other countries, the feasibility of various transition paths to restore solvency, the administrative aspects of a system of individual accounts, and the impact of reform on workers and beneficiaries.[3] The disappearance of the projected budget surpluses has not diminished interest in Social Security reform.

To date, there has been no comprehensive discussion of the likely effects of Social Security reform on employer-provided pensions. That is a critical omission. Secure retirements often are depicted as a stool with three legs—Social Security, employer-provided pensions, and personal savings. Changing any one of the legs may require changes in the others if the stool is to remain stable.

There are several possible channels through which firms and workers might modify the system of employer-provided pensions in response to Social Security reform. First, because the Social Security system is funded by a tax on labor earnings paid by employers as well as employees, closing the financial gap in Social Security will raise the cost of employing workers. That increased cost will result partly in lower employment and partly in a reduction in compensation in all forms, including aggregate pension contributions from employers.

Second, because pensions plans are used primarily to accumulate wealth for retirement, the effects of Social Security reform on pension plans depend on the way reform affects workers' demand for retirement saving. For example, a standard life-cycle model predicts that reforms that reduce the disposable income of workers will reduce their demand for pension plans because they will have less of a need to transfer resources from their working years to their retirement years. Reforms that reduce expected retirement income will increase workers' demand for pension plans because they will have more of a need to make those transfers.

---

3. See Samwick (1999) for a review of the literature as well as a discussion of my other research on Social Security reform. Two influential contributions to the recent debate are Aaron and Reischauer (1998) and Schieber and Shoven (1999). The Office of the Chief Actuary at the Social Security Administration maintains a list of reform plans that it has evaluated at www.ssa.gov/OACT/solvency/index.html.

The overall effect of reform on demand for pension plans clearly depends on the particular combination of tax increases and benefit cuts that is implemented.

Third, there is considerable heterogeneity in the reasons why people save and in how well their pension plans help them to achieve their goals. While some may save for retirement, others may save to ensure that they can maintain their desired level of consumption in the face of uncertain income, to accumulate a downpayment on a home, or to finance their children's education; workers therefore may differ in their desired combination of pension benefits and other forms of compensation. However, pension plans by their nature cover groups of workers who share a common employer; they cannot be tailored to the preferences of each individual worker. If workers could freely sort themselves across firms on the basis of the combination of wages and pensions the firms offer, then the distinction between the group and the individual would not be relevant to the effect of Social Security reform on private pensions. However, if there are impediments to complete sorting, such as search costs or government imposed nondiscrimination rules, then Social Security reform will affect pension plans also through changes in the relative demands for pensions by different groups of workers at a firm.

The primary objective of this chapter is to identify important channels through which employers and employees might modify employer-provided pension plans in response to Social Security reform. Background information is given on the nature of the problem facing Social Security, and a range of possible solutions that have been suggested in recent academic, legislative, and presidential campaign proposals are examined. A model of saving and sorting in the labor market is presented that characterizes how pension plans are distributed in the work force, and the particular effects of Social Security reform on pension plans that are formally integrated with the Social Security system are discussed. Integrated pension plans base their contributions or benefits on a feature of the Social Security system, such as the maximum taxable earnings level or the typical replacement rate for a given worker; although it may appear that such plans are particularly susceptible to Social Security reform, the model suggests that that is not the case. The likely impact of proposed policy reforms on pension plan design is assessed, and directions for future research are suggested.

The Problem Facing Social Security

Figure 6-1 demonstrates the magnitude of the financial imbalances inherent in the Social Security program according to projections in the 2003 Trustees' Report.[4] The relatively flat line indicated by dashes represents the forecasted

4. See Samwick (1999) for a more extensive discussion of the financing crisis in Social Security.

Figure 6-1. *Estimated Income and Cost Rates, Intermediate Assumptions*

Percent of taxable payroll

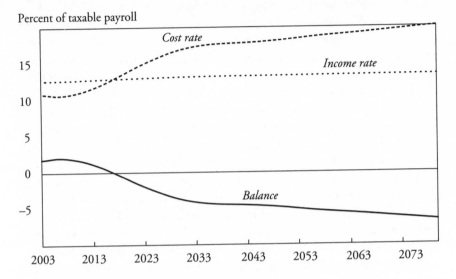

income rate. The income rate reflects revenue received by the Old-Age, Survivors, and Disability Insurance (OASDI) program from the payroll tax of 12.4 percent and the income tax on current benefits. Income tax on benefits currently equals 0.30 percent of taxable payroll, making the income rate 12.70 percent in 2003.[5] In 2077, income tax on benefits will equal 1.03 percent of payroll, resulting in an income rate of 13.43 percent.[6]

The curve at the top represents the cost rate, or Social Security payments made to beneficiaries. The cost rate in 2003 was 10.89 percent of payroll, generating a 1.81 percent (12.70 percent – 10.89 percent) annual balance in the program: the annual balance is graphed at the bottom. Over time, the cost rate increases substantially, reaching a value of 20.09 percent of payroll in 2080,

5. The income and cost rate figures are reported in table IV.B1, p. 47, of the 2003 Trustees Report. The portion of the income rate due to the income taxation of benefits is reported in Table IV.B10, p. 69.

6. The amount increases over time because the threshold level of modified adjusted gross income that must be reached before benefits are taxed is not indexed for inflation, so a greater number of beneficiaries will surpass this threshold over time. For single (married) taxpayers, 50 percent of benefits become eligible for taxation once a threshold of $25,000 ($32,000) is reached, with 85 percent of benefits becoming taxable when a threshold of $34,000 ($44,000) is reached. The income tax from the first 50 percent is allocated to Social Security. The income tax from the remaining 35 percent is allocated to Medicare. See Internal Revenue Code, Section 86.

when the annual balance will be –6.67 percent (13.43 percent – 20.09 percent) of payroll (rounded to 6.67 in the Trustees Report). Unless the Social Security system is reformed before that time, the payroll tax would have to rise from 12.40 percent to 19.07 percent to pay all the benefits promised in current law. Such an increase would represent a 50 percent increase in required revenues. Alternatively, benefits could be reduced by 33 percent to equal payroll tax revenues.

Public discussion commonly associates the financial crisis in Social Security with the approaching retirement of the baby boom generation. However, the problem is more fundamental than the aging of an unusually large birth cohort. In 2080, even the youngest baby boomer will be 116 years old. Almost all benefits paid in that year will go to retirees who were born after the baby boom. Even if no baby boomer pays another dollar in taxes or receives a dollar in benefits, the –6.67 percent balance in 2080 would be only trivially smaller. The retirement of the baby boom generation does have an important impact on the system's finances, which can be seen clearly in figure 6-1. The period of rapid increase in the cost rate (and decline in the annual balance) occurs during the two decades following 2008, when the baby boomers begin to retire. The annual balance over that period deteriorates by 5 percentage points of payroll, but note that it does not improve over the remainder of the seventy-five-year period. The retirement of the baby boom generation does not cause the financial crisis, but it does make the long-term problem appear in 35 years rather than 75 years. In so doing, it may have served as to raise the issue of reform in the policy arena.

Policy Options for Restoring Solvency

Solvency can be restored to the Social Security system in only two ways: reducing outflows or increasing inflows. However, there are a variety of policies for achieving those ends, and many of them entail a bit of both approaches. A range of policy options that have been suggested in academic and legislative proposals over the past several years, including some reforms that were proposed during the 2000 presidential campaign, follow below. They are summarized in table 6-3 later in this chapter.

Benefit Cuts

To reduce outflows, benefits could be cut by a uniform fraction at all benefit levels. As noted above, the benefit cut required to restore full solvency will reach approximately one-third by the end of the seventy-five-year projection period in the trustees' report. A legislative proposal by Representatives Jim Kolbe (R-Ariz.)

and Charles Stenholm (D-Tex.) in 1999 included a provision to (modestly) reduce benefits for all workers directly through the benefit formula.[7]

There also are less direct ways that benefits can be cut. One method is to reduce the link between postretirement benefits and the consumer price index (CPI). As an example, consider a policy in which imperfect indexation erodes 1 percent of the real value of benefits each year. If benefits were paid to retirees for an average of twenty years, that policy would reduce average benefits by approximately 10 percent each year.[8] The Kolbe-Stenholm proposal discussed above included a provision to reduce the cost-of-living adjustment by 0.33 percentage point per year.

Another way to reduce benefits is to increase the number of years that are averaged to calculate average indexed monthly earnings (AIME). Currently, the AIME is based on the average of the 35 highest indexed years of earnings.[9] Raising the number of years in the calculation necessarily reduces the average, since the added years are lower than the years already included. A legislative proposal by Senators Daniel Patrick Moynihan (D-N.Y.) and J. Robert Kerrey (D-Neb.) in 1999 contained a provision that would have increased the number of years in the AIME calculation to 38.[10] That provision also was included in the reform plan presented in Aaron and Reischauer (1998). The incidence of a benefit cut achieved in this way falls disproportionately on workers who have spent more time out of the labor force, whose earnings in those marginal years will be low or zero.

A third way to cut aggregate benefits is to increase the normal retirement age (NRA) at which Social Security benefits can be received. The NRA was 65 when the program was introduced in 1935, and only now is it being increased gradually to 67, following legislation passed in 1983.[11] At one extreme, all workers could retire two years later and receive the same benefits (apart from changes in

---

7. "The 21st Century Retirement Act," introduced as H.R. 1793. An earlier version, coauthored with Senators Judd Gregg (R-N.H.) and John Breaux (D-La.), was introduced in 1998 as H.R. 4256 and S. 2313. Under current law—Social Security Act, Section 215(a)(1)(A)—a worker's average indexed monthly earnings are converted to her primary insurance amount (PIA) in a piecewise-linear fashion at rates of 90, 32, and 15 percent. These ratios would have been reduced to 76.3, 16.8, and 7.9 percent for beneficiaries who were newly eligible in 2044 and later (see Copeland, VanDerhei, and Salisbury 1999, p. 20). The reductions were less severe at lower benefit levels to shift the burden more to higher income households. See Copeland, VanDerhei, and Salisbury (1999) for a description and simulation analysis of four proposals that were under consideration in 1998 and 1999.

8. As noted by Brown (2002), imperfect indexation undoes some of the annuitization inherent in the program. This policy can only be preferred to a uniform benefit cut of equal magnitude on distributional grounds—higher-income people tend to live longer and would therefore be disproportionately affected by imperfect annuitization.

9. Social Security Act, Section 215(b)(2).

10. The Social Security Solvency Act of 1999, introduced as S. 21.

11. Social Security Amendments of 1983, P.L. 98–21.

their AIME due to the extra two years of work) that they currently do. Aggregate benefit payments would be reduced because two more age cohorts would not be collecting each year, and payroll tax revenues would increase because those same cohorts still would be working and paying the payroll tax. At the other extreme, workers could retire at exactly the same ages that they would with an NRA of 65 and face greater penalties for early retirement. Those penalties would reduce total benefits paid each year.

Given the increase in average life expectancy that has occurred since the program's inception and that is projected to continue in the next century, as well as the reduction in the share of manual labor jobs in the economy, there is room to increase the NRA without compromising Social Security's objective of insuring workers against poverty in old age. The Kolbe-Stenholm bill included a provision to accelerate the increase in the NRA to 67 for those reaching age 62 in 2011 and thereafter to index it to average life expectancy. The Aaron-Reischauer proposal included that change in the normal retirement age and a provision to increase the early retirement age from 62 to 64 and to maintain the three-year difference between the two ages thereafter.

Tax Increases

An obvious option for increasing Social Security system revenues is to raise the payroll tax from 12.4 percent or the maximum taxable earnings (MTE) on which it is paid ($87,000 in 2003). The Moynihan-Kerrey plan included a provision to increase the MTE to $99,900 and, by 2060, to increase the payroll tax rate to 13.7 percent. Another option is to increase the size of the payroll tax base by requiring state and local government workers who are not covered by the Social Security program to participate. The Moynihan-Kerrey and Aaron-Reischauer proposals required all newly hired state and local government workers to be brought into the system.

Still another option to raise revenues is to increase the fraction of retirement benefits subject to the income tax or to lower the threshold income level at which benefits become taxable. The Moynihan-Kerrey proposal also included a provision that would make 80 percent of benefits taxable as income for all recipients. The Aaron-Reischauer proposal included a provision to tax benefits in the same manner as private pension income. However, that source of financing is more properly thought of as a benefit cut, since the money is paid when participants receive benefits, not when they pay the payroll tax.

The prospect of simply increasing the size of the existing PAYGO tax has not received much public consideration, in part because the cost rate will not exceed the income rate for the next fifteen years. A recent reform plan detailed by Diamond and Orszag is an exception.[12]

12. Diamond and Orszag (2004).

In the wake of the Advisory Council's 1997 report, proposals to reform the system through investments in the debt and equity of private companies also have been discussed. The recent Presidential Commission to Strengthen Social Security (2001) provided three such plans. Investing in private securities to substitute for a portion of PAYGO benefits would increase both the expected return on payroll contributions and the riskiness of investing for retirement. Whether the portfolio change is thought of more appropriately as a tax increase or a benefit cut depends on how the risk is shared. For example, if beneficiaries were simply to forgo one-third of their PAYGO benefits in exchange for a PRA that on average would have a sufficient balance to fund those benefits, then the portfolio shift is analogous to a benefit cut. The magnitude of the cost of the cut to beneficiaries is equal to the lesser of the utility loss incurred by exposure to the increased risk and the costs incurred by beneficiaries to obtain insurance against that risk.[13] The government could provide that insurance directly by establishing a minimum benefit guarantee; the cost of funding the guarantee presumably would be borne by workers in the form of higher and more variable payroll taxes.[14]

Other Reforms

The discussion of policy options thus far indicates that, to address just the solvency of the Social Security system, reform probably will include increases in contributions, reductions in future benefits, and changes in the riskiness of retirement investments. Major reform also is likely to encourage other changes in the system that are not directly related to rectifying its actuarial imbalance.

The 2000 presidential campaign provides examples of other reforms proposed by both major political parties. The reform plan put forward by George W. Bush permitted a portion of the assets in PRAs to be bequeathed rather than annuitized.[15] The same is true of the plans put forward by the 2001 Presidential Commission. Mandatory and full annuitization has been a central feature of the Social Security system since its inception.

The reform plan advocated by Al Gore was similar in its treatment of the system's solvency to the plan proposed by President Bill Clinton in his 1999 State of

13. Feldstein and Ranguelova (2000) show how this could be done using put and call options. Beneficiaries might also lessen their risk by changing the portfolio allocations in their privately held portfolios.

14. Whether the pure portfolio change is an efficient way of implementing the tax increase or benefit reduction generally boils down to the explanation for the equity premium puzzle. See Abel (1999), Smetters (2001), and Feldstein, Ranguelova, and Samwick (2001) for three different approaches to investment risk in the evaluation of Social Security reform.

15. See *A Blueprint for New Beginnings*, pp. 45–47.

the Union Address.[16] It included two provisions unrelated to financial solvency. The first would give parents credit toward Social Security benefits for up to five years spent raising children, assigning a value to the time spent of up to one-half the average wage in the calculation of the AIME (approximately $16,500 in 2001). The second provision would increase the widow(er)'s benefit to 75 percent of the combined couple's benefit, capped at the average Social Security retirement benefit. Currently, the lesser-earning spouse receives between one-half and two-thirds of the couple's combined benefit.[17]

As with the Clinton administration's proposal for universal savings accounts (USAs), the Gore plan proposed a new system of individual accounts *outside* the Social Security tax and benefit system. The Gore plan called for the establishment of retirement savings plus accounts (RSPAs), which would enjoy the same tax treatment as 401(k) plans and traditional IRAs, with tax-deductible contributions, tax-free accumulations, and withdrawals taxed as ordinary income. Preretirement withdrawals would be permitted for college expenses, first-home purchases, and catastrophic medical expenses. Household contributions to RSPAs would be matched by the government at rates that were comparable or even superior to those offered by traditional 401(k) plans, especially for low-income households.[18] The generosity of the match rate makes this proposal particularly significant in discussing the impact of proposed reforms on the design of employer-provided pension plans.

Saving and Sorting in the Labor Market

As noted above, Social Security reform may directly affect the availability and generosity of private pension plans in two ways. The first is through supply,

16. For an analysis of the Clinton administration's proposal, see Copeland, VanDerhei, and Salisbury (1999). Details of the Gore proposal can be found in Richard W. Stevenson, "Gore Is Pursuing His Case for Retirement Savings Plan," *New York Times,* June 21, 2000, p. A19, and Katharine Q. Seelye, "Gore to Announce $200 Billion Plan to Aid Retirement," *New York Times,* June 19, 2000, p. A1. Unlike the Clinton proposal, the Gore plan does not include any Social Security trust fund investments in equities.

17. The Aaron-Reischauer proposal included the same provision, financed in part by reducing the dependent spouse benefit from one-half to one-third of the retired worker benefit.

18. For a married couple making up to $30,000 annually, each spouse could contribute up to $500 annually to his or her own account. The refundable tax credit would be $1,500, for a total contribution of $2,000 each. For married couples making between $30,000 and $60,000, the $2,000 contribution would be split evenly between the couple and the government match. For those earning between $60,000 and $100,000, the $2,000 contribution would be split $1,500 from the couple and $500 from the government. The match rates in the RSPAs are 300, 100, and 33 percent for the lowest, middle, and highest income groups, respectively. Match rates in typical 401(k) plans are seldom more than 100 percent.

because employers will have less money with which to compensate workers in all forms. The second is through demand, with demand for pensions increasing to the extent that benefits are reduced and decreasing to the extent that payroll taxes are raised. Restoring financial solvency also may change some features of Social Security (for example, reducing the annuitization of benefits), increasing demand for those features in private pension plans.

A less direct but potentially significant effect that Social Security reform may have on the distribution of private pension entitlements results from the way that the combination of pension benefits and other forms of compensation adjusts to restore equilibrium to the labor market after the reform. Social Security reform may affect the relative demands for pensions by groups of workers, and that change in *relative* demands also can affect the *overall* level of pension provision. Two factors are of paramount importance in the argument: heterogeneity in preferences for saving and impediments to complete sorting of workers across firms in the labor market.

Heterogeneity in Life Cycle and Other Motives for Saving

Saving in all of its forms is designed to transfer resources from periods when income is relatively high to periods when income is relatively low. A period can be defined in many ways. Life-cycle saving transfers resources from the working years, when income is predictably higher, to the retirement years, when income is predictably lower. Precautionary saving transfers resources from a state of nature when income is certain to a state when income is uncertain. Dynastic saving transfers resources from parents' lifetimes to children's lifetimes through bequests.

It is clear from even a quick look at surveys of household wealth that there is considerable heterogeneity in household saving behavior. Some indication of that heterogeneity can be gained from an examination of self-reported household motives for saving. Table 6-1 reports the responses to the question "What is your (family's) most important reason for saving?" from the Survey of Consumer Finances, 1998.[19] Households could list up to six reasons why they saved, in order of importance. The sample consists of all survey respondents and respondents' spouses if they reported nonzero income. Each member of a two-earner couple was included separately.

The responses were aggregated into ten groups, and the workers were divided into six age categories. For each of the five age groups over age 25, retirement was cited most frequently as the primary reason for saving; for workers younger than 25, uncertainty was cited most frequently. Overall, those two categories

19. The Survey of Consumer Finances is a triennial survey of household wealth in the United States. See Kennickell (2000) for a description of the 1998 survey.

Table 6-1. *Household Reasons for Saving, by Age*[a]

	Age category							
Reason for saving	Under 25	25–34	35–44	45–54	55–64	Over 65	Primary reason[b]	Any mention[b]
Retirement	11.83	31.06	37.73	49.69	56.38	39.25	39.61	57.17
Uncertainty	20.59	18.22	19.61	19.56	18.93	28.53	19.47	32.84
Home purchase	17.72	9.52	3.72	1.57	0.08	0	4.94	9.75
Other housing	17.43	15.43	14.18	8.20	1.78	1.98	11.50	22.99
Transfers to family	4.67	1.65	1.55	1.62	3.46	2.93	2.02	6.88
Special purchases	8.62	7.64	11.71	9.03	4.74	6.40	8.92	23.80
Investment/ business	0.54	0.21	0.80	0.02	0.59	0	0.41	1.60
Cover expenses	3.86	1.95	1.17	1.30	1.72	3.96	1.69	3.49
Good idea/ get ahead	13.55	11.82	7.83	7.15	10.76	9.76	9.39	12.79
Don't/can't save	1.19	2.49	1.69	1.87	1.55	7.18	2.05	2.08
Population share	5.49	25.47	31.20	23.53	11.50	2.82	100.00	

Source: Author's calculations from the Survey of Consumer Finances, 1998.
a. Sample consists of all respondents and spouses who earn non-zero income.
b. Percentage for all age categories.

accounted for 60 percent of the primary responses.[20] However, the last column shows that 43 percent of the workers did not report retirement as a motive for saving even with six opportunities to do so. In addition, the primary reasons for saving can change over the life cycle—purchases of homes or other housing and special purchases (like durable goods) are, in most cases, more important to people below age 45 than to those above it.

Samwick (1998a) shows that many of the nonretirement motives for saving, including precautionary saving against uncertainty, can give rise to target saving of the sort described by the buffer stock model of saving in Carroll (1997). In that model, households are impatient, in the sense that they would borrow against future income if it were certain. However, they also are prudent, in the sense that they have a precautionary motive to save in the presence of uncertainty. Buffer stock saving generates a target ratio of wealth to income. Households use

20. Samwick (1998a, table 1, p. 624) showed similar tables for the SCF 1992 in which, for most age groups, the relative positions of uncertainty and retirement motives were reversed. A possible explanation is the difference in the points in the business cycle for the two years. During the weak recovery of 1992, households were relatively more concerned with job market risk, whereas in the stock market boom of the late 1990s, households were thinking more about enjoying their retirements.

this buffer stock primarily to insulate their level of consumption against near-term fluctuations in income. Impatience prevents wealth from becoming too great, while prudence keeps it strictly greater than zero.

Buffer stock saving can be caused by a sharply rising age-earnings profile in addition to a stronger preference for consuming more now than for consuming more later (a high rate of time preference). Buffer stock saving therefore is more prevalent early in the life cycle. If income is expected to be much higher in the future than it is today, there is no life-cycle reason to save; saving will be done for precautionary reasons. Samwick (1995) showed that when households in the buffer stock mode were given a noncontributory pension, they did not reduce their stock of nonpension wealth. Buffer stock savers prefer to receive their compensation in cash instead of pension contributions, even with a modest tax disadvantage, because illiquid pension wealth is a poor substitute for the liquid wealth that they need for precautionary reasons. In contrast, households actively saving for retirement prefer to take the compensation in the form of a pension contribution because the tax advantage of the pension facilitates the saving that they would like to do.[21] Those workers can be expected to reduce their other saving somewhat, even if total saving increases.

Variations in household intertemporal budget constraints and underlying rates of time preference therefore can generate heterogeneity in the value that different households place on an employer's pension contributions. Samwick (1998b) uses a stochastic life-cycle model that encompasses both retirement and precautionary saving to estimate the distribution of time-preference rates from the distribution of wealth-to-income ratios in the Survey of Consumer Finances, 1992. The estimates imply that as much as one-third of the residual variation in wealth (controlling for age, income uncertainty, and retirement replacement rates) can be attributed to variation in rates of time preference.

Incomplete Sorting of Workers across Firms

The evidence from survey questions about motives for saving and the wide distribution of wealth and underlying preference parameters suggest that there will be heterogeneity—much of which cannot be ascertained systematically by the employer—in the relative values that a random cross-section of workers place on pension contributions, wages, and other forms of compensation. An employer

---

21. Samwick (1995) further shows that, even for households who begin their working careers in a buffer stock mode, the income drop at retirement is a sufficiently "negative income growth rate" that they begin saving for life-cycle reasons as retirement approaches. This prediction is borne out in the increasingly frequent citing of retirement as the primary reason for saving as age increases in table 1.

Table 6-2. *Pension Coverage and Saving Horizons*[a]

Saving horizon	Probability of pension coverage	Fraction of pension-covered workers	Median earnings (thousands)	Median age
Next few months	45.10	13.46	25	37
Next year	41.05	9.01	26	38
Next few years	51.80	26.76	28	40
Next five to ten years	59.78	28.98	34	45
Over ten years	63.56	21.80	36	39
Total	53.70	100.00	30	41

Source: Author's calculations from the Survey of Consumer Finances, 1998.
a. Sample consists of all respondents and spouses who earn non-zero income.

cannot design a pension plan that offers each worker his or her desired amount of tax-advantaged saving; at best, the employer only can establish a plan that provides optimal benefits for a large subset of employees, perhaps those that the firm is most interested in retaining.

However, given the limited ability of the employer to ascertain which employees want a particular pension plan and which do not, the employer's contributions can be funded only by reducing the wages of all workers covered by the plan. Workers can search across potential employers for the combination of wages and pensions that best suits their preferences for the tax advantage provided by pension plans. Workers with low rates of time preference would choose firms with generous pension plans, and impatient workers would choose firms with less generous or no pension plans.[22]

Table 6-2 provides some evidence on the extent of sorting. Households in the Survey of Consumer Finances 1998 were asked, "In planning your (family's) saving and spending, which of the time periods listed on this page is most important to you?" Possible responses, ranging from "the next few months" to "over ten years," are listed in the left column of the table. Samwick (1998b) showed that households that reported longer time horizons had lower estimated rates of time preference. Responses therefore could be used as a proxy to determine an underlying preference for pension benefits relative to wages. The next column reports the probability of pension coverage for each saving horizon

22. Ippolito (1997, chapter 9, pp. 107–28)) derives a model in which patience is an unobservable but productive trait. Firms offer 401(k) plans with match rates to attract and retain patient workers. Since patient workers would like to save more than impatient workers, the employer match allows patient workers to receive more in total compensation from the employer.

group. As expected, the probability of pension coverage was lower for workers who reported shorter horizons, at 45 percent for "next few months" and 41 percent for "next year," compared with a sample average probability of 54 percent. The probability of pension coverage increased with the saving horizon, to 52 percent for those reporting a horizon of "next few years," to 60 percent for those reporting "next five to ten years," and to 64 percent for those reporting "over ten years." The positive correlation between having pension coverage and having a longer saving horizon is evidence that on average, pensions are more likely to be offered to workers with longer saving horizons or that workers with longer saving horizons are able to select jobs that offer pensions.

The third column of the table shows that the sorting is not perfect. Among workers covered by a pension plan, 22 percent report saving horizons of the "next few months" or the "next year." Another 27 percent report a saving horizon of the "next few years." Given the variety of saving motives shown in table 6-1 that could give rise to short saving horizons, there are clearly a substantial number of households whose saving objectives cannot be met by the illiquid assets or entitlements in their pension plans.[23] The remaining two columns of the table show that on average those workers have lower incomes and are younger than those who report longer saving horizons.

Imperfections in the labor market are required to support this allocation of workers to pension-covered jobs. One possible imperfection is that the labor market is not competitive enough to offer an identical job with the same total compensation that offers more of that compensation as wages than as pension contributions. Given an overall rate of pension coverage of only 54 percent and the costs to the employer of administering a pension plan, that explanation is doubtful. Alternatively, such a job may exist, but a high cost of searching for that better combination of wages and pensions keeps impatient workers in jobs with pension coverage that they value very little.

Another possible labor market imperfection is that workers with short saving horizons do not have to give up wages (or other fringe benefits that they do value) in order to receive pension contributions from the employer. A complicated set of nondiscrimination rules requires rough parity of coverage, participation, and contributions across different categories of employees if the contributions are to be tax advantaged. In the case of pensions, the categories are highly and non–highly compensated workers.[24] Regulations such as nondiscrimination

---

23. Strictly speaking, the table applies only to the pension-covered population as a whole and not individually to each firm that offers a pension. It could be that, within the set of firms that offer pensions, workers with short saving horizons are in pensions with low employer contributions and generous loan and withdrawal provisions and those with long horizons are in generous pensions with less immediate liquidity.

24. See chapter 5 of McGill, Brown, Haley, and Schieber (1996) for a description of nondiscrimination rules.

rules are common when an exception is made to the income tax code in order to ensure that the benefits of the exception are distributed in a way that is deemed to be equitable.

Table 6-2 shows that compensation is correlated with the saving horizon, so it is reasonable to expect those rules to be binding. That prediction is confirmed by Garrett (1997), who demonstrated large effects of the rules on non–highly compensated workers compared with highly compensated workers. Further evidence on the effects of nondiscrimination rules is presented in Carrington, McCue, and Pierce (2000). They use firm-level data on compensation packages to analyze variation in pensions, wages, and other fringe benefits. Their two main findings are consistent with an effect of nondiscrimination rules on the distribution of pension entitlements: First, they found that only 36 percent of the total variation in pension entitlements across all workers in their sample could be explained by the fact that pension entitlements differ for different workers in the same firm. That is substantially less than the corresponding estimate of 53 percent for the within-firm component of wage variation.[25] Nondiscrimination rules appear to make pension entitlements more homogeneous than wages. Second, they show that, keeping an employee's total compensation constant, the share taken as a pension benefit increases with the average compensation of the other workers at the firm.[26] In the absence of nondiscrimination rules or other impediments to perfect sorting, the average compensation of other workers would have no effect on the pension entitlements of a given worker.

In effect, nondiscrimination rules are a tax on the employment of workers who have high rates of time preference, because pension contributions are favored by the tax code. Employment costs are increased without a corresponding benefit to the firm or to those workers. To the extent that they can be identified, workers with high rates of time preference may bear the incidence of that tax through lower wages and reduced employment opportunities. To the extent that they cannot be identified or that nondiscrimination rules are binding, the incidence of the tax can be shifted to workers with low rates of time preference or to the employer.

Implications for Social Security Reform

To summarize, there is evidence that workers differ in their patience, or rates of time preference. Less patient workers have less willingness to forgo wages for pension contributions. Those differences are not necessarily observable by outsiders such as the employer and so cannot be made an explicit part of the employment contract. However, the correlation between patience and income

---

25. Carrington, McCue, and Pierce (2000, table 2, p. 28).
26. Carrington, McCue, and Pierce (2000, table 3, p. 29).

and the progressive income-tax rate schedule both suggest that high-income workers at a given firm are the natural clientele for compensation taken in the form of pension benefits. Imperfections in the labor market, abetted by nondiscrimination rules, prevent complete sorting of workers into jobs that offer them their optimal combination of wages and pension benefits, given their productivity. In equilibrium, both the employer and the patient, generally high-income workers bear some of the incidence of subsidizing the contributions of the impatient, generally low-income workers.

Social Security reform therefore can affect private pensions by changing the magnitude of that subsidy, apart from how it affects overall supply and demand for pension contributions. For example, consider a simple reform of Social Security that cuts benefits only for low-income workers. Compared with high-income workers, low-income workers become more willing to accept lower wages in exchange for higher pension contributions. The direct effect of their increased demand is for the employer to make the pension more generous for the low-income workers. If the employer previously was constrained by nondiscrimination rules, then that constraint will be relaxed, making it possible for the employer to offer high-income workers a compensation package that consists of more pension contributions and lower wages. Because of the tax advantage of pensions, that change also will raise the firm's profits.

The increase in pension contributions on behalf of high-income workers even though their Social Security benefits were not changed by the reform illustrates the mechanism through which Social Security reform can affect the distribution of pension entitlements by changing the *relative* demands for pensions by low- and high-income workers.

Pension Plan Integration

Whenever there is a change in Social Security provisions, employers are induced to change their pension plans because, in light of the change, another plan design may better help workers to achieve their savings objectives. All pension plans therefore are implicitly linked to Social Security, since the optimal use of the tax advantage of the pension plan depends on other resources available to retirees. In addition, some plans are explicitly integrated with features of the Social Security system. The defining characteristic of integrated plans does not pose any additional substantive challenge for ascertaining the effects of reform on pension plans.

Pension plans can be formally integrated with features of the Social Security program through the "offset" method and the "excess" method. Under the offset method, defined benefit pension plans can deduct a percentage of a retiree's Social Security benefits from his or her pension benefits. In most cases, the plan uses an estimate of benefits rather than the actual benefits paid to each individual. Since the Social Security benefit formula yields higher income replacement rates at lower earnings levels, integrating the plan by the offset method has the effect of allowing the firm to devote its resources to higher-paid employees. Not surprisingly, nondiscrimination rules determine how much the benefit offset can affect low-earning compared with high-earning workers. There also are rules that prevent an employee's entire pension from being eliminated, and the maximum offset is 50 percent of Social Security benefits. For example, if a retiree's pension and Social Security benefits were $10,000 and $4,000 per year, an offset rate of 25 percent would leave him or her with a total retirement income of $13,000 instead of $14,000.

Under the excess method, a defined benefit pension plan can provide higher replacement rates on pension-covered earnings above Social Security maximum taxable earnings than on earnings below the MTE. Nondiscrimination rules limit the differential between those replacement rates. For example, consider a worker who retires with final average compensation of $100,000 and 20 years of service. If the plan credited years of service below the MTE at 0.75 percent per year and years of service above the MTE at 1.25 percent per year, then the retiree would receive (in 2003, when the MTE was $87,000):

$$20*0.0075*87,000 + 20*0.0125*(100,000 - 87,000) =$$
$$13,050 + 3,250 = \$16,300.$$

Defined contribution (DC) pension plans can be integrated in a manner similar to the excess method, with higher contribution rates on earnings above the MTE and with nondiscrimination rules that restrict the amount of the differential.

Ostensibly, integrated pension plans attempt to provide workers of all earning levels with roughly equal benefits from the combination of pension and Social Security benefits or with roughly equal contribution rates of the employer to the combination of pension plan and Social Security system. In practice, pension plan integration can be used by employers to direct their resources toward higher-income workers as the model in the previous section suggests is in their interest. Tabulations of the 1992 Health and Retirement Study in Slusher (1998) indicate that of respondents age 51 to 61, 64.2 percent had a pension on a current or past job. Of those workers, 38.8 percent had participated in at least one pension plan that was integrated; 18.9 percent had an offset plan and 23.0 had an excess plan or an integrated DC plan.[27]

The explicit link between pensions and Social Security benefits in integrated plans seems to suggest that pension benefits will change automatically in

27. Slusher (1998, table 1, p. 23).

response to reductions in benefits or increases in the MTE.[28] For example, a reduction in benefits would reduce the amounts deducted from offset plans. The percentage offset in the plan is the fraction of the Social Security benefit cut that would be recouped by the beneficiary.[29] Merton, Bodie, and Marcus (1987) discussed how that type of integration could serve in theory as insurance against the uncertainty in provision of Social Security benefits if the employer was firmly committed to providing a replacement rate that included the worker's actual Social Security benefit. In practice, pension plans are integrated to achieve cross-sectional redistribution toward high-income workers who get low replacement rates from the existing Social Security benefit formula—not as insurance against the risk that all workers will receive a lower replacement rate from the Social Security system after fundamental reform.

Any differences between integrated plans and others in their sensitivities to Social Security reform are more apparent than real. Because an integrated plan relies explicitly on a feature of the Social Security system to generate its distribution of replacement rates, a change in that feature requires the firm to specify whether the new feature applies to the old pension formula. For example, if the MTE is increased as part of Social Security reform, then the firm must clarify whether the integration will occur at the old or the new MTE.[30] However, a more important effect of a change in the MTE is that it changes the anticipated distribution of retirement replacement rates across the workers. The model discussed previously suggests that a change in the MTE will cause *all* pension plans to change their provisions to restore a distribution of pension benefits that achieves the firm's objectives.

It would not be surprising, however, if some of the most dramatic responses to fundamental Social Security reform were found in plans that currently are integrated with the Social Security system. Pension plan integration is likely to be an indicator that the employer is aware of the potential for redistributing benefits and targeting workers through the pension plan. Integration might also indicate the existence of a group of low-income workers who are content with a plan that gives them comparatively less of a pension benefit than it gives their higher-income colleagues.[31]

---

28. Slusher (1998) and Bender (1999) analyze the characteristics of workers covered by integrated pension plans and discuss the implications of Social Security reform for integrated pension plan design.

29. In contrast, increases in the MTE make the pension plan appear less generous to high-income workers because the higher replacement (or contribution) rate on compensation above the MTE applies to a smaller excess amount.

30. Historically, major tax and regulatory changes, such as the Social Security Amendments of 1983 and the Tax Reform Act of 1986, have precipitated changes in integration rules. See chapter 15 of McGill, Brown, Haley, and Schieber (1996) for a description of pension plan integration.

31. Slusher (1998) notes that if Social Security reform includes a switch to individual accounts that are invested in risky securities, then integration under the offset method becomes more difficult

Impact of Reform on Employer-Provided Pensions

Table 6-3 summarizes the broad range of possible reforms discussed previously; benefit cuts are listed first, followed by tax increases, individual accounts, and other reforms. The columns of the table summarize the channels through which reform can affect private pensions; discussion of each of the columns provides the organizing framework for the analysis.

The first column pertains to the impact that reform can have on the supply of pensions by changing the resources available to employers to make pension contributions. Not surprisingly, only reforms that increase taxes paid into the existing PAYGO system or a new system of individual accounts will affect the supply of pensions. Greater contributions to Social Security or individual accounts will lower employers' contributions to pensions; reductions of future benefits will not have any effect. Those entries in the table are denoted by an ellipsis (...).

The second column in table 6-3 pertains to the impact that reform can have on the overall demand for pensions through changes in lifetime budget constraints of workers. That column illustrates the direct effect of reform due to life-cycle saving and does not distinguish between different types of workers. All reforms tend to reduce the amount of resources that households have available over their lifetimes; the key aspect of the reform is when that reduction occurs. If it occurs during retirement, then the need for life-cycle saving increases and so too does the overall demand for pensions. That is the case with any reform that cuts benefits, including an increase in the income tax on benefits. In contrast, the two reforms listed at the bottom of the table—crediting earnings for years spent in caregiving and increasing widow(er)'s benefits—increase postretirement income and thereby decrease the need for life-cycle saving and demand for pensions.

If the reduction in worker resources occurs before retirement, as would be the case with higher taxes or individual accounts, then the need for life-cycle saving decreases, reducing overall demand for pensions. Some of the reforms that are listed as tax increases embody a small expansion in future benefits as well. For example, if newly hired state and local government workers are brought into the system, they will pay higher taxes today and receive higher benefits in the future. For both reasons, they will demand less of an employer-provided pension. That proposed reform nonetheless is treated as a tax increase because those workers were not helping to finance the payments to current retirees in the PAYGO system. On balance, their lifetime resources are lower because a portion of their savings is now taken for that purpose by taxes.

---

to implement. Employers wishing to integrate their pensions would be more inclined to use the excess method.

Table 6-3. *Summary of Major Social Security Reform Proposals*

Possible reform	Direct effect on employer resources	Direct effect on worker resources — Pre-retirement	Direct effect on worker resources — Post-retirement	Wage level of workers with larger change in demand	Other effects on pension plan design
Benefit cuts					
Percentage reductions in PIAs	...[a]	...[a]	Lower	Low	...[a]
Less generous COLAs	...	...	Lower	High	More annuitization
Include more years in AIME	...	...	Lower	Ambiguous	...[a]
Increase normal retirement age	...	...	Lower	Ambiguous	Accommodate
Increase income tax on benefits	...	...	Lower	High	...
Tax increases					
Include new state and local employees	Lower	Lower	Higher	Ambiguous	...
Increase maximum taxable earnings	Lower	Lower	Higher	High	...
Increase payroll tax rate	Lower	Lower	...[a]	Low	...
Individual accounts					
Used to replace some PAYGO benefits	Lower	Lower	...	Ambiguous	Less financial risk
Replacement, with a benefit guarantee	Lower	Lower	Higher	Ambiguous	...
Used to supplement PAYGO benefits	Lower	Lower	Higher	Low	...
Other proposed reforms					
Credit earnings for years of caregiving	...	...	Higher	Low	...
Increase widow(er) benefits	...	...	Higher	Ambiguous	...

a. Ellipsis denotes no effect.

Establishing a system of individual accounts also can affect budget constraints in both the pre- and post-retirement periods. If the individual accounts serve only to replace PAYGO benefits with an equivalent payout from the account, then there will be no change in postretirement income. Such a system requires the accounts to be invested in riskless, inflation-protected securities and paid out as annuities; if instead the accounts are invested in risky securities, then the effects on postretirement income will be ambiguous unless the government also provides a benefit guarantee. In such a scenario, postretirement income will be higher because the retiree will have more options for collecting income (risky investing or the guarantee). Similarly, individual accounts that supplement the existing PAYGO system, such as the RSPAs proposed during the presidential campaign in 2000, will increase retirement income and thereby reduce the demand for employer-provided pensions.

The next column in table 6-3 pertains to the effect of reform on pensions through changes in the relative demands for pensions by different groups of workers. As discussed, the critical element in each case is the incidence of the change in Social Security on the two groups of workers, patient and impatient, recalling that the former tends to have higher income than the latter. When the demand for pensions increases more for low-income workers than for high-income workers, the nondiscrimination rules are less likely to bind, enabling the employer to offer a greater share of compensation as pensions to all workers, not just low-income workers.

That effect appears twice—first when postretirement income is reduced disproportionately for low-income workers through benefit cuts. Reducing benefits through across-the-board reductions in the primary insurance amount (PIA) clearly affects the benefits of low-income workers more than those of high-income workers. Making the cost-of-living adjustment (COLA) less generous reduces the benefits of high-income workers by more, given the positive correlation between lifetime income and longevity. Taxing more of benefits or increasing the rate at which they are taxed also affects high-income workers more than low-income workers. The effect is ambiguous for the other two benefit cuts listed in the table. It is not clear which group's marginal years of earnings are lower relative to their average earnings. Nor is it clear which group would be more affected by an increase in the normal retirement age for Social Security. Ultimately, those questions must be resolved empirically.

The effect of reform through changes in relative demands for pensions appears again when taxes are raised disproportionately on high-income workers. As noted above, the tax increase reduces their demand for pensions because of life-cycle considerations. However, that initial reduction in their pension contributions relaxes nondiscrimination constraints if they are binding. In that case, the employer can reduce pension contributions made on behalf of low-income workers. Thus, part of the higher tax burden on high-income workers can be offset by reducing the implicit cross-subsidy of low-income workers. Pensions of low-income workers are scaled back, even if their tax rates are not specifically changed by reform.

Thus tax increases or contributions to individual accounts that are financed disproportionately by high-income workers create larger reductions in pension coverage than do tax increases financed disproportionately by low-income workers. Increases in the maximum taxable earnings level disproportionately affect high-income workers, whereas increases in the payroll tax rate disproportionately affect low-income workers. For the individual account reforms, the effect is ambiguous for those that use the account to substitute for a portion of the PAYGO benefits. However, if the individual accounts are similar to the USA or RSPA plans, then they clearly have the effect of increasing retirement benefits by more for low-income workers. In that case, they tend to make the nondiscrimination rules more likely to bind.[32]

The last column of the table considers the effects that Social Security reform may have on the form that pensions take, rather than on their overall level of generosity. Some reform proposals reduce benefits by reducing the cost-of-living adjustment. As noted, reducing the COLA has the effect of reducing the degree of annuitization in Social Security, because the real value of benefits is lower at higher ages. That particular type of benefit cut may increase the desirability of annuities for receiving pension benefits. That increase in the desirability of annuities might also lead to a more generous COLA on defined benefit pension plans.[33]

Increasing the Social Security normal retirement age presents several possible complications for pension plans. If the NRA is increased without a parallel increase in the early retirement age (ERA), then the critical effect occurs at the current ERA of 62, as most workers with a pension are retired before they reach the Social Security NRA. Under the current system, the hazard rate of retirement is sharply higher at age 62 than at other ages; that spike in retirement rates is probably due to the need for liquidity in income among potential retirees. DB

---

32. The interaction between government-sponsored accounts and nondiscrimination rules has been examined. Salisbury (1999) presents evidence from a large survey of 401(k) plan sponsors on the likely effect of the Clinton USA plan on the ability of the plan sponsors to meet the nondiscrimination rules. Salisbury's estimates indicate that between 13 and 26 percent of plans would fail the nondiscrimination rules if eligible workers stopped making voluntary contributions to their 401(k) plan in favor of the new account. As a result, the Gore proposal for RSPAs included provisions to give relief from the nondiscrimination rules if the failure is due to participation in RSPAs by low-income workers. Despite this relief, there still remains the possibility that RSPAs make low-income workers less willing to accept lower wages in exchange for pensions, because the RSPA decreases their current income and increases their retirement income.

33. Some defined benefit pension plans have a formal cost-of-living adjustment in the plan. Other plans give periodic, ad hoc increases to retirees at the plan sponsor's discretion.

pension plans also have early and normal retirement ages, and those ages typi-cally are lower than the ERA and NRA for Social Security. For example, a com-mon ERA for pensions is age 55. DB pension formulas often are structured to offer employees financial incentives to remain with the firm until the ERA and then to depart shortly thereafter; doing so is facilitated by supplementing the early retirement pension by an extra amount in the years between the plan ERA and the Social Security ERA.

If the Social Security ERA does not change, then the effect of a higher Social Security NRA is to reduce the level of the benefit available at age 62. Workers are less likely to retire at age 62, but, if they want to retire at 62, they prefer to have less of a supplement from their DB plan and more of a benefit continuing beyond the ERA. If the ERA increases along with the NRA, then workers absorb the benefit cut largely by postponing retirement until they reach the new ERA. The natural response for the employer is to increase the ERA in the pen-sion plan to maintain the same number of years of supplemental payment or to reduce the benefit that continues beyond the new ERA in favor of offering more years of the supplement before the new ERA.

By far the most dramatic reforms that have been proposed pertain to the establishment of individual accounts to replace a portion of Social Security ben-efits that otherwise would have to come from the pay-as-you-go system. In the typical setup, individual accounts differ from a straight increase in the payroll tax in that funds are invested in higher-return, higher-risk portfolios. That allows the expected replacement rate to be funded with a lower annual contribu-tion than would be required by a payroll tax hike, at the cost of greater financial risk to a portion of retirement income.[34]

The effect of a portfolio shift from Social Security to an individual account[35] comes primarily from the ways that workers will attempt to prepare for that risk. Precautionary behavior can be expected to manifest itself in two ways. First, workers will attempt to reduce the riskiness of their other financial assets to temper the amount of total risk that they face. They can be expected to allo-cate defined contribution funds to safer investments. Second, the added risk will encourage a greater level of total saving, particularly among patient workers who already are saving for retirement. They will seek to increase their pension contri-butions to provide higher income in retirement, when their total income is sub-ject to more risk. Since the impatient workers as a group will have less of an inclination to increase retirement saving, nondiscrimination rules may bind

34. See Feldstein, Ranguelova, and Samwick (2001) for simulations of the distribution of bene-fits from individual accounts under a variety of transition scenarios.

35. As discussed in McHale (2001), evidence on unanticipated benefit reductions from a vari-ety of countries suggests that it is incorrect to think of the Social Security benefits promised under current law as if they were riskless.

more severely when high-income workers attempt to make higher pension contributions. On the whole, attempts to offset the effects of individual accounts will reduce both risk and expected returns on pensions but increase total assets in the pension system.

Conclusions

This analysis establishes a framework for assessing the likely impact of Social Security reform on employer-provided pensions that incorporates standard effects on the supply of pension contributions by employers and life-cycle demand for pensions by workers. Its main analytical contribution is to incorporate in this framework heterogeneity in tastes for saving and imperfections in the way workers and firms are matched on the basis of workers' desired mix of wages and pensions.

Any pension plan is likely to cover two types of workers. Those in the first group have saving horizons that extend to retirement, and they therefore are willing to accept lower wages in exchange for pension benefits. Those in the second group have much shorter saving horizons and therefore are unwilling to forgo wages to obtain pension benefits. The two groups can coexist if the employer and the workers in the first group are willing to devote some of their tax savings to make contributions on behalf of the workers in the second group. The key to understanding the full effect of any potential reform on employer-provided pensions is to determine how it changes the relative demands for tax-advantaged saving by each of the two groups.

There are several important areas for future research. First, the public debate on Social Security reform requires more specifics from policymakers on how the long-term annual gap in finances will be closed. Some suggestions along those lines are set forth in Social Security Advisory Board (1999).

Second, because the employer decides which pension plan model is used, data must be collected at the employer level and supplemented with detailed demographic and economic data about employees and financial and economic data about the employers. Think, for example, of a dataset that links the Bureau of Labor Statistics' Employee Benefits Survey, the Health and Retirement Study, and Compustat. The data collected by EBRI that are used in Salisbury (1999) and even data of a single firm, as used in Kusko, Poterba, and Wilcox (1998), are good starting points.

Third, more work clearly is needed to understand the full model of saving. Extending the deterministic life-cycle model to include uncertainty was important, as was the introduction of target saving behavior.[36] But even that model is incomplete. Recent theoretical advances in habit formation and nonexponential

---

36. Carroll (1997).

discounting clearly are relevant to the way that households save, as are behavioral models that rely on psychological factors other than the standard utility maximization paradigm in economics. In addition, research on portfolio allocation over the life cycle is even less comprehensive than research on the size of the portfolio. As employer-provided pensions and eventually Social Security rely more heavily on individual accounts, informed policy requires a more thorough understanding of how households choose to allocate their retirement portfolios.

David A. Wise

Andrew Samwick thoughtfully addresses a very hard problem, one that is hard in part because the conventional theory of saving leaves much of saving behavior unexplained. For example, I believe that payroll deduction is perhaps the most important reason for the higher participation rate observed in 401(k) plans than in IRAs, but standard theory does not recognize this effect.

Samwick first presents a nice summary of options for Social Security reform and then a framework for analyzing the effects of reform on private pensions. The framework encourages us to think about how representative the framework might be and about the likely quantitative importance of the predictions. The framework also encourages us to think about the reverse effect—that of changes in private retirement saving on the Social Security system.

The Framework

In Samwick's framework, workers are patient savers or impatient nonsavers. Workers select high-pension jobs or low-pension jobs. Saver heterogeneity within firms is important: all firms include savers and nonsavers. The assumption is that (on average) firm pension arrangements are optimal given their mix of workers and the current Social Security system. If the Social Security system changes, the firm system would no longer be optimal; therefore every firm would want to change to a new optimal use of the tax advantage of the pension. An initial question is how nonoptimal the new situation might become. For a small divergence from optimality (assuming the current situation is optimal), will it typically be worthwhile to incur the transaction cost of changing to a private pension plan?

Empirical Analysis That Might Inform the Framework

The Samwick framework raises many empirical questions. Heterogeneity and sorting play a key role in the framework. That workers within a firm are heterogeneous seems clear, but the nature of sorting or self-selection of jobs is perhaps less clear. Venti and Wise show that persons with similar lifetime earning have very different tastes for saving, no matter what their lifetime earnings.[1] Some are savers, some are nonsavers. Persons with similar earnings are likely to fill jobs that are similar in many ways. If persons are sorted into jobs with similar earn-

---

1. Venti and Wise (2001).

ings, how much of the sorting represents a stronger preference for pension than wage compensation? How much of the sorting reflects job options? Persons with little education have more options among short-term, low-wage, low-pension jobs. A high degree of education provides more opportunity for long-term, high-wage, high-pension jobs. Do low-education workers choose low-pension jobs? Or are those the jobs available to them?

With respect to sorting by pension, how common is it, for example, for a worker to leave a job to substitute a 401(k) plan for a higher wage? Or to do the reverse? Empirical evidence on the question would be helpful. Perhaps the answer is difficult to identify: persons who seem to be nonsavers may in fact choose a job with a 401(k) payroll deduction option to protect themselves from their nonsaver selves—an example of the out-of-sight, out-of-mind syndrome.

The Samwick framework leads to several plausible predictions. One is that an increase in the Social Security normal retirement age or in the early retirement age would have an effect on the provisions of private pension plans. The provisions of the typical employer-provided defined benefit plan now incorporate strong incentives to retire early, often before the Social Security early retirement age. According to Lumsdaine, Stock, and Wise, the current planned increase in the Social Security normal retirement age would have little effect on retirement under the current provisions of the typical defined benefit employer plan.[2] Has there been any employer response to the planned increase in the Social Security normal retirement age from 65 to 67? Have the provisions of company plans changed to coincide with the Social Security increase?

The option for early retirement at age 62 was introduced in 1961. Was there a corresponding change in employer-provided defined benefit plans? A decline in the employer-provided defined benefit early retirement age? One might also search for "natural experiments" in Japan and the United Kingdom, where private pension systems are important and where there also have been important changes in the social security systems.

The Samwick framework suggests that in response to "risky Social Security personal accounts," workers would adjust their asset allocation in an employer-provided (defined contribution) plan and increase their saving in the employer plan. Many workers, especially low-income workers, are not eligible for a 401(k) plan that, for example, allows asset allocation. For higher-income workers, who are more likely to be eligible for a 401(k) account, the account would tend to dominate the Social Security account, in dollar terms (Poterba, Venti, and Wise 1998, 2001).[3] Thus the incentive to adjust the private plan allocation to relatively small changes in the Social Security system may be reduced.

2. Lumsdaine, Stock, and Wise (1997).
3. Poterba, Venti, and Wise (1998, 2001).

In addition, with respect to risk, many may consider the 401(k) plan—and perhaps Social Security personal accounts as well—to be less risky than promised Social Security benefits. Therefore they may not reduce 401(k) risk and increase 401(k) saving as the framework would suggest. Finally, 401(k) asset allocation may be determined by company options more than by careful analysis.

Effect of Private System Change on Social Security

It seems plausible that the effect of private pension plan change on Social Security may be as important as the reverse. There has been enormous and rapid change in the private pension system over the past two decades. In 1980, 92 percent of pension plan contributions were to employer-provided plans and 64 percent of those contributions went to defined benefit plans. Today, perhaps more than 65 percent of contributions go into personal accounts and—counting employer-provided conventional defined contribution plans—more than 80 percent of contributions go into individual-controlled accounts. Today 401(k) plans are the most important form of retirement saving. About 50 percent of households are eligible to contribute and more than 70 percent of them do. Poterba, Venti, and Wise project that 401(k) assets by 2035 are likely, on average, to be much larger than Social Security assets—75 to 250 percent of Social Security assets depending on the allocation of 401(k) assets and assuming no change in current Social Security provisons.[4] In seems clear that private personal retirement saving is progressing more quickly than any resolution of the Social Security personal account debate. Universal 401(k) coverage would indeed look much like a partially privatized Social Security system. This trend might well dominate any reaction of the pension system to Social Security reform.

Personal retirement plans have none of the early retirement incentive effects of defined benefit plans. Therefore any incentive to change the normal or early retirement ages of defined benefit plans in response to changes in Social Security retirement ages, for example, does not apply to the rapidly expanding personal retirement accounts.

How employees will view the relative risks of personal retirement and defined benefit accounts is not clear. The market risk inherent in personal accounts must be weighed against the job-change risk in defined benefit accounts. Job change can erode a very large fraction of the defined benefit retirement income that would accrue to a person who spent his or her working life in the same job, as discussed in Kotlikoff and Wise.[5] Indeed, many may view personal retirement accounts as less risky than promised Social Security benefits. It therefore seems plausible that a potential reallocation of assets in a 401(k) plan, for example,

4. Poterba, Venti, and Wise (1998, 2001).
5. Kotlikoff and Wise (1989).

may be outweighed by the dollar magnitude of 401(k) assets and by the problematic relative risk of Social Security and private retirement plan assets.

In Summary

Samwick has presented a carefully considered framework within which to think about the potential effects of Social Security reform on private pensions. An important question now is how representative the framework might be and how quantitatively important its predictions. I have suggested some directions for empirical analysis that might shed light on the question. In addition, thinking along the lines suggested by Samwick indicates to me that it might also be fruitful to take the opposite direction, in order to predict the effects of private pension reform on Social Security reform.

References

Aaron, Henry J., and Robert D. Reischauer. 1998. *Countdown to Reform: The Great Social Security Debate.* New York: Century Foundation Press.

Abel, Andrew B. 2001. "The Social Security Trust Fund, the Riskless Interest Rate, and Capital Accumulation." In *Risk Aspects of Investment-Based Social Security Reform,* edited by John Y. Campbell and Martin Feldstein, 153–93. University of Chicago Press.

Advisory Council on Social Security. 1997. *Report of the 1994–1996 Advisory Council on Social Security.* Washington.

Bender, Keith A. 1999. "Characteristics of Individuals with Integrated Pensions." *Social Security Bulletin* 62 (3): 28–40.

Board of Trustees of the Federal Old-Age and Survivors Insurance and Disability Insurance Trust Funds. 2003. *Annual Report.* U.S. Government Printing Office.

Brown, Jeffrey R. 2002. "Differential Mortality and the Value of Individual Account Retirement Annuities." In *The Distributional Aspects of Social Security and Social Security Reform,* edited by Martin S. Feldstein and Jeffrey B. Liebman, pp. 401–46. University of Chicago Press.

Campbell, John Y., and Martin S. Feldstein, eds. 2001. *Risk Aspects of Investment-Based Social Security Reform.* University of Chicago Press.

Carrington, William J., Kristin McCue, and Brooks Pierce. 2000. "The Efficacy and Impact of Non-Discrimination Rules." Bureau of Labor Statistics (June).

Carroll, Christopher D. 1997. "Buffer Stock Saving and the Life Cycle/Permanent Income Hypothesis." *Quarterly Journal of Economics* 112 (February): 1–55.

Copeland, Craig, Jack VanDerhei, and Dallas L. Salisbury. 1999. "Social Security Reform: Evaluating Current Proposals: Latest Results of the EBRI-SSASIM2 Policy Simulation Model." Issue Brief 210. Employee Benefit Research Institute (June).

Diamond, Peter A., and Peter R. Orszag. 2004. *Saving Social Security: A Balanced Approach.* Brookings.

Executive Office of the President of the United States. 2001. *A Blueprint for New Beginnings: A Responsible Budget for America's Priorities.* Government Printing Office.

Feldstein, Martin, Elena Ranguelova, and Andrew Samwick. 2001. "The Transition to Investment-Based Social Security when Portfolio Returns and Capital Profitability Are Uncertain." In Campbell and Feldstein, eds., *Risk Aspects of Investment-Based Social Security Reform,* 41–81.

Garrett, Daniel M. 1997. "The Effects of Nondiscrimination Rules on 401(k) Contributions." Stanford University, Department of Economics, and Cornerstone Research (January).

Ippolito, Richard A. 1997. *Pension Plans and Employee Performance: Evidence, Analysis, and Policy.* University of Chicago Press.

Kennickell, Arthur B. 2000. "Codebook for the 1998 Survey of Consumer Finances, 1998." Board of Governors of the Federal Reserve System (February).

Kotlikoff, Laurence J., and David A. Wise. 1989. *The Wage Carrot and the Pension Stick.* W. E. Upjohn Institute for Employment Research.

Kusko, Andrea L., James M. Poterba, and David W. Wilcox. 1998. "Employee Decisions with Respect to 401(k) Plans." In *Living with Defined Contribution Pensions: Remaking Responsibility for Retirement,* edited by Olivia S. Mitchell and Sylvester J. Schieber, 98–112. University of Pennsylvania Press.

Lumsdaine, Robin L., James H. Stock, and David A. Wise. 1997. "Retirement Incentives: The Interaction between Employer-Provided Pension Plans, Social Security, and Retiree

Health Benefits." In *The Economic Effects of Aging in the United States and Japan*, edited by Michael Hurd and N. Yashiro. University of Chicago Press

McGill, Dan M., Kyle N. Brown, John J. Haley, and Sylvester J. Schieber. 1996. *Fundamentals of Private Pensions*, 7th ed. University of Pennsylvania Press.

McHale, John. 2000. "The Risk of Social Security Benefit-Rule Changes: Some International Evidence." In *Risk Aspects of Investment-Based Social Security Reform*, edited by John Y. Campbell and Martin Feldstein, 247–82. University of Chicago Press.

Merton, Robert C., Zvi Bodie, and Alan J. Marcus. 1987. "Pension Plan Integration as Insurance against Social Security Risk." In *Issues in Pension Economics,* edited by Zvi Bodie, John B. Shoven, and David A. Wise, 147–69. University of Chicago Press.

Poterba, James M., Steven F. Venti, and David A. Wise. 1998. "Implications of Rising Personal Retirement Saving: Implications for 401(k) Asset Accumulation." In *Frontiers in the Economics of Aging*, edited by David A. Wise. University of Chicago Press.

———. 2001. "Pre-Retirement Cashouts and Forgone Retirement Saving: Implications for 401(k) Asset Accumulation." In *Themes in the Economics of Aging*, edited by David A. Wise. University of Chicago Press.

Salisbury, Dallas L. 1999. "Social Security's Goals and Criteria for Assessing Reforms." Statement before the Subcommittee on Social Security of the House Committee on Ways and Means, 106 Cong. 1 sess., March 25.

Samwick, Andrew A. 1995. "The Limited Offset between Pension Wealth and Other Private Wealth: Implications of Buffer Stock Saving." Dartmouth College, Department of Economics (December).

———. 1998a. "Tax Reform and Target Saving." *National Tax Journal* 51 (September): 621–35.

———. 1998b. "Discount Rate Heterogeneity and Social Security Reform." *Journal of Development Economics* 57 (October): 117–46.

———. 1999. "Social Security Reform in the United States." *National Tax Journal* 52 (December): 819–42.

Schieber, Sylvester J., and John B. Shoven. 1999. *The Real Deal: The History and Future of Social Security*. Yale University Press.

Slusher, Chuck. 1998. "Pension Integration and Social Security Reform." *Social Security Bulletin* 61 (3): 20–27.

Smetters, Kent. 2001. "The Effect of Pay-When-Needed Benefit Guarantees on the Impact of Social Security Privatization." In Campbell and Feldstein, eds., *Risk Aspects of Investment-Based Social Security Reform*, 91–105.

Social Security Act of 1935. P.L. 271. 74 Cong. 1 sess.

Social Security Advisory Board. 1999. "Report of the 1999 Technical Panel on Assumptions and Methods." Washington, D.C. (November).

Social Security Amendments of 1983. P.L. 98–21. 98 Cong. 1 sess.

Venti, Steven F., and David A. Wise. 2001. "Choice, Chance, and Wealth Dispersion at Retirement." In *Aging Issues in the United States and Japan,* edited by S. Ogura, T. Tachibanaki, and David Wise. University of Chicago Press.

7

Pension Choices with Uncertain Tax Policy

JOEL M. DICKSON

T raditionally, almost all pension plans and tax-preferred saving incentive vehicles in the United States contained what has become known as front-loaded tax incentives. In particular, the initial contribution was deductible from income, and the investment returns generated no tax liability until they were withdrawn, when they were taxed as ordinary income. Examples of front-loaded plans include defined benefit pensions, 401(k) plans, Individual Retirement Accounts (IRAs), and Keogh plans.

Recently, the United States has experimented with back-loaded saving incentives. The canonical back-loaded plan is the Roth IRA. Like traditional saving incentive plans, Roth IRAs feature tax-free buildup of investment returns in the account. Unlike traditional plans, however, contributions to Roth IRAs are not deductible and withdrawals are not taxable. The Roth IRA was established in 1997. A Roth 401(k) plan was established in 2001 tax legislation, to take effect in 2006. In 2003 and again in 2004, the Bush administration proposed a massive expansion of back-loaded incentives, including the creation of Lifetime Saving Accounts and Retirement Saving Accounts.[1]

A natural question is why front- and back-loaded saving incentives should exist in the same tax system. One concern is the possibility of creating opportunities for

1. Department of Treasury (2003).

221

investors to game the system. A second concern is that back-loaded incentives may have negative implications for long-term government revenue.[2]

This paper proposes a risk-based justification for allowing both front- and back-loaded incentives to exist at the same time and expounds on some of the implications. Although both front- and back-loaded incentives allow for tax-free accrual of funds, they create an important trade-off between present and future tax rates. Given an initial post-tax contribution, an investor will be indifferent to the choice between back- and front-loaded plans if it is known that the tax rate will be the same when contributions are made as when withdrawals are made. The investor will benefit more from the back-loaded plan than the front-loaded plan to the extent that the investor's future tax rate is higher than the current tax rate. But future tax rates are uncertain and vary with changes in income and legislation.[3] Thus, the benefit of investing in a front-loaded plan is uncertain relative to a back-loaded plan, and the simultaneous existence of both types of programs allows investors to hedge against the risks of future tax rate increases or decreases. Specifically, the Roth IRA allows investors to hedge against future tax rate increases by paying taxes today (when tax rates are known) and eliminating any future tax liability.

Investor Choice with Known Future Tax Rates

Holding the after-tax contribution constant, traditional and Roth vehicles will generate equal amounts of after-tax future wealth if tax rates are constant over time. But the vehicles can differ in other ways. First, under current law, contributions to traditional and Roth IRAs are capped at $3,000 ($3,500 for individuals age 50 and older), but the Roth contribution is made with after-tax funds, whereas the traditional IRA contribution is made with pre-tax funds. As a result, part of the contribution to a traditional IRA is really a deferred tax liability. This implies that the effective contribution to a Roth IRA is higher, because the investor gets to keep all of the proceeds of the contributions made to a Roth. Second, Roth 401(k) proceeds, as proposed, can be rolled over to Roth IRAs, which are not subject to required minimum distributions during the owner's lifetime, unlike traditional IRAs. As such, Roth 401(k)s may provide additional deferral possibilities for many investors. For the most part, this paper ignores these additional features and focuses on the key role played by the relation between current tax rates and expected future tax rates.

---

2. The budget issue arises because the costs of back-loaded plans do not show up in government revenue figures until well into the future. In addition, the advent of back-loaded plans has coincided with incentives to cash out traditional plans, pay taxes on the balances, and put the funds in the back-loaded plans, which actually raises revenue for the government in the short run, though several observers have argued that this approach may reduce revenue by even more in the long term (Halperin 1998, Steuerle 1997, and Burman, Gale, and Orszag 2003).

3. Burman, Gale, and Weiner (1998, 2001).

The basic arithmetic with known future tax rates is simple. Consider an investment of $1 (after-tax) in either a traditional or a Roth IRA. Let r be the pre-tax rate of return on the investment, t_0 and t_1 be the current and future marginal income tax rates, respectively, and T be the number of years before the balances are withdrawn. Under these assumptions, the after-tax funds available after all taxes for consumption spending in T years are e^{rT} in the Roth account and $e^{rT} * (1 - t_1)/(1 - t_0)$ in the traditional account.[4]

The difference between the Roth and traditional plan is determined solely by the difference between current and future tax rates. When future tax rates are higher than current rates, the Roth plan provides more after-tax wealth than the traditional plan. When future tax rates are lower than today, the traditional IRA generates higher after-tax wealth. Unless current and future tax rates are constant, the investor chooses an extreme allocation: either all of the contributions go to the traditional plan or all go to the back-loaded plan.

One of the potentially testable implications of this result is that individual savings behavior will depend on assumptions about the difference between current and future tax rates. Other things constant, those with higher expected retirement income (that is, higher current assets) should tend to prefer back-loaded vehicles to front-loaded vehicles.

The example above assumes that one tax rate applies to all contributions and another tax rate (which is possibly the same value) applies to all withdrawals. In a multiperiod context, income and hence tax rates can evolve over time, and the choices can be somewhat more complex. This is illustrated in figure 7-1 by tracing the real pre-tax income of an individual throughout his thirty-year working career. The straight line is the real, pre-tax annuitized value of his savings assuming a twenty-year distribution period. Given the assumptions of 2 percent real wage growth, 6 percent real return, and 15 percent total contribution to a retirement plan, the figure shows that for the first twelve years of the career, the annuity value is higher than the real income. This suggests that for this portion of his career, the investor may face a higher tax rate in retirement than his current rate in those years. Later in the career, the investor would likely expect a lower future tax rate, hence the decision between Roth and traditional would switch.

Investor Choices with Uncertain Future Tax Rates

The example above assumes that future tax rates are known. In reality, of course, they are not, and evidence suggests that tax rates can vary substantially over time.[5] Because investors are typically risk-averse, the uncertainty of future tax rates will make the traditional IRA less attractive relative to the back-loaded IRA.

---

4. The analysis ignores the possibility of an employer matching contribution.
5. Burman, Gale, and Weiner (1998).

Figure 7-1. *Real Pre-Tax Income over a Hypothetical Life Cycle*

Real income (dollars)

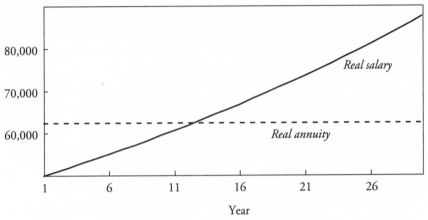

Source: Author's calculations.

To examine the effects of uncertainty in future tax rates, I consider a very simple extension of the previous example. Suppose the future tax rate (t_1) equals $t_0 - \varepsilon$ with probability p and $t_0 + \varepsilon$ with probability $1 - p$. Note that when $p = 0.5$ (that is, when a tax rate increase of a given size is just as likely as a tax rate decrease of the same size), a risk-averse investor would allocate the entire contribution to the Roth. This occurs because a risk-averse investor will always choose a safe asset over a risky asset that has the same expected return. In this case, the traditional 401(k) is the risky asset, and the Roth 401(k) represents a safe asset in terms of future tax rate changes.[6] Obviously, if the probability of a lower future tax rate is less than 0.5, the investor would choose to invest in the Roth. As p increases above 0.5, however, the investor will allocate progressively more of his savings to the traditional 401(k) vehicle. That is, over some probability range, the optimal choice is to invest in both the traditional and Roth 401(k) versions. Given the individual's risk aversion, there is a probability p^* between 0.5 and 1 above which all savings would be allocated to the traditional 401(k).

Figure 7-2 shows how the investor would allocate assets among the plans for different levels of risk aversion, assuming the investor's preferences can be modeled using a power utility function as described in appendix 7A. In this exercise, $t_0 = 30$ percent and $\varepsilon = 5$ percent. As the investor becomes more risk-averse,

---

6. This paper takes a narrow view of tax code risk; namely, that there is a risk of future tax rate changes. In a more general sense, tax code risk can also affect the choices between Roth and traditional 401(k)s to the extent that minimum distribution requirements or the general taxation of the Roth were to change in the future. Of course, the biggest risk for the Roth investor would be the introduction of a consumption-based taxation scheme that would result in double taxation of the Roth investment.

Figure 7-2. *Allocating among Both Traditional and Roth IRAs*[a]

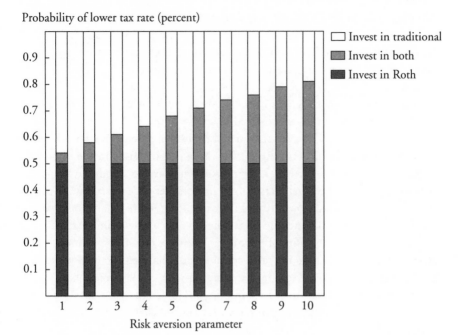

Probability of lower tax rate (percent)

Risk aversion parameter

Source: Author's calculations
a. Tax rate = 30 percent; tax rate moves +/– 5 percent in future.

she is more likely to allocate funds to both types of investment vehicles in order to hedge against the risk of a higher future tax rate that would reduce future consumption.

Even this extremely simple manner of introducing uncertainty generates significant differences in both preferred investment choice and the intuition regarding that choice. The treatment of uncertainty can be expanded as well. A richer way of modeling uncertainty is to consider the possibility of moving to a lower tax bracket in the future, combined with an expected tax increase that is less than the difference in tax rates between brackets.[7] The lower tax bracket is motivated by the view that, for most people, income when retired is lower than income during the working years. There are several reasons to consider higher

7. Considering the possibility of a lower tax bracket but a constant or lower tax rate for all brackets is somewhat uninteresting in this model because it would lead the individual to allocate all of his investment to the traditional 401(k). That is, future tax rates would be no higher than today, but could be lower. Similarly, if the expected tax increase were higher than the decline in tax rates from changing brackets, then the investor would face a higher future tax rate, implying that all investments should be made to the Roth.

tax rates, not the least of which is the potential for a significant long-term fiscal shortfall facing the country.[8]

In this case, the future tax rate equals $t_0 - (\alpha - \varepsilon)$ with probability p and $t_0 + \varepsilon$ with probability $1 - p$.[9] Figure 7-3 shows how the investor's allocation will change for different values of α and ε. The top panel shows an investor with some probability of moving from a 28 percent bracket to a 25 percent bracket, but who also faces an expected tax rate increase of 2 percentage points. The bottom panel considers the case of someone moving from the 25 percent bracket to the 15 percent bracket and an expected bracket increase of 3 percentage points.

One implication of this analysis is the likelihood of heterogeneity in the allocation between traditional and Roth 401(k)s among investors in the same federal tax rate bracket. In particular, an investor with taxable income in the lower part of the 25 percent federal marginal tax rate bracket may allocate more of her current savings to a traditional 401(k) than to a Roth 401(k) than would someone with current taxable income in the higher part of the same bracket. This occurs because the probability of realizing a lower tax rate in the future is more likely, and a relatively large tax rate increase would have to occur to make this "bet" unattractive.[10] Conversely, investors currently in the 31 percent tax bracket may not allocate as much to the traditional 401(k), for a given p, because the relatively modest decrease in tax rates between brackets could be offset by changes to the tax rates for all brackets.

A second implication concerns the presence of employer matching contributions in 401(k) plans. Consider an individual who has access to an employer-sponsored 401(k) plan with a match, but whose optimal allocation is to invest in the Roth IRA. The decision rule for this individual would be to forgo investing unmatched amounts in the 401(k) until he had contributed the maximum possible amount to the Roth IRA. For any reasonable match, the investor should still take advantage of the employer-sponsored plan up to the matched level. These results can provide testable implications about how investors choose deferral percentages within traditional 401(k) plans and whether or not an investor chooses to invest in a Roth IRA.

Another investor, whose optimal solution is to invest all proceeds in the traditional 401(k), would invest in the Roth IRA only after maximizing contributions to the 401(k) and a traditional IRA (if possible). If he were ineligible for a traditional IRA, he would then invest in a Roth IRA to the extent additional tax-deferred savings were desired.

---

8. Auerbach and others (2003); Gokhale and Smetters (2003).

9. As derived in the appendix, α is the percentage point difference between the old and new tax rate brackets.

10. In terms of the model, not allocating toward the 401(k) would suggest that the future tax rate increase (ε) is large relative to the rate difference between the brackets (α).

Figure 7-3. *Allocating among Both Roth and Traditional IRAs*

a. Moving from 28 percent rate to 25 percent bracket; 2 percent increase

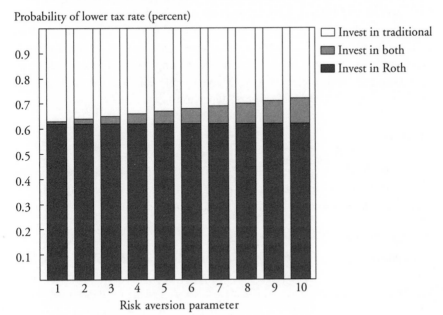

b. Moving from 25 percent rate to 15 percent bracket; 3 percent increase

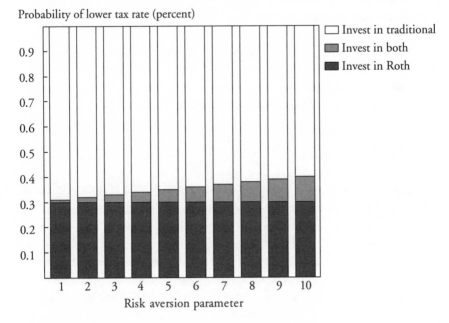

Source: Author's calculations.

Conclusion

This paper shows that back-loaded saving plans can provide a potentially valuable way for taxpayers to hedge a risk that is typically very difficult to insure against, namely, the risk of future tax increases. The availability of Roth IRAs and, in the future, Roth 401(k)s may represent a significant benefit to risk-averse individuals saving for retirement. Depending on an investor's risk tolerance and expected future tax rate, Roth investment vehicles could represent part or all of an investor's retirement saving allocations.

Appendix 7A

This appendix derives the mathematical results underlying the discussion in the text. Consistent with the text, the appendix compares situations where future tax rates are known to those where future rates are uncertain.

Known Future Tax Rates

The consumer's utility function is assumed to be time-separable and concave. The investor chooses a level of after-tax savings (S_0) and a savings allocation between two investment vehicles—a front-loaded pension plan—traditional 401(k)—and a back-loaded tax deferral plan—Roth 401(k)—in period 0. Amounts saved from a given income level (Y_0) earn a real rate of return r, and the price of the single consumption good remains fixed in real terms. Consumption in period 1 is equal to wealth in period 1. Marginal tax rates in each period are denoted by t_0 and t_1, with t_1 known.

Let x represent the proportion of savings allocated to the traditional 401(k). S_0 and x are the individual's choice variables in this optimization problem. I can represent the chosen after-tax savings amount as $S_0 = x S_0 + (1 - x) S_0$. Multiplying and dividing the first term on the right side by $(1 - t_0)$ yields:

$$(7\text{-}1) \qquad S_0 = (1 - t_0) \frac{x S_0}{1 - t_0} + (1 - x) S_0.$$

Under this representation, the amount contributed to the traditional 401(k) is represented by the first term on the right side of equation 7-1. That is, $x S_0 / (1 - t_0)$ is the pre-tax equivalent of the after-tax savings amount allocated to the traditional 401(k), and the saver's consumption is reduced by $(1 - t_0)$ of this amount in the first period because of the front-loaded tax benefit of the traditional 401(k). The amount contributed to the Roth 401(k) is represented by the second term on the right side of the equation. Given the allocation of current-period savings, real wealth (hence, consumption) in period 1 is the after-tax values of the traditional and Roth investments and can be represented by:

(7-2)
$$W_1 = S_0(1 + r)\left[x\left(\frac{t_0 - t_1}{1 - t_0}\right) + 1\right],$$

and the consumer's maximization problem is:

(7-3)
$$\underset{S_0, x}{Max} \; U(c_0, c_1) = U(c_0) + \frac{1}{1 + \delta} U(c_1)$$

s.t. $c_0 = (1 - t_0)Y_0 - S_0; \; c_1 = W_1$
$S_0 \geq 0; \; 0 \leq x \leq 1.$

Under the case of certainty (that is, t_1 is known), this maximization problem is straightforward to solve. The first-order conditions are:

(7-4)
$$\frac{\delta U}{\delta x} : \frac{1}{1 + \delta} U'(c_1)S_0(1 + r)\left(\frac{t_0 - t_1}{1 - t_0}\right), \text{ and}$$

(7-5)
$$\frac{\delta U}{\delta S_0} : -U'(c_0) + \frac{1}{1 + \delta} U'(c_1)S_0(1 + r)\left[x\left(\frac{t_0 - t_1}{1 - t_0}\right) + 1\right].$$

Under the assumption that the utility function is concave, it is readily apparent that the second derivatives with respect to each of the choice variables are nonnegative. The sign of 7-4 is determined solely by the difference in present and future tax rates. Given that x must lie between zero and one, the choice of x will be:

$$x^* = 1 \text{ for } t_1 < t_0$$

(7-6)
$$x^* = 0 \text{ for } t_1 > t_0$$

$$x \in [0,1] \text{ if } t_1 = t_0.$$

In other words, the consumer invests the entire savings amount in the traditional 401(k) if the future tax rate is less than the current rate, and all of his savings in the Roth 401(k) if the future tax rate is higher than the current rate. If tax rates today and in the future are equal, then the optimal choice of x is not uniquely defined because any value for x will result in the same period 0 and period 1 consumption amounts.

The optimal savings level is derived from equation 7-5 and satisfies:

(7-7)
$$\frac{U'(c_0)}{U'(c_1)} = \frac{1 + r}{1 + \delta}\left(x \; \frac{t_0 - t_1}{1 - t_0} + 1\right).$$

Using equation 7-6, equation 7-7 simplifies to $(1 + r)/(1 + \delta)$ when $t_1 > t_0$ because the optimal amount allocated to the traditional 401(k) is zero. In other words, the consumer saves in order to account for the differences between real asset growth and the discount rate.[11]

Let utility be defined by the power utility function, with constant relative risk aversion parameter $\gamma > 1$.[12] Hence,

$$U(c) = \frac{1}{1 - \gamma} c^{1 - \gamma}.$$

Using equations 7-6 and 7-7 and the simplifying assumption that $r = \delta$, the optimal level of savings can be obtained:[13]

$$S_0^* = \frac{(1 - t_0) Y_0}{(1 + r)\tau + 1} \; ; \text{ where } \tau = \left[\frac{1 - t_1}{1 - t_0} \right]^{(\gamma - 1)/\gamma} \qquad t_1 < t_0$$

$$= \frac{(1 - t_0) Y_0}{2 + r} \qquad t_1 \geq t_0.$$

The availability of the Roth 401(k) clearly expands the consumer's opportunity set. The savings rate increases (or current consumption declines) as the future tax rate increases in order to smooth consumption over the two periods. That is, $\delta S_0^*/\delta t_1 > 0$. The introduction of the Roth makes the savings rate independent of the future tax rate when the future rate exceeds the current marginal tax rate. In other words, although the first-period savings rate will be no higher with the introduction of the Roth (and could be lower), the ability to "avoid" higher future tax rates allows for increased consumption in both periods. This is also a result of the modeling of this problem; namely, that the two investment options are close substitutes. In short, the introduction of the Roth 401(k) would have two effects: an income effect (lifetime wealth may rise, thereby affecting the current-period savings decision) and a substitution effect (dollars that would have been invested in the traditional 401(k) may be shifted to the Roth version).

With uncertain future tax rates, the problem and solution change. As noted in the text, let the future tax rate (t_1) equal $t_0 - \varepsilon$ with probability p and $t_0 + \varepsilon$ with probability $1 - p$. In this case, the consumer maximizes the expected utility version of equation 7-3, where

$$EU(c_1) = pU(c_{1, \varepsilon}) + (1 - \rho)U(c_{1, -\varepsilon}),$$

11. The special case when $r = \delta$ is a familiar one in that the consumer saves in order to equate consumption in each period.

12. When $\gamma = 1$, the utility function is represented by log utility, that is, $U(c) = \ln (c)$.

13. Making this simplifying assumption does not alter any of the comparative static results discussed.

where $c_{1,-\varepsilon}$ denotes period one consumption when $t_0 - t_1$ equals ϕ. The solution for the proportion allocated to the traditional 401(k), x, is represented by the first-order condition:

$$pU'(c_{1,\varepsilon})S_0(1 + r)\left(\frac{\varepsilon}{1 - t_0} + 1\right) - (1 - p)U'(c_{1,-\varepsilon})S_0(1 + r)\left(\frac{\varepsilon}{1 - t_0} + 1\right) = 0,$$

or, equivalently,

$$\frac{U'(c_{1,\varepsilon})}{U'(c_{1,-\varepsilon})} = \frac{1 - p}{p}.$$

If investor preferences exhibit power utility, then the proportion of savings allocated to the traditional 401(k) can be shown to satisfy:

(7-8) $x^* = (1 - t_0)(1 - \rho^{1/\gamma})/\varepsilon(1 + \rho^{1/\gamma})$, where $\rho = (1 - p)/p$.

Note that at $p = 0.5$, the investor would allocate his entire savings to the Roth. The case of $\gamma = 1$ implies log utility preferences, and expression 7-8 simplifies to $x = (1 - t_0)(2p - 1)/\varepsilon$.

Another way to model the uncertainty is to let the future tax rate equal $t_0 - (\alpha - \varepsilon)$ with probability p and $t_0 + \varepsilon$ with probability $1 - p$. Assuming the power utility representation, solving for x yields a formula similar to 7-8:

$$x = (1 - t_0)(1 - \rho^{1/\gamma}\xi^{1/\gamma})/\varepsilon(1 + (\alpha - \varepsilon)\rho^{1/\gamma}\xi^{1/\gamma}), \text{ where } \rho = (1 - p)/p; \xi = \varepsilon/(\alpha - \varepsilon).$$

Selected results using this equation are shown in figure 7-3.

Peter R. Merrill

Joel Dickson's paper advances the theory of optimal portfolio choice by treating the investor's future marginal tax rate as subject to uncertainty. Previous papers, cited by Dickson, have analyzed portfolio choice on an after-tax basis but have treated only asset prices and not individual income tax rates as stochastic. Dickson's paper illuminates the consequences of stochastic tax rates in a simple model in which pre-tax returns are deterministic.

An investor's future marginal income tax rate may vary from expectations because of tax code changes (legislative uncertainty) and fluctuations in the investor's income (income uncertainty). Legislative uncertainty includes not only changes in tax brackets, but also changes in the alternative minimum tax (AMT) and in various phase-ins and phase-outs that can affect an investor's marginal income tax rate. For retirement savers, the phase-in of Social Security benefit taxation is particularly significant. Where applicable, the phase-in of Social Security benefit taxation can increase the marginal tax rate on unrelated income—such as withdrawals from a traditional IRA—by up to 85 percent.

Tax bracket changes are hardly an insignificant factor for U.S. investors. Since 1980 the top tax rates on interest, dividends, and long-term capital gains income have undergone frequent changes (table 7-1). The number and width of tax brackets has changed as well, and the brackets were indexed for inflation in 1981. There is little prospect that marginal tax rates will become more stable or predictable over the next twenty-five years. A statutory sunset applies (in 2009) to the reduced tax rates on stock dividends and capital gains enacted in 2003. The ordinary tax rate reductions enacted in 2001 sunset in 2011. Moreover, the AMT will apply to a growing percentage of taxpayers over time because the exclusion amount is not indexed. Many commentators believe that Congress will modify the scheduled tax rate sunsets and the increasing bite of the AMT. In addition, the looming fiscal imbalances in the Social Security and Medicare systems will likely result in further adjustments to the tax system within the first quarter of the twenty-first century.

In theory, future income tax rates should affect many types of current economic decisions including labor effort, savings, and the allocation of savings. With respect to portfolio choice, a known increase in income tax rates reduces the relative attractiveness of investment arrangements that defer the taxation of income (such as traditional IRAs, deferred annuity contracts, and installment sales).[1]

1. Investment through tax-deferred savings vehicles such as IRAs, 401(k)s, and deferred annuities has the effect of converting capital gains income into ordinary income, so the attractiveness of these accounts depends on the trajectory of ordinary and capital gains rates.

Table 7-1. *Top Individual Income Tax Bracket Rates: Interest, Dividends, and Long-Term Stock Gains, 1980–2011*[a]

Percent

Year first effective	Interest income	Stock dividends	Long-term stock gains
1980	70	70	28
1981	50	50	20
1987	38.5	38.5	28
1988	28	28	28
1991	31	31	28
1994	39.6	39.6	28
1997	39.6	39.6	20[b]
2001	39.1	39.1	20[b]
2002	38.6	38.6	20[b]
2003	35	15	15
2009	35	35	20[b]
2011	39.6	39.6	20[b]

a. Reflects legislation enacted as of December 31, 2003.
b. A top capital gains rate of 18 percent applies for certain property held more than five years.

Where future tax rate changes are known with certainty, investors may engage in "tax rate arbitrage" by shifting income recognition events immediately before or after tax rate change dates. For example, in 1986, capital gains realizations nearly doubled in response to the increase in capital gains tax rates enacted in the 1986 Tax Reform Act (effective in 1987). By contrast, Dickson's paper focuses on future tax rate changes that are subject to uncertainty. An additional element of Dickson's model is irreversible portfolio choice decisions.[2] With irreversible investment choices, tax rate uncertainty would be expected to cause risk-averse investors to reduce their investment in tax-deferred, relative to tax-prepaid, savings vehicles, which is the result that Dickson finds.

Purpose of Savings

The paper implicitly assumes that savings are intended for retirement purposes. The paper does not present any data regarding the proportion of IRA savings that are intended for funding retirement income. To the extent that a substantial portion of IRA balances are withdrawn before age 59-1/2 or, alternatively, pass through estates, the model would need to be extended to address these other

2. Taxpayers generally may recharacterize IRA contributions as either traditional or Roth IRAs up to the due date of the tax return for the year in which the contribution is made. In general, subject to income limitations, amounts in traditional IRAs can be rolled over or converted into a Roth IRA in subsequent years, and converted amounts are included in gross income. However, Roth IRA accounts cannot be converted into traditional IRAs.

types of savings, which have additional tax considerations. For example, unlike traditional IRAs, Roth IRAs are not subject to required minimum distributions, making them more attractive for estate building. As another example, Roth IRA distributions generally do not qualify for tax-free treatment unless a five-year holding period is satisfied, making them particularly unsuitable for short-term (less than five-year) savings. Dickson's model also does not take into account the 10-percent penalty tax that applies to certain distributions made from both traditional and Roth IRAs before age 59 $^1/_2$.

Level of Savings

Dickson's two-period model allows both the amount of savings and the form of savings to vary in response to future tax rates. Dickson's paper, however, focuses only on the impact of tax rate uncertainty on the allocation of savings between traditional and back-loaded pension plans. It does not address how the level of first-period savings is affected. The impact of tax rate uncertainty on the *level* of savings is a matter of considerable policy interest and should be elaborated in further work.

Allocation between Qualified and Nonqualified Accounts

Dickson considers only the allocation of savings between traditional and back-loaded pension plans and not the allocation of savings between qualified and nonqualified accounts. Dickson argues that qualified accounts will likely dominate nonqualified accounts. This conclusion should be reexamined in view of the 2003 Job Growth and Tax Relief Reconciliation Act's reduction of the top tax rates on stock dividends and capital gains to 15 percent. More generally, the model could be extended to allow for more than one asset. In a model with both debt and equity, it would be possible to examine how tax rate uncertainty affects both the asset location decision (that is, whether to put equity or bond investments in qualified accounts) and the choice between types of qualified accounts (that is, traditional or Roth IRAs).

Number of Model Periods

The use of a two-period model, representing the investor's accumulation and retirement periods, has the advantage of simplicity; however, such a model implicitly assumes that tax rates are constant within each of the two periods, each of which may last for thirty or more years. It is unclear (at least to me) how Dickson's results would be affected in a model where tax rates can change during multiple pre- and post-retirement periods. For example, would traditional IRAs look more attractive in a multiperiod model (with stochastic tax rates in each period) due to the traditional IRA investor's option in every period to convert into a Roth IRA, or to postpone withdrawals in any period with unfavorable tax rate outcomes (subject to required minimum distributions and consumption needs)?

Capital Losses

Under present law, itemizers may deduct embedded losses on Roth IRAs upon a complete liquidation of all Roth IRA accounts (subject to the 2 percent of adjusted gross income floor applicable to certain miscellaneous itemized deductions). In a model with stochastic asset prices, the loss deduction feature would make Roth IRAs relatively more attractive.

Constrained Investors

As Dickson notes, the amount of investment in traditional and Roth IRAs is subject to a combined annual dollar cap. For traditional IRA investors contributing the maximum amount, the front-end tax savings cannot be reinvested within the IRA itself and thus must be accumulated in a nonqualified account. A simple modification (to reflect accumulation of tax savings outside of qualified accounts) would allow Dickson's model to be extended to the constrained investor case.

Empirical Research

Dickson has developed a theory of portfolio allocation under tax rate uncertainty with potentially testable results. A direction for future research would be to use data on Roth IRA holdings to test the model. Such an analysis might focus on investors that have made IRA contributions after 1997 when the Roth IRA was enacted. The Survey of Consumer Finance collects data on both types of IRA holdings and could be used for this purpose.[3] Brokerage account data also might be used for this purpose.

Conclusion

Dickson has made an important contribution to the theory of portfolio choice by illustrating the effects of tax rate uncertainty in a simple two-period model with a single nonstochastic asset. The paper opens the way to future research including both theoretical extensions and empirical testing of the model using data on utilization of traditional and Roth IRAs.

3. Such an analysis would need to take into account the income limitation on deductions for traditional IRA contributions where the investor, or the investor's spouse, is an active participant in an employer-sponsored retirement plan, and the separate income limitation on contributions to Roth IRAs.

References

Auerbach, Alan J., and others. 2003. "Budget Blues: The Fiscal Outlook and Options for Reform." In *Agenda for the Nation,* edited by Henry J. Aaron, James M. Lindsay, and Pietro S. Nivola. Brookings.

Burman, Leonard E., William G. Gale, and Peter R. Orszag. 2003. "The Administration's Savings Proposals: Preliminary Analysis." *Tax Notes* (March 3): 1423–46.

Burman, Leonard E., William G. Gale, and David Weiner. 2001. "The Taxation of Retirement Saving: Choosing between Front-Loaded and Back-Loaded Options." *National Tax Journal* 54(September): 689–702.

———. 2001. "The Taxation of Retirement Saving: Choosing between Front-Loaded and Back-Loaded Options." *National Tax Journal* 53 (September): 689–702.

Department of the Treasury. 2003. *General Explanations of the Administration's Fiscal Year 2004 Revenue Proposals.* February.

Gokhale, Jagadeesh, and Kent Smetters. 2003. *Fiscal and Generational Imbalances: New Budget Measures for New Budget Priorities.* Washington: AEI Press.

Halperin, Daniel. 1998. "I Want a Roth IRA for Xmas." *Tax Notes* (December 21): 1567.

Steuerle, C. Eugene. 1997. "Back-Loaded IRAs: Head Taxes Replace Income and Consumption Taxes." *Tax Notes* (October 6): 109–10.

8

The Design and Cost of Pension Guarantees

KENT SMETTERS

The U.S. Social Security system faces a substantial long-term financial shortfall. Some have advocated using personal accounts to help resolve the problem. Others support increasing the extent to which the existing system is prefunded by contributions that are made in advance of benefit payments. It is also possible to combine the two approaches. Much of the academic and policy discussion of these alternatives has proceeded under the assumption that each approach is riskless. Under that assumption, the alternatives generate roughly the same outcomes, so that whichever reform is taken, the results will be similar.

But public pension outcomes are not certain; they are subject to a variety of contingencies, stemming from traditional, market-based risks involving uncertain and variable rates of return, to a variety of political-economic risks. This paper demonstrates that the two approaches to Social Security reform can generate very different results when risks are explicitly taken into account. Personal accounts are typically superior in handling the most important political-economy risks. But expanded prefunding of public accounts can be more effective at reducing market-based risks. This finding suggests that any analysis of

Parts of this paper circulated under a different title in the past, and helpful comments were received from Martin Feldstein, Bill Gale, Olivia Mitchell, Jan Walliser, and seminar participants at the NBER Summer Institute, Berkeley, Michigan State, World Bank, Philadelphia Federal Reserve Bank, Congressional Budget Office, and the American Economic Association meetings.

237

public pension reform needs to consider explicitly the risks involved rather than just the outcomes that are expected to derive in a fully certain environment.

Conceptual Building Blocks

The true costs of any promise to pay future benefits must be measured ex ante—that is, before the value of underlying risks is realized. This cost is not likely to be a readily observable variable like, for example, the price of corporate share. As a result, the costs may be inadvertently ignored in comparing the outcomes of different reform options. In fact, the ex ante cost of risks created can be larger than the *expected* cost of a pension plan. As a result, a pension reform that reduces the expected value of a pension plan's liabilities might actually increase its true liabilities once risk is taken into account.

Funding

In 401(k) plans, the contribution level is defined by formula, and the final retirement benefit level is directly tied to the account balance. In contrast, most public pension plans are defined benefit plans, where the value of the retirement benefit is determined by a formula, typically related to years of service, age, and salary. The disconnect between benefit levels and fund values in defined benefit plans has allowed government to set aside an amount of assets for the public pension plan that is less valuable than outstanding promised benefits. These plans are referred to as underfunded. Since an underfunded pension plan does not hold enough assets to meet promised benefits, the government must use tax revenue collected in a given year to help cover benefits paid in the same year. That is, benefits paid to retired generations in each year are paid, in part, using tax revenue collected from the subsequent generations of workers who are employed in the same year. If the pension plan fund has no assets whatsoever, then the pension is known as a pay-as-you-go plan. In that case, benefits paid to retired generations in each year are fully paid using tax revenue collected from subsequent generations of workers employed in the same year.

The current U.S. Social Security system is underfunded. While the Social Security trust fund is now worth more than $1 trillion, that represents a small fraction of the system's outstanding liabilities. Full funding would require an accumulation of another $10.5 trillion in assets under intermediate projections made by the Social Security Trustees.

Solvency

The U.S. Social Security system is also insolvent over the next seventy-five years. That is, existing projections of payroll tax revenues, plus the combined value of the current trust fund balance and future interest accruals on the balance, are less than legislated benefits over the next seventy-five years. Either payroll contributions will have to be raised, or benefits must be reduced, or both. The insolvency problem gets even worse if the projection horizon is extended beyond seventy-five years.

Insolvency should not be confused with underfunding.[1] All insolvent plans are underfunded, but not all underfunded plans are insolvent. For example, if Social Security payroll tax rates were increased over the next few decades, as needed to pay for current-law benefit levels, Social Security would be solvent, since tax revenue would cover benefits. But this system would still be underfunded since the government would still have to rely on the contributions from workers at each point in time in order to meet the benefit obligations of the elderly.

Rates of Return

The expected rates of return on contributions to an underfunded pension system will typically be less than those earned on a funded system. The reason is that all future generations must pay for the windfall given to early Social Security beneficiaries who received benefits but paid little or nothing into the system during their working years. That windfall is the flip side of the fact that the pension is underfunded, and it illustrates a key point: the benefits to one generation come at the cost of higher expenses to future generations. Indeed, pay-as-you-go financing in particular (and underfunding in general) is best thought of as an intergenerational zero-sum game for the most part.[2] The windfall to some set of beneficiaries equals the costs imposed on other generations.

A higher rate of return to contributions would be possible if Social Security were funded. Payroll contributions would then be invested into real assets earning market rates of return. Retirement benefits could be funded either by establishing personal accounts or by prefunding Social Security itself. No generation would then need to depend on the payroll taxes collected from the next generation; that is, the system would be fully funded.

The Challenge of Prefunding

Just as increasing benefits to earlier generations imposes costs on future generations, so increasing the Social Security resources of future generations requires an equivalent decrease in the present value of resources to some earlier generations.

---

1. As it turns out, however, the unfunded liability in the U.S. Social Security system and the insolvency problem are almost exactly the same. For those familiar with budget concepts, the "closed-group obligation" (CGO) represents the unfunded liability that current and past workers place on future workers. The "open-group obligation" (OGO) corresponds to solvency, that is, system sustainability. By sheer coincidence, both the CGO and OGO have been estimated in the 2003 Social Security Trustees' Report to be equal to $10.5 trillion.

2. This assumes that the economy is so-called "dynamically efficient" and that the government cannot run a Ponzi game. Abel and others (1989) provide strong evidence that the U.S. economy is dynamically efficient. See Geanakoplos, Mitchell, and Zeldes (1998) for more discussion of the zero-sum game.

Additional prefunding would require that some transitional generations make extra contributions, reducing their lifetime resources. These transitional generations would have to pay both for the benefits already promised to existing retirees and for their own future benefits. Future generations, however, would benefit from being born into a funded system that gave them higher rates of return.

To be sure, the present value of resources for all generations could increase after reforming Social Security, but only if greater funding was accompanied by some source of efficiency gain independent of funding itself. That gain could come from an implicit tax reform happening in the background of reform. For example, a move toward personal accounts could generate greater transparency in the link between the taxes that each person pays and the future benefits each person receives. In this case, *effective* net tax rates on labor would be reduced, and government revenue would likely increase somewhat. Funding using personal accounts could also reduce uncertainty about future benefits.

But barring an increase in tax efficiency or some other indirect benefit, increasing the resources of some future generation requires reducing the resources of some transitional generation. The reduction in resources for that intermediate generation might be justified on moral grounds if we believe that future generations are being hit particularly hard under the current public policy baseline.

Even if it is agreed that greater funding is fair to future generations and potentially even efficiency improving, the question arises as to whether the new assets should be held in personal accounts by individuals or in the Social Security trust fund. These options create a variety of risks, in the political and market spheres, that bear on the best choice.

Political-Economy Risks

Political-economy risks are subjective in nature, but could prove to be substantial nonetheless.[3] Instead of calculating a dollar value for each major political-economy risk, table 8-1 summarizes a more qualitative ranking of each risk as high, medium, or low for each risk considered in this section.

Using Retirement Funds for Other Purposes

One important political-economy risk is that assets held by the public pension plan could be spent on other programs, possibly in a roundabout way, given the opaque nature of most government accounting. Funding the existing public pension plan relies heavily on the government being able to store assets in a

---

3. Diamond (1997, 2000a, 2000b); McHale (2000).

Table 8-1. *Political-Economy Risks*

	Reform	
Political risk	*Increasing size of trust fund*	*Private accounts*
Using retirement funds for other purposes	High risk	Low to medium risk
Investment restrictions leading to lower expected returns for a given level of risk	High risk	Low risk
Regulatory conflicts	Low to medium risk	Low to medium risk
Less redistribution	Low risk	Low to medium risk
Setting aside enough money to actually save Social Security	Medium to high risk	Low to medium risk
High administrative costs	Low risk	Low to medium risk

"lock box" to pay for future benefits. A true lock box, however, seems to have eluded policymakers in the United States since the inception of Social Security.[4]

The Social Security trust fund was taken off budget during the 1980s in an effort to raise the transparency of the store of value represented by the trust fund. But policymakers, along with the Congressional Budget Office and the White House Office of Management and Budget, continued to set spending targets based on the unified budget measure that includes income surpluses in the trust fund. To the extent that policymakers target a given unified budget surplus level (say, zero), larger trust fund surpluses will get spent elsewhere and will not lead to an increase in public saving or the nation's preparation for financing future benefits.

Indeed, the late Senator Daniel Patrick Moynihan often argued that the decision to begin building up the trust fund during the 1980s was nothing more than a clever Republican regressive tax reform. In particular, the increase in payroll taxes during the 1980s created higher labor taxes, levied over a limited wage tax base, that were used to afford lower income taxes, levied over a more progressive tax base that includes capital income. Indeed, in 1990 Senator Moynihan even suggested reducing the Social Security payroll tax in order to move Social Security back to a strict pay-as-you-go system. If Moynihan is right, the growth in the Social Security trust fund during the past two decades failed to increase significantly public savings in order to help pay for future benefits.

4. Schieber and Shoven (1999).

Not everyone share's Moynihan's opinion. Diamond, based on his own reading of the political dynamics during the past twenty years, argues that Congress would have essentially allowed for even larger deficits without the Social Security trust fund surpluses.[5] Hence, the trust fund buildup during the 1980s, he believes, probably did lead to a lower level of external debt and, thereby, increased public saving.

Still, the government's continued focus on the unified budget measure gives an important clue that a true lock box might be elusive. Ultimately, the issue of whether a larger trust fund has increased national saving is an empirical one. In another work, I provide evidence that the federal government has indeed diverted trust fund dollars to other fiscal priorities.[6] I also find that the adoption of a "unified budget" framework in the late 1960s appears to play a statistically significant role in this result.

This political-economy problem could be addressed if assets were held in a separate capital account and, therefore, did not appear in the unified budget surplus.[7] But it is not clear if the integrity of separate budget accounts would be maintained over time if politicians want to spend money on other causes, especially in times of great need. For example, during the budget impasse between Congress and the Clinton administration for the 1996 fiscal year, the government's general fund borrowed from the federal employees' Civil Service Retirement fund and the federal Thrift Savings Plan to keep from hitting the legal debt ceiling.[8] Trust fund assets could also easily be leveraged by using pension obligation bonds, like those issued recently by many states. Or the government could focus on a "superunified" budget surplus measure that adds capital account surpluses right back into the spending equation.

The ramifications of using assets held in a capital account for other purposes could go undetected by the public for quite a while because Social Security benefit levels are not directly tied to the value of the trust fund. Hence, an extraction of resources by one generation could be passed along to future generations as indirect debt, undetectable by standard deficit accounting techniques. In table 8-1, therefore, I list the risk that trust fund assets could be spent elsewhere as high.

Another way to prevent the government from spending money intended to fund public pension benefits would be to store the money in personal accounts,

---

5. Diamond (2000b, 2003).

6. Smetters (2003).

7. The current budget rules are not clear as to whether a government investment in equities would show up as an outlay and, therefore, be subtracted from the unified surplus measure (see CBO 2003). Some plans to invest the trust fund in equities explicitly require that the investments not be counted as an outlay in order to avoid the appearance of reducing the surplus. Hence, equity investments could still be matched with less public saving elsewhere.

8. GAO (1996). In this particular case, those funds were replenished once a budget deal was struck. In essence, the government unofficially temporarily "defaulted" on one set of bonds to temporarily reduce the outstanding debt.

which are more directly tied to future retirement benefits. Confiscation of personal assets by the government for other uses would be quite explicit and, therefore, probably much less likely to happen.

Still, those assets could be spent by consumers themselves who lobby the government for the right to use those assets for other reasons, such as college expenses or the purchase of a new home. For example, continuing legislative proposals attempt to waive tax penalties for people who use money in their 401(k) accounts for certain nonretirement purposes. Of course, 401(k) accounts are not first-tier retirement benefits for most people, and so it is not clear if that discussion is informative in the current context. To be sure, college and housing expenses are productive investments. But allowing people to spend retirement resources for other reasons would essentially defund the retirement system, causing a larger liability to be passed to future generations who will be called upon to support the elderly.

Chile, which privatized its public pension system during the 1980s, restricts how people can use the funds in their personal accounts. People can extract, in a lump-sum fashion, some funds from their personal accounts for any purpose by retiring early. But the remaining account balance must be enough to be able to provide a real-indexed annuity with survivor's protection that pays at least 70 percent of the worker's average salary and 120 percent of the system's minimum guaranteed pension.[9] Similar rules might have to be employed in the United States if personal accounts were heavily relied upon to provide first-tier retirement benefits. Whether these types of rules—which do seem to work in Chile—would be sustainable in the U.S. political system, with its greater emphasis on individual choice, is unclear. For this reason, I view that this risk is low to medium for personal accounts.

Investment Restrictions

Currently, the Social Security trust fund in the United States is required to purchase government bonds. One of the options for reforming the system that received a fair amount of attention during the Clinton administration was to invest a portion of the Social Security trust fund into equities. The main intention of this policy change was to attempt to increase the expected returns earned by the Social Security system, reducing the projected insolvency of the system. This proposal, in fact, was suggested for study in the "Maintain Benefits Plus" plan of the 1994–1996 Social Security Commission, which eventually found its way into President Clinton's 1999 State of the Union Address. This reform raises many issues, one of which is the possibility that the government might invest in "socially responsible" projects or attempt to prop up inefficient industries.

9. CBO (1999).

Empirically, rates of returns to investments made by partially funded public pensions in individual states in the United States and across the world are often lower than investment returns on personal pensions in the same countries. In a recent important cross-country study, Iglesias and Palacios document that public pension plans across the world tend to earn annual rates of return that are as much as several hundred basis points below their personal pension plan counterparts on average.[10] The main reason is that governments often—in fact, typically—restrict where public assets can be invested or direct money to inefficient projects.[11]

In the United States investments in politically sensitive industries, for example, might be prohibited. Already, state-level public pension plans in the United States are prohibited from investing in companies located in countries that violate various human rights; tobacco producers; pollution-causing industries; and even music record companies that produce songs with objectionable lyrics.[12]

Investments might also be too heavily weighted in domestic companies and might directly subsidize inefficiency.[13] If so, less global diversification might occur during a recession when citizens are the most concerned with foreign competition. Moreover, while personal investments would generally flow away from inefficient industries, public investments might flow the opposite direction to prop up politically sensitive, but economically inefficient, industries. Pressures to subsidize inefficient domestic industries could be higher in a national funded public pension system than in many U.S. state-level pensions. In particular, more resources in the national plan could make the ability to conduct industrial policy that much more tempting.

To be sure, assets held by Social Security could be independently managed by a distinct government agency, maybe a counterpart to the Federal Reserve Board. But potential conflicts would still remain. Some people may not want the government to hold assets that they themselves would not hold. They might be willing to accept a lower return and might try to impose those standards on others. And, since benefit obligations are not directly tied to asset returns, people could lobby for investment restrictions and not even bear the cost themselves. As a result, asset underperformance might be largely passed on as a liability to future taxpayers. To be sure, a greater burden could have instead been passed explicitly to future generations via a larger amount of government debt. But portfolio restrictions would be a more hidden way to go about it. For this reason,

---

10. Iglesias and Palacios (2000).

11. Some of the difference in outcomes is simply due to the fact that some government pension systems invested only in government bonds, thereby earning a lower rate of return in exchange for less risk. This difference, of course, is not a source of inefficiency. However, in many cases, the return was lower even on a risk-adjusted basis.

12. Diamond (1997).

13. Iglesias and Palacios (2000).

and based on existing empirical evidence outlined above, I view the political-economy investment restriction risk as high for funded public pension plans.

Investment restrictions could also be placed on personal accounts. One type of investment restriction could require agents to hold a broad set of assets. But this restriction would probably be quite sensible. It would reduce moral hazard by people who invest speculatively in just a few companies and later lose, thereby becoming wards of the state. But the government could also limit investments to politically desirable or domestic enterprises, or both, in the same way that it might limit investments of a public fund. However, this political risk is probably much smaller for personal accounts since retirement benefits would be more closely tied to the performance of funds held in personal accounts. As a result, people who lobby for investment restrictions would also have to bear part of the cost. Moreover, people who object to investing in certain companies could avoid those companies in their own account, without forcing others to follow.

Empirically, very little pressure seems to exist in defined contribution plans to pass laws that limit how tax-preferred 401(k) accounts can be invested. This fact is interesting since current 401(k) assets do not even constitute first-tier retirement income for many people. Moreover, 401(k) account coverage is not universal, and so some of the population could lobby for investment restrictions and not bear the cost. Nonetheless, little pressure seems to exist to restrict how these accounts are invested, despite the tax subsidy that they receive. For this reason, I view the risk of investment restrictions as low for personal accounts.

Regulatory Enforcement

Assets held by a public trust fund could lead to other types of governmental conflicts of interest as well including, for example, antitrust enforcement. In essence, antitrust enforcement would involve the government suing itself as part shareholder. As a result, the government might choose not to sue itself, especially if a decrease in the value of a moderately sized public pension trust fund required a near-term increase in politically unpopular distorting taxes or a reduction in retirement benefits. This risk might be heightened if the government's portfolio is already restricted to a small subset of domestic companies. I, therefore, view this risk as medium for a public pension system.

For funded personal accounts, regulatory enforcement risk is probably on the low to medium end. It is possible that owners of personal accounts would also lobby the government not to enforce competitive-based regulations, fearing a decrease in the value of their personal accounts. But individuals investing for retirement are also able to take a long horizon and to reap the long-term benefits of greater economic efficiency. To be sure, older investors might lobby for reduced regulatory enforcement since they might bear short-run costs of enforcement without realizing the long-term benefits. Empirically, however, there did not seem to be much of a public outcry against the government's antitrust case against Microsoft, despite the popularity of the company and its cofounder Bill Gates. The same was basically true regarding the breakup of AT&T a few decades ago. Hence, there probably is a risk that regulation would not be sufficiently enforced after more personal accounts were established. But that risk is probably fairly modest.

Less Redistribution

Social Security currently commingles old-age insurance with redistribution, and funding the current system would probably have little impact on this redistribution. Redistribution is accomplished through the benefit computation formula. It gives individuals with lower lifetime (covered) wages a retirement life annuity payment that replaces a larger fraction of their average pre-retirement wages relative to those with higher wages. However, since the annuity payment is not increased to compensate poor people for living a shorter life on average, Social Security benefits might not be as progressive as once thought.[14]

A move to personal accounts would tend to make Social Security's redistribution more explicit. Progressivity could be maintained if personal contributions were subsidized by, for example, matching the contributions made by the poor.[15] Another approach would prop up asset values of poor agents upon retirement. In either approach, redistribution would be quite explicit.

Defenders of the current form of Social Security worry that any type of explicit redistribution program will lose political support. This notion was expressed eloquently by Wilbur Cohen, the first employee of the Social Security Administration who later become its chief administrator. In a now classic debate with Milton Friedman, Wilbur Cohen noted that "a program for poor people will be a poor program."[16] Interestingly, even Milton Friedman now concedes the point. Reflecting on Cohen's remark more than twenty-five years later, Friedman noted in a recent interview:

> Now, if you stop and think about it, you ask yourself: 'Isn't that true?' Look at what has happened to public housing: It's a program designed for poor people—it's a poor program. Look at what happened to Aid to Families with Dependent Children: It was a program designed for poor people—it was a poor program. Programs that are designed for the poor will be poor programs. You need to have a universal program to have the backing of society as a whole, in order that it can really be a part of the structure of society.[17]

14. See Coronado, Fullerton, and Glass (2000) for this and other reasons.
15. This approach to subsidization has been analyzed in Kotlikoff, Smetters, and Walliser (1998).
16. Friedman and Cohen (1972). That sentiment is also reflected in Siedman (1999) and Diamond (1997).
17. George Clowes, "An Interview with Milton Friedman," *School Reform News* (www.heartland.org/education/dec98/friedman.htm [1998]).

To be sure, one might argue that a fear of less redistribution should not really be classified as a risk. After all, if the redistribution in the current system is made explicit and it so happens to become unpopular, then that reduction in redistribution simply reflects the will of the people. Indeed, one could argue that the current bundling of old-age insurance and redistribution, as in Social Security, risks having an old-age pension system that does not fully reflect the will of the people.

However, it could also be argued that making old-age insurance and redistribution difficult to untangle is a reasonable social norm for enforcing ex ante risk-sharing agreements between young workers. In particular, young workers have an incentive to pool their future lifetime wages. If, in later years, agents who happened to realize higher lifetime wages could easily vote to undo that risk-sharing agreement, then they could effectively renege on a previous agreement. Knowing that fact ex ante, young agents would not be able to engage in the risk-sharing agreement in the first place. It follows that agents might agree ex ante to a pension system with some redistribution that is difficult to unravel later on.

While subsidizing the accounts of poor people at the point of retirement could be politically unpopular, a progressive government match of contributions would likely not be viewed as a program that focuses on the poor. A government match could be universal, providing at least some match to everyone on a sliding scale. A progressive match would appear similar to the federal government's Earned Income Tax Credit (EITC) program, which provides extra income for working people who earn little income.

Government matching programs like the EITC appear to be both popular with conservative economists, like Gary Becker and Milton Friedman, as well as the general population. The federal EITC program has actually been expanded over time in face of the demise of other government welfare programs like Aid to Families with Dependent Children (AFDC). The EITC program might be relatively more popular with the population at large because it appears to subsidize good behavior (such as working). Programs like AFDC, however, appeared to reward people for bad behavior (such as having children out of wedlock) even though, of course, the point of AFDC was mainly to transfer income to support children who had little choice in the matter.

Even without a government match, holding funds in personal accounts might not lead to a significant decrease in redistribution if personal accounts were mainly used to supplement Social Security benefits. In light of the solvency problem facing Social Security, personal accounts could be used to supplement a reduced Social Security benefit in the future, as in the Feldstein and Samwick plan.[18] In this case, Social Security benefits could be scaled back in a progressive fashion; indeed, in model 2 of the plan offered in 2001 by President Bush's

18. Feldstein and Samwick (2000).

Social Security Commission, many poor would actually fare better than they currently do under Social Security.[19] For these reasons, I rank this political-economy risk as low to medium for personal accounts.

Failure to Set Aside Enough Money

Another political-economy risk facing a plan to fund future Social Security benefits is that the government might actually fail to set aside enough resources to achieve any stated funding objective. Rather than make a large enough initial investment, the government might instead hope for large subsequent investment returns. While it is true that, historically, stocks have appeared to be low risk for long thirty-year holding periods, that stylized fact is based on only a few unique holding periods.[20] Moreover, that stylized fact appears to hold true for U.S. markets and not for most international markets.[21] And many economists believe that stocks are risky even for long holding periods.[22]

Failure to set aside enough money would almost be automatic in a prefunded Social Security system that invested in equities under the revenue projection rules currently used by the Congressional Budget Office and the Office of Management and Budget. For example, revenue projections made by the CBO and OMB of President Clinton's 1999 proposal to invest part of the Social Security trust fund in equities focused on *expected* returns to risky equities, ignoring risk.[23] Hence, prefunding would not occur on a *risk-adjusted* basis.[24]

To be sure, the issue of possibly failing to set aside enough money would be moot *if* a larger Social Security trust fund simply bought more government debt. But there currently is not enough debt available to prefund Social Security significantly (if the government simply printed more debt, then no prefunding would occur). As of the start of the 2003 fiscal year, the debt held by the public was about $3.5 trillion, and "redeemable debt" is estimated to be closer to $2.5 trillion. Social Security, in contrast, faces a present value shortfall closer to $10.5 trillion according to the 2003 Trustees' Report. Hence, at least some resources would have to be invested in the stock market if the government attempted to address Social Security's problems fully. I therefore view this political-economy risk as medium to high for a funded public pension plan.

19. The President's Commission to Strengthen Social Security. 2001. "Strengthening Social Security and Creating Personal Wealth for All Americans." Washington.

20. Siegel and Thaler (1997).

21. Goetzmann and Jorion (1996).

22. Bodie (1995); Jagannathan and Kocherlakota (1996).

23. Bazelon and Smetters (1999); Smetters (2000a).

24. Since the trust fund bears both the upside and downside risk, risk could be properly accounted by projecting future returns using the Treasury yields instead of the expected returns to equities. This approach was, in fact, recommended by the 1999 Technical Panel on Assumptions and Methods to the Social Security Advisory Board (SSAB, 1999) which advises the Social Security Administration. However, it is not government accounting practice.

For personal accounts, I view this risk as low to medium. There is some debate about whether existing private investors are too risk seeking or too risk averse. New personal accounts would likely include many more currently non-active traders who are likely to be risk averse. To be sure, some bounds on investments may be needed to prevent investors from taking too little risk or too much risk. But the market risk in personal accounts would be substantially more transparent than the market risks held by a Social Security trust fund that held equities. The reason is that benefits are more directly tied to contributions and investment returns in a personal account system. This would reduce the ability of the government to focus only on expected values when determining contribution rates.

High Administrative Costs

The current Social Security system appears to have fairly low operational costs,[25] and those costs would unlikely change much if Social Security benefits were funded. Concern, however, has been raised about the administrative costs of personal accounts. Diamond, for example, argues that personal accounts could be plagued with high costs, depending on their design.[26] These costs include expenses associated with collecting contributions, investment management, and fraud.

Goldberg and Graetz estimate administrative costs of personal accounts in detail.[27] Their analysis shows that personal accounts with very few controls could indeed be expensive to administer. However, some of these costs are in exchange for real services that are not currently provided by Social Security, including, for example, account updates. In a low-cost system, investment funds would be approved and regulated by the federal government and would be subject to standard auditing controls to reduce fraud. Maximum account charges might be employed to limit investment charges that are inefficient but not strictly fraudulent. In this case, most of the administrative costs would come from collecting contributions from individual workers. Goldberg and Graetz argue that these collection costs could be quite low if the new system continued to use the collection method currently implemented by Social Security. Once collections are made, contributions could be shifted between various competing and regulated funds electronically, maybe using Internet access or a touch-tone telephone access. Free movements of resources among funds could be limited.

Major costs could thus be avoided. Few Americans would disagree with controls against fraud. Moreover, few Americans appear to object to the specific manner in which payroll contributions are currently collected under Social

25. Mitchell (1998).
26. Diamond (2000a).
27. Goldberg and Graetz (2000).

Security. For these reasons, I view the risk of having high transaction costs as low to medium.

Market-Based Risks

In addition to the political risks created by reform options, market-based risks may also prove to be substantial. This section outlines the market-based risks associated with personal accounts and with prefunding Social Security.

Personal Accounts

Personal accounts in an unfettered economy would require individual retirees to bear significant asset-return risk. The amount of money that risk-averse agents would be willing to pay to avoid that risk could be large. But few observers believe that individuals would really be required to bear that risk. The government would likely bear a significant amount of risk, even as the insurer of last resort.

Many plans to transform Social Security into a system based on personal accounts explicitly state a guarantee role for the government. In most of these plans, the benefit guarantee would be unfunded; that is, the government would not set aside additional assets ahead of time to buffer market downturns. The value of this new unfunded liability could actually be larger than Social Security's existing unfunded liability.[28] Hence, plans that appear to fund Social Security benefits could actually increase the true unfunded liabilities inherited by future generations.

Table 8-2 shows that the long-run reduction in unfunded liabilities from creating personal accounts depends crucially on whether minimum benefit guarantees are provided.[29] The calculations in table 8-2 assume that contributions to personal accounts are invested half in stocks, which earn 9 percent a year, and half in bonds, which earn 3 percent.[30] This portfolio pays an average annual rate of return (including corporate income taxes) of 6 percent. The Social Security payroll tax base is assumed to grow at an annual real rate of 1 percent.[31]

Suppose that the contribution rate for private accounts is chosen so that the expected retirement benefit produced by the private account equals the benefit level currently provided under Social Security. A contribution rate of about

28. Smetters (2002).

29. Details are provided in Smetters (2002). The costs of different types of pension guarantees have also been estimated in Marcus (1987), Pesando (1996), and Pennachi (1999).

30. A bond could be replicated by a "collar," which is a security that combines different rights (options) to buy (call) and sell (put) stocks at different (strike) prices. Collars can also be designed in a more flexible fashion, as in Feldstein and Ranguelova (2000). But collars do not reduce unfunded liabilities any more than does a portfolio with bonds.

31. This assumption is consistent with the 2000 Social Security Trustees' Report, the most recent report available when Smetters (2002) was written.

Table 8-2. *Change in Unfunded Liabilities: Private Accounts*[a]

Expected private benefit/current Social Security benefit (ratio)	*Required contribution rate for private accounts/pay-as-you-go Social Security payroll tax rate required for solvency (ratio)*	*Guaranteed benefit level/current Social Security benefit (ratio)*	*Reduction in unfunded liabilities relative to Social Security's current unfunded liabilities (percent)*
1	.17	0	100.0
1	.17	3/4	53.8
1	.17	1	29.9
2	.34	3/4	70.9
2	.34	1	51.9
2	.34	1 1/4	30.5
2	.34	1 1/2	7.6
3	.51	1	64.5
5	.86	3/4	100.0
5	.86	1	82.9
5	.86	1 1/2	51.1

a. 50 percent investment in broad stock index, 50 percent investment in bonds.

19.5 percentage points of payroll is projected by the Social Security Trustees to be required to keep Social Security solvent over the next seventy-five years.[32] Table 8-2 shows that the corresponding contribution rate for the personal accounts is about 3.3 percent. The significant difference in contributions is attributable to the large differences in expected rates of return between the private account and Social Security, compounded over many years.

If the individual accounts are introduced without a minimum benefit guarantee, Social Security's unfunded liabilities would be reduced by 100 percent. Private agents themselves would fully bear all market risk, none of which would be passed to future generations. The reduction in unfunded liabilities implies that future generations would be better off ex ante.

A strikingly different picture emerges if the introduction of individual accounts is coupled with a government guarantee that promises that pensioners will receive at least the benefit that they would have earned under the previous Social Security system. In this case, table 8-2 shows that unfunded liabilities fall by just 29.9 percent. The reason for the much smaller reduction is that although the individual account on average earns 6 percent a year, it may earn substantially less than that over extended periods of time. Thus, with a minimum benefit guarantee, the government has to make up the difference between investment outcomes and the minimum benefit when private returns are low, but it does

32. Social Security Trustees (2000).

not benefit from reductions in payments when returns are abnormally high. All of the risk is placed on the government, that is, is placed on future generations of taxpayers. As a result, the expected unfunded liability does not fall by very much.

Now suppose the contribution rate and expected benefits for the individual account are raised by *five* times. If the current Social Security benefit level is guaranteed, unfunded liabilities fall by 82.9 percent relative to the case with no individual accounts. In other words, 17.1 percent of Social Security's current $10.5 trillion unfunded liability (or about $1.8 trillion) would still remain. At first, this might seem like a surprising result since the probability of running up against the minimum benefit is indeed much smaller than before. So why should the remaining guarantee costs be so large? The reason is that the guarantee is still valuable and, hence, unfunded liabilities are reduced only a little bit. The reason is that protection against very low returns is still the most valuable part of a benefit guarantee in the presence of risk aversion. Although the probability of using the guarantee is much smaller, its value does not decrease proportionately with increases in the contribution rate.

Increasing the Size of the Trust Fund

As above, the alternative approach would increase the prefunding of the current Social Security system. The accumulation of assets, therefore, is held by the government in a trust fund. Because the benefit provided by Social Security is fixed, returns in excess of those needed to provide that fixed benefit level are passed to future generations in the form of a lower tax liability. Prefunding Social Security, therefore, is more effective than are personal accounts at reducing unfunded liabilities at a given contribution rate. In particular, prefunding Social Security allows the government—and, hence, future generations—to capture fully the upside potential of asset performance instead of just having to subsidize the downside risk, as would happen under the personal account option considered above.

Table 8-3 shows the reduction in unfunded liabilities, as a fraction of Social Security's current unfunded liability, associated with funding Social Security under different policy designs. If the contribution rate is chosen so that the expected retirement benefit equals the fixed benefit level currently provided under Social Security, unfunded liabilities decline by 31 percent when prefunding Social Security, almost exactly the same as the 30 percent decline for the private account design shown in table 8-2. These results are almost identical because, at a low contribution rate, the ex ante value of the government being able to capture the upside potential is quite small.

This result should give budget authorities some pause. Under traditional budgetary revenue projection rules, which focus only on expected returns, it

Table 8-3. *Change in Unfunded Liabilities: Funding Social Security*[a]

Expected benefit that could be paid/current Social Security benefit (ratio)	Required contribution rate in funded Social Security system/pay-as-you-go Social Security payroll tax rate required for solvency (ratio)	Actual fixed Social Security benefit to be paid/current Social Security benefit (ratio)	Reduction in unfunded liabilities relative to Social Security's current unfunded liabilities (percent)
1	.17	$^3/_4$	55.9
1	.17	1	30.9
2	.34	$^3/_4$	86.9
2	.34	1	61.9
2	.34	$1^1/_4$	36.9
2	.34	$1^1/_2$	11.9
3	.51	1	92.8
5	.86	$^3/_4$	179.7
5	.86	1	154.7
5	.86	$1^1/_2$	104.7

a. 50 percent investment in broad stock index, 50 percent investment in bonds.

would appear that Social Security could be fully replaced with a small payroll tax invested in equities. However, table 8-3 shows that once risk is taken into account, the true value of unfunded liabilities is reduced by less than one-third.

If the contribution rate rises by five times but the Social Security benefit is held at its current level, unfunded liabilities are reduced dramatically, by 155 percent, compared with just 83 percent under personal accounts. That is, the system becomes overfunded. Intuitively, at a higher contribution rate, the ex ante value of the potential upside, which is being captured by the government under the plan to fund Social Security, becomes greater. Ex ante unfunded liabilities are reduced by more.

The calculations so far assume that the Social Security trust fund will not be invaded for other purposes. In particular, assets stored in the trust fund are assumed not to be spent elsewhere. As argued in the previous section, this assumption is tenuous. Although the Social Security trust fund can, as a pure accounting matter, increase in size over time, those increases might not correspond to an increase in public saving. If only half of the assets in the trust fund are truly saved, then unfunded liabilities will be reduced by only about half of the 155 percent, or about 78 percent. As a result, personal accounts might, in practice, do a better job of reducing unfunded liabilities if they do not generate very much leakage. This shows that political and market-based risk can interact in the determination of the optimal social security reform.

Conclusion

Many economists believe that future retirement benefits provided by many public pension systems, including the U.S. Social Security system, should be backed by more assets. Disagreement, however, exists about whether those new assets should be held in personal accounts or by the public pension plan itself. This paper concludes that personal accounts are superior in handling important political-economy risks. But public pension plans can be more effective at reducing pension liabilities associated with market-based risks. Although the optimal choice of Social Security reforms depends on many factors, the ability of alternative reforms to handle risk should be of paramount concern.

COMMENT

Yuewu Xu

The paper by Kent Smetters provides a novel analysis of an important topic in pension reform. Proposals to reform Social Security too often focus on expected outcomes, rather than explicitly incorporating the role of risk and uncertainty. Smetters focuses on the role of both political-economic risk and market-based risk in evaluating Social Security reforms. While I believe that the political risks raised are important topics for consideration, my comments focus on the analysis of market-based risks.

Most existing proposals for reform do not explicitly analyze the risks created. This is strange because Social Security is largely intended as a way to reduce risks—including those related to longevity, survivorship, disability, inflation, and career earnings. As a result, a full analysis of Social Security should contain analysis of risk (to the government as well as to the individuals) as one of its central elements.

For example, Feldstein and Samwick show that a system with a contribution rate of 2 percent of payroll into a private account could eventually replace the much larger Social Security tax while producing the same *expected* benefit.[1] The reason is that the rate of return of the equity market is substantially higher than the implied return on Social Security contributions.

The Smetters paper takes Feldstein and Samwick and related proposals one step further toward a full analysis by asking about the risk properties of the proposed solutions. Specifically, one of its key contributions is to ask what happens if the government actually *guarantees* some level of minimum benefit, instead of having a system with just the same expected benefit? Recall that in the original Feldstein and Samwick approach, the economic agent bears all the investment risks, although the proposal has the same expected benefit as the current Social Security system. Given that Social Security is intended as a base of secure retirement income, it makes sense to ask what the effects of guaranteeing a minimum benefit would be, and in particular, how much it would cost the government (that is, the price of risk) to provide such a guarantee.

Smetters shows that providing guarantees can be very costly to the government. This holds even when the agent is required to save at a rate that produces expected benefits as much as five times that of the benefit level under the current Social Security. Hence, from the perspective of reducing the unfunded liability of the current Social Security system, this type of guarantee is not very attractive.

1. Feldstein and Samwick (1997). The long-run rate of return in the equity market is crucial in this approach. This relates to the size of the equity premium. For historical estimates, see Ibbotson (2002) and Dimson, Marsh, and Staunton (2002).

The intuition behind this result is straightforward: investment in equities is risky and therefore the guarantee of a minimum benefit is very valuable. It has long been recognized that the risk involved in equity investments is nontrivial, even with investment horizons as long as thirty years. For example, Leibowitz showed that for an investment horizon of thirty years, there remains a substantial 21 percent probability that stock will fall short of bonds.[2]

These points are not only central to the analysis of a crucial policy issue, their analysis is also well-grounded in the option pricing theory in finance literature. Essentially, guaranteeing a minimum level benefit gives the investor a European put option on the portfolio in his or her private account. A European option gives its holder the right, but not the obligation, to sell a security at a prespecified time for a prespecified price. Hence, if the stock price grows slowly or falls in value over time, the investor can essentially "trade" the stock to the government for a guaranteed benefit at retirement. Under weak assumptions on the return dynamics of the guaranteed portfolio,[3] the value of the investor's European put options can be priced according to the well-known Black and Scholes option pricing formula.[4] The government's liability is just the flip side of this benefit. Since this liability is funded by taxing future generations, it is important to compare it to that of the current Social Security system.

What is the economic meaning of the government liability thus obtained using the option pricing theory? This theoretical value is the exact amount of money that the government would need at the start so that it can exactly offset its obligations in the end—provided it traded continuously in the market according to the Black-Scholes replication scheme to hedge against its liability. In reality, of course, no one would really expect the government to actually trade in the market. Therefore, if the government does not utilize the Black-Scholes continuous replication scheme to hedge its liability, the final *realized* liability for the government could be larger than the theoretical liability obtained from the above analysis.

Thus, there are well-developed tools for analyzing the economic merit of competing policies such at this one. Any guarantee or insurance against a future event is called a contingent claim (or derivatives) in finance. The valuation of such contingent claims is one of the most extensively studied subjects in modern finance. Furthermore, these finance theories undergo real-world tests on a daily basis on Wall Street.[5]

In summary, by elaborating on the role of risk in the analysis of Social Security reforms, the author has analyzed an important dimension of the debate that is frequently ignored. The paper constitutes an excellent example of incorporating the risk factor into the analysis of competing public policies.

---

2. Leibowitz and Krasker (1988).

3. Or equivalently, under similar assumptions on the return dynamics of its equity component. The fixed-income component is assumed to be riskless.

4. Black and Scholes (1973). The strike price is the minimum guarantee level in this case.

5. See Ingersoll (1987) and Merton (1992) for excellent reviews and references.

References

Abel, Andrew, and others. 1989. "Assessing Dynamic Efficiency: Theory and Evidence." *Review of Economic Studies* 56: 1–20.

Bazelon, Coleman, and Kent Smetters. 1999. "Discounting inside the Beltway." *Journal of Economic Perspectives* 13 (Fall): 213–28.

Black, Fischer, and Myron J. Sholes. 1973. "The Pricing of Options and Corporate Liabilities." *Journal of Public Economy* 81 (3): 637–54.

Bodie, Zvi. 1995. "On the Risk of Stocks in the Long Run." *Financial Analysts Journal* 51(May/June): 18–22.

CBO (Congressional Budget Office). 1999. "Social Security Privatization: Experiences Abroad." CBO Paper. Washington.

———. 2003. "Evaluating and Accounting for Federal Investment in Corporate Stocks and Other Private Securities." CBO Paper. Washington. January.

Coronado, Julia, Don Fullerton, and Thomas Glass. 2000. "The Progressivity of Social Security." Working Paper 7520. Cambridge, Mass.: National Bureau of Economic Research.

Diamond, Peter. 1997. "Macroeconomic Aspects of Social Security Reform." *Brookings Papers on Economic Activity* 2:1997: 1–66.

———. 2000a. "Administrative Costs and Equilibrium Charges with Individual Accounts." In *Administrative Aspects of Investment-Based Social Security Reform,* edited by John B. Shoven. University of Chicago Press for the National Bureau of Economic Research.

———. 2000b. "Social Security Trust Funds. In Memoriam: Robert Eisner." Presentation at the 2000 American Economic Association meeting, Boston.

———. 2003. "Social Security, the Government Budget, and National Savings." MIT, Department of Economics. Processed.

Dimson, E., P. Marsh, and M. Staunton. 2002. *Triumph of the Optimists: 101 Years of Global Investment Returns.* Princeton University Press.

Feldstein, Martin, and Elena Ranguelova. 2001. "Accumulated Pension Collars: A Market Approach to Reducing the Risk of Investment-Based Social Security Reform." In *Tax Policy and the Economy,* vol. 15, edited by James Poterba. Cambridge, Mass.: National Bureau of Economic Research.

Feldstein, Martin, and Andrew Samwick. 1997. "The Economics of Pre-Funding Social Security and Medicare Benefits." In *NBER Macroeconomics Annual 1997,* edited by B. Bernanke and J. Rotemburg. MIT Press.

———. 2000. "Allocating Payroll Tax Revenue to Personal Retirement Accounts to Maintain Social Security Benefits and the Payroll Tax Rate." Working Paper 7767. Cambridge, Mass.: National Bureau of Economic Research.

Friedman, Milton, and Wilbur Cohen. 1972. *Security: Universal or Selective?* Washington: American Enterprise Institute.

General Accounting Office. 1996. "Debt Ceiling: Analysis of Actions during the 1995–1996 Crisis." GAO/AIMD-96-130 (August). Washington.

Geanakoplos, John, Olivia S. Mitchell, and Stephen P. Zeldes. 1998. "Would a Privatized Social Security System Really Pay a Higher Rate of Return?" In *Framing the Social Security Debate: Values, Politics, and Economics,* edited by D. Arnold, M. Graetz, and A. Munnell. Brookings.

Goetzmann, William N., and Philippe Jorion. 1996. "Global Stock Markets in the Twentieth Century." Yale School of Management and University of California at Irvine. Processed.

Goldberg, Fred T., Jr., and Michael J. Graetz. 2000. "Reforming Social Security: A Practical and Workable System of Personal Retirement Accounts." In *Administrative Aspects of Investment-Based Social Security Reform,* edited by John B. Shoven. University of Chicago Press for the National Bureau of Economic Research.

Ibbotson, R. 2002. "Stocks, Bonds, Bills, and Inflation." Ibbotson Associates. Chicago.

Iglesias, Augusto, and Robert Palacios. 2000. "Managing Public Pension Reserves. Part I: Evidence from the International Experience." Pension Reform Primer Working Paper Series. World Bank, Washington. Processed.

Ingersoll, J. 1987. *Theory of Financial Decision Making.* Lanham, Md.: Rowman & Littlefield Publishing.

Jagannathan, Ravi, and Narayana Kocherlakota. 1996. "Why Should Older People Invest Less in Stocks than Younger People?" *Federal Reserve Bank of Minneapolis Quarterly Review* 20 (Summer): 11–23.

Kotlikoff, Laurence, Kent Smetters, and Jan Walliser. 1998. "Social Security: Privatization and Progressivity." *American Economic Review* 88 (May, *Papers and Proceedings*): 137–41.

Leibowitz, M., and William Krasker. 1988. "The Persistence of Risk: Stocks versus Bonds over the Long Term." *Financial Analyst Journal* (November/December): 40–47.

Marcus, Alan J. 1987. "Corporate Pension Policy and the Value of PBGC Insurance." In *Issues in Pension Economics,* edited by Zvi Bodie, John B. Shoven, and David A. Wise. University of Chicago Press.

McHale, John. 2000. "The Risk of Social Security Benefit Rule Changes: Some International Evidence." In *Risk Aspects of Investment-Based Social Security Reform,* edited by John Campbell and Martin Feldstein. University of Chicago Press.

Merton, Robert C. 1992. *Continuous-Time Finance.* Oxford, U.K.: Blackwell Publishers.

Mitchell, Olivia S. 1998. "Administrative Costs in Public and Private Retirement Systems." In *Privatizing Social Security,* edited by Martin Feldstein. University of Chicago Press.

OMB (Office of Management and Budget). 2000. *Analytical Perspectives: Budget of the United States Government—Fiscal Year 2001.* Government Printing Office, Washington. Table 12-2 (p. 272).

Pennachi, George. 1999. "Government Guarantees for Old Age Income." In *Prospects for Social Security Reform,* edited by Olivia Mitchell, Robert Myers, and Howard Young. University of Pennsylvania Press.

Pesando, James. 1996. "The Government's Role in Insuring Pensions." In *Securing Employer-Based Pensions: An International Perspective,* edited by Zvi Bodie, Olivia Mitchell, and John Turner. University of Pennsylvania Press.

Schieber, Sylvester, and John Shoven. 1999. *The Real Deal: The History and Future of Social Security.* Yale University Press.

Siedman, Laurence S. 1999. *Funding Social Security: A Strategic Alternative.* Cambridge University Press.

Siegel, Jeremy J., and Richard Thaler. 1997. "Anomalies: The Equity Premium Puzzle." *Journal of Economic Perspectives* 11 (Winter): 191–200.

Smetters, Kent. 2000. "The Equivalency of State-Contingent Taxes and Options and Futures: An Application to Investing the Social Security Trust Fund in Equities." *Journal of Risk and Insurance* 67 (3): 351–68.

———. 2002. "Controlling the Cost of Minimum Benefit Guarantees in Public Pension Conversions." *Pension Economics and Finance Journal* 1 (March): 9–34.

———. 2003. "Is the Social Security Trust Fund Worth Anything?" University of Pennsylvania, Wharton School. Processed.

Social Security Advisory Board (SSAB). 1999. *1999 Technical Panel on Assumptions and Methods* (November). Washington.

Social Security Trustees. 2000. *The 2000 OASDI Trustees Report.* Social Security Administration, Washington.

———. 2003. *The 2003 OASDI Trustees Report.* Social Security Administration, Washington.

9

Effects of Nondiscrimination Rules on Pension Participation

ROBERT L. CLARK, JANEMARIE MULVEY, AND SYLVESTER J. SCHIEBER

One of the central reasons policymakers provide tax subsidies for pensions is to raise pension coverage and benefit levels, especially among low- and moderate-income workers.[1] To achieve this goal, Congress has established and periodically revised nondiscrimination standards that pension plans must meet in order to qualify for tax subsidies. In broad terms, the nondiscrimination rules require that coverage and benefits for low-wage employees maintain at least minimal levels relative to what is available for highly compensated workers.

The central policy question surrounding nondiscrimination rules is whether they are effective in raising coverage and benefits for low-wage workers. The rules may work as intended if, in the absence of such regulations, firms would choose to skew pension subsidies toward highly compensated workers. But the rules may also inadvertently reduce coverage for all workers in general and for low-income workers in particular, in either of two ways. First, the rules are complex and thus

Robert Clark's work on this paper was funded by grants from WorldatWork and the Shannon J. Schieber Retirement Policy Institute of the American Benefits Council. The authors wish to thank Annelise Li and Lex Miller of Watson Wyatt Worldwide for their help in developing the statistical analysis included in this paper. They thank Kyle Brown of Watson Wyatt Worldwide for his comments. A more detailed version of many of the results in the paper may be found in Clark, Mulvey, and Schieber (2000).

1. For an analysis of the size and distribution of pension tax expenditures, see Goodfellow and Schieber (1993) and Clark and Wolper (1997).

may raise the administrative burden of providing a pension, which could reduce overall coverage rates. This problem may especially affect small firms, which tend to disproportionately employ low-wage workers.[2] Second, the rules may bear more heavily on the cost of offering defined benefit plans than on the cost of offering defined contribution plans. Participation rates for low-wage workers are lower in defined contribution plans, where workers choose whether to participate, than in defined benefit plans, where employers determine participation.[3]

To a large extent, the policy debate over nondiscrimination standards has proceeded without evidence.[4] This paper aims to fill that gap. Using twenty years of data from the *Current Population Survey,* we examine the effects of three changes in nondiscrimination rules in the 1980s and 1990s. The primary finding is that stricter nondiscrimination standards did not increase coverage rates of low-wage workers in absolute terms or relative to highly compensated employees. In addition, some of the findings suggest that the rules reduced coverage for low-wage workers relative to others. These results indicate that the nondiscrimination rules enacted in the past not only failed to meet their ostensible goal of helping low-wage workers, but appear to have been counterproductive, reducing participation rates for low-wage workers relative to others. The key policy implication from this research is that giving employers better incentives to sponsor plans, by simplifying the nondiscrimination rules and reducing administrative costs, would likely be more effective than current policy in raising pension coverage levels among low- and moderate-wage workers.

Nondiscrimination Rules: A Primer

Tax-qualified employer-sponsored retirement plans may not discriminate in favor of highly compensated employees in coverage, contributions, or benefits. This simple principle is the basis for an extremely complex set of rules and regulations.[5]

General Provisions

A "highly compensated employee" is defined as anyone who is a 5-percent owner, is paid more than $75,000 in compensation, is paid more than $50,000

---

2. McGill and others (1996) provide a detailed discussion of these standards and the various tests that are required for plans to retain their tax-qualified status.

3. Clark and Schieber (1998) conclude that low-wage workers are less likely to make voluntary contributions to pension plans such as 401(k) plans.

4. For contributions using cross-sectional firm data, see Garrett (1995) and Carrington, McCue, and Pierce (2000). Bankman (1988) provides a conceptual analysis.

5. The seventh edition of *Fundamentals of Private Pensions* dedicates three full chapters to the description of current general rules and part of another chapter to the special provisions covering 401(k) plans (see McGill and others, 1996, chs. 3–5, 12). The discussion of current rules provided here is a far broader overview than that in the *Fundamentals,* and readers needing the full detail should refer to that text or similar ones on pension plan design and regulation.

in compensation and is in the "top-paid group," or is paid more than $45,000 in compensation and is an officer. All of the pay levels are in 1987 dollars. Since 1994 the dollar amounts have been indexed in increments of $5,000, rounded to the next lower increment. The "top-paid group" includes the top-paid 20 percent of employees including those in all businesses under common control. Workers who have short service, are part-time, are nonresident aliens, or are younger than 21 can be excluded from the top-paid group.

To qualify for tax benefits, a plan must meet at least one of two tests relating to pension coverage. A plan qualifies if the proportion of workers covered by the plan who are not highly compensated is at least 70 percent of the proportion of highly compensated workers covered.[6] Alternatively, the plan qualifies if, first, average benefits for nonhighly compensated workers are at least 70 percent, as a percent of pay, of the average benefits provided for highly compensated workers and, second, the proportion of covered workers who are not highly compensated is at least a specified percentage of the covered highly compensated workers.[7] Under each coverage test, there are provisions for safe harbors, for excluding certain workers, for aggregating and disaggregating plans for testing, and so forth.

In addition to coverage tests, a plan must also meet contributions and benefits tests. Safe harbor rules limit the extent to which pension accruals or contributions can vary across workers on the basis of years of service under the plan or a combination of a worker's age and service. For plans that do not meet a safe harbor, extremely complex tests group workers by accrual or contribution rates and then test each group against coverage rules.

Special Treatment of Cash or Deferred Arrangements

Pension rules allow for tax-deductible employer contributions to all tax-qualified plans, but employee contributions are only tax-deductible in cash or deferred arrangement (CODA) plans, the best known of which is the 401(k).[8] Because of concerns that only higher-paid workers would contribute to such plans, thus making the plans discriminatory under existing rules, special rules were adopted. Under these rules, CODA plans cannot require more than one year of service for eligibility and only need to consider eligible employees, not participants.

---

6. Note that covering 70 percent of nonhighly compensated workers automatically guarantees that the ratio test is met.

7. The specified percentage is based on the share of the work force that is highly compensated. Groups of employees may be included or excluded on the basis of job category, hourly or salaried pay classes, geographic location, or other business criteria.

8. Technically, 401(k) plans apply only to the private sector, with similar plans called 403(b) plans applying to the nonprofit sector, 457 plans applying to state and local government, and Thrift Saving Plans applying to federal workers. All of these plans share the general characteristic that employee contributions are tax-deductible.

Table 9-1. *Average Contribution Rates for Nonhighly Compensated Workers and Maximum Allowable Contribution Percentages for Highly Compensated Workers Participating in 401(k) Plans*

Average contribution percentage for non-HCEs	Maximum allowable average contribution percentage for HCEs	Ratio of maximum HCE to non-HCE contributions	Percentage difference
1.00	2.00	2.00	1.00
2.00	4.00	2.00	2.00
4.00	6.00	1.50	2.00
8.00	10.00	1.25	2.00
10.00	12.50	1.25	2.50

Source: Internal Revenue Code, section 401(k).

Elective contributions to 401(k) plans are considered nondiscriminatory if they meet either of two tests based on the actual deferral percentage (ADP), the ratio of elective contributions divided by annual pay. The average ADP for highly compensated workers must either be less than 1.25 times the average ADP for nonhighly compensated workers, or it must be less than two times that of nonhighly compensated workers, with the difference less than two percentage points. Table 9-1 shows the maximum allowable contributions for highly compensated workers given the average ADPs for nonhighly compensated workers.

Safe harbor rules require sponsors to send an annual notice to all eligible workers explaining their rights and obligations under the plan in language that is easily understandable by a typical lay person. In addition, the sponsor either must make nonelective contributions for all eligible workers of at least 3 percent of pay that vest immediately, or must match workers' elective contributions up to 3 percent of pay at 100 percent or more and match contributions on the next 2 percent of pay at 50 percent or more.

Evolution of Nondiscrimination Rules

Because our empirical investigation below hinges on historical changes to the nondiscrimination rules, we briefly review the evolution of these rules, with a particular focus on changes in the 1980s and 1990s.

Although employer-provided pensions have been subject to evolving regulations since the inception of the corporate income tax in 1909, the first explicit set of nondiscrimination rules appeared in 1942 and limited the ability of plan sponsors to favor shareholders, officers, supervisors, and highly compensated workers with respect to pension coverage, benefits, and financing. An extensive regulatory structure developed around these rules over several decades. A plan that covered 70 percent of a sponsor's work force would be qualified if 80 percent of the eligible population participated. Plans could be pooled for qualification purposes. Workers could be excluded if they did not meet the minimum age and service requirements or maximum age limitations. The commissioner of the Internal Revenue Service (IRS) could qualify plans under certain circumstances. Plans were not discriminatory if they limited coverage to salaried or clerical workers. Plan benefits could be integrated with Social Security benefits using any of a variety of methods.

The Employee Retirement Income Security Act (ERISA) of 1974 began a new era of pension regulation. ERISA was intended to expand the reach of employer pensions and to secure benefits for covered workers. ERISA maintained the broad context of coverage and discrimination rules under previous law but also altered several aspects of pension regulation in significant ways. Plan sponsors had to include employees who were working at least half time, were 25 years of age or older, and had one year of service under the plan. Workers hired at ages within five years of the normal retirement age in a plan could be excluded. ERISA also introduced a new funding constraint—the so-called section 415 rules—whose goal was to limit the tax preferences accorded to any individual worker. This provision was largely aimed at highly paid workers and thus was a new element in the nondiscrimination rules.

The Tax Equity and Fiscal Responsibility Act of 1982 reduced the contribution and funding limits significantly. TEFRA also classified as "top heavy" plans where accrued benefits for key employees and their beneficiaries exceed 60 percent of accrued benefits for all employees and their beneficiaries. Key employees included all officers up to a total of fifty employees, or if less, the greater of three employees or 10 percent of all employees. Key employees also include owners who were among the ten employees owning the largest share in the employer, 5-percent owners, or 1-percent owners whose annual compensation exceeded $150,000. Top-heavy plans had to provide minimum benefits or contributions to all participants who were not key employees. These plans faced an additional constraint in that no compensation over $200,000 could be considered for purposes of funding defined benefit plans or making contributions to defined contribution plans. Although the top-heavy provisions were meant to stem pension abuses primarily concentrated in the small employer sector, all plans had to be tested for top-heavy status each year.

In 1984 the Deficit Reduction Act (DEFRA) changed the nondiscrimination rules that had been proposed for 401(k) plans by the IRS. The proposed rules would have allowed 401(k) plans to qualify by passing the general nondiscrimination tests for qualified plans. In addition DEFRA extended the freeze that had been imposed on the section 415 limits by TEFRA for two more years.

The Retirement Equity Act also passed in 1984. This law sought to broaden the distribution of retirement benefits in a number of ways. It reduced the age participation standard that originally had been set in ERISA at 25 to 21. It also required that all service after age 18 had to be considered for vesting purposes.

The Tax Reform Act of 1986 (TRA) included many changes to nondiscrimination rules and the funding and contribution limits. After the passage of the 1986 legislation, the IRS undertook a massive overhaul of the nondiscrimination requirements affecting tax-qualified plans. The 1986 law created a uniform definition of highly compensated workers and applied the nondiscrimination standards. Explicit coverage standards were established to replace the previous set of rules. Additional tests were included to determine that contributions and benefits were not discriminatory. The 1986 tax reform also altered the rules affecting integration between Social Security and private pension plans to reduce the permitted disparity between benefits that could be provided to the highly compensated relative to others.

The Omnibus Budget Reconciliation Act of 1993 (OBRA) significantly reduced the compensation limits. The Small Business Job Protection Act of 1996 simplified and liberalized nondiscrimination standards.

Determinants of Pension Coverage

Aggregate trends in pension coverage are well documented and well understood. Since the early 1970s the share of the aggregate work force covered by pensions has remained roughly constant, with the role of defined contribution plans rising substantially and defined benefit plans falling commensurately. Pension coverage and participation rates rise with workers' age, tenure, marginal tax rate, and earnings. The rates vary across industries and depend in part on regulatory structure. Changes in these factors appear to explain a substantial share of trends in pension coverage and participation.[9]

We take these findings as given and offer three additional perspectives on determinants of pension coverage, relating to the key role of changes in administrative costs over time, the role of funding limits in defined benefit plans, and age-based preferences for defined contribution plans. These added perspectives help provide a more complete view of the determinants of historical trends in pension coverage and participation and will prove useful in interpreting the regression results in subsequent sections.

Administrative Costs

Employers' decisions to offer pensions are based in part on comparing the gains from the preferential tax treatment to the administrative cost of providing a pension plan. To the extent that the gains exceeds the costs, employer will have greater incentives to offer pensions.

---

9. See, for example, Bloom and Freeman (1994), Clark and McDermed (1990), Goodfellow and Schieber (1993), Gustman and Steinmeier (1992), Ippolito (1997), McGill and others (1996), and Schieber (2003).

Table 9-2. *Annual Per Capita Pension Administrative Costs in 1996 Dollars*

Year	Employees in defined benefit plans				Employees in defined contribution plans	
	15	75	500	10,000	15	10,000
1981	$ 194.67	$ 138.97	$ 67.85	$ 23.32	$ 137.13	$ 25.71
1982	194.80	142.21	69.14	23.37	140.87	26.21
1983	210.67	150.04	72.55	24.12	148.73	27.75
1984	232.40	157.63	76.43	24.96	156.73	29.14
1985	262.47	174.36	85.76	31.57	172.73	33.21
1986	307.60	200.07	102.01	43.35	184.53	35.18
1987	321.80	208.57	117.78	44.73	220.60	37.68
1988	529.47	264.65	139.93	57.88	230.40	38.97
1989	507.80	291.65	151.71	63.72	252.33	44.30
1990	526.60	300.81	155.44	63.85	262.33	45.69
1991	548.93	314.73	163.17	67.87	271.40	46.73
1992	561.47	320.25	165.73	68.39	274.60	47.41
1993	566.13	322.43	166.23	67.82	277.20	47.60
1994	608.53	340.15	171.82	68.82	281.13	48.24
1995	615.07	343.39	172.95	68.66	284.53	48.78
1996	619.93	345.68	173.62	68.33	287.20	49.19
Compound annual growth rate (%)	8.03	6.26	6.46	7.43	5.05	4.42

Source: Calculated by authors from Hustead (1998, p. 171).

Table 9-2 shows estimates of the costs of administering pension plans in the 1980s and 1990s for different plan types and sizes. The administrative expenses include "in-house administrative costs, consultant fees, and Pension Benefit Guaranty Corporation premiums. The figures do not include investment expenses or one-time costs to conform to changes in regulations."[10] The table shows that administrative costs per participant rose more in absolute terms for small plans than for large plans, that the percentage increase was higher for very small plans, and that costs rose more rapidly for defined benefit plans than for defined contribution plans. A plausible assessment of these findings is that increasingly burdensome pension regulations drove the cost increases.[11] After all, improvements in computer technology and software should have reduced costs of plan administration had regulatory compliance not become more complex.

This interpretation implies that changes in pension regulations, including nondiscrimination rules, have increased administrative costs and thus may have encouraged firms to terminate pensions or to shift from traditional defined

10. Hustead (1998, p. 166).
11. Hustead (1998).

Figure 9-1. *Present Value of Potential Accruing Pension Benefits for Selected Representative Workers Relative to Administrative Pension Costs for Small Firm in 1996*

Annual amounts in 1996 dollars

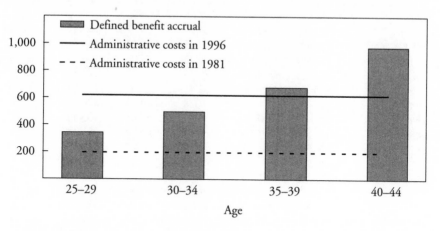

Source: Derived by the authors as described in the text.

benefit plans to less costly defined contribution plans. One useful way to gauge the magnitude of increasing administrative costs over time is to compare the costs to the accruing tax benefits that workers receive. To do so, we estimated pension accruals under a reasonably representative defined benefit plan.[12] Figure 9-1 compares the per-participant administrative costs for a fifteen-employee defined benefit plan in 1981 and 1996 (both in 1996 dollars) relative to the accruing benefits from the representative defined benefit plan for workers of different ages who have between five and nine years of service.

Clearly the economics of pensions changed significantly over the period. Administrative costs were nearly three times as high in 1996 as in 1981. From the employer's perspective in 1996, offering a worker in her late twenties a benefit accrual of roughly $350 with an attendant administrative cost of $620 probably did not make very much sense. Paying the worker in wages would have been much simpler and cheaper.

---

12. The defined benefit plan has a 1.15 percent accrual per year of service with benefits determined on the basis of final five-year salary. The initial pay structure for workers was estimated using the May 1993 *Current Population Survey.* In calculating benefit accruals, we assumed 5 percent pay increases per year of service from the initial pay levels at each age and service combination set in 1996 dollars and discounted benefits from estimated retirement by 6.5 percent per year. For additional details, see Clark, Mulvey, and Schieber (2000).

The economic viability of defined contribution plans was not as threatened by increasing administrative costs both because the cost increases were more moderate and because accruals tend to be more even over the life cycle than in defined benefit plans.

Funding Limits

Changes in defined benefit funding limits may also have encouraged the shift to defined contribution plans. In 2000 the limit of compensation that could be considered was $170,000. As discussed earlier, this limit was reduced in the 1980s and 1990s. Like nondiscrimination rules, funding limits seek to make the distribution of tax preferences for retirement plans more equitable. Funding limits cap the total amount of tax subsidies the highly compensated can obtain. Nondiscrimination rules affect the allocation of subsidies across wage groups.

Funding limits in defined benefit plans create problems because sponsors can only account for anticipated wage growth up to the current compensation limits. For example, a worker who earns $35,000 at age 35 would have a final salary of just under $173,000 upon reaching her normal social security retirement age at age 67, if nominal wages grow at 5.1 percent a year.[13] The sponsor would not be permitted to fund currently the pension for this employee on the proportion of expected final earnings that exceeds the $170,000 limit, which amounts to the top $2,936 of his or her earnings this year.

Instead, these accruals would have to be funded in the future. For large employers with long track records, deferral of pension funding obligations may be manageable. Even so, they might prefer to fund the obligation now to keep their balance sheets clean and future income streams unencumbered. If so, the funding limits would encourage them to shift to defined contribution plans where obligations can be fully funded as they accrue. For smaller employers with less secure future prospects, deferral of funding could be the equivalent of financial suicide. To explore the extent of this phenomenon, we combined the data on twenty-five large companies with about 1 million active defined benefit participants, and with varying benefit levels and in different industries. To focus on full-time workers, we omitted anyone with earnings below $5,000. Table 9-3 shows that significant numbers of workers have their pension accruals slowed by the compensation limits in current law, and that the pay levels for those being affected are hardly exorbitant, especially for middle-aged and younger workers. The average pay level of those workers from ages of 25 to 29 who were affected was below $40,000 in 1999.

---

13. This is the average wage growth assumption used in valuing the final-pay pension plans included in Watson Wyatt's (2000) actuarial assumption survey for the 1999 plan year.

Table 9-3. *Percentage of Workers in Selected Pension Plans Affected by Pension Funding Limits by Age and Their Median Pay Levels in 2000*

Age of workers	Percentage of workers with projected pay above $170,000 limit	Median pay of workers affected by the $170,000 limit
21–24	80.4	$ 33,675
25–29	76.7	39,748
30–34	69.4	47,860
35–39	49.8	58,025
40–44	20.3	76,453
45–49	10.5	93,700
50–54	7.0	113,900
55–59	3.6	137,860
60–64	1.5	183,128

Source: Watson Wyatt Worldwide.

Age-Based Preferences for Defined Contribution Plans

While it is well recognized that pension coverage rises with age, the link between age and preference for type of pension has not been documented as clearly. McGill and others analyzed preferences for type of pension plan by examining workers who were covered by both a defined benefit and defined contribution plan.[14] As shown in table 9-4, younger workers were much more likely to identify their defined contribution plan as their "most important plan." McGill and others interpret this result to mean that younger workers have a strong preference for defined contribution plans.

The combination of age-based preference for defined contribution plans and changes in the age composition of the work force helps explain shifting pension coverage over time. Table 9-5, for example, shows strong growth in the numbers of workers at ages below 45 in the 1970s and 1980s, with the fastest growing cohorts exceeding age 45 in the 1990s.

In combination, tables 9-4 and 9-5 suggest that much of the growth of defined contribution plans in the 1970s and 1980s was driven by worker preferences. Indeed, it is interesting that much of the shift occurred without much public disapproval by workers. In that light, the outcry against recent shifts in plan types might be driven as much by fundamental tastes by an aging work force for alternative plan types as by the reaction to specific plan changes that were adopted.[15] This would be consistent with Quick's conclusion that the

14. McGill and others (1996).
15. Clark and Schieber, in this volume.

Table 9-4. *Indication of Most Important Retirement Plan by Individuals Covered by Both Defined Benefit and Defined Contribution Plans, by Age*
Percent

Respondent's age	Plan identified as most important	
	Defined benefit	*Defined contribution*
21–24	27.9	72.1
25–34	35.6	64.4
35–44	46.1	53.9
45–54	52.4	47.6
55–64	71.5	28.5
65 or over	93.6	6.4
Total	47.9	52.1

Source: Tabulations of the Pension Supplement from the April 1993 *Current Population Survey.*

Table 9-5. *Percentage Change in Numbers of Workers by Age for Selected Decades*
Percent

Age	Change from		
	1970–1980	*1980–1990*	*1990–2000*
16–19	30.6	–21.3	14.9
20–24	50.0	–12.6	–0.7
25–34	72.4	22.2	–10.3
35–44	23.6	56.4	21.6
45–54	0.0	21.3	53.7
55–64	5.3	0.0	20.2
65 and over	–6.1	12.9	8.6

Source: Derived by the authors from annual summary estimates in U.S. Department of Labor, Bureau of Labor Statistics, *Employment and Earnings,* from the January issues 1971, 1981, 1991, and 2001.

switch to defined contribution plans until recently has occurred because employers are trying to meet the needs of their work forces.[16]

Trends in Pension Coverage and Participation

Our empirical analysis is designed to measure the impact of three sets of changes to the nondiscrimination rules during the 1980s and 1990s. As noted above, the Tax Equity and Fiscal Responsibility Act was enacted in 1982 with provisions becoming effective in 1983. The Tax Reform Act of 1986 was implemented over

16. Quick (1999).

several years. The Omnibus Budget Reconciliation Act of 1993 contained provisions becoming effective in 1994. Other legislation passed during this period also affected pension rules but had less direct impact on nondiscrimination standards per se.

The three changes in national pension policy described above were intended, at least in part, to raise the relative participation rates of workers with low earnings. Thus, if the three rule changes were successful, participation rates should have risen among low-wage workers either in absolute terms or relative to other workers after the changes were enacted.

To examine these questions, we use data from the March Supplement to the *Current Population Survey* (CPS) covering 1980 to 1999.[17] Earnings for all years are reported in 1999 dollars. Respondents are divided into four annual earnings categories: less than $15,000, $15,000 to $24,999, $25,000 to $49,999, and $50,000 and more. In each year of the sample, roughly 40 percent of respondents had earnings between $25,000 to $49,999, and each of the other categories accounted for 20 percent of respondents. This stability in the real earnings distribution reflects the lack of growth in real earnings during much of this period.[18]

The CPS asks individuals whether their employer sponsors a pension plan and whether the individual participates in that plan.[19] Following earlier analyses, we consider a worker to be covered if the employer sponsors a plan for which the worker is eligible, and to participate if the worker is actually included in a company-sponsored plan. Figure 9-2 illustrates that coverage and participation rates for all workers in the sample declined through the 1980s and rose during the mid- to late 1990s.

Figure 9-3 shows that coverage rates for low-income workers fell steadily from the late 1970s to 1985 and then began a slow climb that appears to have accelerated at the end of the 1990s. Participation rates similarly declined through the mid-1980s and then stayed relatively flat.

17. The CPS files were obtained from UNICON, a private company that has standardized the CPS records from 1962 forward. The March supplement to the CPS each year solicits information from respondents on their pension participation during the previous year. In that regard, our analysis covers the period 1979 through 1998. When we refer to pension coverage or participation during 1979, the information was gleaned from the 1980 March CPS, and so forth for subsequent years. The analysis is limited to workers in the private sector who were age 21 and older and were working thirty-five or more hours a week.

18. The proportion of the sample in the four earnings categories (from lowest to highest) in 1979 was 21, 24, 39, and 16. The distribution had changed only slightly to 20, 23, 38, and 19 in 1998.

19. This question refers to coverage at any time during the previous year. Most studies of pension coverage have used the May CPS pension supplement, which was conducted in 1972, 1979, 1983, 1988, and 1993. These surveys ask about pension coverage at the time of the survey. Thus, the estimates from the March supplement used in this analysis tend to be slightly higher than those reported in studies using the May supplement; however, the trends in coverage are similar.

Figure 9-2. *Trends in Pension Coverage and Participation*

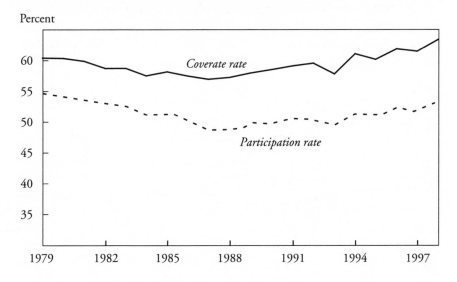

Source: Authors' calculations from March supplement of the *Current Population Survey*, various years.

Figure 9-3. *Pension Coverage and Participation Rates for Workers with Annual Earnings of Less than $15,000*

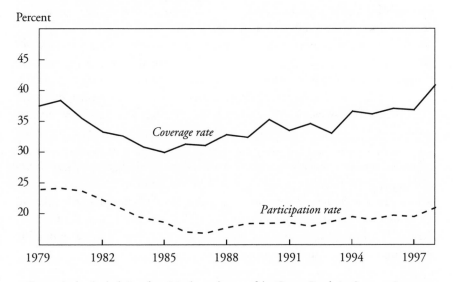

Source: Authors' calculations from March supplement of the *Current Population Survey*, various years.

Figure 9-4. *Pension Participation Rates for Workers with Annual Earnings under $50,000 Relative to Those Earnings over $50,000 a Year for Selected Years*

Ratio

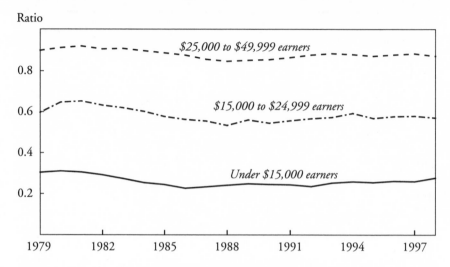

Source: Authors' calculations from March supplement of the *Current Population Survey,* various years.

Participation rates for respondents in other categories followed the same basic pattern over time. Figure 9-4 shows participation rates in the three lowest earnings categories relative to the highest earning category. In each case, participation rates fell for the lower-wage workers relative to workers in the highest-wage category through the 1980s and then remained flat in the 1990s.

The data above show that the strengthening of nondiscrimination standards coincided with modest declines in the pension participation rates of low-wage workers relative to highly compensated workers over the past two decades. Of course, numerous other factors affect these trends as well. The growth in 401(k) plans played an important role in altering the distribution of pension coverage across workers, as the voluntary nature of participation in 401(k) plans has caused participation rates to drop most for workers at lowest earnings levels.[20] Likewise, younger workers, who have lower pension coverage, are more prevalent in the lower earnings groups. Changes in the industrial composition of the work force also influenced pension participation and coverage, and the substantial reductions in marginal tax rates in the 1980s may also have influenced the demand for pensions. To sort out the relative importance of these competing explanations, we turn to regression analysis.

20. Even and McPherson (1994).

Regression Results

We estimate two sets of regressions, one using aggregate time series data, the other using individual records. In neither case does the evidence provide any support for the view that nondiscrimination rules have helped raise pension participation in general or the participation rates of low-income workers in particular.

Time Series Analysis

The dependent variable in the time series regression is the ratio of pension participation rates each year for workers in the three lower earnings categories relative to the highest category. In the first specification, the explanatory variables include the share of workers in the lower earnings category relative to the higher earnings category who are employed in the manufacturing sector; the share of workers in the lower earnings category relative to the higher earnings category who are between ages 35 and 44; and three dummy variables for TEFRA, TRA, and OBRA. The latter variables take a value of one beginning with the year their provisions became effective and ending with the passage of the next act.[21] Thus, the effect of each law is measured against the pre-TEFRA base.

Table 9-6 shows that the age variable does not enter significantly in any of the regressions. Differences in manufacturing employment help explain the participation rates between workers with earnings between $15,000 and $25,000, and workers with wages above $50,000. More important, the coefficients on each of the variables measuring tightening of nondiscrimination rules are negative and significant for each of the lower two earnings groups. This indicates that instead of increasing participation among low-income workers, the implementation of each of these major pieces of legislation is associated with lower pension participation.

An alternative specification tests the importance of institutional factors such as changes in marginal tax rates and increased prevalence of defined contribution plans in addition to the regulatory effects. As shown in table 9-6, marginal tax rates are significant in regressions for the group earning between $15,000 and $25,000, and the extent of defined contribution coverage has a significant effect for the lowest-wage group. TEFRA exerts a negative and significant influence on participation rates of workers with low earnings relative to high earners. Among these workers, the passage of TEFRA led to a 3.3 percentage point decline in participation rates among workers at low relative to high earnings levels. Coefficients on the other regulatory variables are negative but not significant. None of the institutional or regulatory variables had a significant impact

---

21. For example, TEFRA has a value of one for 1983–88 and zero otherwise, TRA86 has a value of one for 1989–93, and OBRA has a value of one for 1994–99.

Table 9-6. *Time Series Results for Pension Participation Equations for Workers in the Three Lower Earnings Groups Relative to Those with Highest Earnings, 1979–98*

| | Ratio of real earnings | | | | | |
| | < $15,000 relative to $50K+ | | $15K to $25K relative to $50K+ | | 25K to $49K relative to $50K+ | |
	Demo-graphically	Institu-tional	Demo-graphically	Institu-tional	Demo-graphically	Institu-tional
Intercept	33.6	37.7	31.3	79.1	80.7	98.5
	(2.7)	(8.9)	(1.3)	(11.2)	(4.2)	(14.0)
Share ages 35 to 44 ratio	–0.04	. . .	0.007	. . .	–.06	. . .
	(–0.3)		(0.3)		(–0.3)	
Share manufacturing ratio	–0.01	. . .	0.4	. . .	0.15	. . .
	(–0.1)		(1.8)		(0.8)	
Marginal tax ratio	. . .	–0.02	. . .	–0.31	. . .	–.025
		(–0.6)		(–2.6)		(–0.63)
Percent participating in DC plans	. . .	–0.17	. . .	–0.10	. . .	–0.14
		(–1.7)		(–0.57)		(–0.94)
TEFRA 82	–5.9	–3.3	–5.0	–3.05	–2.1	–1.49
	(–6.0)	(–2.3)	(–3.5)	(–1.2)	(–1.4)	(–0.68)
TRA 86	–5.7	–1.8	–8.1	–1.8	–3.2	–3.2
	(–6.8)	(–0.9)	(–4.7)	(–0.9)	(–1.3)	(–0.57)
OBRA 93	–3.6	–1.3	–6.6	1.27	–1.1	0.39
	(–2.6)	(0.5)	(–2.0)	(0.48)	(–0.3)	(0.098)
Adjusted R-squared	0.76	0.82	0.59	0.70	0.39	0.41
N	20	20	20	20	20	20

Note: T statistics are in parentheses.
Source: Estimated by the authors from *Current Population Survey* data for selected years.

on participation rates among workers with earnings between $25,000 and $50,000.

Individual Records

The time series analysis is limited in its predictive power by small sample size. Also, the dummies used to proxy for the three regulatory events may merely reflect a time trend or any other factors that vary systematically over time. A stronger empirical test is to estimate the probability that an individual in a given year participates in a pension plan, controlling for the nondiscrimination standards and other factors. To this end, we pool the individual CPS data and estimate participation probabilities for the years 1979 to 1998 using a separate logit equation for each earnings category. The dependent variable indicates whether a particular worker participated in a pension plan in a particular year. Explanatory

Table 9-7. *Predicted Probabilities of Workers Participating in a Private Pension Plan for Select Groups of Workers Ages 35–44 for Selected Years*

Income class and industry	Estimated percentage of workers covered by a private pension					
	1982	*1984*	*1986*	*1989*	*1992*	*1994*
< $15,000						
Wholesale and retail	13	12	11	11	11	13
Manufacturing	24	22	21	20	21	23
Services	21	19	18	17	18	20
Finance, insurance, and						
real estate (FIRE)	23	21	20	19	20	22
$15,000–$24,999						
Wholesale and retail	40	37	35	32	34	37
Manufacturing	57	54	52	48	50	53
Services	60	56	54	51	53	55
FIRE	60	57	55	52	53	56
$25,000–$49,999						
Wholesale and retail	59	57	55	51	54	54
Manufacturing	79	77	76	73	75	75
Services	78	76	76	72	75	75
FIRE	73	71	70	66	69	69
$50,000 +						
Wholesale and retail	65	63	62	60	62	62
Manufacturing	85	84	84	82	84	83
Services	81	79	79	77	79	79
FIRE	74	73	72	70	72	71

Source: Authors' analysis based on the March Supplement to the *Current Population Survey* for various years. Marginal tax rates and percent of plans in defined contribution plans are held constant at average over twenty years.

variables include dichotomous variables indicating the age of the worker (with age 45 to 54 being omitted) and the industry in which the worker was employed (with manufacturing being omitted). We also included year dummies and each individual's marginal tax rate, which was imputed on the CPS file.

The estimated coefficients are used to derive the probability of pension participation for workers of various characteristics in each year. Table 9-7 presents the predicted probabilities for a worker aged 35 to 44 in four industries for each of the four earnings groups for the years before and after each of the policy changes we are examining. We hold constant the effect of changes in marginal tax rates.

Table 9-7 shows that the estimated probability of pension participation declines for the two lowest-income classes following the implementation of TEFRA. Following implementation of TRA, participation rates decline for all but one hypothetical worker. Hypothetical workers between ages 35 and 44 in

Figure 9-5. *Predicted Probability That a Worker Would Be Participating in a Private Pension Plan for Workers in Manufacturing Ages 35–44*

Participation rate

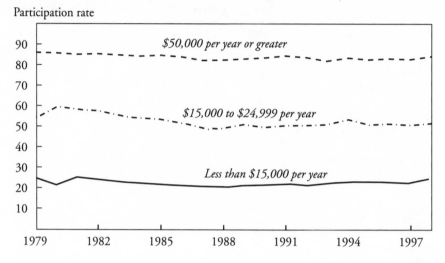

Source: Authors' analysis based on the March supplement of the *Current Population Survey* for various years.

the two higher-income cohorts experience lower probabilities of participation following both TEFRA and TRA, but those declines are smaller in percentage terms than the declines for lower-wage workers. By 1994, following the implementation of OBRA, the probability of participation increases for lower-income categories. Despite these increases following OBRA, pension participation rates do not return to their pre-TEFRA levels for fifteen of the sixteen hypothetical cases. Figure 9-5 plots the predicted participation rate over the entire period for a manufacturing worker age 35 to 44 in the lowest- and highest-income categories.

We also estimate a separate logit equation to control for time trends and the increased participation in defined contribution plans. To do this, we substitute a continuous time trend variable and regulatory dummies representing TEFRA, TRA, and OBRA in place of the year dummies. We also add the annual estimate of the percent of workers in defined contribution plans.[22] The coefficients from the logit estimates are provided in table 9-8. The marginal effects are reported in table 9-9.

The results are consistent with earlier findings and show that the probability of pension participation increases with earnings and age and varies across industries,

22. These data were derived from the Form 5500 data from the U.S. Department of Labor for 1979 to 1996. Estimates for 1997 and 1998 were imputed based on past trends.

Table 9-8. *Logit Coefficients for Estimates of Pension Participation Probabilities, by Earnings Category*

Variable	< $15,000	$15,000–$25,000	$25,000–$50,000	$50,000
Intercept	−1.27*	0.0902	0.856*	0.8773*
Age 21–24	−0.243*	−0.3029*	−0.42*	−0.066*
Age 35–44	0.2508*	0.2268*	0.324*	0.296*
Age 45–54	0.4841*	0.3915*	0.458*	0.46*
Age 55–64	0.6536*	0.5405*	0.473*	0.369*
Age 65+	0.0275	0.0272	−0.2967	−0.567
Agriculture	−0.946*	−0.9525*	−0.76*	−0.372*
Finance, insurance, and real estate	0.188*	0.1962*	−0.0721*	−0.14*
Trade	−0.553*	−0.6457*	−0.7089*	−0.58*
Transportation	0.087*	−0.0894*	0.3763*	0.77*
Manufacturing	0.08*	0.0388*	0.2396*	0.56*
Percent active in DC plans	0.07	0.0445	−0.0682	0.093
Time trend	−0.013*	−0.0227*	−0.0191*	−0.0125*
Marginal tax rate	0.0063*	−0.00328*	−0.00022	0.0003
TEFRA82	−0.164*	−0.126*	−0.0997*	−0.086*
TRA86	−0.118*	−0.0823*	−0.064*	−0.027
OBRA93	0.01	0.102	0.0837*	0.059
Number of observations	223,528	240,522	340,530	161,239

Source: Authors' calculations from the March supplement of the *Current Population Survey*, various years.

*Significant at the 95 percent level.

even after adjusting for time trends, marginal tax rates, and the growth of defined contribution plans. Figure 9-6 shows how the time trend and regulatory effects interact. Beyond the influence of time, we find that TEFRA and TRA had negative and significant impacts on pension participation rates for low-income workers. The results show that the existence of TEFRA lowers participation rates by 2.4 percent for workers with earnings below $15,000 and by 3.1 percent for workers with earnings between $15,000 and $25,000. This is consistent with our earlier time series equations. We also find, however, that TRA also exerted a negative and significant influence on participation rates for the two lowest earnings categories. Following TRA participation rates declined by 1.8 percent for those earning less than $15,000 and by 2.0 percent for those earning $15,000 to $25,000. While TEFRA and TRA had a negative influence on participation rates of higher-income workers, the actual magnitude of the effect was much less than that on lower-wage workers.

Table 9-9. *Marginal Effects from Logit Regression*

Independent variables	< $15,000	Earnings levels $15,000– $24,999	$25,000– $49,999	$50,000+
Intercept	–0.190*	0.022	0.188*	0.159*
Age 21–24	–0.037*	–0.074*	–0.090*	–0.119*
Age 35–44	0.037*	0.056*	0.071*	0.054*
Age 45–54	0.072*	0.960*	0.099*	0.0832*
Age 55–64	0.098*	0.132*	0.108*	0.067*
Age 65+	0.004	0.003	–0.060	–0.100*
Agriculture	–0.141*	–0.233*	–0.168*	–0.067*
Finance, insurance and real estate	0.028*	0.048*	–0.017*	–0.026*
Trade	–0.083*	–0.158*	–0.156*	–0.105*
Transportation	0.013*	–0.022*	0.082*	0.140*
Manufacturing	0.012*	0.010*	0.052*	0.101*
Percent active in DC plan	0.011	0.012	–0.012	0.017
Time trend	–0.002*	–0.006*	–0.037*	–0.002*
Marginal tax rate	–0.001*	–0.001*	0.000	0.000
TEFRA86	–0.025*	–0.031*	–0.025*	–0.016*
TRA86	–0.018*	–0.020*	–0.002*	–0.005*
OBRA93	0.0015	0.0251	0.009	0.018

Source: Estimated by the authors from *Current Population Surveys.*
*Indicates significant at the 95 percent level.

Conclusion

An explicit goal of federal pension policy is to raise the proportion of the labor force, especially among moderate earners, that participates in a pension plan and receives pension benefits in retirement. To reach this goal, Congress established nondiscrimination standards that linked tax preferences for pensions with the requirement that employers include a wide range of workers in pension plans.

Our estimates, however, provide no support for the view that stricter nondiscrimination standards have improved the odds that lower-paid workers will be covered by a pension. Instead, we find that, after the changes in regulatory standards following TEFRA and TRA in the 1980s, pension participation rates fell for both low and high earners, but more for low earners. While participation rates have risen somewhat since the passage of OBRA in 1993, these gains are not concentrated on workers at lower earnings levels, and even after those gains, participation rates remain below pre-TEFRA levels.

The explanation and implications of these results seem clear. The nondiscrimination standards implemented in the 1980s and 1990s, along with other

Figure 9-6. *Isolating the Various Effects over Time for Workers Ages 35–44 in Manufacturing Industry with Earnings Less than $15,000*

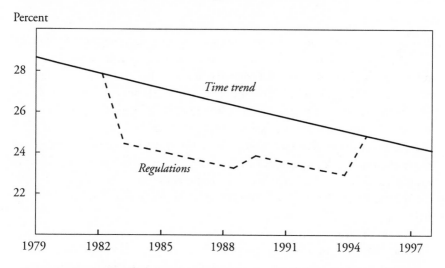

Source: Authors' analysis based on the March supplement of the *Current Population Survey* for various years.

pension regulations, have increased the cost of providing pensions—defined benefit plans in particular. Higher administrative costs offset an increasing share of the tax advantage that pensions generate and thus reduce sponsors' incentives to provide pensions, especially for lower-income workers, whose pension accruals are smaller and for firms with small number of participants, where per capita administrative costs are higher. These regulations are one of the key reasons that participation rates among low-income workers have remained low and why many small employers have terminated defined benefit plans over the past two decades. A better way to expand participation among low-income workers would be to reduce, rather than increase, the regulatory burdens on employers.

Peter R. Orszag

The paper by Clark, Mulvey, and Schieber examines the effects of the nondiscrimination rules applying to qualified pension plans. A somewhat simplified version of the Clark-Mulvey-Schieber argument is that the nondiscrimination rules and other regulations have imposed substantial administrative costs on plan administrators, that as a result many workers and firms do not find the tax benefits from qualified pension plans sufficient to justify the costs, that there is no evidence that the nondiscrimination rules have raised coverage for lower-income workers relative to higher-income workers, and thus that the nondiscrimination rules may have produced exactly the oppose effect intended by policymakers, that is, lower instead of higher coverage rates for low-wage workers.

My comments examine each of these components in the Clark-Mulvey-Schieber argument in turn. As a preview of the most important point, note that evaluating the nondiscrimination rules purely on the basis of participation rates, as Clark, Mulvey, and Schieber do, offers an incomplete perspective on the impact of the rules. In particular, even if the nondiscrimination rules do not affect relative participation rates between lower earners and higher earners, they may well alter the distribution of pension contributions conditional on participation. Indeed, the existence of an entire industry of pension consultants who help corporate decisionmakers find innovative ways of maximizing their own contributions while satisfying the nondiscrimination rules is at least suggestive that those rules may be affecting the distribution of contributions or benefits.

Background

Before examining the Clark-Mulvey-Schieber arguments, some brief background on the nondiscrimination rules may be helpful. As a recent volume co-authored by Schieber notes:

> A fundamental requirement of a tax-favored retirement plan is that the benefits or contributions under the plan must not favor highly compensated employees. Otherwise employers would be able to provide benefits only to highly compensated employees or could provide significant benefits to such employees and *de minimis* benefits to other employees. This is hardly the behavior Congress intended in establishing the tax incentives for retirement plans. Accordingly, the nondiscrimination rules prohibit

plan benefits or contributions from favoring highly compensated employees.[1]

In theory, these nondiscrimination rules could either raise or reduce pension coverage among lower-income workers, depending on whether the positive impact within extant plans dominates the negative impact on the number of plans in existence. As Clark, Mulvey, and Schieber note in their paper, virtually no empirical studies have examined the effects of the nondiscrimination rules. Their paper provides a first step in filling that gap. But the paper is unfortunately somewhat inconsistent regarding the precise objectives of the nondiscrimination rules, making it difficult to evaluate whether those objectives have been achieved. For example, at some points in the paper, the authors suggest that the primary objectives of the nondiscrimination rules are both to increase participation among lower earners and to limit pension tax expenditures for higher earners, whereas at other points in the paper, they suggest that the objective is only the former. To the extent that the nondiscrimination rules have not succeeded in raising participation rates among lower-wage earners, they may nonetheless have succeeded in achieving other objectives (such as altering the distribution of pension contributions or limiting pension tax expenditures for higher earners).

Nondiscrimination Rules and Administrative Costs

The first component of the Clark, Mulvey, and Schieber argument is that administrative costs for pension plans have increased substantially over the past twenty-five years. That is true, but it is not clear from the paper what role the nondiscrimination rules per se have played in contributing to those administrative costs. In particular, Clark, Mulvey, and Schieber highlight the increase in administrative costs associated with the Employee Retirement Income Security Act (ERISA) of 1974. But that act did not change only the nondiscrimination rules. It introduced a wide array of complex rules covering funding requirements, vesting, fiduciary responsibilities, and other matters. For example, ERISA established a mandatory minimum funding standard. The authors presumably support such funding requirements (they write that failing to fund adequately is the equivalent of "financial suicide"). Yet how much of the administrative cost burden is associated with computing the appropriate funding level, relative to evaluating the nondiscrimination tests? If the plan and all participant benefits and wages must be entered into a computer to calculate funding needs,

1. McGill and others (1996, p. 75).

what is the marginal cost of programming the nondiscrimination evaluation also? Furthermore, since defined contribution plans also have to meet the nondiscrimination rules (although, in the case of 401(k) plans, special nondiscrimination tests apply), and since administrative costs for defined contribution plans have increased by much less than defined benefit plans since ERISA was passed, the role of the nondiscrimination rules per se is unclear.

The authors offer no evidence on the marginal cost of the nondiscrimination rules (as opposed to other regulations); they merely argue that they believe that the cost of compliance with these rules has contributed to small firms terminating defined benefit plans and either offering no new pension or establishing defined contribution plans that require voluntary contributions by workers. By contrast, the General Accounting Office recently concluded an examination of the top-heavy rules, which are related to (but distinct from) the nondiscrimination rules. The report concluded that "pension consultants we interviewed estimated the costs to be low in most situations. . . . Practitioners explained that computer software makes running top-heavy tests as routine as hitting a key on a computer."[2] In other words, for most firms, the administrative costs associated with implementing the top-heavy rules appear relatively small. Why are the (marginal) administrative costs associated with the nondiscrimination rules much higher?

It is also worth noting that small employers without pension plans do not appear to place as much emphasis on regulatory burden as Clark, Mulvey, and Schieber do. For example, a recent survey conducted by the Employee Benefits Research Institute suggests that government regulations are not necessarily the dominant explanation for why such firms fail to offer pension plans.[3] Other more important explanations include that workers prefer other forms of compensation (which admittedly could be linked to the administrative cost of the plan) or that the nature of the firm or the industry makes it difficult to adopt pension plans (for example, uncertain revenue combined with a required employer contribution, the absence of an ability to borrow, and risk aversion on the part of the business owner or executive would discourage pension plan adoption). Table 9-10 presents the results from the survey, which should be treated with the same caution as any survey results.

Benefits and Costs of Qualified Pension Contributions

The second component of the Clark, Mulvey, and Schieber argument investigates the relative costs and benefits of contributing to a qualified pension plan. I

2. GAO (2000).

3. EBRI (2001), "The 2000 Small Employer Retirement Survey: Summary of Findings," available at http://www.ebri.org.

Table 9-10. *Reasons for Not Offering a Pension Plan*

Reason	Percent of respondents identifying as most important factor for not offering plan
Employees prefer wages and/or other benefits	21
Workers are seasonal, part-time, or high turnover	18
Revenue is too uncertain	13
Business is too new	11
Costs are too much to set up and administer	9
Required company contributions are too expensive	8
There are too many government regulations	3
Vesting requirements cause too much money to go to short-term employees	3
Benefits for the owner are too small	3
Owner has own deferred compensation arrangement	2
Don't know where to go for information on starting a plan	1
Other reasons	6
Total (with rounding)	100

Source: EBRI, "The 2000 Small Employer Retirement Survey: Summary of Findings," available at www.ebri.org.

agree with the importance of focusing on the net present value of the gain from contributions to a qualified plan. But two points are worth noting.

First, as emphasized above, Clark, Mulvey, and Schieber do not identify the marginal costs associated with the nondiscrimination rules. Their arguments are therefore applicable to the overall pension regulatory regime, not the nondiscrimination rules per se.

Second, the Clark, Mulvey, and Schieber examples are at least partially predicated on a full wage-benefit offset at the level of the individual worker. That is, the after-tax cost to the firm of an extra dollar in pension benefits for an individual worker is assumed to be reflected in the worker's wages. Economists generally concur that the costs of nonwage compensation, such as pensions, will be reflected in wage compensation. But it is unclear whether such shifting occurs at the level of the individual worker, as opposed to large groups of workers or the firm's work force as a whole. As Gruber argues in the context of health insurance, empirical "results confirm that group-specific shifting is possible, but do not offer much insight into how finely that shifting can occur. In particular, can firms go beyond broad demographic categorizations and actually reduce the wages of individual workers who are particularly costly?"[4] Gruber suggests that the answer to that question remains unknown.

4. Gruber (2000), p. 697.

Coverage Rates

The next section of the Clark, Mulvey, and Schieber paper provides an empirical investigation of low-income coverage rates relative to higher-income coverage rates. I have three comments about the evidence presented.

First, as noted above, the authors examine pension participation rates, not amounts. One of the important effects of the nondiscrimination rules may be to alter the share of benefits or contributions flowing to lower-wage earners, rather than higher-wage earners, conditional on participation. If so, we would not necessarily detect any impact of the nondiscrimination rules on participation. Instead, the impact would manifest itself in contribution levels. The paper provides no evidence on the degree to which the nondiscrimination rules have succeeded in raising benefit or contribution amounts conditional on participation.

Second, the empirical analysis evaluates trends in pension coverage rates for workers in four earnings categories (expressed in 1999 dollars). Unfortunately, the minimum threshold for the highest earnings category ($50,000 and above) does not necessarily correspond to the threshold used in nondiscrimination testing. The nondiscrimination rules differentiate highly compensated employees from nonhighly compensated employees. In many cases (such as if the employee was not an owner or officer of the firm, nor in the "top paid" group), an employee could earn well over $50,000 and still not be "highly compensated." Firm-level data are necessary to determine which threshold is applicable for a specific worker; in the absence of such data, it is difficult to know whether the categories chosen by Clark, Mulvey, and Schieber are capable of measuring the potential effects of the nondiscrimination rules, even in terms of participation rates.

Third, the paper mentions, but does not discuss the empirical impact of, the special nondiscrimination rules that apply to 401(k) plans. Data on participation rates in 401(k) plans among lower- and moderate-income workers suggest that a surprisingly large share of lower- and moderate-income workers participate in a 401(k) plan if offered the chance. For example, data from 1993 suggest that 44 percent of workers earning between $10,000 and $15,000 in 1993 (or between $14,000 and $20,000 in 2000, using average wage growth to inflate the values) who were offered the opportunity to participate in a 401(k) chose to do so.[5] Only 21 percent were offered the opportunity, so that the overall participation rate was only 9 percent (table 9-11). Other data sources tell a similar story: The *conditional* participation rate (that is, the participation rate among those workers who are offered the opportunity to save through a 401(k) plan) is surprisingly high, even for lower-income workers. The participation rate in

---

5. It is worth noting that these figures are for earnings, not household income. Some lower-income workers may be from relatively high-income families.

Table 9-11. *Participation Rates in 401(k) Plans*

Implied 2000 earnings[a]	Percent offered a 401(k)	Percent offered who choose to contribute
Under $14,000	10	30
$14,000–$20,000	21	44
$20,000–$28,000	35	55
$28,000–$35,000	43	64

Source: Department of Labor, Social Security Administration, Small Business dministration, and Pension Benefit Guaranty Corporation (1994), table C7.

a. Scales 1993 earnings levels by the percentage change in the Social Security average wage index between 1993 and 2000.

IRAs, on the other hand, is quite low. A recent unpublished Treasury study shows that in 1995 (the latest year for which these data are available), only 4 percent of eligible taxpayers contributed the maximum amount to a conventional IRA in 1995, and only 7 percent made any contribution at all.[6]

The relatively low level of participation in IRAs, relative to the conditional 401(k) participation rate, may reflect a variety of factors, including a positive matching rate, financial education in the workplace (firms often offer such education in conjunction with their 401(k) plans), peer effects, the type of workers offered a 401(k) plan, and the role of the nondiscrimination rules. The impact of the 401(k) nondiscrimination rules, which differ from the generic nondiscrimination rules, is worth further examination. Since two of the co-authors have previously examined 401(k) participation and contribution rates, this topic may be a good one for their attention in the future.[7]

Nondiscrimination Rules Are Counterproductive

The conclusion that Clark, Mulvey, and Schieber draw from their empirical investigation of coverage rates is that these regulations have done little to increase participation among low-income workers over the past twenty years. Workers at low and middle earnings levels actually experienced small declines in pension participation following the adoption of these regulations. The authors argue that if Congress wants to expand participation for low-income workers it should look for ways to reduce, rather than increase, the regulatory burden on employers.

Let us accept for the purposes of argument that the nondiscrimination rules have not significantly affected participation rates among lower-income workers. In other words, the nondiscrimination rules may not have helped very much in

6. Carroll (2000).
7. Clark and Schieber (1998).

terms of raising relative participation rates, but they also do not seem to have hurt much either. Furthermore, they may well have limited the tax expenditures associated with pensions for higher earners. They may also have raised the pension *amounts* flowing to lower earners conditional on participation; remember that the paper offers no evidence on this crucial question.

To the extent that the nondiscrimination rules make the distribution of tax expenditures more equal than it would otherwise be, without reducing participation rates significantly, they could even be viewed as a success from some perspectives. Indeed, from a national saving perspective, the nondiscrimination rules may then have been quite helpful, given the evidence that any dollar of pension saving undertaken by a higher-wage earner is less likely to represent a net addition to national saving than a given dollar of pension saving undertaken by a lower-wage earner.[8]

Two Final Comments

Finally, it is worth noting two important points that the paper does not address. First, the nondiscrimination rules can be viewed as a tax on heterogeneity. (The rules are not binding, for example, for firms with only highly compensated employees.) The welfare implications of such a tax on heterogeneity are more complicated than they may initially appear.[9] Welfare analysis is further complicated because the strength of the wage-benefit offset—that is, the degree to which wages fall in response to an extra dollar of pension contributions—is unclear at the level of the individual worker (as opposed to the firm's entire work force).

Second, the paper does not discuss ways in which the nondiscrimination rules could be simultaneously tightened *and* simplified, thereby reducing their administrative costs. In particular, much of the complexity of the current system—including the rules on permitted disparity and Social Security integration—reflects provisions that allow more "gaming" and raise administrative costs. As just one example, "cross-testing" of pension plans is apparently spreading rapidly among small businesses.[10] Fundamentally, cross-testing allows firms to treat defined contribution plans as defined benefit plans for the purposes of the nondiscrimination test (thus the plans are "cross-tested," since they are defined contribution plans but tested as defined benefit plans). In so doing, cross-testing often allows firms to direct a surprisingly large percentage of benefits toward older, higher-income workers. A newer form of cross-tested plans, called "new comparability plans," often produces even more extreme results.

8. Engen and Gale (2000).
9. Bankman (1988, 1994).
10. Orszag and Stein (2001).

Such plans are complicated to devise and often have high administrative costs (relative to other defined contribution plans). The point is merely that much of the complexity of the nondiscrimination rules may well arise from provisions that allow more, rather than less, skewed benefits or contributions relative to a simple across-the-board percentage-of-pay rule.

References

Bankman, Joseph. 1988. "Tax Policy and Retirement Income: Are Pension Plan Anti-Discrimination Provisions Desirable?" University of Chicago Law Review 55 (Summer):790–835.

———. 1994. "The Effect of Anti-Discrimination Provisions on Rank-and-File Compensation." *Washington University Law Quarterly* 72: 597.

Bloom, David E., and Richard B. Freeman. 1994. "The Fall in Private Pension Coverage in the U.S." In *Pension Coverage Issues for the 90's.* U.S. Department of Labor.

Carrington, William, Kristin McCue, and Brooks Pierce. 2000. "The Efficacy and Impact of Non-Discrimination Rules." Stanford Institute for Economic Policy Research Discussion Paper 00-17. Stanford University.

Carroll, Robert. 2000. "IRAs and the Tax Reform Act of 1997." Department of the Treasury, Office of Tax Analysis. January.

Clark, Robert L., and Ann A. McDermed. 1990. *The Choice of Pension Plans in a Changing Regulatory Environment.* Washington: AEI Press.

Clark, Robert L., and Sylvester S. Schieber. 1998. "Factors Affecting Participation Rates and Contribution Levels in 401(k) Plans." In *Living with Defined Contributions: Remaking Responsibility for Retirement,* edited by Olivia S. Mitchell and Sylvester Schieber. University of Pennsylvania Press.

Clark, Robert L., and Elisa Wolper. 1997. "Pension Tax Expenditures: Magnitude, Distribution, and Economic Effects." In *Public Policy toward Pensions,* edited by Sylvester J. Schieber and John B. Shoven. MIT Press.

Department of Labor, Social Security Administration, Small Business Administration, and Pension Benefit Guaranty Corporation. 1994. *Pension and Health Benefits of American Workers.*

Engen, Eric, and William Gale. 2000. "The Effects of 401(k) Plans on Household Wealth: Differences across Earnings Groups." Working Paper 8032. Cambridge, Mass.: National Bureau of Economic Research.

Even, William E., and David A. MacPherson. 1994. "The Pension Coverage of Young and Mature Workers." In *Pension Coverage Issues for the 90's.* Department of Labor.

Garrett, Daniel M. 1995. "The Effects of Nondiscrimination Rules on 401(k) Contributions." Stanford University (December).

General Accounting Office. 2000. "Private Pensions: 'Top-Heavy' Rules for Owner-Dominated Plans." GAO/HEHS-00-141. Government Printing Office.

Goodfellow, Gordon P., and Sylvester J. Schieber. 1993. "Death and Taxes: Can We Fund for Retirement between Them." In *The Future of Pensions in the United States,* edited by Ray Schmitt. Philadelphia: Pension Research Council.

Gruber, Jonathan. 2000. "Health Insurance and the Labor Market." In *Handbook of Health Economics,* vol. 1A, edited by A. J. Culyer and J. P. Newhouse. Amsterdam: Elsevier.

Gustman, Alan L., and Thomas L. Steinmeier. 1992. "The Stampede toward Defined Contribution Plans: Fact or Fiction?" *Industrial Relations* 31 (2): 361–69.

Hustead, Edwin C. 1998. "Trends in Retirement Income Plan Administrative Expenses." In *Living with Defined Contribution Plans: Remaking Responsibility for Retirement,* edited by Olivia S. Mitchell and Sylvester J. Schieber. University of Pennsylvania Press.

Ippolito, Richard A. 1997. *Pension Plans and Employee Performance.* University of Chicago Press.

McGill, Dan M., and others. 1996. *Fundamentals of Private Pensions,* 7th ed. University of Pennsylvania Press.

Orszag, Peter R., and Norman Stein. 2001. "Cross-Tested Defined Contribution Plans: A Response to Professor Zelinsky." *Buffalo Law Review* 49.

Quick, Carol. 1999. "An Overview of Cash Balance Plans." *EBRI Notes* 20(7).

Schieber, Sylvester J. 2004. "The Evolution and Implications of Federal Pension Regulation." In William G. Gale, John B. Shoven, and Mark J. Warshawsky, eds., *The Evolving Pension System: Trends, Effects, and Proposals for Reform*. Brookings.

Watson Wyatt Worldwide. 2000. *Survey of Actuarial Assumptions and Funding*. Bethesda, Md.

10

Asset Location for Retirement Savers

JAMES M. POTERBA, JOHN B. SHOVEN,
AND CLEMENS SIALM

Deciding how much of a portfolio to allocate to different types of assets is one of the fundamental issues in financial economics. For taxable individual investors, the proliferation of tax-deferred vehicles for retirement saving, such as individual retirement accounts (IRAs), 401(k) plans, Keogh plans, and 403(b) plans, has added a new dimension to the historical asset allocation problem. A taxable investor needs to make choices not just about the amount to hold in various assets but also about *where* to hold those assets. If there are two asset classes, broadly defined as riskless and risky, the asset allocation problem facing tax-exempt investors involves choosing only the fraction of the portfolio to allocate to the risky asset. Taxable investors with a tax-deferred retirement saving account, however, face a more complex problem, since they must decide how much of the risky asset to hold in their tax-deferred account and how much to hold in their taxable account. Shoven (1999), Shoven and Sialm (2004), and Dammon, Spatt, and Zhang (2004) labeled the problem of deciding where to hold a given asset the asset *location* decision.

Poterba, Venti, and Wise (2000) have shown that more than 30 million workers currently participate in 401(k) pension plans; millions more have tax-

We thank Olivia Lau and Svetla Tzenova for assistance with data collection and William Gale, Davide Lombardo, Sita Nataraj, and Paul Samuelson for helpful comments on an earlier draft. James Poterba thanks the National Science Foundation for research support.

deferred assets in IRAs. Virtually all 401(k) plans—and all IRAs—give account holders substantial discretion in choosing the set of assets that they hold. Therefore most account holders who also have other assets outside the tax-deferred accounts face asset location choices. The choices are likely to be most salient for middle- and upper-middle-income households whose tax-deferred assets represent a substantial fraction, but not all, of their financial wealth. Recent legislation prospectively increasing the limits on contributions to tax-deferred retirement saving plans could make the asset location decision more significant for households in higher income and wealth strata, since the legislation will increase the total pool of assets that a household can accumulate in a tax-deferred setting.

How holding an asset in a taxable or tax-deferred account affects long-term wealth accumulation depends on the tax treatment of the asset in question as well as on the other assets available. Given a set of assets that an investor wishes to hold, long-run wealth accumulation generally will be maximized by placing the most heavily taxed assets in the tax-deferred account (TDA) while holding the less heavily taxed assets in the taxable account. We refer to the latter as the conventional savings account (CSA).

The asset location problem is a practical question in applied financial economics that confronts many households as they save for retirement and other objectives. Yet much of the conventional wisdom on asset location for individual investors derives from research on a related problem confronting corporations. Two decades ago, Black (1980) and Tepper (1981) studied the problem of asset allocation for a corporation that could choose to hold its assets in its defined benefit pension plan or in its taxable corporate account. They explored corporate asset location problems with respect to taxable bonds and corporate equities. Taxable bonds were assumed to generate heavily taxed interest income, and corporate equities were assumed to generate lightly taxed returns because capital gains are not taxed until they are realized. The studies concluded that because bonds are taxed more heavily than stocks, a firm could maximize shareholders' after-tax cash flow by placing bonds in the pension account and stocks in the taxable corporate account. The pension account in the corporate setting is equivalent to an individual investor's tax-deferred account. Something like that analysis underlies the suggestion, made by many financial advisers, that individual investors should allocate taxable bonds to their tax-deferred account before holding any such bonds in their taxable account.

However, that analysis neglects two important aspects of the investment decisions that face many taxable investors. First, heavily taxed corporate or government bonds are not the only way for taxable investors to participate in the market for fixed-income securities; they also can choose to hold tax-exempt bonds. Over the last four decades, the average yield on long-term tax-exempt bonds has exceeded the after-tax yield on taxable Treasury bonds for individual investors in the highest marginal tax brackets. Tax-exempt bonds therefore offer taxable investors the potential to hold fixed-income securities with an implicit tax rate that may be lower than the statutory tax rate on taxable bonds.

The second shortcoming of the conventional asset location analysis is that it assumes that investments in corporate stock are lightly taxed. In practice, many taxable investors hold equities through equity mutual funds. Many equity funds, particularly actively managed ones, are managed in a fashion that imposes substantial tax burdens on taxable individual investors. Dickson and Shoven (1995), Dickson, Shoven, and Sialm (2000), Bergstresser and Poterba (2002), Arnott, Berkin, and Ye (2000), and others have computed before-tax and after-tax returns for equity mutual funds in the United States. Their studies suggest that such funds often realize capital gains more quickly than might be desirable if the objective is to defer taxes. Therefore the effective tax rate on equity investments through mutual funds often is substantially greater than that on a buy-and-hold equity portfolio.

Omitting tax-exempt bonds from the asset location analysis and failing to recognize that many investors hold their equities in actively managed mutual funds combine to overstate the tax burden on fixed-income assets compared with that on equities. In this chapter, we investigate whether those two factors are important enough to reverse the conventional wisdom, exploring whether historically investors would have accumulated more after-tax wealth by holding equity mutual funds in a tax-deferred account and municipal bonds in a taxable account than by holding taxable bonds in a tax-deferred account and equity mutual funds in a taxable account.

We use the historical performance of mutual funds to explore the asset location problem. Earlier work on asset location was either theoretical or used hypothetical or simulated mutual funds.[1] Although using historical data provides information on how investors following alternative investment strategies would have fared in past decades, historical data may not describe the future. It is possible that in the future actively managed equity mutual funds may impose lower tax burdens on their investors than they have in the past.

We consider a stylized investor who made equal annual contributions to a tax-deferred account and a conventional savings account over the period 1962–98. We assume that the investor rebalanced his or her portfolio each year to hold half of the total assets in equities and half in fixed-income investments. We also assume that all equity investments were made in one of a set of equity mutual funds for which we collected historical returns and that fixed-income investments could be made in tax-exempt as well as taxable bonds.

1. See Shoven and Sialm (2004), Shoven (1999), and Shoven and Sialm (1998).

We compute the investor's after-tax wealth at the end of 1998 under two different asset location strategies. The first, Defer Stocks First, specified that investments in one of the equity mutual funds in our data set would be given priority for placement in the tax-deferred account. Under that rule, if the total market value of the assets in the TDA were less than half of the combined market value of the assets in the TDA and the CSA, the investor would hold only an equity mutual fund in the tax-deferred account. If the total amount that the investor could hold in the TDA were more than half of the combined value of the TDA and the CSA, then the TDA would hold some fixed-income instruments and the CSA would hold only fixed-income instruments. That would involve holding some taxable bonds in the TDA and tax-exempt bonds in the CSA.

The second asset location strategy, Defer Bonds First, reversed that order. Fixed-income assets were held in the TDA before any such assets were held in a taxable format. In this case, if the total value of the TDA assets were less than half of the combined value of the TDA and the CSA, the investor would hold only taxable bonds in the TDA.

In this chapter, we first describe a simplified one-period model of asset location. While we can find clear results analytically for a one-period asset location problem, we cannot do this for a multiperiod problem; we therefore develop numerical results on the consequences of different asset location decisions for hypothetical multiperiod investors. Next we describe the data on equity mutual fund returns and bond returns underlying our calculations and give our assumptions about the marginal tax rates facing our hypothetical taxable investors. We then present our core findings on the amount of wealth that investors would have accumulated if they had followed the two different asset location strategies over the 1962–98 period. For virtually all of the actively managed mutual funds in our data set, an investor would have had more end of period wealth if he had allocated his mutual fund shares to his tax-deferred account before holding equity mutual funds in his conventional saving account. The differences in end of period wealth between the two asset location strategies are substantial for all of the actively managed funds in our data sample. The differences are much smaller for equity index funds. Our findings stand in contrast to much conventional wisdom, due both to our recognition of the opportunity to hold tax-exempt bonds and to the higher tax burden on corporate stock that follows from holding equities through mutual funds rather than directly.

We also explore the sensitivity of our findings to the particular pattern of equity and bond returns that has characterized the last four decades. We evaluate the robustness of our findings by drawing sequences of thirty-seven returns (with replacement) from each fund's empirical distribution of returns. Our results suggest that while the recent history of returns has been particularly favorable to the Defer Stocks First strategy, for most random draws from the return distribution for the last four decades, this strategy would have generated more after-tax wealth than the Defer Bonds First strategy.

We last introduce inflation-indexed bonds such as Treasury inflation-protected securities (TIPS), which have been available in the United States since 1997. Our analysis assumes that inflation-indexed bonds with a 4 percent real return were available throughout the 1962–98 period. We show that in this case, holding equity mutual funds in the TDA and inflation-indexed savings bonds in the CSA would have given investors a higher expected utility than holding equity mutual funds in their TDA and tax-exempt nominal bonds in their CSA. The chapter concludes with a summary of our findings.

Asset Location in a Simple Setting

Our analysis begins with a one-period example illustrating the effects of asset location on investor returns. We suppose that an investor can hold taxable bonds (B), tax-exempt municipal bonds (M), and stocks (S) in a conventional savings account (CSA) or in a tax-deferred account (TDA). The pretax returns of the three asset classes are r_B, r_M, and r_S, where the bond returns are nonstochastic and satisfy $0 < r_M < r_B$. We assume the effective tax rate of stocks to be lower than the effective tax rate of taxable bonds: $\tau_S < \tau_B$. The implicit municipal bond tax rate equals $\tau_M = 1 - r_M/r_B$. For simplicity, we assume that the tax rates do not change over time, which means that the return on an investment in a TDA equals the before-tax return $r^{TDA} = r$. The after-tax return on taxable assets in a CSA equals $r^{CSA} = (1 - \tau)r$. We take the investor's total wealth in the TDA and the CSA as given, perhaps as a result of constraints on TDA contributions.

In this setting, it is never optimal to hold tax-exempt bonds in the tax-deferred account, because the taxable bond has a higher before-tax return than the tax-exempt bond. In addition, taxable bonds should not be held in the taxable account if the implicit tax rate on municipal bonds τ_M is smaller than the tax rate on taxable bonds τ_B. In this case, the after-tax returns in the CSA would be higher if the investor held tax-exempt bonds.

To analyze the optimal location of stocks in the one-period model, we suppose that an investor with $\tau_M < \tau_B$ holds tax-exempt bonds in the CSA, taxable bonds in the TDA, and stocks in both the TDA and the CSA. The following argument presents conditions under which it is optimal to increase stock exposure in the TDA and to decrease stock exposure in the CSA.

We increase stock holdings in the TDA by \$1 and reduce holdings of taxable bonds in the TDA by \$1. At the same time, we decrease stock holdings in the CSA by \$1/$(1 - \tau_S)$ and increase the holdings of tax-exempt bonds in the CSA by \$1/$(1 - \tau_S)$. This transaction involves no net investment in total financial assets, and it leaves the investor with the same degree of exposure to risky equity as does the initial portfolio.

Before the portfolio shift, the risky component of the portfolio at the end of the period, which we denote W_S, is

$$(1) \qquad W_S = I_{S,\,TDA}[1 + r_S] + I_{S,\,CSA}[1 + (1 - \tau_S)r_S],$$

where initial investments of stocks in the TDA and the CSA are denoted by $I_{S,\,TDA}$ and $I_{S,\,CSA}$, respectively. The riskless component of the initial portfolio, which is the sum of the wealth held in taxable bonds (W_B) and tax-exempt bonds (W_M), is

$$(2) \qquad W_B + W_M = I_{B,\,TDA}[1 + r_B] + I_{M,\,CSA}[1 + r_M].$$

Note that final wealth is $W = W_S + W_B + W_M$.

After the suggested portfolio shift, the values of the risky and risk-free components are

$$(3) \quad W_S' = [I_{S,\,TDA} + 1][1 + r_S] + \left[I_{S,\,CSA} - \frac{1}{1 - \tau_S}\right][1 + (1 - \tau_S)r_S] = W_S - \frac{\tau_S}{1 - \tau_S}$$

and

$$(4) \qquad W_B' + W_M' = [I_{B,\,TDA} - 1][1 + r_B] + \left[I_{M,\,CSA} + \frac{1}{1 - \tau_S}\right][1 + r_M] = $$

$$W_B + W_M + \frac{\tau_S}{1 - \tau_S} + r_B \left(\frac{\tau_S - \tau_M}{1 - \tau_S}\right).$$

The total value of the portfolio after the shift equals

$$(5) \qquad W' = W_S' + W_B' + W_M' = W + r_B \left(\frac{\tau_S - \tau_M}{1 - \tau_S}\right).$$

The suggested portfolio shift increases the wealth level at the end of the period if $\tau_S > \tau_M$. The shift does not involve any risk, and investors should take advantage of the profitable arbitrage opportunity offered until they reach borrowing or other constraints.

The foregoing argument shows that stocks have a preferred location in the TDA (Defer Stocks First) if $\tau_S > \tau_M$. Stocks have a preferred location in the CSA if $\tau_S < \tau_M$. If stocks are highly taxed, then they should replace the taxable bonds in the TDA; if stocks are lightly taxed, then they should replace the tax-exempt bonds in the CSA.

Optimal asset location is considerably more complicated in a model with multiple periods, because asset location choices in one period will affect the amount in the tax-deferred account in future periods. In our one-period example, the terminal value of the TDA changes with the portfolio shift:

$$(6) \quad W'_{TDA} = [I_{S,TDA} + 1][1 + r_S] + [I_{B,TDA} - 1][1 + r_B] = W_{TDA} + r_S - r_B.$$

In a multiperiod setting, having a larger tax-deferred account is beneficial because it allows the investor to shelter a larger proportion of future wealth. Multiperiod asset location choices have to consider the potential long-term effects of current asset location choices on future TDA values.

Simple results like the ones derived above are difficult to obtain analytically in the multiperiod asset location problem. For that reason, we developed numerical results on the wealth that hypothetical investors would have built up after many years of investment if they had pursued various asset location strategies. The remainder of the chapter is devoted to describing those results. While the results depend on the time period that we study, they provide some evidence on how multiperiod investors should analyze their asset location options.

Data on Asset Returns and Investor Tax Rates

Our analysis of the economic effects of different asset location choices relies on data from the 1962–98 period, focusing on hypothetical investors who held equities through actively managed mutual funds rather than through direct equity holdings. We consider the returns on twelve actively managed equity mutual funds that were available to investors for the entire 37-year period; table 10-1 summarizes the total asset values of those funds. The equity funds were sorted according to their total valuation in December 1961 and 1968 as listed by Johnson's Investment Company; the first five funds ("top five funds") were the five largest equity funds at the end of December 1961.[2] Selection and survivorship bias are important because, as Carhart noted, funds with above-average past performance tend to be larger and are less likely to be discontinued.[3] Results using the top five funds are not subject to those biases, whereas results using the other funds might be.

We also collected data for the ten largest equity funds on December 31, 1968, according to Johnson's Investment Company.[4] We augmented that data sample with information on two other funds, the Fidelity Fund and Vanguard Windsor. Our whole sample represents 29.2 percent of the total value of mutual

2. Johnson (1962, 1969).
3. Carhart (1997).
4. Johnson (1969).

Table 10-1. *Equity Mutual Funds in Data Set*[a]

Name	Assets in millions (year-end 1961)	Assets in millions (year-end 1968)	Assets in millions (year-end 1998)
1. MFS Mass. Investors Trust	1,800	2,293	7,142
2. IDS Stock	1,025	2,341	3,257
3. Lord Abbett Affiliated	815	1,805	8,594
4. Fundamental Investors	733	1,391	12,713
5. United Accumulative	601	1,460	1,864
6. MFS Mass. Investors Growth	575	1,264	3,609
7. Fidelity Fund	487	898	10,563
8. Dreyfus	311	2,666	2,591
9. Investment Co. of America	259	1,056	48,498
10. Fidelity Trend	42	1,346	1,198
11. Van Kampen Enterprise	n.a.	953	2,127
12. Vanguard Windsor	n.a.	225	18,188
Summary statistic			
Sum of equity funds	6,647	17,698	120,344
Sum of top five funds in 1961	4,974	9,290	33,570
Total assets of all mutual funds	22,789	52,677	5,525,200
Total number of funds	170	240	7,314

Source: Authors' calculations based on data from Investment Company Institute, Mutual Fund Fact Book, and Johnson's Charts.

a. The top five equity mutual funds correspond to the five largest equity funds at the end of 1961. The results of those five funds should not be subject to survivorship bias. Ten funds (all funds except Fidelity and Vanguard Windsor) were the ten largest equity funds at the end of 1968. The Massachusetts Investors Trust and Massachusetts Investors Growth Funds changed their names to MFS Massachusetts Investors Trust and Growth, respectively. Investors Stock changed to IDS Stock, Affiliated to Lord Abbett Affiliated, the Enterprise Fund to Van Kampen Enterprise, and Windsor to Vanguard Windsor. Investors Mutual and the Wellington Fund were both larger than United Accumulative in 1961; those two funds are not included in our data set because they were balanced funds and held a significant portion of bonds. We excluded the Investors Mutual and the Investors Stock Fund because they were balanced mutual funds in 1968. Moreover, we excluded the ISI Trust Fund because in 1968 it did not issue shares but rather issued ten-year participating agreements.

funds in 1961 and 33.6 percent of the value in 1968. The sample becomes less representative over time, the result of both an increase in the total number of mutual funds and a sharp increase in inflows to equity mutual funds during the 1980s and 1990s. As those inflows were distributed across the funds in existence in those decades, many of which were new entrants that were not available in the 1960s, the share of assets in the "old" equity funds declined. Data from the Investment Company Institute suggest that in 1998 our twelve actively managed mutual funds held only 2.2 percent of the assets invested in mutual funds.[5]

5. Investment Company Institute (2000).

An important issue in interpreting our results is the degree to which the historical performance of the funds we consider is likely to provide guidance on the future performance of today's funds.

The data on the pre- and posttax returns on the equity funds for the years before 1992 are taken from Dickson and Shoven.[6] We updated their data by using Standard & Poor's dividend records (1993–99) and Moody's dividend records (1993–99) for the distributions (dividends and short-, medium-, and long-term capital gains) and by using Interactive Data (part of *Financial Times* Information) for the net asset values of the funds.[7] The annual total return equals the percent change in the value of one mutual fund share purchased at the end of the previous year. The returns are adjusted for splits as necessary. We assume that mutual fund distributions are reinvested on the "ex-dividend date."

To model the taxable and tax-exempt fixed-income investment options available to our hypothetical investor, we use the Vanguard long-term bond fund and the Vanguard long-term municipal bond fund. The annual distributions and net asset values of the two bond funds are taken from Morningstar.[8] Both bond funds paid monthly dividends, and we assume monthly compounding when computing their annual returns. In addition to the twelve actively managed funds that we consider, we also construct a time series of returns that we viewed as corresponding to a passively managed Standard & Poor's (S&P) 500 index fund. When available, we use the returns on the Vanguard 500 index fund for the index fund returns.

Data for the two bond funds and the index fund are available only after the mid-1970s. To indicate the type of returns that investors in such funds would have earned if the funds had been available during the first decade and a half of our sample period, we construct synthetic funds. The returns on the synthetic bond funds are calculated from the year-end yields to maturity of long-term corporate bonds (Moody's AAA-rated bonds) and of long-term tax-exempt bonds (with an average rating of A1) as reported in the *Statistical Release of the Federal Reserve*. The synthetic bond funds are assumed to hold the bonds for one year. The interest income of the funds paid at the end of the year equals the yield to maturity at the issue date minus expenses of 50 basis points. We calculate the capital gain or loss for each bond fund for each year by calculating the capital gain or loss on twenty-year par bonds that were newly issued at the beginning of the year.[9]

6. Dickson and Shoven (1995).

7. Interactive Data (2000), see www.ftinteractivedata.com.

8. Morningstar Principia Plus Database (Chicago: Morningstar Associates, 2000).

9. The capital gain (CG) of the synthetic bond fund between time t and time $t + 1$ was computed as the difference between the price of a nineteen-year bond at time $t + 1$, p_{t+1}^{19}, and the price of a twenty-year bond at time t, p_t^{20}. By convention, bonds are issued at par, so $p_t^{20} = 1$. We defined the yield to maturity of a twenty-year bond at time t and a nineteen-year bond at time $t + 1$ as y_t^{20}

Positive capital gains in the synthetic mutual funds are distributed to the shareholders annually and capital losses are carried forward. To ascertain whether the characteristics of the synthetic funds are similar to those of the actual funds, we computed returns on the synthetic funds for the 1979–98 period, when we also have returns on the actual equity index fund and on the two bond funds. The performance of the synthetic fund did not differ much from the performance of the actual fund.[10]

We create a synthetic index fund corresponding to the Vanguard 500 index fund by using the return data on the large stock index of Ibbotson Associates.[11] The synthetic fund distributed dividends net of expenses, which we assumed to equal 25 basis points. The fund's turnover rate of 5 percent results in short- and long-term capital gain distributions, which are distributed if positive and carried forward if negative. The actual index fund and the synthetic index fund yield very similar returns for the period 1979–98.[12]

To evaluate investor performance over the 1962–98 period, we spliced together the returns on our synthetic bond and index funds for the early part of our sample and used the actual returns on those funds in the later part of the sample. We labeled them spliced funds.

We translate the before-tax returns on the various mutual funds in our sample into after-tax returns by using two sets of marginal tax rates for hypothetical high- and medium-tax individuals. We assume that the high-tax individual has taxable income that is ten times the median adjusted gross income, as reported in the Statistics of Income of the Internal Revenue Service, less the standard deduction for a married couple with three exemptions, in each year. The medium-tax individual has taxable income equal to three times median AGI, again less the standard deduction and three exemptions. The tax rates between 1962 and 1992 are taken from Dickson and Shoven;[13] we update them by using

---

and y^{19}_{t+1}, respectively. We assumed that yields at all maturities were equal, so that $y^{19}_{t+1} = y^{20}_{t+1}$. In this case,

$$CG_{t+1} = p^{19}_{t+1}/p^{20}_t - 1 = (y^{20}_t/y^{19}_{t+1})*[(1 - (1 + y^{19}_{t+1})^{-19}] + (1 + y^{19}_{t+1})^{-19} - 1.$$

The interest return at time $t + 1$ of the synthetic bond fund was set equal to the coupon rate at time t, y^{20}_t.

10. The synthetic bond funds had slightly higher mean returns (0.21 percent for the corporate bond fund and 0.43 percent for the municipal bond fund) and considerably higher standard deviations (3.14 percent for the corporate bond fund and 2.53 percent for the municipal bond fund) than the actual bond funds. The correlation coefficients between the returns of the actual and synthetic funds were 0.94 for the corporate bond fund and .99 for the municipal bond fund.

11. Ibbotson Associates (2000).

12. The average return on the synthetic index fund was slightly higher (by 0.10 percent per year) than that on the actual index fund, and the standard deviation of the synthetic index fund return was 0.05 percent higher than that of the actual index fund return. The correlation between the returns on the actual and synthetic index funds was 0.9997.

13. Dickson and Shoven (1995).

Figure 10-1. *Marginal Tax Rate*[a]

Tax rate

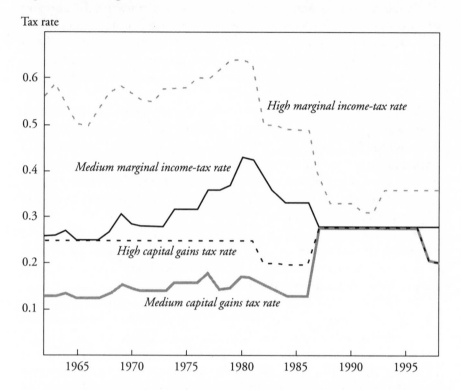

Source: Median AGI was taken from the Statistics of Income of the Internal Revenue Service. The values between 1962 and 1992 were taken from Dickson and Shoven (1995). The tax rates were updated using the instructions to Form 1040 of the IRS (www.irs.gov/forms_pubs/index.html).

a. The time series of the marginal income and long-term capital gains tax rates are depicted for high- and medium-income individuals. Taxable income for a medium-income individual (high-income individual) is computed as three (ten) times the median adjusted gross income (AGI), subtracting the standard deduction for married couples and three exemptions.

tax forms for the years 1993 to 1998. We assume that our medium-tax investor has an income roughly three times the median AGI because stock and bond investors, particularly those with the asset location problem we describe, have much higher incomes than the average household does. We use data on the short- and long-term capital gain distributions of the equity mutual funds in our sample as well as on their dividend distributions to compute after-tax returns. We also consider medium-term capital gain distributions for the applicable years, 1997 and 1998. Figure 10-1 shows the evolution of marginal tax rates for our high-tax and medium-tax investors between 1962 and 1998.

Table 10-2 presents summary statistics on returns for the twelve actively managed equity mutual funds in our sample. They had an average nominal

Table 10-2. *Summary Statistics of Mutual Funds, 1962–98*[a]

Funds	Average return	Standard deviation	Dividend distribution	ST-CG distribution	LT-CG distribution	Total ST proportion distribution	Total proportion distribution
A. Actively managed equity funds							
1. Mass. Investors Trust	0.119	0.152	0.034	0.001	0.069	0.292	0.867
2. IDS Stock	0.107	0.149	0.034	0.003	0.052	0.345	0.833
3. LA Affiliated	0.127	0.141	0.045	0.001	0.059	0.362	0.824
4. Fund Investors	0.119	0.156	0.032	0.002	0.044	0.283	0.650
5. United Accumulative	0.110	0.150	0.031	0.017	0.049	0.437	0.885
6. Mass. Investors Growth	0.125	0.195	0.015	0.007	0.072	0.175	0.754
7. Fidelity Fund	0.135	0.152	0.038	0.020	0.043	0.431	0.749
8. Dreyfus	0.113	0.142	0.031	0.014	0.048	0.395	0.823
9. Investment Co. of America	0.140	0.147	0.034	0.000	0.048	0.247	0.586
10. Fidelity Trend	0.117	0.197	0.016	0.007	0.038	0.202	0.523
11. VK Enterprise	0.169	0.288	0.016	0.010	0.048	0.156	0.438
12. Vanguard Windsor	0.139	0.177	0.039	0.007	0.062	0.329	0.779
All equity funds							
Mean	0.127	0.171	0.031	0.007	0.053	0.304	0.726
Standard deviation	0.017	0.042	0.010	0.007	0.011	0.096	0.144
Top five funds							
Mean	0.117	0.150	0.035	0.005	0.055	0.344	0.812
Standard deviation	0.008	0.006	0.006	0.007	0.010	0.062	0.094
B. Spliced funds							
S&P index fund	0.128	0.159	0.036	0.001	0.013	0.288	0.392
Corporate bonds	0.074	0.083	0.081	0.001	0.003	1.095	1.140
Municipal bonds	0.059	0.112	0.061	0.001	0.006	1.054	1.154
C. Consumer price inflation							
CPI	0.047	0.032					

a. This table reports the annual mean nominal returns, the standard deviations of the annual returns, and the distribution characteristics of the funds. Dividend, ST-CG, and LT-CG distributions are the returns distributed to shareholders as dividends, short-term capital gains, and long-term capital gains. The last two columns show the total proportions of the average returns distributed to shareholders as short-term distributions and as short- plus long-term distributions. It is not possible to get long-run data on the S&P 500 index fund, taxable corporate bond funds, and tax-exempt municipal bond funds. Actual data are available for the Vanguard 500 index fund after 1977 and for the Vanguard long-term corporate bond fund and the Vanguard long-term municipal bond fund after 1978. The synthetic funds use market data to replicate the payoffs of those funds before 1977 and 1978 and the data from the actual funds afterward.

return of 12.7 percent over the 1962–98 period and an average standard deviation of the annual returns of 17.1 percent. Ibbotson Associates reports that the rate of consumer price inflation had a mean of 4.7 percent and a standard deviation of 3.2 percent for the same period.[14]

The mean nominal returns and the standard deviations of the funds differ considerably. The Van Kampen Enterprise Fund had the highest average nominal return (16.9 percent) and the highest standard deviation (28.8 percent). The IDS Stock Fund had the lowest average return (10.7 percent), and the Affiliated Fund had the lowest standard deviation (14.1 percent). The top five funds had a considerably lower mean return than the remaining seven funds (11.7 percent versus 13.4 percent), possibly because of survivorship bias.

Table 10-2 gives particular attention to the division among dividends, realized capital gains, and unrealized capital gains in the composition of returns received by investors. On average the twelve funds distributed 72.6 percent of their total return annually, either as dividends or capital gains, and 30.4 percent of the total average returns were either dividends or short-term capital gains.[15] Capital gains that were not distributed were deferred until the investor sold the mutual fund shares. The most successful fund, Van Kampen Enterprise Fund, distributed only 43.8 percent of its total returns, whereas the relatively poorly performing United Accumulative Fund distributed 88.5 percent of its total return. The top five funds tended to impose somewhat higher tax burdens on their investors than the other funds since they distributed a larger portion of their total returns and since a larger portion of their distributions did not qualify as long-term capital gains.

The passively managed spliced index fund had an average nominal return of 12.8 percent and a standard deviation of 15.9 percent. The average return on the index fund was similar to that for our whole sample of equity funds, and it was considerably higher than the average return on the bias-free top five funds. The passively managed index fund exhibited a smaller difference between pretax and posttax returns than did the actively managed equity funds. On average only 39.2 percent of its total nominal return was distributed to shareholders, and only a small portion of those distributions resulted from the distribution of realized capital gains.

The spliced corporate bond fund had a mean nominal return of 7.4 percent and a standard deviation of 8.3 percent, while the spliced tax-exempt municipal bond fund had a lower mean nominal return (5.9 percent) and a higher standard deviation (11.2 percent). Both bond funds distributed most of their total returns as interest income.

14. Ibbotson Associates (2000).
15. The data sources did not always distinguish between short- and long-term capital gains. We assumed that capital gains were long term if the sources did not indicate the term. That resulted in an overstatement of the actual tax efficiency of the mutual funds.

Asset Location and Investor Returns: Historical Evidence

Our data make it possible for us to compute asset location results for the period 1962–98 for the twelve actively managed equity mutual funds as well as the three spliced funds. The investor is assumed to have made identical contributions (in constant dollars) each year to a tax-deferred pension account and to a conventional taxable savings account. We normalize the total annual contributions to $1.00 in 1998 purchasing power. The actual 1998 contributions were 50 cents to each account, whereas the earlier contributions were less in nominal dollars. The total real investment over the 37-year period was $37 at 1998 prices.

We assume that half of each annual investment was placed in the TDA and half in the CSA and that the investor wants half of his or her total portfolio in stocks and half in bonds.[16] We assume that half of the initial 1962 investments were made in stocks and half in bonds; thereafter, the investor adjusted the portfolio annually to maintain the fifty-fifty balance. Rebalancing is attempted first by adjusting the composition of new investments, and if necessary, assets were sold and bought in order to maintain the desired proportions of stocks and bonds. At the end of the year, the investor is taxed on the taxable mutual fund distributions and the realized capital gains from selling fund shares in the taxable account. Realized losses are carried forward and subtracted from future capital gains. At the end of the sample period, the investor liquidated all assets and pays the necessary capital gains taxes as well as ordinary income taxes on withdrawals from the TDA. The dollar figures shown in our tables thus represent retirement accumulations after the payment of all taxes.

We evaluate two possible asset location rules. The first, Defer Stocks First, gives the equity mutual fund priority for placement in the TDA; the corporate bond fund is held in the TDA only if there were room after all of the investor's desired equity is in the TDA. Municipal bonds have a preferred location in the CSA. The second rule, Defer Bonds First, gives the corporate bond fund priority for placement in the TDA, and the equity mutual fund priority for placement in the CSA. If it were necessary to hold bonds in the CSA to maintain the desired fifty-fifty asset allocation, then the investor would hold the municipal bond fund there.

16. When we computed the stock proportions we did not adjust the value of assets held in the two different accounts to reflect deferred taxes. That raises at least two issues. First, the investor owns only $(1-t)$ of the assets invested in the tax-deferred account, because the government taxes withdrawals from a tax-deferred account at the rate t. Second, the realized returns of assets in the CSA are taxed annually, and that reduces their accumulation. Whether one dollar invested in a TDA is more valuable than one dollar invested in a CSA depends on the investment horizon. One dollar invested in a CSA is more valuable at a sufficiently short investment horizon, and one dollar invested in a TDA is more valuable at a sufficiently long horizon.

Table 10-3. *Asset Location Results*[a]

	High-tax individual			Medium-tax individual		
Type of fund	Wealth at retirement (Defer Stocks First)	Wealth at retirement (Defer Bonds First)	Relative wealth	Wealth at retirement (Defer Stocks First)	Wealth at retirement (Defer Bonds First)	Relative wealth
A. Actively managed mutual funds						
1. Mass. Investors Trust	90.49	84.59	1.070	98.21	93.30	1.053
2. IDS Stock	79.91	74.94	1.066	86.30	83.15	1.038
3. LA Affiliated	91.75	81.20	1.130	99.61	91.93	1.084
4. Fund Investors	89.02	88.26	1.009	96.57	96.84	0.997
5. United Accumulative	81.11	73.07	1.110	87.68	82.91	1.058
6. Mass. Investors Growth	92.70	89.60	1.035	100.72	98.02	1.028
7. Fidelity Fund	100.68	88.31	1.140	109.66	100.86	1.087
8. Dreyfus	74.18	64.56	1.149	79.83	73.73	1.083
9. Investment Co. of America	101.03	96.08	1.052	110.05	106.39	1.034
10. Fidelity Trend	71.21	69.40	1.026	76.49	76.05	1.006
11. VK Enterprise	109.23	98.85	1.105	119.31	108.86	1.096
12. Vanguard Windsor	102.20	87.21	1.172	111.37	100.15	1.112
All funds						
Mean	90.29	83.01	1.089	97.98	92.68	1.056
Standard deviation	11.87	10.59	0.053	13.36	11.45	0.037
Top five funds						
Mean	86.46	80.41	1.077	93.67	89.62	1.046
Standard deviation	5.53	6.39	0.047	6.22	6.28	0.032
B. Index fund						
S&P 500	96.28	97.91	0.983	104.72	106.91	0.980

a. The real wealth levels at retirement are reported for an individual making annual real contributions of $0.50 to both a tax-deferred account (TDA) and a conventional taxable savings account (CSA) during a period of 37 years, from 1962 to 1998. The investor annually adjusts the portfolio to maintain a 50 percent proportion of stock funds; the remaining 50 percent is allocated to either taxable corporate bonds or tax-exempt municipal bonds. The Defer Stocks First strategy gives preference to stocks in the TDA and to municipal bonds in the CSA, and the Defer Bonds First strategy gives preference to corporate bonds in the TDA and to stocks in the CSA.

Table 10-3 shows our basic asset location results. Defer Stocks First yielded higher terminal wealth values than Defer Bonds First for all twelve of the actively managed equity mutual funds for the high-income, high-tax investor and for eleven of the twelve funds for the medium-income, medium-tax investor. The additional wealth accumulated by following the Defer Stocks First rule could be quite large. For the twelve actively managed funds as a whole the average gain from deferring stocks first was 8.9 percent for high-tax retirement accumulators. For the five largest funds in 1961, the gain averaged 7.7 percent. For an investor who contributed $10,000 (1998 dollars) per year to both the CSA and the TDA in each year between 1962 and 1998, the 7.7 percent differential translated to additional wealth of more than $140,000 in 1998.[17]

The equity mutual fund that gained the most from deferring stocks first was the Vanguard Windsor fund. Its before-tax performance was better than average over the 1962–98 period, while it imposed a higher-than-average tax burden on its investors. With Vanguard Windsor, the Defer Stocks First rule resulted in more than 17 percent more retirement wealth than Defer Bonds First. The actively managed fund for which the advantage of deferring stocks first was the smallest was the Fundamental Investors Fund. Its before-tax performance was worse than average, and its investor tax burden was better than average. For high-income investors using Fundamental Investors in a fifty-fifty stock-bond asset allocation plan, Defer Stocks First conferred an advantage of less than 1 percent. For the medium-income investor using Fundamental Investors, Defer Bonds First worked better than Defer Stocks First, although the difference was extremely small. For the eleven other funds, Defer Stocks First yielded between 1 and 17 percent more after-tax wealth than Defer Bonds First.

Interestingly, considering the S&P 500 index fund, the Defer Bonds First rule yielded the highest terminal wealth. The S&P index fund had slightly better before-tax returns than the average actively managed fund, almost all due to its low expenses, and it imposed much lower tax burdens on its investors. In that case the advantage of deferring bonds instead of stocks was considerable. A high-tax investor holding shares in an S&P 500 fund in a TDA and municipal bonds in a CSA would have ended up with 1.7 percent less retirement wealth than a similar investor who put corporate bonds in a TDA and held the index fund in a CSA. That result is important, because it suggests that the rise of relatively tax-efficient mutual funds in the 1990s may affect the applicability of our findings to investors who hold equities through those funds.

One reason that the Defer Stocks First rule yielded greater end-of-period wealth than Defer Bonds First for most actively managed equity funds during our sample period was that equities have experienced higher rates of return than bonds and thus would have generated higher tax bills in a taxable environment. That is related to the well-documented equity premium puzzle described by Mehra and Prescott.[18] One could ask whether Defer Stocks First still would

---

17. While we modeled people who chose a particular equity mutual fund and stuck with it, many investors periodically switch funds. Switching generates taxable capital gains in a CSA, raising the wealth accumulated from applying the Defer Stocks First rule relative to that accumulated from applying Defer Bonds First.

18. Mehra and Prescott (1985).

Table 10-4. *Sensitivity Analysis with Lower Equity Premiums*[a]

Type of fund	Reduction in equity premium (in basis points)					
	0	100	200	300	400	500
A. Actively managed mutual funds						
1. Mass. Investors Trust	1.070	1.048	1.031	1.018	1.008	1.000
2. IDS Stock	1.066	1.048	1.034	1.025	1.017	1.010
3. LA Affiliated	1.130	1.102	1.078	1.059	1.043	1.030
4. Fund Investors	1.009	0.994	0.984	0.978	0.975	0.974
5. United Accumulative	1.110	1.089	1.074	1.063	1.055	1.050
6. Mass. Investors Growth	1.035	1.017	1.004	0.994	0.989	0.984
7. Fidelity Fund	1.140	1.113	1.091	1.072	1.056	1.045
8. Dreyfus	1.149	1.127	1.108	1.093	1.081	1.072
9. Investment Co. of America	1.052	1.033	1.017	1.002	0.992	0.985
10. Fidelity Trend	1.026	1.019	1.014	1.013	1.016	1.020
11. VK Enterprise	1.105	1.091	1.076	1.065	1.055	1.045
12. Vanguard Windsor	1.172	1.147	1.125	1.106	1.089	1.074
All funds						
Mean	1.089	1.069	1.053	1.041	1.031	1.024
Standard deviation	0.053	0.049	0.045	0.041	0.037	0.034
Top five funds						
Mean	1.077	1.056	1.040	1.029	1.020	1.013
Standard deviation	0.047	0.043	0.038	0.034	0.031	0.029
B. Index fund						
S&P 500	0.983	0.966	0.952	0.946	0.945	0.946

a. This table reports the relative wealth levels of the two location strategies for a high-tax individual if the return of the equity funds is decreased. The distributions of the equity funds are adjusted proportionally. The first column corresponds exactly to the third column in table 10-3.

generate higher end-of-period wealth if the average return advantage of equities were lower. Table 10-4 answers that question for our high-tax, high-income investor. Each successive column presents results based on a 100-basis-point reduction in realized fund returns compared with those in the previous column. All fund distributions (dividends and capital gains) are reduced proportionally. Each additional 100-basis-point reduction lowers the average advantage of first deferring stocks, but by decreasing amounts. Even an unrealistically high reduction of 500 basis points (that is, one that eliminates the premium of equity funds over corporate bonds) would leave Defer Stocks First generating higher end-of-period wealth than Defer Bonds First for nine of the twelve actively managed funds. The results in table 10-4 suggest that the difference in wealth accumulated by applying the two location rules would be attenuated if the average return on stocks were lower than that in the 37-year period that we studied.

Table 10-5. *Asset Location without Municipal Bonds*[a]

	High-tax individual			Medium-tax individual		
Type of fund	Wealth at retirement (Defer Stocks First)	Wealth at retirement (Defer Bonds First)	Relative wealth	Wealth at retirement (Defer Stocks First)	Wealth at retirement (Defer Bonds First)	Relative wealth
A. Actively managed mutual funds						
1. Mass. Investors Trust	79.04	84.54	0.935	92.64	93.49	0.991
2. IDS Stock	69.72	74.89	0.931	81.46	83.25	0.979
3. LA Affiliated	80.99	81.21	0.997	94.85	91.75	1.034
4. Fund Investors	78.14	88.17	0.886	91.62	96.68	0.948
5. United Accumulative	70.99	73.07	0.972	83.06	82.87	1.002
6. Mass. Investors Growth	80.87	89.54	0.903	94.80	98.20	0.965
7. Fidelity Fund	88.88	88.26	1.007	104.28	100.88	1.034
8. Dreyfus	64.85	64.47	1.006	75.53	73.71	1.025
9. Investment Co. of America	89.62	94.68	0.947	105.07	105.58	0.995
10. Fidelity Trend	62.05	69.25	0.896	72.15	76.21	0.947
11. VK Enterprise	96.18	96.40	0.998	112.55	108.01	1.042
12. Vanguard Windsor	91.29	85.37	1.069	107.05	98.63	1.085
All funds						
Mean	79.38	82.49	0.962	92.92	92.44	1.004
Standard deviation	10.88	10.08	0.055	12.91	11.15	0.042
Top five funds						
Mean	75.77	80.37	0.944	88.73	89.61	0.991
Standard deviation	5.08	6.37	0.042	6.04	6.23	0.032
B. Index fund						
S&P 500	84.48	97.77	0.864	99.15	106.95	0.927

a. The results in this table differ from those of table 10-3 in that individuals were not allowed to invest in municipal bonds. Corporate bonds were held in both the TDA and the CSA.

The results in table 10-4 derive from both the fact that capital gain distributions on actively managed equity funds raise their effective tax burden and the fact that the implicit tax rate on tax-exempt bonds was below the statutory marginal tax rate throughout our sample. Table 10-5 helps to indicate the relative importance of these two factors. It presents results in which investors did not take advantage of their option to hold municipal bonds; instead, they invested in a single equity mutual fund and a corporate bond fund. The only location decision to be made was whether to give the equity fund preference in the TDA and the corporate bond preference in the CSA, or vice versa. Without the use of municipal bonds, the Defer Stocks First rule generated higher end-of-period wealth for only three of the twelve actively managed mutual funds for the high-income investor. For the other equity mutual funds, Defer Bonds First produced more retirement wealth, often quite a bit more. The average gain of deferring bonds first for the twelve actively managed funds was 3.8 percent. Defer Stocks First yielded higher relative wealth values for the medium-income, medium-tax investor for six of the twelve actively managed equity funds. In fact, even without allowing municipal bonds, average retirement wealth from applying the Defer Stocks First rule was slightly greater than that from applying Defer Bonds First for the medium-tax investor.

Our interpretation of tables 10-3 and 10-5 is that the average actively managed mutual fund produced an effective tax rate for its high-income taxable holders that was higher than the implicit tax rate on municipal bonds. Hence most of the actively managed funds would have gained more from being in a TDA than would corporate bonds, given the availability of tax-exempt bonds for investments in a CSA. The only equity mutual fund that would have generated an effective tax rate significantly lower than the implicit tax rate on municipal bonds was the passively managed index fund. The presence of municipal bonds was less important for the medium-income investors, because the effective tax rate on the equity funds was lower (due to lower tax rates on ordinary income and capital gains), but the implicit tax rate on municipal bonds was the same. Tables 10-3 and 10-5 underscore the fact that the conventional wisdom, which holds that it is best to give preference to corporate bonds for placement in a TDA, is based on analysis that does not consider the availability of municipal bonds.

One caution should be noted in comparing taxable and tax-exempt bond yields and calculating implicit tax rates from those yields. Investors in taxable and tax-exempt bonds may face somewhat different risks, and the differential between the yields on those bonds may reflect both tax considerations and the pricing of those risks. One particularly important risk, noted in Poterba (1989), is that of tax reform. Tax-exempt bonds could experience substantial valuation changes if the current income-tax treatment of taxable and tax-exempt bonds changes. Quantifying the price that investors demand for bearing that risk and modifying the implicit tax rate accordingly is very difficult.

The results in tables 10-3 and 10-5 assume that the then-current tax laws applied to returns generated in each year during our sample period. Since marginal tax rates on dividend and interest income are lower now than at some points in our sample, that assumption may limit the prospective applicability of our findings. To address that concern, in table 10-6 we present findings in which we apply the 1998 tax law to the 1962–98 returns generated by the CSA assets. Table 10-6 shows that the after-tax wealth realized from applying the Defer Bonds First rule would have been much higher compared with that from Defer Stocks First, if the 1998 tax law had been in force throughout the

Table 10-6. *Asset Location Results with Taxes from 1998*[a]

Type of fund	High-tax individual			Medium-tax individual		
	Wealth at retirement (Defer Stocks First)	Wealth at retirement (Defer Bonds First)	Relative wealth	Wealth at retirement (Defer Stocks First)	Wealth at retirement (Defer Bonds First)	Relative wealth
A. Actively managed mutual funds						
1. Mass. Investors Trust	90.78	90.24	1.006	98.45	96.25	1.023
2. IDS Stock	80.18	79.20	1.012	86.52	85.29	1.014
3. LA Affiliated	92.01	87.60	1.050	99.84	94.61	1.055
4. Fund Investors	89.32	93.18	0.959	96.80	99.33	0.975
5. United Accumulative	81.41	76.66	1.062	87.89	84.24	1.043
6. Mass. Investors Growth	93.02	94.49	0.984	100.97	100.02	1.009
7. Fidelity Fund	100.96	93.81	1.076	109.91	102.68	1.070
8. Dreyfus	74.41	68.74	1.083	80.03	75.48	1.060
9. Investment Co. of America	101.29	101.63	0.997	110.28	108.23	1.019
10. Fidelity Trend	71.45	72.40	0.987	76.68	77.69	0.987
11. VK Enterprise	109.52	104.93	1.044	119.53	111.31	1.074
12. Vanguard Windsor	102.46	94.73	1.082	111.58	102.82	1.085
All funds						
Mean	90.57	88.13	1.028	98.21	94.83	1.035
Standard deviation	11.88	11.46	0.043	13.37	11.67	0.036
Top five funds						
Mean	86.74	85.37	1.018	93.90	91.94	1.022
Standard deviation	5.53	7.13	0.041	6.22	6.78	0.031
B. Index fund						
S&P 500	96.57	101.86	0.948	104.97	108.43	0.968

a. The results in this table differ from those in table 10-3 in that tax rates from 1998 were used instead of the historical taxes from 1962 to 1998.

1962–98 period, particularly for high-income investors. Nonetheless, Defer Stocks First still would have yielded higher end-of-period wealth for eight of the twelve actively managed mutual funds. The counterfactual tax assumption of table 10-6 affects the results less for the medium-income investor, with Defer Stocks First still generating more retirement wealth for ten of the twelve actively managed mutual funds.

Table 10-6 does not describe what actually would have happened if the 1998 tax code had prevailed over the entire 37-year period. We did not adjust the implicit tax rate on municipal bonds even though it presumably would have dropped in the presence of lower marginal tax rates on high-income households. Similarly, we did not adjust the before-tax rates of return of any of the assets, even though a significant tax change presumably would have substantial general equilibrium effects. It also is possible that with different tax rates, the proportions of dividends and capital gains in equity returns would have differed from historical values.

Asset Location and Investor Returns: Simulation Evidence

The foregoing asset location results show the performance of different strategies using historical data over the period 1962–98, a period that in many respects was unrepresentative: equity returns were relatively high; the rate of inflation was high and very volatile; and marginal tax rates changed considerably. To determine whether our results are robust, we ran some bootstrap simulations. Each simulation proceeded in two steps: first we selected one mutual fund from our sample at random, and then we drew a random sequence of years with replacement. For each year selected, we drew the selected fund's return, the returns of two bond funds, the inflation rate, and the tax rate. We computed the level of wealth of investors making constant real annual contributions to a CSA and TDA for 37 years, as described above. All the simulations were repeated 10,000 times.

Our bootstrap returns address only the issue of the sequencing of returns during the 1962–98 period. They do not address what is likely to be a more important source of uncertainty, namely the possibility that future returns will be generated from a different return distribution than the one observed over the last four decades.

Figure 10-2 shows the probability distributions of real wealth levels at retirement of the two asset location strategies for a high-tax individual choosing from the set of the five largest mutual funds in December 1961. The Defer Stocks First rule outperforms Defer Bonds First at all probability levels except in the four lowest of the 10,000 simulations. That means that the probability of reaching a particular wealth level or higher was almost always greater with Defer Stocks First than with Defer Bonds First.

Table 10-7 shows numerical values corresponding to several points in the probability distribution shown in figure 10-2. The real wealth level of Defer Stocks First exceeded that of Defer Bonds First by 3.7 percent at the 1st percentile, by 6.1 percent at the median, and by 16.4 percent at the 99th percentile. The portfolio selection of this investor is quite risky. There is a more than 20 percent probability that the real wealth level accumulated at retirement will not exceed the 37 real dollars invested and there is a more than 20 percent probability that retirement wealth under Defer Stocks First will exceed twice the total real investments (74 real dollars).

Figure 10-2. *Wealth Distribution of the Two Asset Location Strategies with Bootstrap Simulations, Top Five Funds*[a]

Cumulative distribution

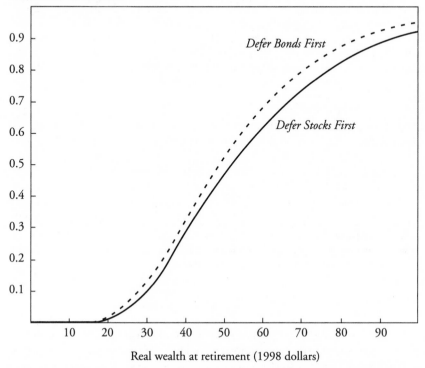

Real wealth at retirement (1998 dollars)

a. The cumulative distribution of real wealth at retirement resulting from saving $1.00 per year for thirty-seven years is depicted for the two asset location strategies. The investor chooses randomly among the five largest mutual funds in each of the 10,000 bootstrap simulations.

The median wealth level at retirement achieved by applying the Defer Stocks First rule was $51.81, considerably lower than the $86.46 from table 10-3 that was computed using the actual history instead of simulated returns. A realization of $86.46 would be an outcome at the 87th percentile in our bootstrap simulations. The main reason for that discrepancy is the ordering of the returns between 1962 and 1998. The ordering of the identical returns had a substantial effect on the wealth level at retirement for investors making contributions over many years to their savings account. The arithmetic average of the real returns of the S&P 500 index fund was 2.2 percent during 1962–79 and 13.9 percent during 1980–98. The computations that used actual historical returns had the low returns in the first half of our investment horizon (when the accumulated

Table 10-7. *Wealth Distribution with Bootstrap Simulations*[a]

	Cumulative distribution						
Type of fund	*0.001*	*0.010*	*0.100*	*0.500*	*0.900*	*0.990*	*0.999*
A. All actively managed funds							
Wealth (Defer Stocks First)	14.80	20.31	31.16	55.87	107.53	195.71	343.71
Wealth (Defer Bonds First)	13.81	19.65	30.13	53.65	101.00	186.57	312.93
Relative wealth	0.686	0.780	0.885	1.050	1.228	1.397	1.577
B. Top five actively managed funds							
Wealth (Defer Stocks First)	14.55	19.46	29.94	51.81	93.73	155.08	211.14
Wealth (Defer Bonds First)	13.81	18.76	28.55	48.82	84.98	133.24	188.42
Relative wealth	0.762	0.820	0.920	1.069	1.24	1.411	1.579
C. Index fund							
Wealth (Defer Stocks First)	14.98	20.24	32.01	57.18	106.92	182.06	264.07
Wealth (Defer Bonds First)	14.82	19.95	32.44	58.05	105.26	173.70	259.52
Relative wealth	0.706	0.762	0.854	0.995	1.152	1.298	1.460

a. The probability distributions of the real wealth levels of a high-income individual are shown for the two location strategies. Individuals randomly chose one equity fund and contributed as described in table 10-3. The returns of the assets were bootstrapped 10,000 times.

contributions were relatively small) and the high returns in the second half (when the accumulated contributions were large). Those back-loaded returns generated higher wealth levels at retirement compared with the distribution of returns that occurred in the bootstrap simulations.[19]

If we let history run backward (that is, the 1998 returns occur first, the 1997 returns second, and the 1962 returns last), then we accumulate a real wealth level of $32.70 under the Defer Stocks First rule, which corresponds to the 15th percentile of the bootstrap distribution. That is because the low returns occur when the investor has a large accumulated asset balance.

Table 10-7 also summarizes the distribution for investors who randomly chose funds from the whole set of twelve actively managed equity funds and who chose the spliced index fund. Defer Stocks First outperformed Defer Bonds First at all indicated points of the cumulative distribution for the actively man-

19. The ordering of the returns r_t was irrelevant if investors made only a single contribution to an account. In that case the final wealth level was simply the product of the return relatives $W_T = \prod_{i=0}^{T}(1 + r_i)$. Ordering had a significant effect on accumulated wealth levels for investors making multiple contributions to an account. We can think of the portfolio with multiple contributions as the sum of a sequence of single-contribution portfolios with decreasing maturities $\sum_{t=0}^{T}[W_t] = \sum_{t=0}^{T}[\prod_{i=t}^{T}(1 + r_i)]$. The returns during the last years affected most of the single-contribution portfolios, whereas the returns during the first years affected only a few of them.

Figure 10-3. *Wealth Distribution with Bootstrap Simulations, Index Fund*[a]

Cumulative distribution

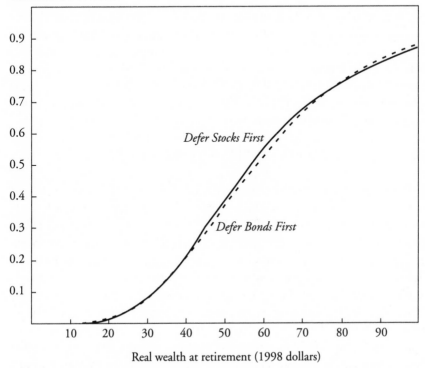

Real wealth at retirement (1998 dollars)

a. The cumulative distribution of real wealth at retirement resulting from saving $1.00 per year for thirty-seven years is depicted for the two asset location strategies. The investor holds a spliced Standard & Poor's 500 index fund.

aged equity funds. The probability distribution function for the whole sample of twelve funds usually lies to the right of the one for the top five funds, because the five largest funds did not perform as well as the seven other funds. Figure 10-3 shows that the distributions of the two location strategies are quite close if an investor held a passively managed index fund, underscoring our earlier point that asset location is less important in that case than in the case of actively managed funds.

To facilitate comparison of the different cases, we summarize the whole probability distribution of the 10,000 simulations by computing the certainty equivalent wealth level of an individual with a constant relative risk aversion (CRRA) utility function. The expected utility of real wealth $EU = E[U(W)]$ of the investor is defined as

$$\text{(7)} \qquad EU = E[U(W)] = \frac{1}{n} \sum_i \frac{W_i^{1-\alpha}}{1-\alpha}.$$

Simulations are indexed by i, the real wealth level is W_i, and we denote the risk aversion coefficient by α and the total number of bootstrap simulations by n. The certainty equivalent wealth level is the certain wealth level for which an individual is indifferent between that wealth and the distribution of wealth outcomes from the random 10,000 simulations. We assume that income from assets accumulated in the CSA and the TDA is the only source of income during retirement. The certainty equivalent is given by

$$\text{(8)} \qquad CE(EU) = U^{-1}(EU) = [(1-\alpha)EU]^{1/(1-\alpha)}.$$

Table 10-8 summarizes the certainty equivalents for five levels of risk aversion. The values with a risk aversion of $\alpha = 0$ equal the expected wealth levels. Most economists think that coefficients of relative risk aversion between 1 (log-utility) and 5 are plausible. The average real wealth level at retirement for investments in the five largest mutual funds applying the Defer Stocks First rule equaled $58.09; investing in all twelve mutual funds and in the index fund resulted in considerably higher average wealth levels. All the certainty equivalents for the actively managed equity funds were larger if stocks instead of bonds were deferred first. Defer Stocks First resulted in a 5.2 percent higher certainty equivalent for an individual with a risk aversion of 3 investing in the top five funds; however, Defer Bonds First yielded higher certainty equivalents for intermediate levels of risk aversion if investors held the index fund, which has a higher certainty equivalent than the actively managed funds. Those results confirm the deterministic results above.

Figure 10-4 shows the relationship between the real wealth levels of the two location strategies using exactly the same simulation results as in figure 10-2. The 45-degree line represents the cases in which the wealth levels were identical for the two location strategies. There are 7,116 points (of 10,000) below the 45-degree line and 2,884 points above. Thus, Defer Stocks First outperformed Defer Bonds First 71.2 percent of the time. The distribution of the relative wealth levels of the two strategies is summarized in the third row of table 10-7. Defer Stocks First outperformed Defer Bonds First in 64.0 percent of the simulations if investors chose among all twelve funds and in 48.5 percent of the cases with the index fund.

The previous results analyze the optimal asset location choice for an asset allocation of 50 percent stocks and 50 percent bonds, a rule-of-thumb allocation that is not necessarily optimal. Moreover, the optimal stock proportion for an investor might depend on his or her location strategy, since the two strategies

Table 10-8. *Certainty Equivalents of Bootstrap Results*[a]

Type of fund	Coefficient of relative risk aversion				
	0	*1*	*3*	*5*	*10*
A. All actively managed funds					
CE (Defer Stocks First)	64.86	57.20	45.96	38.02	26.11
CE (Defer Bonds First)	61.64	54.67	44.23	36.67	25.46
Relative CE	1.052	1.046	1.039	1.037	1.026
B. Top five actively managed funds					
CE (Defer Stocks First)	58.09	52.46	43.30	36.31	24.90
CE (Defer Bonds First)	53.78	49.11	41.16	34.82	24.73
Relative CE	1.08	1.068	1.052	1.043	1.007
C. Index fund					
CE (Defer Stocks First)	64.89	57.93	46.80	38.57	26.63
CE (Defer Bonds First)	64.86	58.27	47.23	38.66	26.44
Relative CE	1.001	0.994	0.991	0.998	1.007

a. This table records the certainty equivalents (CE) of the bootstrap simulations of the two location strategies for a high-tax individual with a constant relative risk aversion (CRRA) utility function. The wealth resulting from the investment in the two accounts is the only source of income at retirement. The returns were bootstrapped 10,000 times.

have different effective stock exposures. To provide some illustrative calculations of the expected utilities associated with different stock-bond allocations, we performed bootstrap simulations for eleven different stock proportions (0.0, 0.1, . . . , 1.0) and computed the corresponding certainty equivalents of the two location choices. Figure 10-5 plots the results for high-tax individuals with risk aversions of 3 and 5 who invested in the five largest actively managed mutual funds. Note that asset location is irrelevant in the cases in which the investor holds either only bonds or only stocks, since the same assets are held in both locations.

We found that the certainty equivalent of the Defer Stocks First rule usually was higher than that of Defer Bonds First. At a risk aversion of 3, the certainty equivalent was maximized at a stock proportion of between 80 and 100 percent with Defer Stocks First and of 100 percent with Defer Bonds First. At stock proportions that high, the effect of optimal asset location is smaller than when the stock proportion is 50 percent.

Asset location was more important if investors had a risk aversion of 5 than if they were more risk tolerant. Asset location increased the certainty equivalent by 4.9 percent (the maximal certainty equivalent wealth level was 37.21 with Defer Stocks First and 35.46 with Defer Bonds First). A 100 percent stock portfolio

Figure 10-4. *Relationship between the Wealth Levels of the
Two Location Strategies, Top Five Funds*[a]

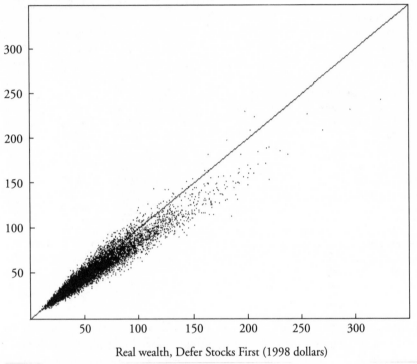

Real wealth, Defer Bonds First (1998 dollars)

Real wealth, Defer Stocks First (1998 dollars)

a. The relationship between real wealth levels at retirement between the two asset location
strategies is depicted. The investor chooses randomly among the five largest mutual funds in each
of the 10,000 bootstrap simulations. The simulation results are identical to those in figure 10-2.

had a higher certainty equivalent than a 100 percent bond portfolio for both
levels of risk aversion.

Asset Location with Inflation-Protected Bonds

The corporate and municipal bond funds in the previous asset allocation and
asset location analysis are exposed to at least three risks that can be reduced with
recently introduced government securities. These risks are the default risk of
individual issues; inflation risk; and reinvestment risk. Reinvestment risk results
from the fact that the bond or bond fund investor cannot be sure of the terms
on which future interest payments can be reinvested. Inflation risk results from

Figure 10-5. *Certainty Equivalents of Different Asset Allocations*[a]

Certainty equivalent (1998 dollars)

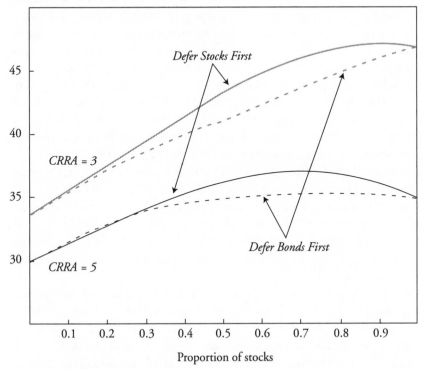

Proportion of stocks

a. The certainty equivalent wealth levels are computed for different asset allocations (stock proportions range between 0 and 100 percent) and different asset locations (either the stocks or the taxable bonds are deferred first). The certainty equivalents are shown for coefficients of relative risk aversion (CRRA) of 3 and 5.

the fact that corporate and municipal bonds are nominal contracts. While investing in high-grade securities can control default risk, corporate and municipal borrowers usually are considered riskier than the U.S. government.

Since 1997, the U.S. government has issued inflation-indexed bonds, which essentially eliminate all of the risks just described. There are two forms of inflation-indexed bonds. The first are Treasury inflation-protected securities (TIPS), which are U.S. government bonds with fixed maturities (so far, five-, ten-, and thirty-year bonds have been issued), real interest payments, and a principal amount adjusted to reflect inflation in the consumer price index (CPI). Both the interest payment and the adjustment in the principal amount are fully taxable if TIPS are held in a conventional savings account, but those considerations are not relevant in a TDA. TIPS essentially eliminate the default and inflation risks of corporate and municipal bonds, but they still are subject to reinvestment risk. Investors also may bear some risk associated with potential redefinition of the consumer price index. The real return on TIPS in 2000 is near 4 percent.

The other U.S. government inflation-indexed security is the Series I savings bond, which is issued in denominations of from $50 to $10,000. Like all savings bonds, I bonds are zero coupon instruments with taxation deferred until redemption, and, as with all federal notes, bills, and bonds, the interest on I bonds is exempt from state and local income tax. I bonds are nontransferable and nonmarketable, but they are redeemable at par at any time; three months' interest is forfeited if the bonds are redeemed in less than five years. Interest is compounded monthly and accrues for up to 30 years. Investors are limited to purchasing $30,000 of Series I savings bonds per year. Series I bonds have one other unusual feature, which they share with Series EE savings bonds: the interest realized on redemption can be exempted from taxation if it is used for college tuition expenses. That tax-free redemption feature is available to households with an adjusted gross income of less than roughly $80,000; above that amount, the tax-free option is phased out until it is completely eliminated for AGIs exceeding roughly $110,000.

The features of various forms of bonds are listed in table 10-9. The primary advantage of Series I bonds for retirement accumulators holding bonds in a CSA is their tax-deferred status. The combination of zero coupon status (and therefore no reinvestment risk) and redeemability at par at any time up to 30 years also is an advantage. Neither TIPS nor I bonds are completely inflation protected when they are held in a CSA because the taxable interest increases with inflation and therefore the after-tax real return is lower at higher rates of inflation. In a TDA, either TIPS or Series I bonds offer a true inflation-indexed real return. Currently I bonds yield 40 basis points less than TIPS. Given that modest interest-rate discount, I bonds (with their tax-deferred feature) would result in more long-term wealth accumulation than TIPS for investors holding bonds in a CSA, while TIPS could generate greater long-term wealth accumulation in a TDA. Holding I bonds in a TDA would render the tax-deferral feature of the bonds worthless.

We repeated the asset location computations with the historic returns used above by replacing the municipal bonds in the taxable CSA with Series I bonds and the corporate bonds in the TDA by TIPS.[20] We assumed in the base case a real return of 3.6 percent for I bonds and a 4 percent real return for TIPS, which corresponds closely to the current real yields. Care should be used in

---

20. Series I bonds currently are available only with a maximum maturity of 30 years. Our computations assumed that the tax on those bonds could be deferred until retirement. The benefits of holding I bonds would decrease if taxation of the bond returns could be deferred for only 30 years.

Table 10-9. *Features of Various Types of Fixed-Income Securities*

Feature	Corporate bonds	Municipal bonds	TIPS	Series I bonds
Inflation protection	No	No	Yes	Yes
Call option	Callable	Callable	Noncallable	Noncallable
Coupon or zero	Coupon and zeros	Coupon and zeros	Coupon	Zeros
Marketability	Market traded	Market traded	Market traded	Nontransferable; redeemable at par
Maturity	Fixed	Fixed	Fixed	Flexible (up to 30 years)
Taxation	Federal, state, and local taxation	Can be exempt from all taxation	Federal taxation only; exempt from state and local tax	Tax deferred; exempt from state and local tax
Accumulation limit	None	None	None	$30,000 per year
Special features	None	None	None	Tax-free if used for college tuition by qualifying households

comparing earlier results with these. Previous results were based on actual real returns of bonds, whereas these are based on hypothetical real returns for inflation-protected bonds and the returns are held at their current level for the entire sample period. Corporate bonds had a real return of only 2.7 percent between 1962 and 1998, while the simulations reported here assume that indexed bonds offered a 4 percent real return.

Table 10-10 summarizes our findings when we used historic returns on equity mutual funds and allowed investors to hold inflation-protected bonds with three different assumptions about the real yields. Panel C shows the accumulated real wealth levels in the base case with a real return of 3.6 percent for Series I bonds and a 4 percent real return for TIPS. On average, the Defer Stocks First rule outperformed Defer Bonds First by 5.3 percent for a high-tax investor and by 6.1 percent for a medium-tax investor. Those gains are similar to the ones in table 10-3 with nominal bonds. With inflation-protected bonds, Defer Stocks First was relatively more beneficial for medium-tax individuals than for high-tax individuals. The tax advantage of I bonds over stocks was greater for medium-tax investors than for high-tax investors. Defer Bonds First was again superior for the index fund.

Table 10-10. *Asset Location Results with Inflation-Protected Bonds*[a]

	High-tax individual			Medium-tax individual		
Type of fund	Wealth at retirement (Defer Stocks First)	Wealth at retirement (Defer Bonds First)	Relative wealth	Wealth at retirement (Defer Stocks First)	Wealth at retirement (Defer Bonds First)	Relative wealth
A. RI = 2.6% RT = 3.0%						
All actively managed funds	82.88	77.80	1.064	92.72	86.37	1.072
Top five actively-managed funds	78.60	75.04	1.048	88.08	82.98	1.062
Index fund	88.30	91.28	0.967	99.14	99.00	1.001
B. RI = 3.1% RT = 3.5%						
All actively managed funds	86.90	82.01	1.059	97.43	91.20	1.066
Top five actively managed funds	82.26	78.97	1.042	92.42	87.56	1.056
Index fund	92.50	96.34	0.960	104.09	104.85	0.993
C. RI = 3.6% RT = 4.0%						
All actively managed funds	91.15	86.51	1.053	102.42	96.36	1.061
Top five actively managed funds	86.15	83.11	1.037	97.02	92.44	1.050
Index fund	96.85	101.68	0.953	109.28	110.97	0.985

a. This table reports the average wealth levels of the two location strategies if the real return of the bonds is changed. RT denotes the real return of TIPS; RI denotes the real return of Series I bonds. The base case is summarized in panel C.

Panels A and B of table 10-10 report the average wealth levels at retirement for different real yields of the inflation-protected bonds. Wealth levels decreased as the real yield decreased. However, the Defer Stocks First strategy still outperformed Defer Bonds First for all cases using actively managed mutual funds. The relative advantage of deferring stocks first increased slightly as the real yield of the bonds fell, because sheltering bonds in the tax-deferred account was less beneficial if bonds paid a lower yield. Holding the passively managed index fund in the CSA continued to generate higher after-tax wealth at the end of the period than holding the fund in the TDA.

The most significant benefit of TIPS and Series I bonds is protection against inflation. To quantify that benefit, we performed bootstrap simulations with the two real securities. We used the same method that we used in the previous simulations, although randomization was irrelevant for the real yields on the inflation-protected bonds since we assumed that those yields were fixed.

Figure 10-6 depicts the wealth distribution at retirement for a high-tax individual investing for 37 years in the largest five funds and following the Defer Stocks First rule. The figure shows the cumulative distribution functions for an

Figure 10-6. *Wealth Distribution of Inflation-Protected and Nominal Bonds, Top Five Funds, Defer Stocks First*[a]

Cumulative distribution

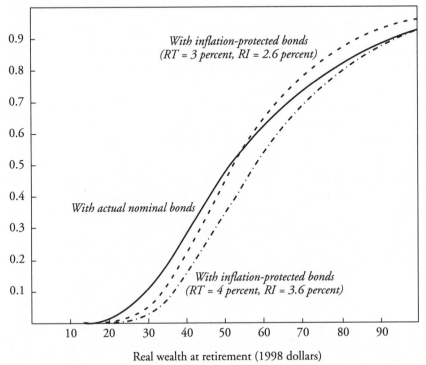

Real wealth at retirement (1998 dollars)

a. The cumulative distribution of real wealth at retirement using inflation-protected and nominal bonds is depicted. The investor chooses randomly among the five largest mutual funds in each of the 10,000 bootstrap simulations. Only the wealth levels of the strategy Defer Stocks First are shown. The wealth levels with inflation-protected bonds are shown for real returns of RT = 3 percent and RT = 4 percent for TIPS and RI = 2.6 percent and RI = 3.6 percent for Series I bonds.

environment with the historic nominal returns on municipal and corporate bonds and with the hypothetical inflation-protected bonds at two different real return levels. The high-return case assumed real returns of 3.6 percent for Series I bonds and 4 percent for TIPS, and the low-return case assumed real returns of 2.6 and 3 percent, respectively. The distribution function for the nominal bonds was exactly identical to the one in figure 10-2. Introducing inflation-protected bonds increased the outcomes at the lower tail significantly. The cumulative distribution function shifted to the left if the bonds had lower real yields.

Table 10-11 summarizes the probability distribution of the two location strategies with inflation-protected bonds with real returns of 3.6 percent (I bonds) and

Table 10-11. *Wealth Distribution with Inflation-Protected Bonds*[a]

Type of fund	Cumulative distribution						
	0.001	*0.010*	*0.100*	*0.500*	*0.900*	*0.990*	*0.999*
A. All actively managed funds							
Wealth (Defer Stocks First)	20.54	27.26	38.31	63.01	111.28	198.80	377.03
Wealth (Defer Bonds First)	20.15	26.63	38.47	62.05	101.29	182.25	323.20
Relative wealth	0.742	0.807	0.900	1.018	1.202	1.35	1.444
B. Top five actively managed funds							
Wealth (Defer Stocks First)	20.81	26.15	37.10	58.00	94.50	136.87	173.80
Wealth (Defer Bonds First)	19.92	25.06	37.04	57.01	85.26	115.59	138.19
Relative wealth	0.800	0.844	0.922	1.026	1.194	1.312	1.391
C. Index fund							
Wealth (Defer Stocks First)	22.93	28.41	40.29	65.07	108.25	158.02	208.13
Wealth (Defer Bonds First)	21.67	28.01	42.09	67.18	103.16	145.13	178.67
Relative wealth	0.746	0.783	0.862	0.975	1.156	1.251	1.307

a. The probability distribution of the real wealth levels of a high-income individual is shown for the two location strategies. Individuals randomly chose one equity fund initially and contributed as described in table 10-3. The returns of the assets were bootstrapped 10,000 times. The annual real return of I bonds is 3.6 percent and of TIPS is 4 percent.

4 percent (TIPS). Panel B of table 10-11 summarizes the probability distributions of the two location strategies for a high-tax individual investing in one of the top five funds. The two functions were quite close at low wealth levels, but Defer Stocks First dominated Defer Bonds First at higher wealth levels. Defer Stocks First usually dominated Defer Bonds First for the actively managed mutual funds but not for the passively managed index fund. Comparing panel B of table 10-7 with the same panel in table 10-11 shows that the wealth level increased with the Defer Stocks First strategy by 34.4 percent at the 1st percentile and by 23.9 percent at the 10th percentile. It was almost identical at the 90th percentile and decreased by 11.8 percent at the 99th percentile.

Table 10-12 shows certainty equivalent results like those in table 10-8, although now we allow for index bonds. Comparing this with table 10-8 shows that the certainty equivalent of an investor with a risk aversion of 3 who invested in the top five funds increased by 19.4 percent when real rather than nominal bonds were available. Risk-averse investors value protection against inflation because they put a much higher weight on the lower tail of the probability distribution. The certainty equivalents from table 10-12 indicate that deferring stocks first was preferable to deferring bonds first at all listed levels of risk aversion for the actively managed mutual funds. The opposite held for the index fund unless individuals were extremely risk averse. By comparing panel C

Table 10-12. *Certainty Equivalents with Inflation-Protected Bonds*[a]

Type of fund	Coefficient of relative risk aversion				
	0	*1*	*3*	*5*	*10*
A. All actively managed funds					
CE (Defer Stocks First)	70.93	64.41	54.87	47.97	36.81
CE (Defer Bonds First)	67.88	62.58	54.18	47.40	35.76
Relative CE	1.036	1.029	1.013	1.012	1.029
B. Top five actively managed funds					
CE (Defer Stocks First)	62.62	58.62	51.69	46.03	35.97
CE (Defer Bonds First)	59.54	56.52	50.64	45.13	34.56
Relative CE	1.052	1.037	1.021	1.020	1.041
C. Index fund					
CE (Defer Stocks First)	70.52	65.57	57.036	50.25	39.04
CE (Defer Bonds First)	70.62	66.50	58.56	51.26	38.35
Relative CE	0.992	0.986	0.974	0.980	1.018

a. Table summarizes the certainty equivalents (CE) of the bootstrap simulations for the two location strategies using a constant relative risk aversion (CRRA) utility function.

in table 10-12 with the other two panels, we again see that using the index fund usually had a higher certainty equivalent outcome than using a randomly selected actively managed fund.[21]

Conclusion

Our findings suggest that asset location decisions are very important for retirement accumulators who hold assets in both tax-deferred pension accounts and in taxable saving accounts. The improvement in the average or certainty equivalent outcome from following an optimal asset location strategy can be as high as 9 percent. With particular actively managed funds, the ex-post gain can be as high as 17 percent.

Our results suggest two conclusions regarding the after-tax wealth that high-income and medium-income investors would have accumulated over the 1962–98 period if they had invested in both stocks and bonds and held assets in both pension and taxable accounts. First, if an investor invested in stocks

21. In results not reported here, we explored the importance of asset location for investors with different desired stock-bond holdings in an environment with inflation-indexed bonds. As in the case with nominal bonds, optimal asset location was most important for an investor who was planning to hold a nearly equal mix of bonds and stocks.

through an actively managed equity mutual fund like the ones we consider, then after-tax wealth was maximized by holding as much of the equity mutual fund as possible in the pension account. Such an investor would have held corporate bonds in the pension account only if there was room for them, while holding municipal bonds in taxable accounts. Our results are based on a small sample of actively managed equity mutual funds that were available for our entire sample period, but we suspect that they would apply to most other actively managed funds available during the last four decades. Second, an investor who used a passively managed equity index fund for stock investments would have accumulated wealth most quickly by first locating corporate bonds in the tax-deferred account and holding the index fund in the taxable account.

Our results show that the tax burden that equity mutual funds, particularly actively managed funds, impose on their investors and the availability of both municipal bonds and inflation-protected Treasury securities as alternatives to corporate bonds need to be factored into the asset location strategy. At least historically, most actively managed equity funds imposed an effective tax rate on their shareholders that was higher than the implicit tax on municipal bonds. Therefore the gain from holding a typical actively managed fund in a TDA rather than a CSA was greater than the gain from holding a corporate bond in a TDA rather than a tax-exempt bond in a CSA. This analysis is reversed with index funds, although it appears that the stakes from optimal location are lower in that case. Passively managed index funds impose a low enough tax burden on their investors that what they gain from being held in a pension account is less than the after-tax yield differential of corporate bonds over municipal bonds.

Even though it was not our purpose to enter the debate over actively managed and passively managed equity funds, our simulations do shed light on the relative advantage of the two fund types for someone saving consistently over 37 years. Our bootstrap simulations indicate that a risk-averse retirement accumulator would have fared better overall with an index fund held in a taxable setting than with a randomly chosen actively managed fund held in a tax-deferred account. Of course, the historical pattern may provide only limited insight on future patterns of returns.

One important issue that arises in using historical results to predict the future concerns the extent to which managers of actively managed funds recognize the tax consequences of their decisions for taxable investors. If they become more aware of taxes in the future—as the recent emergence of tax-managed funds and other financial products that are designed to reduce investors' tax burden suggests that they might be—then our findings may be attenuated. Although the financial press today devotes some attention to the question of how taxes affect after-tax mutual fund returns for individual investors, tax-managed mutual funds currently account for less than 1 percent of the total assets held by equity mutual funds. If the tax efficiency of a typical actively managed equity fund improves in the future, it could have important implications for the future applicability of our analysis.

While most of our analysis concerns a rule-of-thumb, fifty-fifty stock-bond asset allocation, we did look at the outcome for different allocations in our bootstrap simulations. Not surprisingly, an investor's optimal asset allocation is a function of his or her risk aversion. Still, given the well-known equity premium puzzle and the fact that even our bootstrap results were based on realized returns from 1962 to 1998, mildly risk-averse retirement investors would have achieved their highest certainty equivalent outcomes by allocating substantially more than 50 percent of their portfolio to stocks. Whether such results will obtain going forward is not clear.

We also looked at the asset location issues associated with the relatively new inflation-protected Treasury bonds such as TIPS and Series I savings bonds. TIPS have a real coupon rate and an inflation-adjusted principal amount; both the coupon and the principal adjustment are taxable income. Series I bonds are zero coupon inflation-protected bonds; taxation is deferred until sale. Given those features, inflation-linked securities pose their own location question. Our results suggest that the answer depends on the type of equity mutual fund that the investor holds. If index bonds had been available for the last four decades and their yields had been similar to those on current index bonds, then investors would have generated more wealth by holding actively managed funds in a pension account (with Series I bonds held outside) than by following other strategies for those funds. Investors who wished to hold index funds, however, would have accumulated more wealth by holding them outside their retirement accounts, with TIPS in their pension accounts.

Leslie E. Papke

In an important contribution to the pension finance literature, both Fischer Black and Irwin Tepper noted that firms that offer a defined benefit (DB) pension plan could choose to hold the assets in their pension plan account—a tax-deferred account—or outside the pension plan in the corporate account, where the income would be fully taxable.[1] They concluded that more heavily taxed assets should be held in the pension plan account and the less heavily taxed assets in the taxable corporate account. Since the view was that corporate bonds generally were taxed heavily relative to stocks, their advice implied that bonds should be held in the corporate DB plan and equities in the corporate account. This investment strategy—bonds inside and stocks outside—became the conventional wisdom.

As participant-directed defined contribution (DC) plans have become common, plan participants who also save outside their pensions face an analogous asset allocation problem: if they plan to hold both stocks and bonds, should they hold predominantly stocks in their tax-deferred plan or should they defer bonds first?

In this chapter, Poterba, Shoven, and Sialm consider plan participants who want to hold half of their assets in fixed-income securities and the other half in equities. The authors' contribution lies in noting that actively managed equity mutual funds often generate substantial tax liability and that tax-free municipal bonds are also available. They calculate returns to two strategies: the first gives preference to stocks in the tax-deferred account, a 401(k) plan, for example; the second gives preference to bonds. By calculating the end-of-period returns using historical data from 1962 to 1998, they demonstrate that the stock-bond distinction in the traditional Black-Tepper recommendation is too general.

The following are their major conclusions:

—If investors choose to hold actively managed equity mutual funds that generate substantial tax liability, their total return will be higher if they hold those funds in their 401(k) plan and tax-free municipal bonds outside. For the twelve actively managed funds, the average gain from this strategy (deferring stocks first) is 8.9 percentage points for investors with high marginal tax rates. Essentially, the actively managed funds result in a higher effective tax rate for high-income investors than the implicit tax rate on municipal bonds.

Including municipal bonds as an investment option plays a key role in this result. If investors are limited to corporate bonds, then deferring bonds first—

---

1. Black (1980); Tepper (1981).

the usual Black-Tepper recommendation—outperforms the other strategy for nine of twelve actively managed equity funds.

—If investors choose to hold a passively managed equity index fund like the S&P 500 index, which is more tax efficient, the conventional wisdom wins—returns are higher if bonds are held in the 401(k) account and stocks outside. The difference in returns from the two strategies is smaller in this case, only 1.7 percentage points. Passively managed funds are sufficiently tax efficient that they gain less from the pension environment than the premium of corporate bond yields over municipal bonds.

—If investors also choose to hold U.S. government inflation-indexed bonds, the basic results in one and two above are unchanged. The strategy with the highest return depends on which type of equity stock fund is held.

This chapter provides a thorough demonstration of the high tax costs incurred by actively managed equity mutual funds. These tax costs are high enough to reverse the traditional investment advice that bonds should be held in a tax-deferred pension plan and stocks outside (if the investor is willing to hold municipal bonds as well). The tax consequences of churning are often discussed in the newsletters of some investment companies, but the numerical results in this chapter quantify how large this difference can be over a thirty-seven-year time horizon.[2]

This exercise also usefully demonstrates the efficiency of the equity index fund. If an investor holds this type of fund, the preferred strategy would have been to hold it outside the pension account, but with either strategy the difference in returns would have been under 2 percentage points. Further, bootstrap simulations indicate that risk-averse investors would have fared best historically with an index fund held outside their pension plan than with a randomly chosen actively managed account held in their plan.

Although the chapter has no clear policy implications, it does give useful cautionary information to high-income investors with pensions: that actively managed equity funds should be considered heavily taxed and therefore held in tax-deferred accounts. Investors can simplify their lives if they hold an index fund instead—whether this type of fund is held inside the pension plan or outside is much less important. This may have relevance for plan participants who have limited choice, or no choice at all, in their pension asset allocation.

The focus of the chapter is the finding that if an investor chooses to hold an actively managed equity index fund, then—if he or she is also willing to hold municipal bonds—returns to the stocks inside/bonds outside strategy would maximize after-tax returns. In my comments on the original version of this

---

2. See, for a recent example, Vanguard Group, "For Investors, Increased Activity Translates into Lower Returns," *In the Vanguard* (Summer 2000).

chapter, I discussed two reasons why one might expect the future differences in returns from the two strategies to narrow in this case. First, high marginal tax rates magnify the difference between using a tax-deferred versus a conventional savings account, and marginal tax rates were relatively high over this period. The rapid inflation of the 1970s and early 1980s (see figure 10-1) led to bracket creep, driving individuals into higher tax brackets and diminishing the real value of the personal exemption and deductions. The average marginal tax rate rose from 21 percent in 1975 to 27 percent in 1981 without legislated increases in rates.[3] Average marginal tax rates were higher in 1981 than in any other year from 1962 to 1995. The 1981 Economic Recovery Tax Act substantially reduced marginal tax rates and provided for bracket indexing in 1985. So, there was no bracket indexing for twenty-four of the thirty-seven years analyzed here.

The authors test the sensitivity of their results to alternative tax rates first by applying 1998 tax law to the 1962–98 returns, but since they are unable to calculate the substantial general equilibrium effects on the before-tax returns, this comparison is of limited usefulness. It is not possible to suggest a path of tax rates that might be more typical since any choice would be arbitrary. My point is not to quibble about the typical path of future tax rates, only to argue that we are unlikely to see a return to the rates that prevailed before brackets were indexed.

The authors, noting that their findings may be sensitive to the particular pattern of equity and bond returns that occurred over the period, simulate returns to equity mutual funds, drawing sequences of thirty-seven returns with replacement and doing 10,000 replications. Since they sample actual empirical returns and do it 10,000 times, they find, on average, what they found earlier, although the difference in strategies is a bit smaller.

A second reason to expect that the differences between the two strategies will narrow when an actively managed equity fund is held is that funds are expected to become more tax efficient. With the rise in participant-directed individual accounts, information on investment funds and their tax consequences is proliferating. Patrick McGeehan and Danny Hakim profiled fund managers and brokerage firms that offer customized baskets of stocks called folios.[4] These folios can be created to be tax efficient, so they need not be held in a pension fund. Innovative investment management firms will find it profitable to offer wealthy clients customized, tax-efficient equity funds.[5] Indeed, a shift to more tax-efficient funds than the ones studied here may already have occurred. Their

3. See Auerbach and Feenberg (2000).

4. Patrick McGeehan and Danny Hakim, "Two Fund Giants to Introduce Self-Directed Portfolios for Investors," *New York Times*, February 14, 2001, pp. C1–2.

5. For example, see the discussion in TIAA-CREF, "TIAA-CREF Trust Company Brings Personal Touch to Investment Management," *Institute Forum*, vol. 4 (September 2000), pp. 1–5.

Table 10-13. *Nonpension Investment in Stock*[a]

Pension asset holdings	Percent of nonpension financial assets in stock			
	Mean	10th percentile	25th percentile	50th percentile
Nonpension investment in stock by pension asset allocation				
Mostly stock	87.66 (24.71)	49	89	100
Mostly bonds	87.10 (30.52)	12.28	100	100
Even split	91.70 (23.00)	75	100	100

Pension asset holdings	Percent of stock held outside based on income of		
	< $30,000	$30,000–$60,000	> $60,000
Nonpension investment in stock by income and pension asset allocation			
Mostly stock	77.65 (44.00)	84.37 (30.76)	89.39 (20.97)
Mostly bonds	66.67 (51.64)	85.75 (32.80)	91.14 (24.13)
Even split	92.86 (26.73)	96.49 (15.86)	88.42 (25.73)
Observations	25	90	187

Source: Author's tabulations of the 1992 Health and Retirement Study in 1994.

a. The unconditional frequency distribution of the three asset categories in pension plans is mostly stocks (26.90 percent), mostly bonds (25.99 percent), and even split (47.11 percent). Nonpension financial assets equal the sum of household holdings of net stocks and bonds.

sample of funds represented about one-third of the total value of mutual funds in the 1960s, but by 1998, the sample had fallen to only 2.2 percent of the market.

The authors acknowledge this point in their revision but add that the so-called tax-managed funds are still a small part of the equity market. However, tax-managed mutual funds plus the individualized folios should offer plenty of opportunities for tax-efficient investments for wealthy, tax-savvy investors.

Finally, to see what sort of investment patterns can be observed in individual data, I tabulate investment information from the 1992 Health and Retirement Study. The study reports three choices for pension assets for participants of defined contribution plans with choice over their asset allocation: mostly stocks, mostly bonds, or an even split. Respondents also were asked about the net worth of financial assets held outside their pension funds: "Excluding IRA and

Keogh accounts, do you own shares of stock in publicly held corporations, mutual funds, investment trusts? Do you own corporate, municipal, government, foreign bonds, or bond trusts?" The responses relating to participants' primary defined contribution plan indicate that of those with DC plans, 712 participants reported choice over their asset allocation and 738 reported no choice.

First, I find that pension participants with outside stock or bond investments were clearly better off. Mean household income in 1991 for those who held assets outside was $98,712.18 (standard deviation of $111,962), with a median of $73,000 (319 observations). Those who had no outside stocks and bonds had mean household incomes of $58,186 (41,766), with a median of $50,000 (393 observations).

The unconditional frequency distributions of the three asset categories in pension plans are 26.90 percent mostly stocks, 25.99 percent mostly bonds, and 47.11 percent even split. In table 10-13, I sum up the value of stocks and bonds held outside the pension fund and present the three pension holding categories by the percent of stock held outside. It appears that regardless of how a pension is allocated, predominantly stocks are held outside. Further, a regression of the percent of stock held outside on dummies for the pension asset allocation categories, plus a quadratic in income, shows no relationship between the allocations. Of course, these data are crude—they cannot distinguish the types of equity funds or bonds held. But it appears that only about 26 percent of participants could be following the traditional prescription.

References

Arnott, Robert D., Andrew L. Berkin, and Jia Ye. 2000. "How Well Have Taxable Investors Been Served in the 1980s and 1990s?" *Journal of Portfolio Management* (summer): 84–93.

Auerbach, Alan J., and Daniel Feenberg. 2000. "The Significance of Federal Taxes as Automatic Stabilizers." *Journal of Economic Perspectives* 14 (3): 37–56.

Bergstresser, Daniel, and James Poterba. 2002. "Do After-Tax Returns Affect Mutual Fund Inflows?" *Journal of Financial Economics* 63: 381–414.

Black, Fischer. 1980. "The Tax Consequences of Long-Run Pension Policy." *Financial Analysts Journal* (July-August): 21-28.

Carhart, Mark M. 1997. "On Persistence in Mutual Fund Performance." *Journal of Finance* 52 (1): 57–82.

Dammon, Robert, Chester Spatt, and Harold Zhang. 2004. "Optimal Asset Location and Allocation with Taxable and Tax-Deferred Investing." *Journal of Finance,* forthcoming.

Dickson, Joel M., and John B. Shoven. 1995. "Taxation and Mutual Funds: An Investor Perspective," In *Tax Policy and the Economy,* edited by James M. Poterba, 151–80. MIT Press.

Dickson, Joel M., John B. Shoven, and Clemens Sialm. 2000. "Tax Externalities of Equity Mutual Funds." *National Tax Journal* 53 (3/2): 607–28.

Ibbotson Associates. 2000. *Stocks, Bonds, Bills, and Inflation: 2000 Yearbook.* Chicago: Ibbotson Associates.

Investment Company Institute. 2000. *Mutual Fund Fact Book.* Washington.

Johnson, Hugh A. 1962. *Johnson's Investment Company Charts.* Buffalo: Johnson and Company.

Mehra, R., and E. C. Prescott. 1985. "The Equity Premium: A Puzzle." *Journal of Monetary Economics* 15 (2): 145–61.

Moody's Investors Service. 1993–98. *Annual Dividend Record.* New York.

Poterba, James. 1989. "Tax Reform and the Market for Tax-Exempt Debt." *Regional Science and Urban Economics* 19 (1989): 537–62.

Poterba, James, Steven Venti, and David Wise. 2000. "Saver Behavior and 401(k) Retirement Wealth." *American Economic Review* 90 (May): 297–302.

Shoven, John B. 1999. "The Location and Allocation of Assets in Pension and Conventional Savings Accounts." Working Paper 7007. Cambridge, Mass.: National Bureau of Economic Research.

Shoven, John B., and Clemens Sialm. 1998. "Long-Run Asset Allocation for Retirement Savings." *Journal of Private Portfolio Management* 1 (2): 13–26.

———. 2004. "Asset Location in Tax-Deferred and Conventional Savings Accounts." *Journal of Public Economics* 88: 23–38.

Stanford University, Economics Department.

Standard and Poor's. 1993–98. *Weekly Dividend Record. Annual Issue.* New York.

Tepper, Irwin. 1981. "Taxation and Corporate Pension Policy." *Journal of Finance* 36: 1–13.

11

Longevity-Insured Retirement Distributions from Pension Plans: Market and Regulatory Issues

JEFFREY R. BROWN AND MARK J. WARSHAWSKY

The method of funding retirement in the United States is in the midst of a major transition, one that is placing greater responsibility on individuals for managing their own retirement assets. The past two decades have witnessed a large shift away from defined benefit to defined contribution pension plans, a trend that appears likely to continue for the foreseeable future. According to some estimates, the average retiree's balance in 401(k) plans alone will rise tenfold over the next thirty years and will rival Social Security as the major source of retirement wealth.[1]

While defined benefit and defined contribution plans differ along many margins, one of the most important is the method of distributing retirement income. Traditional defined benefit plans typically paid benefits in the form of a life annuity and thus provided retirees with a form of insurance against outliving their resources. According to standard economic life-cycle theory, this longevity

The authors thank William Gale, Stuart Gillan, Evan Giller, Ted Groom, David Gustafson, Michael Hurd, Estelle James, Olivia Mitchell, Michael Packard, Milly Stanges, Peter Weinberg, and conference participants for helpful discussions and comments. They also thank Stuart Sirkin and Steven Boyce of the Pension Benefit Guaranty Corporation for providing data from the PIMS simulation model, Ann Combs of the American Council of Life Insurers for providing survey data, and Mary DiCarlantonio for research assistance. Any opinions expressed are those of the authors alone and not their affiliated organizations.

1. Poterba, Venti, and Wise (2000).

insurance is quite valuable to consumers, because it provides a higher sustainable level of consumption than is available in the absence of this insurance. Defined contribution plans, on the other hand, are much less likely to offer life annuities to retirees. Instead, defined contribution plans offer some form of lump-sum payment and/or "phased withdrawal" options upon retirement. While these alternative distribution methods offer retirees a high degree of flexibility and liquidity, they fail to provide a formal mechanism by which individuals can insure against the risk of outliving their resources, the central issue of this paper.

Individual responsibility for retirement asset decumulation has also emerged as a policy issue in the debate about supplementing or partially replacing the current Social Security system with an individual accounts program. The existing system is currently the primary source of annuitized income for the majority of U.S. households and is the only meaningful provider of inflation-indexed annuities. As such, any plans to alter the existing Social Security benefit structure could affect the desirability of alternative distribution methods from private pension plans.

This paper examines the extent to which individuals can and do insure themselves against longevity risk in defined contribution plans. This issue is of policy concern for several reasons. The distribution method chosen can directly affect the extent to which retirees are able to finance consumption in old age—particularly those individuals who live significantly longer than they anticipated at retirement. Also, increasing average longevity and the trend toward earlier retirement presumably make the problem of ensuring adequate resources throughout individuals' old age more widespread among the population. The adequacy of old-age income directly affects the extent of poverty rates among the elderly, a problem that is especially acute for elderly widows.[2] In addition, if individuals fail to provide adequately for old-age consumption needs, the financial pressure on means-tested social assistance programs such as SSI (Supplemental Security Income) and Medicaid could increase. Finally, the distribution method chosen can significantly affect the size of intergenerational transfers taking place in the economy and thus the wealth distribution of the next generation.

This paper focuses on five issues. First, we review the welfare gains from annuitization that result from a standard life-cycle model. We then discuss several reasons why households may choose not to annuitize despite these theoretical welfare gains, including the presence of Social Security, pricing of annuities in the market, bequest motives, inflation risk, health uncertainty, ignorance, and regulatory impediments. Third, we demonstrate that one result of the shift from defined benefit to defined contribution plans is a reduction in opportunities to annuitize retirement wealth; the majority of defined contribution plans do not

2. Hurd and Wise (1989).

offer an annuity payout option. Fourth, we indicate that even though the fraction of retiree wealth that is annuitized will likely decline, the individual annuity market will likely experience substantial growth in the coming decades as households who desire longevity insurance are forced into the individual market with their retirement assets. One likely implication of this shift toward individual markets is a reduction in the annuity income available per dollar of retirement wealth, because annuity payouts in the individual market may be lower than those in the group market. Finally, we discuss the pros and cons of a number of regulatory options available, including annuity mandates, tax incentives, and government provision, for increasing annuitization of defined contribution account balances.

The Welfare Benefits of Annuitization

Annuities play a central role in the economic theory of wealth decumulation. By trading a stock of wealth for a life-contingent income stream, healthy individuals are able to sustain a higher level of consumption than in the absence of annuities and are assured that this income cannot be outlived.

Individuals who do not have access to annuitization must allocate their retirement wealth in a manner that trades off two competing risks. The first is the risk that if individuals consume too aggressively, they increase the likelihood of facing a future period in which they are alive with little or no income. The second is the risk that if individuals self-insure by setting aside enough wealth to be certain it cannot be outlived, then they risk dying with assets that could have been used to increase consumption while alive.

The economic value of annuitization in a life-cycle model with uncertain lifetimes was first demonstrated in 1965, and this framework has been used extensively to value the insurance benefits of annuities.[3] The basic result is that life-cycle consumers will always choose to purchase actuarially fair annuities to finance retirement consumption and absent a bequest motive, will annuitize 100 percent of their resources.[4] The intuition for this result is straightforward— annuities pay a rate of return that is equal to the riskless rate plus a mortality premium. The mortality premium arises from the positive probability that the insured individual will not be alive to receive future payments. Because this mortality premium is always positive, it means that the annuity rate of return strictly dominates the riskless return. In addition, because the annuity income cannot be outlived, individuals are completely insured against an outcome in

---

3. Yaari (1965).

4. In a simple life-cycle model with no other savings motives besides retirement consumption and bequests, an individual with bequest motives will invest the bequest portion of wealth in riskless bonds, and will annuitize the rest.

Table 11-1. *Annuity Equivalent Wealth with Preexisting Annuity Wealth*

	Annuity equivalent wealth	
Coefficient of relative risk aversion	*No preexisting annuities*	*Preexisting annuities*
1	1.502	1.330
2	1.650	1.441
5	1.855	1.623
10	2.004	1.815

Source: Brown, Mitchell, and Poterba (1999).

which they are alive in some future state without sufficient resources to fund ordinary levels of consumption.

The welfare gains from annuitization can be put into dollar terms using an expected utility framework (interested readers will find a more formal treatment of this model in appendix A). Consider a 65-year-old consumer facing an uncertain date of death, who maximizes a lifetime utility function given a fixed amount of retirement wealth. We first allow this individual to fully annuitize in an actuarially fair market, and we calculate the utility level that this individual achieves. We then take away access to the annuity market, and ask the question: "How much additional wealth must we give this individual to make him as well off (that is, to put him on the same expected utility curve) in the absence of annuities as he would be if he were permitted to fully annuitize his wealth?"

In previous work, the ratio of nonannuitized to annuitized wealth that puts one on the same expected utility curve has been labeled as annuity equivalent wealth, or AEW.[5] For example, an AEW equal to 1.20 means that an individual would be indifferent between $120,000 of nonannuitized wealth and $100,000 of fully annuitized wealth.

The middle column of table 11-1 reports the AEW for an individual, inflation-indexed annuity purchased by a 65-year-old male with mortality expectations consistent with that of the 1933 birth cohort (which turned 65 in 1998). Because the value of annuitization rises with risk aversion, we report values of the AEW for several different levels of the risk aversion parameter in the utility function.[6] For the case of log utility (CRRA = 1), the AEW is 1.502, indicating that this consumer would be indifferent between obtaining access to a real annuity or having a 50.2 percent increase in nonannuitized wealth. For higher levels of risk aversion, the increase is even more substantial. With risk aversion

5. Brown and Poterba (2000); Brown, Mitchell, and Poterba (1999); Brown (1999b).
6. With CRRA utility, the reciprocal of the risk aversion parameter is the elasticity of substitution in consumption across periods. A low risk aversion coefficient corresponds to a high willingness to substitute consumption intertemporally.

of 10, having access to an actuarially fair annuity is equivalent in utility terms to a doubling of wealth.

Within this life-cycle model, the gains from annuitization are substantial. Given this, economists have been somewhat puzzled by the limited extent of annuitization outside of defined benefit plans and Social Security. A substantial literature has examined a number of possible explanations, which we review in the next section.

Why Don't Individuals Fully Annuitize?

Social Security, itself a real annuity, is the major asset in the portfolio of most retired individuals.[7] Because Social Security provides a minimum level of income that lasts for life, recipients are already protected against completely outliving their resources. Therefore, the benefits from additional annuitization are reduced. However, the benefits from additional annuitization do not fall to zero, because in the simple life-cycle framework, 100 percent annuitization of retirement assets is still optimal in the absence of bequest motives.

The life-cycle model can be adapted to account for the presence of preexisting annuities, such as Social Security. As reported in the last column of table 11-1, the gains from additional annuitization are smaller, but still substantial. For example, consider the case of an individual with log utility who has $100,000 of nonannuitized wealth and is also entitled to a flow of Social Security benefits with an expected present value of $100,000. In other words, 50 percent of this individual's net worth is already annuitized. In this case, the person is indifferent between annuitizing the $100,000 of financial wealth or having $133,000 of nonannuitized wealth (or an AEW of 1.330). While this is lower than the 1.502 AEW in the absence of preexisting annuity wealth, it is nonetheless substantial. Thus, while the presence of Social Security and defined benefit pension plans may lessen the value of additional annuitization, that cannot, by itself, explain why individuals do not choose to annuitize all of their retirement resources.

Individual Annuity Markets Do Not Offer Actuarially Fair Prices

One important explanation for the lack of annuitization is that annuity prices are unattractive for the average person in the population. Price deviations from their actuarially fair level can be expected to arise for two basic reasons. First, insurance companies selling annuities need to cover administrative and marketing expenses and earn a competitive accounting profit. Second, to the extent that individuals who choose to annuitize have longer life expectancies than the general population, insurance companies need to adjust their prices to reflect this fact.

---

7. Mitchell and Moore (1999).

Friedman and Warshawsky were the first to document the extent to which private market annuity prices deviate from an actuarially fair level by calculating a money's-worth ratio using both population and annuitant mortality tables.[8] The money's-worth ratio is a measure of the expected discounted present value of future annuity payments per dollar of premium that individuals can expect to receive if they were to participate in the individual annuity market. This pricing analysis has been extended using more recent data.[9] In 1999 a 65-year-old male (female) with a mortality rate like that of actual annuitants could expect to receive approximately 97 cents (95 cents) on the dollar, when discounted using the Treasury yield curve. This suggests that administrative costs account for a 3–5 percent reduction in annuity payouts. However, when an annuity is valued using population-average mortality rates, a 65-year-old male (female) could expect to receive only 85 cents (87 cents) on the dollar. This suggests that adverse selection is responsible for an 8–12 percent reduction in annuity payouts. Therefore, to the extent that annuities are priced unattractively, it is attributable to selection effects more so than to administrative costs. Note, however, that the observed load factors are not large enough by themselves to explain the almost complete lack of annuity demand by U.S. households.

Bequest Motives and Risk Sharing within Families

The original life-cycle model of annuity valuation recognized that if retirees wish to leave bequests to their children, full annuitization is no longer optimal.[10] Walliser shows that if bequests enter the utility function in a CRRA form and are weighted so that optimal bequests are about four times annual consumption, then with actuarially fair annuity markets and a risk aversion coefficient of 2, it would be optimal to annuitize only 60 percent of one's wealth at age 65.[11] Furthermore, the optimal allocation to annuities would fall with age. Sufficiently strong bequest motives, combined with the existence of Social Security and the fact that private annuity markets are not actuarially fair, could explain the limited amount of annuitization.

An extremely large economics literature on the subject of bequest and transfer behavior has failed to come to a consensus on whether bequest motives have an important effect on household asset allocation and consumption decisions.[12] For example, Hurd shows that couples with children do not decumulate their retirement assets any faster than couples without children, and he interprets this

---

8. Friedman and Warshawsky (1988, 1990).
9. Mitchell and others (1999); Brown, Mitchell, and Poterba (2000).
10. Yaari (1965).
11. Walliser (2001).
12. A much more complete survey of the bequest and transfer literature is provided by Gale and Slemrod (2001).

as evidence against bequest motives.[13] In related work, Hurd estimates a bequest parameter from the consumption patterns of individuals and finds that it is not significantly different from zero.[14] On the other hand, Laitner and Juster report data on TIAA-CREF participants that is suggestive of some limited bequest behavior.[15] Bernheim suggested that individual bequest motives were strong enough that 25 percent of elderly households were overannuitized by Social Security and were purchasing life insurance to undo the effects of mandated annuitization.[16] A recent reexamination of this approach, however, suggests that this is unlikely to be the case.[17] Specific to the context of defined contribution plans, Brown reports on empirical findings from the Health and Retirement Survey (HRS) that bequest motives do not appear to affect household decisions about whether or not to annuitize defined contribution plan balances.[18]

Even if bequests to one's children are not important determinants of annuitization behavior, it may be the case that married couples engage in a form of mortality risk sharing between themselves. Kotlikoff and Spivak show that two individuals sharing a common budget constraint can capture nearly half of the utility gains achievable through actuarially fair individual annuities.[19] Hurd also discusses a life-cycle model for couples and the interaction between bequests and family self-insurance.[20] Brown and Poterba demonstrate that, as a result of this risk sharing, the utility gains associated with the purchase of joint-and-survivor annuities are substantially lower than the utility gains outlined above for a single individual.[21]

Table 11-2 reports some representative results from Brown and Poterba for a married couple consisting of a 65-year-old husband and a 62-year-old wife.[22] As for the case of a single individual, the annuity equivalent wealth is calculated assuming access to actuarially fair annuities for individuals facing general population mortality tables. The main feature of these results is that the AEW for couples is significantly below that of individuals. For example, a married couple with log utility has an AEW of only 1.175, significantly below the AEW for a 65-year-old single man. Given that most individuals entering retirement are married, within-couple risk sharing may partially explain the lack of annuity demand.

13. Hurd (1987a).
14. Hurd (1989).
15. Laitner and Juster (1996).
16. Bernheim (1991).
17. Brown (1999a).
18. Brown (1999b).
19. Kotlikoff and Spivak (1981).
20. Hurd (1999).
21. Brown and Poterba (2000).
22. Brown and Poterba (2000).

Table 11-2. *Annuity Equivalent Wealth for Couples*[a]

	Annuity equivalent wealth	
Coefficient of relative risk aversion	*Nominal annuities*	*Real annuities*
1	1.175	1.202
2	1.244	1.295
5	1.339	1.446
10	1.407	1.600

Source: Brown and Poterba (2000).
a. Assumes no preexisting annuities and the survivor benefit ratio is 0.5.

Lack of Inflation Protection in Commercially Available Annuities

The results presented so far have assumed that individuals are able to obtain annuities that are not subject to inflation risk. Although the current Social Security system essentially provides real annuities by indexing benefits to the Consumer Price Index, outside of this system there are very few opportunities to purchase annuities that are protected from inflation uncertainty.

Inflation has two undesirable effects on fixed nominal annuity streams.[23] First, even modest rates of inflation will erode the real value of the income stream over time. For instance, at a 3.2 percent annual rate (which is the average U.S. inflation rate over the 1926–97 period), the real value of a constant nominal annuity will be cut in half in twenty-two years. The erosion from a constant and expected rate of inflation, however, is easily remedied through the use of graded or escalating annuity products that increase the nominal payout by a fixed percentage each year. The second effect arises from the uncertainty about inflation. If inflation varies from year to year, then the real income available to retirees will vary, even in escalating products. When Brown, Mitchell, and Poterba extend the annuity valuation model to account for persistent inflation, they find large differences between the valuation of real versus the valuation of fixed nominal annuities.[24]

Table 11-3 presents results from Brown, Mitchell, and Poterba for single individuals facing inflation uncertainty. They considered two alternative inflation processes, one with independent draws each year (independent and identically distributed), and one in which inflation follows a stylized simple autoregressive [AR(1)] process and thus exhibits some persistence. Not surprisingly, the results indicate that inflation uncertainty reduces the value of a nominal annuity, more so when inflation is persistent. Notice that for more risk averse individuals, the impact of inflation uncertainty is an even greater consideration.

23. Brown, Mitchell, and Poterba (1999).
24. Brown, Mitchell, and Poterba (1999).

Table 11-3. *Annuity Equivalent Wealth (AEW) for Nominal Annuities with Uncertain Inflation*[a]

Coefficient of relative risk aversion	Individual with no preexisting annuity wealth			Individual with half of initial wealth in preexisting real annuity		
	Real annuity	Nominal annuity: i.i.d. inflation	Nominal annuity: persistent inflation	Real annuity	Nominal annuity: i.i.d. inflation	Nominal annuity: persistent inflation
1	1.502	1.451	1.424	1.330	1.304	1.286
2	1.650	1.553	1.501	1.441	1.403	1.366
5	1.855	1.616	1.487	1.623	1.515	1.450
10	2.004	1.592	1.346	1.815	1.577	1.451

Source: Brown, Mitchell, and Poterba (1999).

a. The AEW for the nominal annuity is calculated under the assumption that inflation takes one of six possible values, roughly capturing the distribution of inflation outcomes over the 1926–97 period. Inflation shocks are independent across periods in the i.i.d. (independent and identically distributed) case, and follow a stylized AR(1) process in the persistent inflation case.

A caveat should be added to explanations for the lack of annuity purchases invoking market imperfections (as opposed to preferences). Market imperfections can be absolute (that is, costs of a product are so high as effectively to eliminate its consideration for most households) as well as relative (that is, other products do the same or almost the same things as the product being examined and are less expensive). Administrative costs and incomplete inflation protection are features of most investment and insurance products and not only annuities. Hence, market imperfection explanations invoking these considerations have to claim that the problems arising from these features are more severe or important for annuities than for other somewhat similar products.

Table 11-4 demonstrates the cumulative impact of the factors mentioned so far. It reports the annuity equivalent wealth for a couple consisting of a 65-year-old man and a 62-year- old woman who have 50 percent of their total wealth annuitized through Social Security. They are assumed to purchase a joint and 50 percent survivor annuity that is fixed in nominal terms in an environment of 3.2 percent annual inflation. In addition, due to a combination of administrative costs and selection effects, the nominal annuity is assumed to have a money's worth of 0.88, that is, the couple faces a 12 percent load factor on their annuity purchase.

The results indicate that couples with low levels of risk aversion now have an annuity equivalent wealth that is close to one. In fact, for a risk-aversion coefficient of one, complete annuitization would actually lower utility.[25] For higher

25. This does not necessarily mean that some additional annuitization on the margin would not be valued, only that complete annuitization is clearly not optimal in this case.

Table 11-4. *Annuity Equivalent Wealth for Couples with 50 Percent Preexisting Annuity Wealth and a 12 Percent Load Factor (Money's Worth = 0.88)*

Coefficient of relative risk aversion	Nominal annuity with fixed 3.2 percent inflation
1	0.972
2	1.011
5	1.069
10	1.157

Source: Authors' calculations.

levels of risk aversion, the gains from annuitization are still positive, but much smaller than the gains found in a simple life-cycle model of a single individual purchasing actuarially fair real annuities. These results show that while no single factor may explain the lack of annuity demand, several factors working in combination can substantially lessen or even eliminate the value of annuitization.

Health Uncertainty and the Irreversibility of Annuitization

The annuitization decision is largely irreversible. Insurance companies do not allow individuals to cancel an annuity agreement once it is in place; otherwise, adverse selection would obviously occur as individuals acquire additional information about their expected longevity. Furthermore, annuitization imposes a liquidity constraint on individuals, meaning that in each period they have access only to that period's annuity income (and any unconsumed previous payments). Thus, if individuals face significant uncertainty about future expenditure needs, they may be reluctant to fully annuitize.

Uninsured long-term care expenditures are arguably the most important source of financial uncertainty facing most elderly retired individuals. Although Medicare, supplemented by Medigap and retiree health insurance, adequately insures a large proportion of medical expenses for most elderly Americans, it covers only 100 days of long-term care and only in certain limited circumstances, leaving this important source of financial risk uninsured for most elderly. Similarly, Medicaid imposes strict income- and asset-based eligibility tests that generally require individuals to exhaust their personal assets and apply all but a trivial amount of their income to cover nursing home expenses.

Among those age 65 and over, an estimated 60 percent will need some long-term care in their remaining lifetime.[26] Long-term care needs include critical care that must be supplied in a nursing home, as well as a less critical need for simple assistance with daily activities. According to Murtaugh and others, current projections indicate that more than 40 percent of the 65 and over population

26. Warshawsky, Granza, and Madamba (2000).

will spend some time in a nursing home.[27] The likelihood of spending some time in a nursing home at some point during the remainder of life increases with age (from 39 percent at age 65 to 56 percent at age 85). Murtaugh and others estimate that the average expected stay in a nursing home among users of all ages is 2.4 years.[28] The expected stay for most is less than a year; but for almost 20 percent of users, it is more than five years. The mean number of years of nursing home use declines with age, from 2.8 years in the 65-to-74 age group to 1.9 years in the 85 and over age group.

According to the Lewin-VHI, Brookings-ICF Long-Term Care Financing Model, the average lifetime home health care use is just over 200 visits.[29] About half of those expected to use home health care will use fewer than 90 visits during their lifetime, while 12 percent can expect to use more than 730 visits.

The escalating cost of typical long-term care services presents a substantial financial risk to individuals and their families. Cohen reports that the average annual cost for a stay in a nursing home rose from $38,000 in 1995 to $44,500 by 1998.[30] Assisted living facilities currently charge, on average, $26,000 a year. It is clear that older Americans recognize health care costs as an important source of financial risk. Venti and Wise report results from the Health and Retirement Survey on the question "In thinking about your financial future, how concerned are you with health care costs?"[31] Fifty-two percent of respondents indicated a high level of concern—a significantly larger proportion than the proportion concerned with other sources of uncertainty such as job loss or financial market collapse.

Even though nursing home care represents the greatest source of financial uncertainty for most elderly households, very few are insured against this risk. According to Murtaugh, Kemper, and Spillman, about 30 percent of the elderly population are unhealthy enough that current underwriting criteria would prevent the purchase of long-term care insurance.[32] Warshawsky and others estimate that less than 8 percent of the elderly population owns an individual long-term care insurance policy, and group employer-sponsored coverage is still quite uncommon.[33] Therefore, retired individuals may be reluctant to fully annuitize their retirement resources because they wish to retain a buffer stock of wealth that they can use to pay for possible future long-term care expenses.[34]

27. Murtaugh and others (1997).
28. Murtaugh and others (1997).
29. As quoted in Health Insurance Association of America (1997, table 1.3).
30. Cohen (1998).
31. Venti and Wise (1997).
32. Murtaugh, Kemper and Spillman (1995).
33. Warshawsky, Spillman, and Murtaugh (2002).
34. Warshawsky, Spillman, and Murtaugh (2002) analyze an idea to combine long-term care insurance with the life annuity in order to reduce adverse selection and underwriting, and make both LTC insurance and annuities more attractive and available to middle-class elderly households.

Lack of Consumer Understanding of Annuitization

Thus far, we have been working primarily within the framework of a rational life-cycle consumer who chooses an optimal consumption path with full knowledge of his or her own survival probabilities. In 1999, however, the Task Force on Annuity Messages of the American Council of Life Insurers (ACLI) concluded that "consumers have very little knowledge about annuities or understanding of how the product works."[35]

The ACLI task force conducted a number of qualitative focus groups among consumers. These groups indicated that "the term annuity is somewhat familiar to people, but many cannot define it." Furthermore, the focus group findings suggested that "virtually no consumer fully understands how a lump-sum distribution can be converted to an annuity. While older Americans are generally aware that annuities involve some type of payment stream, few really grasp how it works. Most Americans don't know that annuity payments are a combination of principal and investment return, or how the insurance feature can promise these benefits for a lifetime."[36]

The report goes on to suggest that the least understood aspect of annuities is how risk sharing can allow insurers to offer lifelong income. Consumers tended to focus on the risk of dying early and therefore receiving less in return from the annuity than they paid in, while overlooking the fact that they may live longer than expected and receive much more than they paid. In fact, some consumer focus group participants equated lifetime annuity payments with gambling on their lives and believed that the odds in the gamble favored the insurance company. Viewing insurance as a source of increased risk is not consistent with the standard economic model of consumers using annuities to reduce risk by equating the marginal utility of consumption across different states of nature.

This qualitative research by ACLI suggests that consumers simply do not understand the longevity insurance benefits provided by a life annuity. Clearly, for any consumer who equates the purchase of longevity insurance with gambling, the life-cycle model is unlikely to represent their preferences. Moreover, the strong desire felt by some individuals to control, manage, and invest wealth for its own sake, and perhaps even for some entertainment value, is not well explained by traditional economic models. Although previous work has shown that the predictions of the simple life-cycle model are correlated with intended annuitization decisions on the margin, much of the variation in this decision has been left unexplained.[37] One potentially fruitful area for future research is to

35. ACLI (1999, p. 16).
36. ACLI (1999, p. 16).
37. Brown (1999b).

consider whether any behavioral models of decisionmaking have the potential to improve our understanding of household decisions about annuitization.

Institutional Barriers and Legal Issues

Federal law categorizes employer-sponsored tax-qualified retirement plans into three categories: pension, profit-sharing, and stock bonus plans. Defined benefit plans and money purchase defined contribution plans are considered by law to be pension plans, while most 401(k) plans and other thrift-type plans are considered profit-sharing plans.[38] This distinction is important because pension plans are required to "provide systematically for the payment of definitely determinable benefits to employees over a period of years, usually for life, after retirement."[39] Defined benefit and money purchase plans typically meet this requirement by providing a life annuity as the normal form of payment.[40]

By contrast, 401(k) plans and other profit-sharing or stock bonus plans are not required to offer an annuity as a payout option. Hence, plans that we generally refer to as defined contribution plans, with the minor exception of money purchase plans, are not required by federal law to offer life annuities to participants. Indeed, as we show in the next section, most defined contribution plans do not offer such an option to their employees.

Even though most defined contribution plans are not required to offer annuities, there are no explicit legal constraints against doing so. There are several possible reasons arising from the legal and regulatory environment, however, that may discourage sponsors of defined contribution plans from offering annuities. The first reason is the increase in administrative complexity that offering an annuity brings. Since 1984 federal law has required all retirement plans that provide life annuities to pay these benefits automatically to married employees in the form of qualified joint-and-survivor annuities (QJSA).[41] The law also requires that pension plans must provide a qualified pre-retirement survivor annuity (QPSA) to the spouse of any participant if the participant dies after becoming entitled to a vested benefit but before the normal annuity starting date. These requirements were put into place in response to concerns that husbands were selecting single life annuities, which pay higher benefits than joint-and-survivor annuities. The selection of single life annuities meant that wives, who typically

38. Money purchase plans are funded by employer contributions based on a fixed formula. Profit-sharing and stock bonus plans (which includes employee stock ownership plans) have discretionary employer contributions and are therefore not considered to be pension plans (that is, plans meeting a definitely determinable benefit requirement). All of these plans, however, are defined contribution plans in that the ultimate benefits are based upon the accumulated employer contributions and earnings and losses thereon.

39. Treasury Regulation Section 1.401-1(b)(1)(i).

40. McGill and others (1996).

41. The qualified annuity must provide income to the surviving spouse that is not less than one-half of the amount of the annuity payable during the joint lives of the participant and his spouse.

survive their husbands, were not adequately protected against the loss of pension benefits upon the death of their husbands. The joint and survivor requirement can be waived with the consent of the spouse, but the consent must be in writing and witnessed by a plan representative or a notary public and sufficient time before the annuity starting date must be given for this consent to occur.

The law permits the plan sponsor to make actuarially fair adjustments in benefit levels to recoup the cost of survivor annuities, that is, by reducing the benefits for the participant and his or her spouse compared with the benefits in a single life annuity. According to McGill and others, many plans do reduce benefits to reflect approximately the cost of joint-and-survivor annuities, although most do not do so for pre-retirement survivor annuities.[42] Although actuarial adjustments are allowed, the legal requirements for survivor annuities have added to the costs and potential liabilities of pension plan sponsors by increasing administrative burdens. Overall, there is a sense among professionals who advise plan sponsors, that is, plan practitioners, that the requirements have discouraged sponsors of plans from offering life annuities as a payment form unless they are currently required to do so.

A second institutional barrier that may limit the offering of annuitization opportunities by plan sponsors is the uncertainty among plan practitioners about the attitude of the Internal Revenue Service (IRS) toward the payment of life annuity benefits from a trust held for participants in a profit-sharing plan. Defined benefit pension plans can be either insured or trusteed; money purchase plans are insured plans, and profit-sharing plans are trusteed plans. If a pension plan is insured, it is funded through contracts with a life insurance company; life annuities made available to participants are underwritten by the insurance company, either through individual contracts or through a group contract. If the defined benefit pension plan is funded through a trust, the plan sponsor's contributions to the plan are invested and reinvested in a variety of assets. In a trusteed defined benefit pension plan, retirement income benefits can be provided either through (individual or group) annuities purchased from an insurance company, or they may be paid directly from the trust fund.

The regulatory uncertainty arises about the ability of plan sponsors to offer annuities directly from profit-sharing plan trusts, a possibly desirable arrangement. If an employer sponsors both a pension and profit-sharing plan, the plan participant can transfer assets accumulated in the profit-sharing plan to purchase additional retirement benefits (that is, a life annuity) through the pension plan, if the plan sponsor allows such transfers. If the employer does not offer a pension plan, it is nevertheless possible, because of the number and characteristics of plan participants or particular efficiencies and skills possessed by the benefits staff, that a profit-sharing plan itself could offer annuities paying higher

42. McGill and others (1996).

rates than available through an insurance company. Because the assets in a trust for a profit-sharing plan are matched to market-value accounts owned, and often controlled, by plan participants, however, it is unclear what security could be offered for the interest and mortality rate guarantees implicit in the payment of determinable annuity benefits. Either the annuities would have to be completely participating (as opposed to nonparticipating) or the plan sponsor or the plan itself would have to guarantee rates, perhaps backed up by a reinsurance contract or through a captive insurance company. The view of the IRS concerning these arrangements is unknown.

A third consideration for plan sponsors relates to the regulatory burden imposing a liability for the evaluation of the claims-paying ability of the insurance company providing annuities. The Department of Labor, in Interpretive Bulletin 95-1, has stated that a plan fiduciary must evaluate a potential annuity provider's claims-paying ability and generally must select the safest annuity available, although the cost of the annuity may also be considered in the final selection. Some plan practitioners have claimed that this requirement has led to a decline in the level of benefits payable, as competition in the market may have been impaired.

Summary of Barriers to Annuitization

The gains to annuitization suggested by the simplest version of the Yaari life-cycle model are substantial. When one jointly considers the role of Social Security, risk sharing within families, and health uncertainty, all of which ought to reduce the value of annuities, it is possible to explain why many households do not annuitize. However, it appears that the gains from annuitization should still be large enough to stimulate more demand for annuities than we observe in the private market. To explain the limited market for annuities, one must turn to other factors, including market imperfections, limited consumer understanding of the benefits of annuitization, and institutional and regulatory barriers to the provision of annuities. Importantly, if consumers would benefit from annuitization but are unable to do so because of market imperfections or regulatory constraints, or if consumers fail to understand the risk of not annuitizing, then public policies that encourage annuitization may be welfare improving.

The Current State of Retirement Plan Distributions

Since the mid-1970s, there has been explosive growth in the number and importance of defined contribution plans. As indicated in table 11-5, the number of private sector defined contribution plans has more than doubled from 1977 through 1996. The number of defined benefit plans rose from 1977 through the mid-1980s, but then fell dramatically. As a result, defined contribution plans represented 92 percent of all private sector employer-sponsored pension

Table 11-5. *Number of Employer-Provided Pension Plans and Plan Participants, by Type of Plan*

Plans and participants	1977	1982	1987	1992	1996
Total plans (thousands)	403	594	733	708	696
Defined benefit	122	175	163	89	64
Defined contribution	281	419	570	620	633
Defined contribution as					
percent of total	70	71	78	88	92
Total participants (millions)	50	63	78	82	92
Defined benefit	35	39	40	40	41
Defined contribution	15	25	38	42	51
Defined contribution as					
percent of total	30	40	49	51	55

Source: U.S. Department of Labor (1999–2000, tables E1 and E5).

plans in 1996. The growth in the number of participants in defined contribution plans is even more striking, rising from approximately 15 million in 1977 to more than 51 million in 1996. The number of participants in defined benefit plans also grew during this period, from 35 million to 41 million, but by the early 1990s, defined contribution plans accounted for more than half of all pension plan participants.

Table 11-6 further illustrates these trends by examining the fraction of the U.S. work force covered by defined benefit and defined contribution pension plans. In 1978, 38 percent of wage and salary workers were covered by defined benefit plans, while only 7 percent had primary pension coverage in the form of a defined contribution plan. By 1996 the fraction covered by defined benefit plans had fallen to only 22 percent of the work force, while primary defined contribution coverage had increased to 23 percent of workers. In addition, the share of workers covered by a supplemental defined contribution plan rose from 11 percent to 16 percent. Thus, by virtually every measure, it is clear that defined benefit plans are declining in importance as a source of retirement income, while defined contribution plans are becoming ever more important.

The Availability of Alternative Payout Options

Although most defined benefit participants still receive benefits as an annuity, the fraction of defined benefit plans permitting lump-sum withdrawals at retirement grew during the 1990s. As shown in table 11-7, the Department of Labor reports the fraction of defined benefit participants with access to any type of lump-sum option grew from 14 percent to 23 percent in just six years (1991 to 1997). Even more striking, the fraction of participants with access to a 100 percent lump-sum payment rose from 9 percent to 22 percent. Other sources

Table 11-6. *Estimated Private Wage and Salary Worker Participation Rates under Primary and Supplemental Pension Plans*[a]
Percent, unless otherwise specified

Year	Number of wage and salary workers	Fraction of workers covered by defined benefit plan	Fraction of workers covered by primary defined contribution plan	Fraction of workers covered by supplemental defined contribution plan
1978	75,939	38	7	11
1980	78,349	38	8	13
1982	82,318	36	10	15
1984	86,732	34	11	18
1986	90,267	32	14	18
1988	93,012	30	15	16
1990	94,772	28	17	17
1992	96,577	26	20	17
1994	101,077	24	21	16
1996	104,313	22	23	16

Source: U.S. Department of Labor (1999–2000, table E4). Number of workers taken from Employment and Earnings, Bureau of Labor Statistics, and includes both employed and unemployed wage and salary workers. The number of workers in primary and supplemental plans are estimates derived from annual Form 5500 reports filed with the IRS for plan year.

a. For workers covered under both types of plan, the defined benefit plan is designated as the primary plan unless the plan name indicates it provides supplemental or only past service benefits.

giving estimates of lump-sum availability within defined benefit plans vary widely; some suggest that up to half of all defined benefit participants have a lump-sum option, although nearly all sources report an increasing trend during the 1990s.[43]

A lump-sum distribution option is nearly universal in defined contribution plans, covering more than 90 percent of all participants. As reported in table 11-8, 91 percent of full-time participants in savings and thrift plans in 1997 had access to a lump-sum withdrawal option at retirement, and 41 percent of participants had access to an installment payment plan. Strikingly, only 25 percent of participants in these plans had access to an annuitization option within the plan.

43. A 1992 study by Hewitt Associates reported that 34 percent of surveyed companies with a DB plan for salaried employees provide a lump sum option. EBRI (1996) reports that as many as 64 percent of DB plans made lump-sum distributions available to employees in 1993, although this includes plans offering only *de minimis* lump sum payments. KMPG-Peat Marwick reported that 53 percent of defined benefit pension plans, covering 50 percent of participants, offered a lump-sum distribution option for payments in excess of the de minimis level, up from 46 percent in their 1997 study. We thank Mike Packard for pointing out these alternative estimates.

Table 11-7. *Lump-Sum Availability within Defined Benefit Plans*

Category	Percent of full-time participants			
	1991	*1993*	*1995*	*1997*
Percent with lump sum	14	10	15	23
Full amount	9	9	15	22
Amount limited	5	3	5	1

Source: Mitchell (2000, table 17).

Table 11-8. *Distribution Methods: Savings and Thrift Plans*

Distribution method	Percent of full-time participants with distribution option							
	1985	*1986*	*1988*	*1989*	*1991*	*1993*	*1995*	*1997*
Life annuity	29	25	25	28	30	30	17	25
Installments	59	52	49	52	52	48	30	41
Lump sum	99	98	95	96	99	98	85	91

Source: Mitchell (2000, table 29).

Table 11-9. *Distribution Methods: 401(k) Plans*

Distribution method	Percent of full-time participants with distribution option		
	1993	*1995*	*1997*
Life annuity	34	21	27
Installments	49	34	41
Lump sum	98	92	91

Source: Mitchell (2000, table 30).

Table 11-9 reports nearly identical results for 401(k) plans. While 91 percent of 401(k) participants had access to lump-sum options, and 41 percent had access to installment options, only 27 percent had the option to purchase a life annuity in 1997. Note that in both tables 11-8 and 11-9, the estimates of the fraction of employees with access to each distribution option vary greatly from year to year. This variability is quite likely attributable to sampling error rather than high-frequency changes in employee payout options.[44]

The overall trend regarding options for annuitization is clear. Defined benefit plans are on the decline, and those that still exist are making it easier to take a lump-sum distribution. Defined contribution plans are growing, but 70 percent

44. This is one of several "data deficiencies" that will be mentioned in this paper. Clearly, better data on the distribution phase of employer-provided plans are needed.

or more of them do not offer participants a life annuity option. Therefore, opportunities for insuring against longevity risk through employer-provided pensions appear to be on the decline. Now we turn to a review and an assessment of other information about the fall in annuitization rates in recent years.

Annuitization of Current Retirement Assets

Available evidence suggests that a declining fraction of retirement income is being paid in the form of a life annuity. We rely on two primary sources of information to make this determination: the Current Population Survey, including supplemental surveys, sponsored by the Department of Labor (DOL), and Form 5500 filings with the IRS by qualified private plan sponsors.

The Department of Labor periodically sponsors supplemental surveys connected to the Current Population Survey to determine the extent of pension and health benefits of workers ages 40 and over, and retirees. One particular aspect that the DOL has examined through its surveys is the shift in the form in which pension benefits are being received. According to the 1994 survey, among persons 40 and over who were employed in the private sector and received a pension benefit resulting from this employment, 48 percent reported receiving an annuity (10 percent report receiving both an annuity and a lump-sum distribution and 38 percent an annuity only) and 51 percent received only a lump-sum distribution.[45] This distribution in the form of benefits is substantially different from what was reported just five years earlier in a DOL-sponsored supplemental survey. In 1989, 60 percent of recipients reported the receipt of an annuity (52 percent annuity only and 8 percent annuity and lump sum).

The aggregate numbers associated with this trend away from pension annuities further highlight its significance. According to survey information, in 1989, 7.5 million private sector retirees and workers were receiving annuity benefits, and 6 million had received lump-sum payments from pension plans at some earlier point. In 1994 the number of annuity recipients had decreased by 4 percent to 7.2 million, while the number of lump-sum recipients had increased to 9.1 million. These statistics imply that the annuitization *rates* through private pension plans have declined at an even greater rate than the decline in the number of annuitants.

Other information, aggregate and over a longer time period, about the shift in benefit form is available from the Form 5500 reports. This information, however, is more indirect than the survey information, because only plan type and not benefit form is reported, and, as explained above, the once nearly one-to-one correspondence between defined benefit plan type and annuity benefit form has eroded. According to the Department of Labor, private defined benefit plans disbursed $15.2 billion in benefits in 1977, presumably almost entirely in annuity

45. DOL (1995).

form.[46] That year, private defined contribution plans disbursed $7.7 billion in benefits, presumably mostly in lump-sum form. Hence, in 1977, the estimated ratio of annuity (defined benefit) to lump-sum (defined contribution) benefit form payments was approximately 2 to 1. By 1996 the ratio had become 4 to 5: $96.9 billion in benefits from defined benefit plans and $116.5 billion from defined contribution plans. In 1996, 8.9 million retired or separated participants received benefits from private defined benefit plans; this had increased only from 7.7 million participants in 1989.[47]

Utilization of the Annuity Option with Defined Contribution Plans

Given the rapid growth in defined contribution plans, it is of interest to know to what extent employees with access to an annuity option choose to use it. Unfortunately, after an extensive review of available data sources, we have found that very limited information exists to permit reliable estimates of the fraction of retirees that choose to annuitize when the option exists.[48] As we show, those estimates that are available vary widely across data sources. Whether these disparities are attributable to real differences in the annuitization propensities of individuals in different plans or to errors or misreporting in the data is not always possible to ascertain. The sources of data that we examine include the Health and Retirement Survey, TIAA-CREF administrative records, and the federal Thrift Savings Plan. In addition, we discuss the growing market for variable annuity products, as well as evidence on annuitization decisions within the Social Security system.

We first turn to the 1992 wave of the Health and Retirement Survey (HRS). Brown reports that of those households with at least one worker covered by a defined contribution plan who had the option to withdraw the funds as an annuity or installments, 48 percent *intended* to annuitize at least a portion of their account balances.[49] It is still too early to know whether or not *intended* annuitization will translate into *actual* annuitization within the defined contribution plan, because respondents were on average seven years away from their expected retirement date. This calculation is further complicated by the fact that even individuals who ultimately annuitize may not do so immediately at retirement.

---

46. DOL (1999–2000).

47. DOL (1999–2000). Although the Form 5500 and Current Population Survey give a nearly identical number of participants receiving annuity/DB benefits in 1989, the two sources of information give different numbers for 1996 and 1994, respectively. Leaving aside the obvious explanation of different reporting periods for the discrepancy, there is also the explanation that by 1996, many DB plans were allowing participants to receive their benefits in lump-sum form. Also the Survey only reports on workers above age 40, whereas the Form 5500 reports on workers of all ages.

48. An effort is currently under way to collect information on the availability of life annuity payout options from employer Summary Plan Descriptions as part of the Health and Retirement Survey.

49. Brown (1999).

In addition, even individuals who choose to take their account balances as a lump sum could use the proceeds to purchase an immediate life annuity in the individual market.[50]

More detailed information is known about annuity options available to and choices made by participants in the Thrift Savings Plan (TSP), a relatively new supplemental defined contribution plan for federal government employees. As of October 1998, the TSP had 2.4 million individual accounts and $71.5 billion in investment assets; during 1997 it received $7 billion in contributions and disbursed almost $1.4 billion in benefits.[51] In dollar terms, most benefit payments are disbursed as transfers to Individual Retirement Accounts and other qualified plans; the second and third largest disbursement categories are lump sums and death benefits. Federal law requires that several different types of life annuities be made available, including level and increasing payment, single and joint life (50 and 100 percent to survivor), and cash refund and ten-year-certain options. No variable payout options are available, however. The annuities are sold by an insurance company selected according to the criteria set forward in a Request for Proposal issued by the TSP. The TSP annuity payout rates are quite competitive compared with individual life annuities sold by commercial companies through agents.[52] Nevertheless, annuitization rates in the TSP are extremely low, with approximately 1.2 percent of retiring and separating federal workers choosing to annuitize.[53] Most currently retiring federal workers are still in an old retirement system, however, and therefore the TSP represents a relatively unimportant component of their retirement resources. As the TSP system matures, it will become clearer whether life annuities will become a more popular disbursement method.

In contrast to the TSP, TIAA-CREF, the principal and long-standing defined contribution retirement system for the nation's education and research sectors, represents a mature defined contribution pension plan system, where the plans are the primary source of retirement security for their participants. As of October 1998, there were 1.8 million TIAA-CREF participants in the accumulation phase and almost 300 thousand participants receiving annuity income; investment assets totaled almost $230 billion. TIAA-CREF life annuities are available with a wide variety of features and at attractive rates. Furthermore, the system has a long history of educating its participants on the advantages of life

---

50. The limited size of the individual annuity market makes it clear that this is not done very often. According to ACLI, only 112,000 immediate annuity contracts were issued in 1998 outside of pension plans, accounting for roughly $8 billion in premiums. Even this overstates the market, however, since it includes non-life contingent products as well as annuities for structured settlements.

51. Poterba and Warshawsky (1999).

52. Poterba and Warshawsky (1999).

53. Personal communication from Eric Linder, Metropolitan Life Insurance Company, July 25, 2000.

annuities.[54] In fact, before 1988, all TIAA-CREF basic pension plans allowed for distributions only through a life annuity or death benefit. Since then, a variety of distribution methods have been made available. Most TIAA-CREF participants, however, still choose a life annuity; of the 16,300 participants converting their accumulations into streams of periodic income in 1997, 11,700 chose a life annuity.

Ameriks confirms the high rate of annuitization among TIAA-CREF participants.[55] Nearly 60 percent of individuals age 65 retiring in 1994, 1995, and 1996 started their first life annuity income within one year of retiring. Nevertheless, Ameriks also noted, the frequency at which participants are choosing to begin a life annuity immediately following retirement has declined steadily as the number of alternative options available to TIAA-CREF participants has expanded. Many participants retiring at ages 62 to 68 are postponing distribution of their retirement assets until later ages. According to Ameriks, unexpected increases in retirement wealth and other assets may have played an important role in the drop in annuitization rates. Indeed, the data indicate that the decline in annuitization rates has been slightly larger among individuals with greater equity allocations.

Yet another source of information about the likelihood of annuitizing retirement assets is the market for individual deferred variable annuities. This market has seen phenomenal growth over the last decade, with investors pursuing high stock market returns and favorable tax treatment. According to successive issues of the American Council of Life Insurers *Fact Book*, over the 1989 to 1998 period, the number of persons covered by these annuities grew from 2.7 million to 14.6 million. Annual premium volume increased from $6.3 billion to $49.2 billion, and reserves increased from $42 billion to $354 billion. Table 11-10 shows statistics on the number of persons covered by individual variable annuity plans, premium considerations, and annuities in course of payment for the period 1971 through 1996.

There is no requirement that these products ever be converted into a life annuity income stream, and indeed, annuitization rates have remained relatively low over the entire period for which we have data: 1971 through 1996. As shown in figure 11-1, the ratio of the number of persons receiving payments to the total numbers of persons covered by individual variable annuities has ranged from 0.6 percent to 1.9 percent, with the most recent rate at 1.1 percent. As seen in figure 11-2, the ratio of total annualized income to total premiums contributed has ranged from 0.8 percent to 3.2 percent, with the most recent rate at 1.0 percent. Of course, these numbers definitely understate the probability that any one contract will be converted to a life annuity. At any given point in time,

54. Poterba and Warshawsky (1999)
55. Ameriks (1999).

Table 11-10. *Summary Statistics for Individual Variable Annuity Plans in the United States, 1971–96*

Statistic	1971	1976	1981	1986	1991	1996
In force year-end						
Number of persons						
covered	171,600	663,170	797,730	1,913,750	2,838,270	8,156,500
Considerations						
(thousands of dollars)	128,975	565,600	1,862,150	5,283,190	8,388,040	39,700,680
Variable annuities						
in course of payment						
Number of persons						
receiving payments	1,421	6,130	11,460	29,640	54,400	91,700
Annualized income						
(thousands of dollars)	1,571	7,770	19,300	71,910	184,400	381,580

Source: American Council of Life Insurers (1972–97).

the vast majority of these contracts are held by individuals who are still working and accumulating assets. This is especially true given the rapid growth of this market. Consistent with this fact, annuitization rates rose in the late 1970s and again in the late 1980s when growth in the variable annuity market slowed somewhat. Nevertheless, it is clear that regular payments from variable annuities, which either can be fixed or can vary with current value of investments on which the annuity is based, are relatively small.

Figure 11-1. *Comparing Those Receiving Payments to Total Number of Individuals with an Individual Variable Annuity Plan*

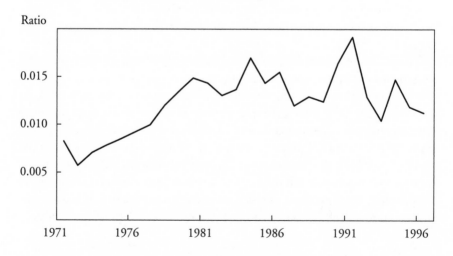

Source: American Council of Life Insurers (various years).

Figure 11-2. *Comparing Total Annualized Income to Total Premium Contributions in Individual Variable Annuity Plans*

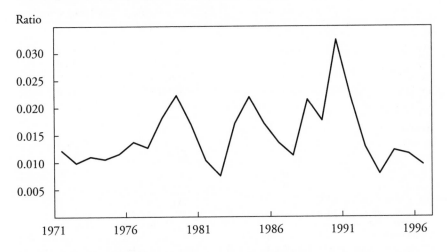

Source: American Council of Life Insurers (various years).

A final source of information on the likelihood of annuitization comes from the Social Security program. Although individuals do not have the opportunity to take Social Security benefits in a nonannuity form, they do have the ability to choose when to claim benefits. By delaying this claim, an individual can trade a lower immediate payout annuity for a deferred annuity with larger payouts in the future. Analysis of claiming decisions suggests that of men who retire before age 62, only 10 percent delay claiming benefits for at least one year after eligibility.[56] While the patterns of who delays is generally consistent with the theory, the fraction of men delaying is much lower than what the theory would predict. This suggests that most individuals are not taking advantage of the opportunity to purchase additional annuitization, even when the annuities are inflation-indexed and close to actuarially fair for the average person in the population.

In summary, it is difficult to determine a single reliable estimate of annuitization probabilities. At the high end, the majority of retirees in the TIAA-CREF system purchase a life annuity with their accumulations. At the low end, the federal Thrift Savings Plan has seen minuscule annuitization rates. In between these extremes, a large fraction of HRS respondents intend to annuitize, but there is very little research on the determinants of actual annuitization behavior. This is clearly an area that is ripe for future research.

56. Coile and others (2002).

Table 11-11. *Mortality Rates*

Deaths per 1,000

Gender	General population	Group annuitants	Individual annuitants
Males			
Age 65	21.5	14.4	11.0
70	30.3	22.1	18.0
75	44.0	33.9	29.1
80	70.0	58.0	47.2
85	111.7	93.1	75.6
Females			
Age 65	13.3	9.0	7.0
70	19.7	14.2	11.0
75	29.6	22.5	18.9
80	45.9	37.7	33.1
85	75.0	63.6	57.8

Sources: General population mortality rates from the 2000 Trustees' Report of the Social Security Administration. Group annuitant mortality rates are from the Society of Actuaries (1995). Individual annuitant mortality rates are from Johansen (1996). The annuitant tables have been converted into cohort tables for the 1935 birth cohort as described in text.

Relative Payouts of Annuities in the Two Types of Plans

In addition to lessening opportunities for annuitization, one of the implications of the shift from defined benefit to defined contribution plans is that annuity payouts per dollar of premium may be lower in a voluntary defined contribution framework. This is possible for two reasons. First, in traditional defined benefit plans without a lump-sum option, participants are unable to self-select out of the annuity pool, and the pool will thus, on average, have higher mortality rates than the defined contribution pool in which individuals choose to participate. Second, administrative costs are likely to be lower in a group plan.

The difference in mortality rates between these two mortality pools can be seen in table 11-11, which reports mortality rates for several representative ages. Three sets of rates are reported. First, mortality rates for the general population are taken from the 1935 birth cohort table from the Social Security Administration's 2000 Trustees' Report, which is appropriate for individuals turning age 65 in the year 2000. Next we report mortality rates for group annuitants, as reported in the Society of Actuaries 1994 Group Annuitant Mortality Table, updated to the year 2000. Finally, we report mortality rates for individual annuity market participants, as reported in Johansen.[57] For both of the annuitant tables, mortality tables are converted into cohort tables for the 1935 birth cohort by applying

57. Johansen (1996).

Table 11-12. *Monthly Annuity Payment Available from a $100,000 Actuarially Fair Annuity under Alternative Mortality Assumptions*

Assumption	General population	Group annuitant	Individual annuitant
Real (3 percent)	$508.41	480.41	459.99
Nominal (6 percent)	679.33	651.65	632.78

Source: Authors' calculations as described in text.

the mortality improvement rates implicit in the difference between Social Security's year 2000 period table and the 1935 birth cohort table.[58]

As the table indicates, mortality rates for the group annuitant table lie between the population and the individual annuitant mortality rates. Whereas in the general U.S. population, 21.5 deaths per 1,000 65-year-old males were expected in the year 2000, only 14.4 out of a group of 1,000 annuitants will die at this age, and only 11 out of 1,000 individual annuitants.

To measure the importance of these mortality differences for the pricing of annuities, we have computed the actuarially fair monthly payout that would be provided in a joint-and-full survivor annuity for a couple, both of whom were 65-year-olds, assuming an initial annuity premium of $100,000. That is, we calculate the monthly payment *A*, according to the following equation:

$$(1) \qquad \$100,000 = \sum_{j=1}^{12*(115-age)} \frac{A \cdot (P_j^m + P_j^f - P_j^m \cdot P_j^f)}{\prod_{k=1}^{j}(1 + i_k)},$$

where P_j^m and P_j^f are the cumulative probability of surviving *j* months beyond age 65 for males and females respectively, and i_j is the interest rate for month *j*. When one determines the payout of a fixed nominal annuity, i_j is the nominal interest rate, and when one determines the initial payout of a fixed real annuity, i_j is the real interest rate.

Table 11-12 reports the initial value of the payout for an actuarially fair real and nominal annuity, assuming a real interest rate of 3 percent and a nominal interest rate of 6 percent. Of most relevance here is the comparison of the group and individual annuitant payout rates. For nominal annuities, using the group annuitant table (as would be the norm in a defined benefit plan), the 65-year-old couple could expect to receive $651.65 a month. Using the individual annuitant table, as would be the norm if individuals were required to annuitize on their own, this same couple would expect to receive only $632.78 a month, or approximately 3 percent less. For an inflation-indexed annuity, the difference in payouts is approximately 4 percent.

58. Readers interested in more detail on this process should consult Mitchell and others (1999).

The role of administrative costs probably increases the difference between the payouts available in group versus individual annuity markets. Administrative costs would reduce the payout of both group and individual annuities. If, however, there are economies of scale in the cost of servicing group annuity contracts relative to individual contracts, then one would expect the individual annuitant prices to be reduced by more.

Thus, it appears that the shift from defined benefit to defined contribution plans means that individuals have fewer opportunities to annuitize their resources. It also probably means that those who do annuitize through their defined contribution plan are likely to receive somewhat less monthly income under the plan per dollar invested than they could have under a group defined benefit plan.

Future Trends in Pension Distributions

Given the trends away from defined benefit and toward defined contribution pension plans, the possibility exists that future retirees will have a smaller fraction of their retirement assets annuitized than current retirees. To assess the extent of these changes, we have undertaken several illustrative calculations. First, using data provided by the Pension Benefit Guaranty Corporation (PBGC), based on runs of its simulation model of single-employer defined benefit plans, we calculate the expected number of participants, benefit payment amounts and plan liabilities for these defined benefit plans for 1999 and the next twenty years. Second, we have constructed some estimates of future annuitization levels from 401(k) plans.

Future Defined Benefit Annuitization Trends

The PBGC uses a stochastic simulation model—the Pension Insurance Modeling System (PIMS)—to evaluate its exposure and expected claims. For the universe of private single-employer defined benefit plans, the model produces, among other variables, the number of participants (total, active, terminated vested, and retired), benefit payment amounts, and plan liabilities. Values of the variables can be averaged over thousands of runs of the model to represent the most likely outcomes in the future. Under the assumptions that the long-term Treasury bond yield will tend to 6.35 percent, the inflation rate will tend to 4.26 percent, and the wage growth rate will tend to 5.31 percent, we calculated the likely number of participants, benefit payment amounts, and plan liabilities for 1999 and the next twenty years.[59] These calculations were based on data runs provided to us by PBGC staff.

59. Readers should be cautioned that the simulation sample weights provided to us by the PBGC are more appropriate to the liability statistics than the participant and benefit amount statistics. In order to give some indication of the extent of the universe of private single-employer DB plans, however, we have used the weights for all variables being studied. It should also be noted

Table 11-13. *Participants, Annual Benefits Paid, and Plan Liabilities for Private Single-Employer Defined Benefit Plans: Most Likely Forecast*

	Participants (millions)			Annual benefits paid (millions of 1999 dollars)		Plan liabilities (millions of 1999 dollars)
Year	Total	Active	Terminated vested	Retired	Only life annuities	Lump sums	
1999	23.9	11.0	4.8	8.1	93.9	83.7	1,477,049
2009	26.5	11.0	5.3	10.2	119.1	117.2	1,949,258
2019	28.8	11.0	5.6	12.1	159.8	132.3	2,287,435

Source: Authors' calculations based on data provided from the PIMS simulation model of the Pension Benefit Guaranty Corporation.

The benefit payment amounts were calculated under two diametrically opposed assumptions: all benefits are paid as life annuities; and all new and future benefits are paid as lump-sums while payments to current retired annuitants continue for their lives.

The results are shown in table 11-13, in inflation-adjusted terms where appropriate.[60]

According to the calculations, the number of participants in private single-employer defined benefit plans is forecast to increase minimally over the next twenty years, from 24 million to 29 million, and even that increase occurs only in the terminated vested and retired segments of the participant population, as the entire private defined benefit plan sector ages. Annual benefits paid as life annuities grow from $94 billion in 1999 to $160 billion (inflation-adjusted) in 2019. Given the increasing tendency of defined benefit plans to pay benefits as lump sums, this forecast is probably on the high side. If current and future benefits are paid entirely as lump sums, that amount grows from $84 billion to $132 billion (inflation-adjusted) over the period, while benefits paid to current annuitants (not shown in the table) decline from $77 billion to $22 billion.

To provide some context for these figures, consider forecasts done in 1999 by the Office of the Actuary for the Social Security OASI program. In 1999, $341 billion was paid out in life annuity benefits from Social Security; private defined benefit plan annuity benefits therefore would currently represent 27.5 percent of Social Security benefits. In 2019, under the intermediate assumptions of the

---

that active participant counts are not the result of a stochastic simulation but rather represent the assumption of PBGC staff on the likely or median future path of the system.

60. We do not have access to similar forecasts for multiemployer and government worker retirement plans; the trend in these sectors, however, like the private sector, is toward defined contribution plans.

Actuary, $602.2 billion (inflation-adjusted) in Social Security annuity benefits will be paid out. According to the calculations cited above, defined benefit plan annuity benefits will represent no more than 26.5 percent of Social Security benefits in 2019, and probably less given current trends in plan distribution options and choices.

Future Defined Ccontribution Annuitization Trends

According to Poterba, Venti and Wise, 401(k) plans are now the most important form of retirement saving, accounting for 55 percent of all contributions to employer-sponsored plans in 1998.[61] Poterba, Venti, and Wise constructed synthetic cohorts of households using earnings history information from the Current Population Survey and constructed an algorithm to forecast future 401(k) balances for cohorts attaining age 65 in 2025. Their results suggest that 401(k) wealth will be an extremely important component of household portfolios in the coming decades. For example, among those reaching retirement in 2025, assuming that plan assets are invested in a 50-50 stock-bond portfolio, Poterba, Venti and Wise report that average 401(k) plan assets would be $133,400 (in 1992 dollars), or roughly 1.10 times Social Security wealth.

Not surprisingly, these 401(k) wealth levels vary by earnings decile, varying from virtually nothing among low earners to substantially more than double Social Security wealth at the higher end of the earnings distribution. Using these estimates and information on the size of the cohort reaching age 65 in 2025, one can estimate an aggregate amount of wealth held in 401(k) accounts by this cohort. Using data household projections for the year 2020 from the Joint Center on Housing Studies,[62] combined with mortality rate information from the Social Security Administration's 2000 Trustees' Report, we estimate that approximately 2.35 million households will turn age 65 in the year 2025.[63] If we again update the 50-50 stock/bond portfolio estimate of $133,400 (in 1992 dollars) to January 2000 dollars using the Consumer Price Index-Urban (which rose approximately 20 percent from the end of 1992 to the end of 1999), we produce an estimate of aggregate 401(k) wealth holdings by the cohort age 65 in year 2025 of $376 billion (in 2000 dollars). Recall that in 1997, an estimated 27 percent of 401(k) participants had access to an annuity option. This was higher than that reported for 1995, but lower than that for 1993, and thus it is difficult to ascertain whether there is any trend in the data. Furthermore, we do not know whether newly created 401(k) plans will be more or less likely to offer a life annuity option. If we assume that 27 percent of all 401(k) plans will offer

---

61. Poterba, Venti, and Wise (2000).
62. Masnick (2000).
63. This is quite likely an overstatement of the relevant population, because it includes individuals who were never in the labor force due to disabilities, and so on.

a life annuity option to participants, and if the probability of having this option is the same across all income deciles, then approximately $101 billion of 401(k) assets in 2025 will be in plans that have an annuity option.

As previously discussed, it is quite difficult to determine a precise measure of a household's propensity to annuitize its assets. Brown's tabulations from the HRS suggest that 48 percent of households with a 401(k) plan intend to annuitize at least *a portion* of their accounts. If we were to assume that those households that do annuitize do so with half of their account balances, then approximately $24 billion of wealth would go into the purchase of immediate life annuities each year. For perspective, this is roughly ten times larger than the approximately $2 billion flowing into the individual immediate annuity market in 1998.[64]

Although these estimates are quite speculative, they nonetheless suggest two broad conclusions. First, the private individual annuity market will likely undergo substantial growth over the coming decades. Second, the size of the individual annuity market will remain small relative to Social Security as a source of annuitized income. Combined with the declining importance of defined benefit plan payouts relative to Social Security, it seems clear that, absent institutional and regulatory changes, overall rates of annuitization will fall in the future, potentially exposing retirees to substantial longevity risk.

Evaluation of Options to Encourage Annuitization

In this section, we evaluate a range of policy options related to the annuitization of account balances in defined contribution plans. These options extend from mandating minimum levels of annuitization, to tax incentives, to the establishment of a government-sponsored program/organization where plan participants can purchase annuities. It is assumed that the laws and regulations currently applying to annuities from pension plans, such as joint-and-survivor requirements, will be extended to defined contribution plan annuities. We do not discuss other policy proposals that have been made to improve the functioning of pension annuities, such as inflation indexing or the enhancement of joint-and-survivor rules.

The evaluation of policy options will clearly differ depending on what one believes is the underlying reason for why individuals do not choose to annuitize more of their wealth. As discussed earlier, there are many possible reasons that individuals may not annuitize, and it is highly unlikely that any one reason is

---

64. As discussed in Brown, Mitchell, and Poterba (2000), the $7.9 billion individual annuity market reported by the ACLI significantly overstates the extent of annuitization because it includes structured settlements as well as non-life contingent annuities. We estimate the actual size of the retirement life annuity market to be on the order of two to three billion dollars in premiums per year.

sufficient to explain the lack of annuitization. It could be that rational actors are making an optimal decision based on their expectations about future health expenditure needs and preferences toward risk and bequests. If so, then the lack of annuitization may not be viewed as a major problem for policymakers, and it should be left to the private market to design products accommodating individuals' needs and preferences. Alternatively, it may be that rational actors would like to annuitize but simply do not have access to fairly priced annuities because their defined contribution plan does not offer them and the private market for individual annuities suffers from adverse selection. In this case, policymakers may wish to require that defined contribution plan sponsors offer an annuity option. They might even consider mandating annuities to overcome the adverse selection problem; otherwise, many individuals would be at risk of relying on government assistance if they live longer than expected and exhaust their resources.

If, however, individuals are not behaving rationally at all, but rather are failing to purchase welfare-enhancing annuities due to myopia or a lack of understanding of the benefits of annuitization, then paternalistic policymakers might wish to simply mandate annuitization. Unfortunately, existing evidence does not allow us to specify what fraction of the population falls in each category. Therefore, we will explore a range of policy alternatives and discuss under what assumptions each policy does or does not make economic sense.

Mandate a Minimum Level of Annuitization

An obvious and highly controversial way to increase annuitization levels would be to mandate that every tax-qualified employer-sponsored retirement plan provide that any benefits payable to a participant below a certain dollar level be paid entirely in life annuity form. Such a mandate could apply to all types of plans, including pension, profit-sharing, and stock bonus plans. For example, one might select the dollar level so that the (joint-and-survivor) lifelong annuity income produced at the normal retirement age would be sufficient, when combined with Social Security benefits, to keep retirees above some minimum income level. If the account balance/plan benefit fell below this (age-adjusted) level, the entire account would have to be annuitized; if it were above this level, discretion for the disposition of the remaining account balance would be left to the plan participant.[65]

An annuity mandate would greatly increase annuitization rates in tax-qualified, especially defined contribution, plans. Therefore the mandate would improve the retirement income security of many plan participants and reduce the adverse selection problem affecting the life annuity market (thereby enhancing annuity payout rates).

---

65. Nondiscrimination requirements presumably would have to be amended to allow the differential treatment of participants by size of account.

However, an annuity mandate has several important negative effects as well. Annuitization may be inappropriate and even harmful for many plan participants, such as those in poor health, or those who wish to leave a large estate. In addition, a mandate has the potential to be administratively burdensome. It is also likely to be politically very unpopular in the United States because it severely restricts individual choice.

Some recent policy discussions in the United Kingdom are relevant to these proposals. Current pension law in the United Kingdom requires that those with personal or occupational pension plan assets must buy a life annuity by the age of 75.[66] The main aim of the law is to cure the moral hazard problem, that is, the possibility that pensioners will spend their assets quickly and fall back on state welfare provision. Recent declines in annuity rates owing to falling interest rates, as well as chafing at the (perceived and real) inflexibility and illiquidity inherent in life annuities, have led to demands that these requirements be softened. A semi-official Retirement Income Working Party recently issued a report recommending that the obligation for total annuitization should be changed to a requirement that when an individual retires, he or she purchase an inflation-indexed annuity to meet a minimum retirement income.[67] The minimum income would be set at a level related to eligibility for state welfare support. Formulas would be established to determine that individuals had pension entitlements, from both state and private sources, sufficient to deliver the minimum retirement income on an inflation-adjusted basis going forward.[68]

Make Annuitization the Default Option for Defined Contribution Plan Distributions

A less drastic proposal is to mandate that employers make annuitization the default distribution option in defined contribution plans. Plan distributions other than in annuity form would require the active and affirmative choice of the plan participant. This is the recommendation of the Department of Labor Advisory Council Working Group: "Require that all defined contribution plans offer annuities as the primary form of benefit for all distributions in excess of $5,000 and comply with the joint and survivor rules, unless the participant elects otherwise in conformance with the joint and survivor rules, including spousal consent."[69] To reduce the administrative burden on plan sponsors and

66. Under present rules, however, 25 percent of the pension account can be taken as a tax-free lump sum distribution. Prior to age 75, the plan participant can choose to substitute "income drawdown" for the purchase of an annuity. In income drawdown, the capital sum remains invested and individuals are allowed to draw an income from the account, as long as the income drawdown level stays within strict guidelines set forth by the government regulator.

67. Retirement Income Working Party (2000).

68. The enforcement mechanism for the current and proposed requirements, however, is left unclear in the Report.

69. U.S. Department of Labor (1998).

providers, defined contribution plans that are not primary plans might also be exempted from the default option mandate.

This proposal has several advantages and disadvantages compared with the proposals for mandatory annuitization and current practice. Clearly, the element of compulsion is missing and therefore freedom of choice and flexibility is preserved. Yet annuitization is encouraged, and this presumably would lead to some improvement in the functioning of annuity markets. Still, an additional administrative burden would be imposed on hundreds of thousands of plans that heretofore have avoided offering the annuity payment form.

There is empirical evidence that creating a default option has a powerful affect on plan participant behavior. Madrian and Shea examined the impact of a shift in one large 401(k) plan from affirmative election of participation to automatic enrollment with the right to decline.[70] No other economic feature of the plan changed and therefore it might be thought that behavior would not change. They found, however, that participation is significantly higher under automatic enrollment: the overall participation rate increased by twenty-five percentage points and the variation in participation rates with respect to demographic characteristics was reduced considerably. Similarly, the default contribution rate and fund allocation chosen by the plan sponsor had a significant influence on the behavior of plan participants. Madrian and Shea make reference to psychological factors such as procrastination, framing, and anchoring in explaining these results. This evidence implies that mandating an annuitization default option would probably substantially increase the selection of life annuities by plan participants.

Mandate or Encourage Primary Defined Contribution Plans to Offer Life Annuities

A less stringent requirement than mandating plans to provide annuitization as the default option is to require that primary defined contribution plans simply offer annuities as one of many distribution options. Alternatively, tax credit incentives could be given to plan sponsors to offer annuities through their plans. Such tax credits have been proposed for small employers to cover the administrative costs of sponsoring a new retirement plan.

It is unclear whether the mere fact that the retirement plan offers an annuity option would be sufficient to increase annuitization rates. Hence, it is uncertain whether this proposal would result in substantial public welfare gains. Furthermore, the requirement to offer annuities presumably would result in some increase in administrative burden for plan sponsors, at least initially. Clearly,

70. Madrian and Shea (2000).

however, it is the least intrusive on participant choice; indeed, it effectively expands the choice set available to most retirement plan participants.[71]

Although any annuity from a retirement plan is currently subject to the joint-and-survivor rules, unless the annuity is the default distribution option, other distributions from the retirement plan are not subject to the joint-and-survivor requirements. This exemption could be viewed either as an advantage or disadvantage. It is an advantage in that it results in a smaller administrative burden on the plan sponsor or provider; it is a disadvantage in that it exposes spouses to unexpected impoverishment in retirement.

Encourage Plan Participants to Choose Life Annuities for Asset Distribution

Under this proposal, distributions from retirement plans would receive favored tax treatment if they occurred through life annuities. For example, capital gains rates could be applied to the entire annuity payment or to the percentage of the distribution attributable to investment gains. Alternatively, a flat dollar amount or a percentage of annuity payments could be exempted from income taxation, similar to the current treatment of Social Security retirement annuity payments.

Although this alternative approach would presumably encourage annuitization, it would not be a mandate on either plan sponsors or a constraint on participant choice and therefore might be more attractive than some of the proposals mentioned above. The demand from plan participants for annuities, as well as the current legal requirement that retirement plans be run in the interests of their participants, would presumably be sufficient cause for many defined contribution plans to offer life annuities. Of course, there would be a revenue loss of unknown magnitude to the federal government from the change.[72] Furthermore, placing a tax wedge between alternative distribution options could lead to pure efficiency losses if it distorts the decisions of individuals who would otherwise rationally choose not to annuitize.

Create a Government-Sponsored Agency to Provide Life Annuities to Plan Participants

The last proposal we examine, which either could operate independently or in conjunction with the proposals listed above, would be to create an agency or

---

71. Of course, a plan participant can currently roll over 401(k) assets to an individual retirement annuity; this economically equivalent action, however, requires significant effort, particularly in search costs. A plan sponsor, who has already conducted a search for the best plan provider and investment manager, presumably is better capable of doing the search and negotiating the best deal possible.

72. Another approach that would increase government revenues and still encourage annuitization would be to penalize, say by the imposition of an excise tax, retirement plan distributions, both pre- and post-retirement, *not* in the form of life annuities.

organization sponsored by the federal government to offer life annuities to retirement plan participants. An analogy might be the TSP or the Federal Employee Group Life Insurance program for federal government workers. Theoretically, this organization could lower transaction and search costs and could underwrite product research and innovation to encourage annuitization, which in turn would lead to reduced adverse selection. There would be no increased burden on plan sponsors. A government-sponsored organization might be viewed as unfair competition to tax-paying and regulated commercial insurance companies, particularly those efficiently run and already providing safe and low-cost annuities to retirement plan participants. Warshawsky, writing in the context of Social Security reform, discussed the possibility of creating a federal board of overseers of annuity providers as well as a national clearinghouse for commercially sold annuities.[73] This mechanism would be analogous to the health plan for federal government workers; annuities from competing insurers could be offered in a clear and rational platform.

Conclusions

Annuities play the important economic role of insuring individuals against the financial risks associated with longevity uncertainty. In the absence of opportunities for annuitization, retirees are required to balance the risk of outliving their resources with the desire to increase consumption while alive. Those who choose to consume conservatively forgo the extra utility they could have achieved from a higher consumption level. Those who consume too aggressively risk finding themselves with insufficient resources at older ages. As a result of their ability to resolve these risks, annuities play a central role in the life-cycle theory of wealth decumulation.

One important implication of the shift from defined benefit to defined contribution pension plans is a reduction in opportunities for retirees to annuitize their retirement assets, because only a minority of defined contribution plans include a life annuity as one of the payout options. Even in those plans that offer an annuity option, the fact that it is optional means that individuals who do choose to annuitize will likely receive lower monthly income due to the lower mortality characteristics of the individual annuitant pool.

Policymakers interested in increasing annuitization rates, either out of concern for the welfare of individual retirees or to avoid excessive old-age dependence on government assistance programs, have a number of options available to them. Mandating annuitization is the most extreme measure and runs the risk of forcing annuitization on households that rationally do not value it. Alternatively, one could simply mandate that firms offering defined contribution

73. Warshawsky (1997).

plans offer an annuity as a payout option, possibly even as the default option. This approach preserves and enhances individual choice by expanding the set of distribution options available to individual retirees. Various tax incentives could also be used to encourage firms to offer and retirees to use annuity options. The downsides of this approach are lost government revenues and the potential tax distortions that this would introduce into the distribution decision. Government provision of annuities is also an option, although one that would clearly crowd out a growing private annuity market.

Appendix 11A
Calculation of Annuity Equivalent Wealth

The calculation of annuity equivalent wealth begins with a representative individual who is assumed to maximize an expected utility function V, by choosing an optimal consumption path (C_t) from time 0 to time T (the maximum possible life span), given a rate of time preference ρ and a vector of cumulative survival probabilities (P_t):

(1)
$$\underset{\{C_t\}}{\text{Max}} \sum_{t=0}^{T} \frac{P_t U(C_t)}{(1 + \rho)^t}.$$

The budget constraint facing this individual depends on whether he has access to annuities. In the absence of annuities, the constraint is that the present value of future consumption, discounted using the riskless interest rate r, be equal to the individual's initial wealth, W_0:

(2)
$$W_0 = \sum_{t=0}^{T} \frac{C_t}{(1 + r)^t}.$$

If this individual is able to purchase actuarially fair annuities, the budget constraint becomes:

(3)
$$W_0 = \sum_{t=0}^{T} \frac{P_t C_t}{(1 + r)^t}.$$

The difference between equation 2 and equation 3 is the role of survival probabilities. In equation 2, the present value of all future consumption must not exceed the initial wealth level. With annuities in equation 3, the budget constraint is that the *expected* present value of the consumption must equal initial wealth. This budget constraint assumes that the insurance company provides an actuarially fair annuity whose payout path exactly equals the consumption path chosen by the individual. In actuality, there may be additional constraints on the structure of the annuity path that make it suboptimal in some circumstances.[74]

Even before solving for the optimal consumption path, it is easy to see why annuities will be preferred in this model. One way to view the difference in the two budget constraints is to interpret the survival probabilities in equation 3 as the relative price of future consumption when annuities are available versus when they are not available. Viewed this way, the price of future consumption is always lower when annuities are available, since the value of $P_t < 1$ for all $t > 0$.

It is common to assume that the one-period utility function, $U(C_t)$, exhibits constant relative risk aversion, and can thus be defined as follows:

$$(4) \qquad U(C_t) = \frac{C_t^{1-\beta}}{1-\beta},$$

where β is the Arrow-Pratt coefficient of relative risk aversion, and $1/\beta$ is the elasticity of intertemporal substitution in consumption.

By maximizing equation 1 subject to equation 2 or 3, one can solve for the individual's optimal consumption path with or without access to annuities annuities. Each optimal C_t^* can be found as a function of W_0, ρ, r, β, and the full set of survival probabilities $\{P_t\}$, as follows:

$$(5) \qquad C_t^{no\ annuities} = W_0 \left(\frac{1+r}{1+\rho} \right)^{t/\beta} P_t^{1/\beta} \left(\sum_{j=0}^{T} \frac{(1+r)^{j(1-\beta)/\beta}}{(1+\rho)^{j/\beta}} P_j^{1/\beta} \right)^{-1}, \text{ and}$$

$$(6) \qquad C_t^{annuities} = W_0 \left(\frac{1+r}{1+\rho} \right)^{t/\beta} \left(\sum_{j=0}^{T} \frac{(1+r)^{j(1-\beta)/\beta}}{(1+\rho)^{j/\beta}} P_j \right)^{-1}.$$

To gain some intuition for the difference between these equations, it is useful to consider the special case in which the consumer has log utility ($\beta = 1$) and in which the interest rate and rate of time preference are equal to one another ($r = \rho$). In this case, equations 5 and 6 reduce to:

$$C_t^{no\ annuities} = P_t W_0 \left(\sum_{j=0}^{T} \frac{P_j}{(1+r)^j} \right)^{-1}, \text{ and}$$

$$C_t^{annuities} = W_0 \left(\sum_{j=0}^{T} \frac{P_j}{(1+r)^j} \right)^{-1}.$$

---

74. Yagi and Nishigaki (1993).

In this special case, the difference in the consumption at time t is proportional to the cumulative survival probability to time t. Since $P_0 = 1$ by definition, the level of consumption at time 0 is the same whether annuities are available or not. In the case with no annuities, consumption declines over time due to falling survival probabilities, whereas with annuities, the consumption profile is level for the rest of the individual's life. Thus, consumption with annuities is greater than or equal to consumption without annuities in all periods, and thus utility is higher.

By plugging the optimal consumption rules from equations 5 and 6 back into the lifetime utility function (1), one can construct the indirect utility functions, $V(.)$, that correspond to each budget constraint. These indirect utility functions express the maximum utility the individual can achieve by following the optimal consumption path as a function of the parameters W_0, r, ρ, β and $\{P_t\}$:

$$V_0(W_0)^{no\ annuities} = \frac{1}{1-\beta}\ W_0^{1-\beta}\left(\sum_{j=0}^{T} \frac{(1+r)^{j(1-\beta)/\beta}}{(1+\rho)^{j/\beta}}\ P_j^{1/\beta}\right)^{\beta}, \text{ and}$$

$$V_0(W_0)^{annuities} = \frac{1}{1-\beta}\ W_0^{1-\beta}\left(\sum_{j=0}^{T} \frac{(1+r)^{j(1-\beta)/\beta}}{(1+\rho)^{j/\beta}}\ P_j\right)^{\beta}.$$

As already indicated, for a given level of wealth W_0, an individual achieves a higher level of utility with annuities than without. It is possible to state this utility gain in dollar terms by determining how much additional wealth would need to be given to an individual without annuities to make him as well off as if he had annuities. This is done by finding the α such that:

$$V_0(\alpha W_0)^{no\ annuities} = V_0(W_0)^{annuities}.$$

The α is what we call the annuity equivalent wealth. In the case shown here, it is easy to solve for α analytically. However, once one begins to incorporate additional complexities, such as the presence of preexisting annuities, liquidity constraints, or other sources of uncertainty, solving for α must be done through dynamic programming solution techniques.[75]

75. Readers interested in the details of the dynamic programming algorithms should see Mitchell and others (1999) for the case of a single individual, Brown and Poterba (2000) for the case of couples, and Mitchell, Brown, and Poterba (1999) for the case in which returns, inflation, or both are uncertain.

Michael D. Hurd

Why do people not annuitize? There are at least four areas in which people could annuitize: they might purchase annuities in the private market; they might consume some of their home equity through a reverse annuity mortgage; they might choose to delay claiming Social Security benefits after retirement, which has the effect of increasing their Social Security annuity; and they might annuitize a pension right. On the first three options, the evidence is pretty clear: rather small fractions of the population annuitize: few purchase annuities; few choose a reverse annuity mortgage rather than a lump-sum; and few delay claiming Social Security benefits after retirement. Whether people choose to annuitize pension rights is one of the topics of the Brown and Warshawsky paper, and the topic is well chosen because of our relative lack of knowledge of the basic facts and because of the importance of the choice for the future economic status of the elderly.

At a basic level, more facts are needed. What fraction of workers who have defined benefit plans actually have a choice of a lump-sum cash-out rather than a pension? What fraction of workers who have defined contribution plans have a choice to annuitize within an employer's risk pool as opposed to purchasing an annuity on the private market? Among those who actually have a choice, how many choose to annuitize, and what are the characteristics of those who do annuitize? The Brown and Warshawsky paper makes clear that there are widely varying estimates of these basic facts. Therefore, this paper is very welcome.

Before we can understand whether we should expect people to annuitize pension rights when they are given the choice to annuitize or cash out, we need to understand from a theoretical point of view the circumstances under which annuitization increases lifetime utility, and what determines the magnitude of the gain. Brown and Warshawsky discuss a number of the determinants of the gain, and the discussion is valuable because it quantifies some basic facts such as the load factor in the private pension market. I will not have anything to say about this aspect of their discussion because I agree with it. Rather, from a somewhat different perspective, I will expand their discussion of the theoretical model. The objective is to show what additional factors determine the decision to annuitize. I conclude that there are good reasons for the low levels of annuitization, again leaving aside annuitization within the pension system where knowledge of the levels is lacking.

Figure 11-3. *Consumption Path*

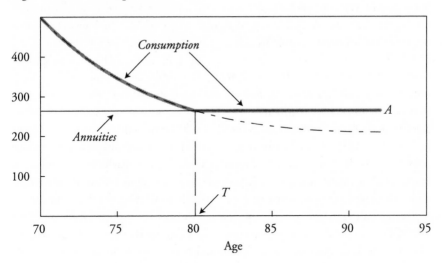

Life-Cycle Model of Consumption

Figure 11-3 shows a typical consumption path under the life-cycle model. An annuity stream, which for most people would be Social Security benefits, is given by A. At age T, which in this example is 80, bequeathable wealth would have been consumed, and from that age on consumption would be A. Before T, consumption follows the optimal path that would be found from the first-order conditions for utility maximization.

Typically the value of an annuity stream is found by calculating the expected present value, which depends on the survival curve and on an interest rate. In the simplest situation one dollar of wealth purchases about one dollar's worth of an actuarially fair annuity. Yet, as explained in the appendix to Brown and Warshawsky, the annuity will finance a higher level of consumption than the bequeathable wealth, so it seems obvious that everyone will always want to annuitize all of his wealth. For a given level of annuities, however, the consumption path does not follow the optimal consumption path after T, which causes the annuity to produce less utility than it would were the optimal consumption path to be followed. The consumption path does not follow the first-order conditions after T because of a side condition that bequeathable wealth cannot be negative.

The utility value of a marginal purchase of annuities by an individual who has a given level of bequeathable wealth and a predetermined level of annuities can be expressed as a marginal rate of substitution (MRS), which gives the number of dollars of bequeathable wealth that someone would be willing to pay for one dollar of annuity wealth. In most circumstances the MRS will be greater than one, and when mortality risk is high, it could be considerably greater than one. Brown and Warshawsky have some examples of the discrete trade-off between bequeathable wealth and annuity wealth, what they call annuity equivalent wealth. Were the MRS constant, it would be the same as annuity equivalent wealth. As the examples in their tables 11-1 through 11-4 show, annuity equivalent wealth varies with economic resources, particularly the mix between bequeathable wealth and annuities. For example, a comparison of columns 2 and 5 of table 11-3 shows that someone with half of initial wealth in annuities would be willing to pay considerably less per dollar to annuitize completely than would someone with no initial annuities. This implies that the MRS is not constant but declines gradually as an individual continues to annuitize. Stated differently, in a population there will be a distribution of the MRS even among individuals who have identical tastes.

In a life-cycle model estimated over data from the Retirement History Survey, I calculated the mean MRS in the population ages approximately 68–74 to be 1.41. That is, on average the survey population would have been willing to pay $1.41 for $1 of expected present value of annuities. If annuities are priced to be actuarially fair, the cost would be $1, so on average there would be considerable gain from increased annuitization.[1] The ninetieth percentile of the MRS was 1.62 and the tenth percentile was 1.27. This variation is based purely on the variation in the mix between bequeathable wealth and annuities that was observed in the survey: utility function parameters and the interest rate were assumed to be the same for all survey cohort members.

In general, the MRS is large when T in figure 11-3 is large. This happens because large T means that the individual would not be forced off his optimal consumption path for many years, and the effect of the distortion would not have large effects on lifetime utility due to discounting. The example in figure 11-3 can be used to illustrate which parameters and variables determine the value of T and, therefore, of an annuity. If bequeathable wealth is high relative to the level of annuities, T will occur only very late in life, which implies that there will be a low probability that the actual consumption path will differ from the optimal path. Thus, a high level of bequeathable wealth increases the value of an annuity and the MRS. In a similar way, anything that flattens the consumption path causing T to increase will increase the value of an annuity. A reduction in mortality risk (increase in life expectancy), a reduction in the

---

1. Hurd (1987b). The assumed interest rate on the annuities was 3 percent.

subjective time rate of discount, and an increase in risk aversion will all act to increase T, and, therefore, will increase the MRS and the desirability of annuitizing bequeathable wealth on the margin.

The conclusion is that the value of annuitizing will vary from individual to individual because of variations in economic status and also because of variations in tastes as reflected in the subjective time rate of discount and in risk aversion. Although the annuity equivalent wealth figures given in the tables of Brown and Warshawsky are all greater than one, the MRS can be less than one. For example, someone who has little bequeathable wealth and whose subjective time rate of discount is greater than the interest rate will have an MRS less than one. Such a person would prefer to sell some annuity rights at the actuarially fair rate.

There are at least two other causes of variation in the value of annuitization that I believe could be quite important in explaining the low levels of annuitization. We need to distinguish between a population morality rate, which could be the mortality rate of the entire population in the case of Social Security and of the actual purchasers of annuities in the case of the private market, and the perceived mortality rate of an individual. The population mortality rate enters the pricing of an annuity: when the mortality rate is high, the cost of a given stream of annuity payments is low. For an individual the value of an annuity depends on his subjective survival probability: greater subjective survival causes an annuity to be more valuable because it acts like a reduction in the subjective time rate of discount, flattening the consumption path in figure 11-3 and increasing T. Subjective survival is generally not observed, but it is queried in the Health and Retirement Study. It is positively correlated with observable correlates of longevity, and it is predictive of actual survival.

A second cause of variation in the value of annuitizing is a possible difference between the interest rate that is used to price the annuity and the interest rate that is available for investments of bequeathable wealth. As is well known, over long periods of time the returns in the stock market have dominated returns in the bond market by a very substantial amount. To the extent that individuals view the alternative use of bequeathable wealth to be investments in the stock market rather than in annuities, there could be a large wedge between the annuity interest rate and the return on alternative investments. Because annualized mortality risk is fairly low at retirement, individuals with access to the stock market or to other investments with high rates of return may believe that alternative investments absolutely dominate the annuity market in the sense that the alternative will produce a higher flow of investment income even without invading the principal. The alternative investment has the further advantage of satisfying a precautionary motive and of being bequeathable. I have used the stock market as an example, but I am sure that at other times long-term corporate debt would have absolutely dominated the annuity market. In this situation no one would purchase an annuity.

Table 11-14. *Effects on the Propensity to Annuitize*

Life table mortality	increase
Subjective mortality	decrease
Interest rate on annuities	increase
Interest rate on bequeathable wealth	decrease
Initial bequeathable wealth	increase
Initial annuities	decrease
Subjective time rate of discount	decrease
Risk aversion	increase

Note that it is the perceived rate of return on alternative investments that helps determine whether annuitization is desirable. But the perceived rate is not observable and is likely to vary from individual to individual. Because of the very large gains in the stock market during the late 1990s, it is not unreasonable to suppose that many individuals believe that an appropriate rate of return on an alternative investment is in the double digits.

Table 11-14 summarizes this discussion: it indicates the effect of changes in a number of factors on the desirability of annuitizing. From the table it is evident that a person who would want to annuitize would have a high ratio of bequeathable wealth to initial annuities, would have high subjective survival, a low subjective interest rate on alternative investments, high risk aversion, and a low time rate of discount.

The most obvious candidate for annuitizing would be a high-wealth person. However, such an individual may view the alternative investment to be stocks, where, according to Kent Smetters in this volume, the rate of return might be 0.09 (real) versus 0.03 (real) in annuities. Furthermore, such a person is likely to have rather low risk aversion: indeed someone with low risk aversion is more likely to have invested in stocks, causing him to have accumulated more wealth. On the other side, a typical characterization of a high-wealth person is that he has a low discount rate and high objective as well as subjective survival.

In addition to the factors quantified by Brown and Warshawsky, a bequest motive for saving and a precautionary motive for holding wealth also reduce the desire to annuitize. While it is difficult to know the magnitudes, they would reduce the propensity further among some fraction of the population.

The conclusion is that individuals who, on the basis of observed wealth status, might gain a good deal from annuitization have other unobserved characteristics that would reduce and could even eliminate the gain from annuitization. Heterogeneity is important: the correlations between observable and unobservable characteristics are such that the analysis of a representative person is likely not to be very informative.

Claiming of Social Security Benefits

It has been pointed out that claiming of Social Security benefits after retirement is the same kind of decision as that involved in the purchase of annuities.[2] Someone who retires at age 62 has the option of taking Social Security immediately or delaying claiming. If someone delays claiming for a year, financing consumption out of bequeathable wealth, his or her Social Security benefit will be increased by approximately 8 percent at age 63. Thus, the delay involves the implicit marginal purchase of 8 percent more in Social Security annuities by the expenditure of a year's Social Security benefits. The aim of the 8 percent increase in benefit was to make the implicit purchase actuarially fair, and as the calculations in Coile and others show, that is approximately the case for a single male based on population life tables and a real interest rate of 3 percent.[3]

The fact that Social Security is approximately fair is not, however, the determinant of whether someone should "purchase" additional Social Security benefits by delaying claiming. The determinant is whether expected lifetime utility is increased. Based on a life-cycle model that has the same features as the model that generated figure11-3, Coile and others find that for representative single men, there is a gain from delaying claiming, and the gain varies with bequeathable wealth and risk aversion in the way I have discussed. The authors give no information about the MRS at age 62, but because for many cases the optimal claiming delay is less than thirty-six months (the number of months between age 62 and 65), I infer that the MRS is not very large initially. I infer this from the fact that at the optimal claiming age, the MRS is one; yet to decline from its initial value, which is determined by Social Security benefits at age 62, to one requires an increase in Social Security benefits of less than 25 percent.[4] Nonetheless, conditional on the assumed parameters, the simulations predict substantial delays in claiming.

Based on data from a 1982 survey, Coile and others find, however, that very few delay claiming. Among those who retired before age 62, 81 percent claimed within the first month of reaching age 62, and 91 percent within the first year. Just 3 percent delay claiming until age 65, at which age the implicit price becomes no longer actuarially fair.

The authors conclude that "part of the population simply claims immediately without sufficient consideration of intertemporal choice issues." An alternative point of view, which is plausible because of the importance of tastes and

2. Coile and others (2002).
3. Coile and others (2002).
4. At age 62 the Social Security benefit is 80 percent of the primary insurance amount, and if claiming is delayed until 65 the benefit is 100 percent of the primary insurance amount. Thus delaying until 65 results in an increase of 25 percent in the Social Security benefit.

perceptions, is that observable characteristics combined with unobservable tastes and subjective beliefs mean that for most retirees it is not optimal to delay, and that as in other types of empirical analysis we can learn about unobserved tastes and perceptions by studying claiming behavior. Social Security claiming behavior provides important information about the desire to annuitize because we understand completely the Social Security rules and we know the population to which the rules apply. This is in distinction to private pensions where we have limited information about who is eligible to annuitize and to the private market for annuities where pricing varies from firm to firm, and the characteristics of the target population are unknown.

Furthermore, as a vehicle to insure against longevity risk, Social Security dominates both privately purchased annuities and pension annuities. First, based on a life table for the entire elderly population, the implicit price of additional Social Security benefits is approximately actuarially fair. The effect of basing it on the general population life table rather than on a selected life table can be seen in table 11-12 of Brown and Warshawsky: based on the general population an annuity would pay about 6 percent more than one based on group annuitants (such as an employer's defined contribution plan beneficiaries), which in turn would pay about 4 percent more than one based on individual annuitants. Second, Social Security benefits are indexed. Third, at least historically there has been no risk about the payment of Social Security benefits. Yet, even with these three advantages the implicit purchase of additional Social Security annuities through delayed claiming is not common. Therefore, it is not surprising to find few purchases of annuities in situations lacking these advantages.

Evidence from the HRS

Brown and Warshawsky cite results from wave 1 of the Health and Retirement Survey (HRS) about intentions to annuitize: about 48 percent of respondents intend to annuitize at least part of their defined contribution accounts. Yet in actual annuitizations observed between waves 1 and 2, 2 and 3, and 3 and 4 of the HRS, just 3 percent of defined contribution plan dispositions were annuitized: the remainder were either cashed out or maintained in some way.[5] Taking the annuitization rate to be a two-year steady-state hazard of annuitizing, I estimate that about 15 percent of defined contribution dispositions will eventually be annuitized. In view of the lack of knowledge that the general population has about annuities, I have more confidence in actual annuitizations than in intentions to annuitize, and so I will characterize the evidence from the HRS as showing rather low levels of lifetime annuitization from defined contribution accounts.

5. Hurd and Panis (2003).

Rates of Annuitization from DC accounts

The rates of annuitization vary but are low in two of the studies cited by Brown and Warshawsky. In the Thrift Savings Plan, it apparently is 1.2 percent a year, which is fairly close to the rate observed in the HRS (a two-year rate of 3 percent). Figure 11-1 in Brown and Warshawsky shows very low fractions receiving annuity payments, and although I realize the system might not be in steady state, it indicates that annuitization will not be the norm. The rate estimated by Hurd and Panis based on the HRS is just 15 percent, and the marginal rate based on Social Security claiming behavior is just 20 percent.[6] The exception to these findings is TIAA-CREF, which is a highly selected, relatively high-wealth pool and so is unlikely to be representative of the general population. Furthermore, because of its relatively high wealth, the economic status of TIAA-CREF participants is not the object of most policy concern. My conclusion is that the rate of annuitization from defined contribution plans is much lower than the implicit rate from defined benefit plans. Further analysis can show how much of this low rate is due to unavailability of group annuities in defined contribution plans and how much is due to unwillingness to annuitize given availability. The Social Security results, however, do not suggest a large role for a lack of availability.

Future Rates of Annuitization

Brown and Warshawsky conclude that the proportion of economic resources represented by annuitized wealth will fall as new cohorts reach retirement age. I agree and believe the decline could be substantial. Although there is some uncertainty about the present rates of annuitization from defined contribution plans conditional on availability, I expect the low rates I have discussed to be verified when more complete data and studies are available. First, the population of obvious annuitizers is likely to be small. Second, observed behavior, particularly Social Security claiming, points to low rates. Third, other factors outside of the life-cycle model, such as a precautionary saving motive, would further reduce the rates. There is, of course, considerable uncertainty about this forecast. There is uncertainty about the right to annuitize within defined contribution plans, and availability could increase. Furthermore, cohort studies based on the HRS indicate that the cohorts retiring in, say, ten years will have more bequeathable wealth than the cohorts retiring today: Their higher wealth levels should make annuitization more valuable, leading to higher rates than observed in data today.

6. Coile and others (2002).

Public policy should be concerned about the possible effect of a decline in annuitization on the economic status of the oldest-old. Of the policy measures discussed by Brown and Warshawsky, encouraging defined contribution plans to provide an attractively priced annuity option would seem to be relatively low cost and not to be overly intrusive. As such this policy should be tried first; but, if, as is likely, availability is not an important cause of the low levels of annuitization, the choice of further policies would become more difficult.

References

American Council of Life Insurers (ACLI). Various years. *Life Insurance Fact Book*. Washington.

———. 1999. "Positioning and Promoting Annuities in a New Retirement Environment." Task Force on Annuity Messages. Washington.

Ameriks, John. 1999. "The Retirement Patterns and Annuitization Decisions of a Cohort of TIAA-CREF Participants." *Research Dialogues* issue 60. TIAA-CREF Institute, New York. August.

Bernheim, Douglas D. 1991. "How Strong Are Bequest Motives? Evidence Based on Estimates of the Demand for Life Insurance and Annuities." *Journal of Political Economy* 99: 899–927.

Brown, Jeffrey R. 2001. "Are the Elderly Really Over-Annuitized? New Evidence on Life Insurance and Bequests" In D. Wise, ed., *Themes in the Economics of Aging*. University of Chicago Press.

———. 2001. "Private Pensions, Mortality Risk, and the Decision to Annuitize." *Journal of Public Economics* 82 (1): 29–62.

Brown, Jeffrey R., and James M. Poterba. 2000. "Joint Life Annuities and Annuity Demand by Married Couples." *Journal of Risk and Insurance* 67 (4): 527–53.

Brown Jeffrey R., Olivia S. Mitchell, and James M. Poterba. 2001. "The Role of Real Annuities and Indexed Bonds in an Individual Accounts Retirement Program." In J. Campbell and M. Feldstein, eds., *Risk Aspects of Investment-Based Social Security Reform*. University of Chicago Press.

———. 2002. "Mortality Risk, Inflation Risk, and Annuity Products." In O. Mitchell and others, *Innovations in Retirement Financing*. University of Pennsylvania Press.

Cohen, Marc A. 1998. "Emerging Trends in the Finance and Delivery of Long-Term Care: Public and Private Opportunities and Challenges." *Gerontologist* 38 (1): 80–89.

Coile, Courtney, and others. 2002. "Delays in Claiming Social Security Benefits." *Journal of Public Economics* 84 (3): 357–85.

Employee Benefit Research Institute (EBRI). 1997. *EBRI Databook on Employee Benefits*, 4th ed. Washington.

Friedman, Benjamin, and Mark Warshawsky. 1988. "Annuity Prices and Saving Behavior in the United States." In Zvi Bodie, John Shoven, and David Wise, eds., *Pensions in the U.S. Economy*. University of Chicago Press.

———. 1990. "The Cost of Annuities: Implications for Saving Behavior and Bequests." *Quarterly Journal of Economics* 105 (February):135–54.

Gale, William G., and Joel Slemrod. 2001. "Overview." In William G. Gale, James R. Hines Jr., and Joel Slemrod, eds., *Rethinking Estate and Gift Taxation*. Brookings.

Health Insurance Association of America. 1997. *Long-Term Care: Knowing the Risk, Paying the Price*. Washington.

Hurd, Michael D. 1987a. "Savings of the Elderly and Desired Bequests." *American Economic Review* 77 (3): 298–312.

———. 1987b. "The Marginal Value of Social Security." Working Paper 2411. Cambridge, Mass.: National bureau of Economic Research.

———. 1989. "Mortality Risk and Bequests." *Econometrica* 57 (4): 779–813.

———. 1999. "Mortality Risk and Consumption by Couples." NBER Working Paper 7048. Cambridge, Mass.: National Bureau of Economic Research.

Hurd, Michael D., and Constantijn Panis. 2003. "The Choice to Cash out Pension Rights at Job Change or Retirement." RAND typescript.

Hurd, Michael D., and David A. Wise. 1989. "The Wealth and Poverty of Widows: Assets before and after the Husband's Death." In David Wise, ed., *The Economics of Aging*. University of Chicago Press.

Johansen, R. 1996. "Review of Adequacy of 1983 Individual Annuity Mortality Table." *Transactions of the Society of Actuaries* 47: 101–23.

Kotlikoff, Laurence J., and Avia Spivak. 1981. "The Family as an Incomplete Annuities Market." *Journal of Political Economy* 89 (April): 372–91.

Laitner, John, and F. Thomas Juster. 1996. "New Evidence on Altruism: A Study of TIAA-CREF Retirees." *American Economic Review* 86: 893–908.

Madrian, Brigitte C., and Dennis F. Shea. 2001. "The Power of Suggestion: Inertia in 401(k) Participation and Savings Behavior." *Quarterly Journal of Economics* 116(4): 1149–87.

Masnick, George. 2000. "Projected Tenure Choice." Paper prepared for Harvard University Joint Center for Housing Studies.

McGill, Dan M., and others. 1996. *Fundamentals of Private Pensions, Seventh Edition*. University of Pennsylvania Press for the Pension Research Council of the Wharton School.

Mitchell, Olivia S. 2000. "New Trends in Pension Benefit and Retirement Provisions." Pension Research Council Working Paper 2000-1. University of Pennsylvania, Wharton School.

Mitchell, Olivia S., and James F. Moore. 1998. "Can Americans Afford to Retire? New Evidence on Retirement Saving Adequacy." *Journal of Risk and Insurance* 65 (3): 371–400.

Mitchell, Olivia S., and others. 1999. "New Evidence on the Money's Worth of Individual Annuities." *American Economic Review* 89 (December): 1299–1318.

Murtaugh, Christopher, Peter Kemper, and Brenda Spillman. 1995. "Risky Business: Long-Term Care Insurance Underwriting." *Inquiry* (Fall): 271–84.

Murtaugh, Christopher, and others. 1997. "The Amount, Distribution, and Timing of Lifetime Nursing Home Use." *Medical Care* 35 (3): 204–18.

Poterba, James M., and Mark J. Warshawsky. 1999. "The Cost of Annuitizing Retirement Payouts from Individual Accounts." NBER Working Paper 6918. Cambridge, Mass.: National Bureau of Economic Research.

Poterba, James M., Steven F. Venti, and David A. Wise. 2000. "Saver Behavior and 401(k) Retirement Wealth." *American Economic Review* 90 (May): 297–302.

Retirement Income Working Party, United Kingdom. 2000. "Choices—An Independent Report to Encourage the Debate on Retirement Income. " (www.bbk.ac.uk/res/pi/reports).

Social Security Trustees. 2000. "The 2000 OASDI Trustees Report." Social Security Administration, Washington.

Society of Actuaries. 1995. "Report of the Group Annuity Experience Committee: Group Annuity Mortality."

U.S. Department of Labor. Various years. *Employee Benefits in Medium and Large Firms.*

U.S. Department of Labor, Advisory Council on Employee Welfare and Pension Benefits. 1998. "Are We Cashing Out Our Future?" Report of the Working Group on Retirement Plan Leakage, November 13. (www.dol.gov/dol/pwba/public/adcoun/leaknew1.htm).

U.S. Department of Labor, Pension and Welfare Benefits Administration, Office of Policy and Research. 1999–2000. "Private Pension Plan Bulletin: Abstract of 1996, Form 5500 Reports. " (No. 9, Winter).

U.S. Department of Labor, Pension and Welfare Benefits Administration, Office of Research and Economic Analysis. 1995. "Retirement Benefits of American Workers: New Findings from the September 1994 Current Population Survey." (July.)

Venti, Steven, and David A. Wise. 2000. "Choice, Chance, and Wealth Dispersion at Retirement." NBER Working Paper 7521. Cambridge, Mass.: National Bureau of Economic Research.

Walliser, Jan. 2001. "Regulation of Withdrawals in Individual Account Systems." In *New Ideas about Old Age Security,* edited by Robert Holzman and Joseph Stiglitz. Washington: World Bank.

Warshawsky, Mark J. 1997. "The Market for Individual Annuities and the Reform of Social Security." *Benefits Quarterly* (third quarter): 66–76.

Warshawsky, Mark J., Lee Granza, and Anna Madamba. 2000. "Financing Long-Term Care: Needs, Attitudes, Current Insurance Products, and Policy Innovations." TIAA-CREF Institute *Research Dialogues* 63 (March).

Warshawsky, Mark J., Brenda Spillman, and Chris Murtaugh. 2002. "Integrating the Life Annuity and Long-Term Care Insurance: Theory, Evidence, Practice, and Policy. " In Olivia Mitchell and others, eds., *Innovations in Retirement Financing.* University of Pennsylvania Press.

Yaari, Menahem E. 1965. "Uncertain Lifetime, Life Insurance, and the Theory of the Consumer." *Review of Economic Studies* 32: 137–50.

Yagi, Tadashi, and Yasuyuki Nishigaki. 1993. "The Inefficiency of Private Constant Annuities." *Journal of Risk and Insurance* 60(3): 385–412.

Glossary

To help readers without extensive background in pensions to understand some of the technical terms mentioned in the papers published in this volume, we have reproduced, with permission and with slight modifications, a number of pension terms from *Employee Benefit Plans: A Glossary of Terms,* 10th edition, 2000, edited by Judith A. Sankey and published by the International Foundation of Employee Benefit Plans, Brookfield, Wisconsin.

Accrual of Benefits In the case of a defined benefit pension plan, the process of accumulating pension credits for years of credited service, expressed in the form of an annual benefit to begin payment at normal retirement age. In the case of a defined contribution plan, the process of accumulating funds in the individual employee's pension account.

Accrued Benefits For any retirement plan that is not a defined benefit pension plan, a participant's accrued benefit is the balance in his or her plan account, whether vested or not. In the case of a defined benefit pension plan, a participant's accrued benefit is his or her benefit as determined under the terms of the plan expressed in the form of an annual benefit commencing at normal retirement age. Under ERISA, three alternative methods of benefit accrual are allowed. See *Back-Loading.*

Actual Contribution Percentage (ACP) In a qualified retirement plan, the average of the ratios of aggregate contributions (matching contributions and after-tax employee contributions) to compensation. It is figured for two groups: highly compensated employees and nonhighly compensated employees. The ratio for each employee is calculated, and then it is averaged for the group. See also *Aggregate Limit; Alternative Limitation.*

Actual Deferral Percentage (ADP)   In a qualified retirement plan such as a 401(k) plan, the average of the ratios of elective contributions to compensation is figured for two groups: highly compensated employees and nonhighly compensated employees. The ratio first is figured for each employee, and then averaged for each group. See also *Aggregate Limit; Alternative Limitation.*

Actuarial Accrued Liability   (1) The actuarial accrued liability of a pension plan at any time is the excess of the present value, as of the date of valuation, of total prospective benefits of the plan (plus administrative expenses if included in the normal cost) over the present value of future normal cost accruals, determined by the actuarial cost method in use. (2) That portion, as determined by a particular actuarial cost method, of the actuarial present value of pension plan benefits and expenses that is not provided for by future normal costs. The presentation of an actuarial accrued liability should be accompanied by reference to the actuarial cost method used.

Actuarial Assumptions   Factors used by the actuary in forecasting uncertain future events affecting pension cost. They involve such things as interest and investment earnings, inflation, unemployment, mortality rates, and retirement patterns.

Actuarial Soundness   (1) An actuarial concept relating to the degree of assurance (existing under an employer's program for funding pension cost) that the funds set aside under a pension plan will be sufficient to meet the pension payments provided for in the plan. Actuaries have not defined objective standards for determining actuarial soundness. (2) The statement that the money set aside under a pension plan will be sufficient to meet the pension payments as calculated.

Actuarial Valuation   (1) An examination of a pension plan to determine whether contributions are being accumulated at a rate sufficient to provide the funds out of which the promised pensions can be paid when due. The valuation shows the actuarial liabilities of the plan and the applicable assets. (2) The determination, as of a valuation date, of the normal cost, actuarial accrued liability, actuarial value of assets, and related actuarial present values for a pension plan.

Age Discrimination in Employment Act (ADEA)   Protects workers over age 40 from compulsory retirement at any age so long as they are capable of performing their jobs adequately. It also protects them from adverse job actions based on age (for example, refusal to hire; discriminatory layoff) and against benefits discrimination. Employers are subject to ADEA if they engage in an industry affecting interstate commerce and had 20 or more employees in each working day of 20 or more weeks in the current or preceding calendar year.

Aggregate Limit   In nondiscrimination testing, this is used to determine inequalities in the deferral or contribution rates of highly versus nonhighly compensated employees when at least one highly compensated employee is eligible to participate in a 401(k) plan. The aggregate limit is a combination of the ADP and ACP of the nonhighly compensated employees: 125 percent of the higher percentage and the lower percentage plus two points (the higher percentage can be up to 200 percent of the lower percentage). The sum of ADP and ACP of the highly compensated cannot exceed the aggregate limit. See also *Alternative Limitation.*

Alternative Limitation   An alternate nondiscrimination test. The ACP and ADP percentage of highly compensated employees cannot be more than double the ACP and ADP of nonhighly compensated employees. In addition, the difference cannot exceed 2 percentage points. See also *Aggregate Limit.*

Annuity   (1) A contract that provides an income for a specified period of time such as a number of years or for life. (2) The periodic payments provided under an annuity contract. (3) The specified monthly or annual payment to a pensioner. Often used synonymously with *pension.*

Asset Reversion   Following the termination of a pension plan, the recovery by the sponsoring employer of any pension fund assets in excess of those required to pay accrued benefits. The recovered assets are subject to regular corporate income tax as well as an excise tax of either 20 percent or 50 percent, depending on subsequent retirement arrangements made for employees.

Back-Loading   The practice of providing a faster rate of benefit accrual after an employee has attained a specified age or has completed a specified number of years of service. For example, back-loading occurs in a plan that provides a benefit of 1.5 percent of compensation for each year of service before age 50 and 2 percent a year thereafter. The practice is limited under ERISA. See also *Accrued Benefits.*

Cash Balance Plan   A defined benefit plan that simulates a defined contribution plan. Benefits are definitely determinable, but account balances are credited with a fixed rate of return and converted to a monthly pension benefit at retirement.

Compulsory Retirement   When the employee must retire when he or she reaches a given age. Now prohibited under ADEA if based solely on age, except for certain executives or where public safety outweighs individual protection (such as airline pilots). Also known as *automatic* or *mandatory retirement.*

Contribution   The transfer of funds or property by either an employer or an employee to an employee benefit plan.

Contribution Limit   The maximum dollar limit on annual additions (employer contributions, certain employee contributions, and forfeitures) for an employee under defined contribution plans of an employer.

Current Liability   Money owed and payable by a company, usually within one year.

Defined Benefit Plan   Both ERISA and the Internal Revenue Code define a defined benefit plan as any plan that is not an individual account plan. Under a defined benefit plan, there is a definite formula by which the employee's benefits will be measured. This formula may provide that benefits be a particular percentage of the employee's average compensation over his or her entire service or over a particular number of years; it may provide for a flat monthly payment; or it may provide a definite amount for each year of service, expressed either as a percentage of his or her compensation for each year of service or as a flat dollar amount for each year of service. In plans of this type, the employer's contributions are determined actuarially. No individual accounts are maintained as is done in the defined contribution plans. (Defined benefit plans are subject to regulation by the Pension Benefit Guaranty Corporation and are "pension plans" under the Internal Revenue Code. That is, they are designed primarily for retirement.)

Defined Contribution Plan   A defined contribution or individual account plan is defined by the Internal Revenue Code and ERISA as a plan that provides for an individual account for each participant and for benefits based solely on (1) the amount contributed to the participant's account plus (2) any income, expenses, gains and losses, and forfeitures of accounts of other participants that may be allocated to the participant's account. 401(k), 403(b) and 457 plans are defined contribution plans.

Early Retirement   A termination of employment involving the payment of a retirement allowance before a participant is eligible for normal retirement. The retirement allowance payable in the event of early retirement is often lower than the accrued portion of the normal retirement allowance.

Employee Retirement Income Security Act of 1974 (ERISA)   Federal statute that requires persons engaged in the administration, supervision, and management of pension monies to have a fiduciary responsibility to ensure that all investment-related decisions are made (1) with the care, skill, prudence, and diligence that a prudent man familiar with such matters would use and (2) by diversifying the investments so as to minimize risk. This wording mandates two significant changes in traditional investment practice: the age-old "prudent man" rule has been replaced by the notion of a prudent "expert"; and the notion of a prudent investment has been replaced by the concept of a prudent portfolio.

ERISA also established the Pension Benefit Guaranty Corporation (PBGC), an insurance program designed to guarantee workers receipt of pension benefits if their defined benefit pension plans should terminate. ERISA includes requirements for funding, bonding, trusts, claims procedures, reporting and disclosure, and prohibited transactions. It regulates the majority of private pension and welfare group benefit plans in the United States.

Employee Stock Ownership Plan (ESOP)   A qualified stock bonus plan or a qualified stock bonus and money purchase plan. Like a stock bonus plan, the contributions need not be dependent on profits, and benefits are distributable in the stock of the employer corporation. Typically, the ESOP is used as a financing vehicle for the employer corporation: The plan borrows money from the employer or uses the employer's credit, and purchases employer stock. The borrowed money is paid to the employer for its stock. The loan is repaid with annual employer contributions.

Enrolled Actuary (EA) A person who performs actuarial service for a plan and who is enrolled with the federal Joint Board for the Enrollment of Actuaries.

Entry Age Actuarial Cost Method Also called *entry age normal actuarial cost method.* A method under which the actuarial present value of the projected benefits of each individual included in an actuarial valuation is allocated on a level basis over the earnings or service of the individual between entry age and assumed exit age(s). The portion of this actuarial present value allocated to a valuation year is called the *normal cost.* The portion of this actuarial present value not provided for a valuation date by the actuarial present value of future normal costs is called the *actuarial accrued liability.* Under this method, the actuarial gains (losses) are reflected as they occur in a decrease (increase) in the unfunded actuarial accrued liability.

Excise Taxes An employer that contributes to a qualified plan will be subject to an excise tax liability for failing to contribute the amount determined to be an accumulated funding deficiency (excess of total charges over total credits in funding the standard account). The tax initially is to be 5 percent of the accumulated funding deficiency at the end of the plan year.

Fiduciary (1) Indicates the relationship of trust and confidence where one person (the fiduciary) holds or controls property for the benefit of another person. For example, the relationship between a trustee and the beneficiaries of the trust. (2) Under ERISA any person who (a) exercises any discretionary authority or control over the management of a plan or the management or disposition of its assets, (b) renders investment advice for a fee or other compensation with respect to the funds or property of a plan, or has the authority to do so, or (c) has any discretionary authority or responsibility in the administration of a plan. (3) One who acts in a capacity of trust and who is therefore accountable for whatever actions may be constructed by the courts as breaching that trust. Under ERISA, fiduciaries must discharge their duties solely in the interest of the participants and beneficiaries of an employee benefit plan. In addition, a fiduciary must act exclusively for the purpose of providing benefits to participants and beneficiaries in defraying reasonable expenses of the plan.

Final Pay Plan (Final Pay Formula) A benefit formula that bases benefits on the employee's compensation over a specified number of years near the end of the employee's service period or on the employee's highest compensation periods. For example, a plan might provide annual pension benefits equal to 1 percent of the employee's average salary for the last five years (or the highest consecutive five years) for each year of service. A final pay plan is a plan with such a formula.

Flexible Benefit Plan   A benefit program under Section 125 of the Internal Revenue Code that offers employees a choice between permissible taxable benefits, including cash, and nontaxable health and welfare benefits such as life and health insurance, vacation pay, retirement plans, and child care. Although a common core of benefits may be required, the employee can determine how his or her remaining benefit dollars are to be allocated for each type of benefit from the total amount promised by the employer. Sometimes employee contributions may be made for additional coverage.

Form 5500   A joint agency financial form developed by the IRS, Department of Labor, and PBGC that may be used to satisfy the annual reporting requirements of the IRC and Titles I and IV of ERISA.

401(h) Plan   A provision of a pension or annuity plan that provides for the payment of benefits for sickness, accident, hospitalization, and medical expenses, of retired employees, their spouses, and their dependents, subject to certain requirements.

401(k) Plan   A plan under which employees can elect to defer income by making pretax contributions. The plan also may allow for employer matching contributions. A Section 401(k) plan is a defined contribution plan.

403(b) Annuity   An annuity that provides retirement income for employees of certain tax-exempt organizations or public schools. Also known as a *tax-sheltered annuity.*

457 Plan   An elective contribution tax-deferred arrangement available to states, political subdivisions of a state, or any agency or instrumentality of a state under Code Section 457.

Frozen Plan   A qualified retirement plan that has stopped employer contributions and benefit accrual by participants. The plan sponsor continues to distribute plan assets and maintain the trust.

Fully Funded   (1) A specific element of pension cost (for example, past service cost) is said to have been fully funded if the amount of the cost has been paid in full to funding an agency. A pension plan is said by some to be fully funded if regular payments are being made under the plan to a funding agency to cover the normal cost and reasonably rapid amortization of the past service cost. (2) If a specific part, or benefit, is fully paid for (such as the past service cost), then this item is fully funded. The total plan is considered fully funded if there are sufficient assets to make all payments due at particular times. This can apply either to level funding or to entry age calculations, provided that both are the normal costs and the conservative amount of amortization costs for the past services have been paid.

Funded Ratio   Ratio of the assets of a pension plan to its liabilities.

Funding Method   Any of the several techniques actuaries use in determining the amounts of employer contributions to provide for pension costs. An actuarial cost method.

Funding Policy The program regarding the amounts and timing of contributions by the employer(s), participants, and any other sources (for example, state subsidies or federal grants) to provide the benefits a pension plan specifies.

Hardship Withdrawal A withdrawal of an employee's contributions to a 401(k) plan prior to retirement at age 55 or attainment of age 59. A hardship withdrawal may be made only in cases of financial emergency provided there are no other sources available to meet the need; the withdrawal is taxable as an early distribution and subject to a 10 percent excise tax.

Highly Compensated Employee (HCE) Either a 5 percent owner or a person who earned more than $80,000 during the current or preceding year. Discrimination in favor of this group is prohibited.

Individual Retirement Account (IRA) Individuals, whether they are covered by a pension or not, are now permitted to save money on a tax-deferred basis in a qualified IRA plan. Although money can be withdrawn, a 10 percent penalty has been placed on those assets withdrawn prior to the individual turning 59, in addition to the normal taxes, which must be paid upon withdrawal. An individual can set up his or her own plan with a bank, insurance company, brokerage house, or mutual fund. A company can also deduct an agreed-upon amount from employees' paychecks and send it along to a designated agent or set up its own plan where managers are selected to manage the assets.

Integration with Social Security (1) A plan wherein benefits are integrated with the Social Security benefit. Under regular corporate plans, the regulations define the percentages applicable to the various benefits. Under a self-employed program, the only offset permissible is the amount of Social Security tax paid for the employee. If more than one plan is instituted for the same company, only one program may be integrated. (2) The basic concept of integration is that the benefits of the employer's plan must be dovetailed with Social Security benefits in such a manner that employees earning more than the taxable wage base will not receive combined benefits under the two programs that are proportionately greater than the benefits for employees earning less than the taxable wage base.

Keogh Plan A qualified retirement plan for self-employed persons and their employees to which yearly tax deductible contributions up to a specified limit can be made, if the plan meets certain requirements of the Internal Revenue Code. Keogh plans, also known as HR 10 plans, include defined benefit and defined contribution plans.

Lump-Sum Distribution A distribution that qualifies for forward averaging or rollover treatment. The requirements include that the distribution include the entire balance to the credit of the employee, and that it be made on account of the employee's death, attainment of age 59, separation from service (except for the self-employed), or disability (self-employed persons only).

Maximum Benefit The highest annual or lifetime benefit that can be paid by a qualified defined benefit plan.

Minimum Participation Standards   In general, the maximum amount of time a qualified retirement plan can require an employee to work before becoming eligible to participate is one year of service and the highest age a plan may require a participant to have attained before being admitted is 21. There are exceptions made for plans maintained by tax-exempt educational institutions and for plans that feature immediate vesting upon participation.

Multiemployer Plan   Under ERISA a multiemployer plan is one that requires contributions from more than one employer and is maintained pursuant to a collective bargaining agreement. They are also known as jointly administered or Taft-Hartley plans. The Multiemployer Pension Plan Amendments Act of 1980 (MPPAA) made substantial changes to ERISA and the Internal Revenue Code which had the effect of enhancing the funding requirements for multiemployer pension plans, providing new rules for multiemployer plans, and revising the termination insurance provisions applicable to these plans.

Nondiscrimination Rules   The requirements in section 105(h) of the Internal Revenue Code that self-funded employee benefit plans not provide significantly greater benefits to higher paid employees and owners than to lower-paid employees. Although some disparity is permitted, there are limits which, if crossed, result in the benefits being deemed taxable income to the beneficiaries. Similar rules apply to 401(k) plans, flexible benefit plans, and pension plans.

Nonqualified Deferred Compensation Plan   An agreement whereby one person (or legal entity) promises to compensate another for services rendered currently with actual payment for those services delayed until sometime in the future. Such agreements are almost invariably reduced to writing and are mutually supported by the employer's promise to pay deferred benefits and the employee's promise to render services in exchange therefore. Such plans do not receive tax advantages.

Normal Retirement   A termination of employment involving the payment of a regular formula retirement allowance without reduction because of age or service and with special qualifications such as disability.

Pension Benefit Guaranty Corporation (PBGC)   The federal agency, established as a nonprofit corporation, charged with administering the plan termination provisions of ERISA Title IV and the Multiemployer Pension Plan Amendments Act of 1980. Employers pay a premium to the PBGC, which guarantees benefits up to a specific maximum for participants and beneficiaries when defined benefit plans terminate.

Portability   (1) Any provision for retaining pension rights and credits when changing from one employer to another. Vested rights are nonforfeitable. The retention of nonvested (contingent) rights depends upon remaining within the scope of a multiemployer plan or its reciprocating plan under a reciprocal agreement. (2) The ability of the consumer to take health insurance from job to job.

(3) The right of an employee to take with him or her, upon separation from the employer, the total accumulation of monies carried in his or her account.

Projected Benefits   Those pension plan benefit amounts that are expected to be paid at various times under a particular set of actuarial assumptions, taking into account such items as the effect of advancement in age and past and anticipated future compensation and service credits. That portion of an individual's projected benefit allocation attributable to service to date, determined in accordance with the terms of a pension plan and based on future compensation as projected to retirement, is called the *credited projected benefit*.

Qualification Requirement   The rules and regulations issued in order to determine whether a proposed pension or profit-sharing plan will be fully deductible for tax purposes.

Replacement Ratio   The portion of pre-retirement earnings under any retirement plan that is replaced by benefits following retirement.

Required Distributions   (1) Payments that must be made once a participant reaches age 70 or retires (whichever is later); they are calculated to span his or her life expectancy. (2) When a participant dies, the payments that must be made to the participant's beneficiary.

Service   Employment taken into consideration under a pension plan. Years of employment before the inception of a plan constitute an employee's past service; years thereafter are classified in relation to the particular actuarial valuation being made or discussed. Years of employment (including past service) prior to the date of a particular valuation constitute prior service; years of employment following the date of the valuation constitute future service; a year of employment adjacent to the date of valuation, or in which such date falls, constitutes current service (included in future service).

Simplified Employee Pension Plan (SEP)   A SEP is a simplified alternative to a profit-sharing or 401(k) plan. A SEP is a pension plan to which contributions are made by the employer to an individual retirement account or annuity (IRA) established by an employee (subject to special rules on contributions and eligibility).

Surviving Spouse Benefit   Payments to the spouse of a deceased participant.

Thrift Plan   A defined contribution plan to which employees make contributions on an after-tax basis, usually as a percentage of salary. Incentive matching or partially matching contributions are also made on behalf of the participating employees by the employer.

Top-Heavy Plan   A qualified plan in which the share of benefits allocable to key employees is more than 60 percent. The plan may be subject to special accelerated vesting provisions and minimum contribution rates.

Unit Credit Actuarial Cost Method   (1) A method of computing pension benefits based on certain units, such as percentage of salary and years of service.

(2) An acceptable actuarial cost method under which the plan's normal cost for a year is the present value of the benefit credited to all participants for service in that year and the accrued liability is the present value at the plan's inception of the units of benefits credited to participants for service before the plan's inception. This method is also known as the *accrued benefit cost method*.

Vested Benefits   Accrued benefits of a participant that have become nonforfeitable under the vesting schedule adopted by the plan.

Vesting Schedules   Under the Tax Reform Act of 1986, there are two minimum schedules: 100 percent vesting after five years of service; and graduated vesting beginning after three years, with 100 percent vesting after seven years. The ten-year cliff, 5-15 year rule, rule of 45, and class year vesting are no longer permitted. If a plan has immediate 100 percent vesting, the eligibility period may be two years of service.

Contributors

Jeffrey R. Brown
Harvard University

Robert L. Clark
North Carolina State University

Joel M. Dickson
The Vanguard Group

William Even
Miami University of Ohio

William G. Gale
Brookings Institution

Jagadeesh Gokhale
American Enterprise Institute

Alan L. Gustman
Dartmouth College

Michael D. Hurd
RAND

Richard A. Ippolito
George Mason University School
of Law

Laurence J. Kotlikoff
Boston University

Dean M. Maki
JPMorgan Chase

Peter R. Merrill
PricewaterhouseCoopers

Janemarie Mulvey
Watson Wyatt Worldwide

Peter R. Orszag
Brookings Institution

Leslie E. Papke
Michigan State University

James M. Poterba
Massachusetts Institute of Technology

Andrew A. Samwick
Dartmouth College

Sylvester J. Schieber
Watson Wyatt & Company

John Karl Scholz
University of Wisconsin

John B. Shoven
Stanford University

Clemens Sialm
University of Michigan

Kent Smetters
Wharton School, University
   of Pennsylvania

Thomas L. Steinmeier
Texas Tech University

Annika Sundén
Boston College

Mark J. Warshawsky
TIAA-CREF Institute

David A. Wise
Harvard University

Yuewa Xu
TIAA-CREF Institute

Acknowledgments

The editors would like to thank Julia Niemiec, Catherine McLoughlin, and Shannon Leahy for expert assistance. In addition, thanks go to Valerie Norville, Eileen Hughes, and Marty Gottron for providing editorial support as well as Carlotta Ribar for proofreading and Enid Zafran for indexing.

Index